THE SERMON ON THE MOUNT AS AN IDEOLOGICAL INTERVENTION

A RECONSTRUCTION OF MEANING

Sjef van Tilborg

VAN GORCUM 1986
Assen/Maastricht, The Netherlands
Wolfeboro, New Hampshire, U.S.A.

Library of Congress Cataloging-in-Publication Data (applied for)

ISBN 90 232 2243 1

Layout: Van Gorcum, Assen, The Netherlands
Printed by Van Gorcum, Assen, The Netherlands

in memory of Roberto Quijada

fighter for the freedom
of the Philippino people
anonymously buried in the
rice fields of San Luis
Agusan del Sur

TABLE OF CONTENTS

INTRODUCTION

There is at the moment no dearth of studies on the Sermon on the Mount: a vivid sign of the existence of an ideological debate around this theme. What is in question is 'the doing of justice': Christianity is a religion where values demand to be actualised notwithstanding all the differences of opinion and all the varieties of interests involved in the question. The Sermon on the Mount is not a text which easily allows interests to remain hidden. This seldom happens in the studies.

This study proposes an argument in the context of this larger social debate. It offers a reconstruction of meaning of the text as reaction against and addition to all those interpretations which more one-sidedly or even exclusively emphasize the points which are relevant for an individualistic ethic and/or a christological dogmatic doctrine. The intention is not to replace as much as to question certain topics. A different perspective can bring to light shades of meaning in an identical text which till now have not been given enough attention. It is this reader's position which is new: as a reader to be directed towards the pragmatic functioning of the text, towards all those social realities which develop because human beings live together in a social context.

I need to elaborate a good deal to show which hermeneutic and literary theory lies at the basis of the project of this study. The specific points of departure demand that. The study uses L. Althusser's philosophical theory of the practical functioning of an ideology as a literary device for the interpretation of (this part of) biblical literature. To say it in a nutshell: the individual sayings of the Sermon on the Mount are always seen as 'ideological interventions in the context of an existing social practice'. This need some further explicitation which probably is not possible if I do not explain the central points of Althusser's theory. To prevent the reader from drowning in abstract philosophical language I will add examples of used literary applications(1).

1. the definition of ideology

Althusser gives his definition of what he means by the word 'ideology' in a language which, for him, is unusually clear. Since this definition is the point of departure for all further considerations, I want to quote this, together with the context in which he places it, even though I think that the discussion on its value belongs in a much broader discourse than is possible here and now. He writes: 'To use a marxist language: if it is true that the representation of the real conditions of the individuals who occupy the acting positions in the production, the exploitation, the repression, the formation of ideology and the scientific practice, ultimately depends on the productive relationships and its dependent relationships, we can say the following: every ideology represents - in a necessarily imaginary deformation - not the existing productive relationships (and its dependent relations), but above all the (imaginary) relation of the individuals to the productive relationships and its dependent relations. Ideology, therefore, does not represent the system of real relationships which affect the lives of individuals, but rather the imaginary relation of these individuals to the real relations under which they live'(2).

In this point of view every ideology has a binary structure. The existing productive relationships are in an ideology the base for the expression of its own relation to these productive relationships, but this expression happens only in the imaginary order - i.e. according to my understanding - in the order of metaphors, symbols, word games etc which obscure the real interest of the people while they do touch it. Structurally ideology encompasses thus an element of recognition and of non-recognition. Every ideological statement is revealing and hiding the truth at the same time. It gives insight because it is based on the existing reality of the productive relationships. But since this insight has to be expressed in language which is part of the imaginary order, it is a deformed insight: deformed because remaining in its own class ideology, one cannot recognise the proper class interests. Ideology is about a relation within a relation. It 'expresses' the relation one has to socially existing, politically realised and economically determined relations between people but this 'expression' is necessarily imaginary because it promotes interests which, within ideology, are not reflected upon.

This general point of departure may give rise to all kinds of reflection, but is not the point of discussion now. Especially open to criticism is Althusser's simple application of religious ideology. There is more to life than he seems willing to consider. This does not diminish the value of his theoretical point of departure. In a text as the Sermon on the Mount it is especially relevant. By taking the individual sayings as ideological pronouncements it is clear how much they participate in the above mentioned binary structure of an ideology. While the content is based on and directed towards the real productive relationships of the society in which Matthew lives, they (hardly ever) reflect these relations. This ambiguity calls forth all the discussions. Or, to say it more explicitly, because the proper interest of the group is not reflected upon in the sayings of the Sermon on the Mount, a well argumented discussion must define which and whose interests are taken in consideration in any given text. Modern research makes a variety of pronouncements on this. It is symptomatic of the fact that the text itself leaves it open. Of course this study gives ample attention to this aspect. It brought me to the complicated conclusion that Matthew's text wants to protect the interests of the poor or even of the poorest section of the population, notwithstanding the fact that his community has progressed socially and economically. In chapter IV which deals with the problems of the rich, I have placed the arguments together, but in reality they are to be found all through the study.

2. every ideology has a material existence

As a proposition it is fairly self-evident that every ideology has its base in a material reality. But since this reality has not been much reflected upon, Althusser's insistence functioned as a new idea and stimulated a lot of research. It links up with the marxist insight that the productive relationships are 'ultimately' determining the superstructure of every society: the juridical, political and ideological constellation of every existing social formation(3). The influence which the economic substructure exerts on the social superstructure will be different from one society to another and from one moment in history to another. It will never be absent. It is interesting in Althusser's proposal that he describes this relationship rather explicitly. In his opinion this material existence of an ideology relates to <u>practices</u> which are tied to <u>rituals</u>, within the material existence of <u>ideological apparatus</u>. He emphasizes the latter and characterises them as state organisations because they take care of state interests, even if they might represent themselves as juridically private organisations. Concretely he points to churches, schools, family, political parties, trade unions, press and cultural organisations. They are all given institutions with which people associate or dissociate themselves whether they are aware of it or not. People find their identity through them because they create people's subjectivity. The main point is that these institutions function primarily and predominantly through an ideology: the intended interests are (almost) never mentioned directly, but always indirectly in an imaginary relation to the productive relationships.

The multiplicity of ideological apparatus which Althusser mentions for modern society responds to the multiplicity of ideological apparatus in ancient society. Many will be mentioned in this study: the Temple organisation, hereditary and hierarchically organised with obvious differences between high priests, priests, levites and temple servants; the more free organisations of the Sadducees, the Pharisees and the Essenes; the beth midrashim and the belonging to the various schools with its consequences towards the functions of scribes and judges; the professional organisations, often organised by heredity; the army of the Roman occupiers; private organisations for the various religious and profane festivities etc. Ancient society was well organised indeed: people were bonded together in many varied ways.

In this study I will return to this time and again, because the text of the Sermon on the Mount is in a sense in continuous conflict with these organisations. I will not treat them as such, but they are the concrete points of reference, because in this study they function within the reconstruction of meaning of the text. Individual sayings get a meaning which otherwise would remain invisible, if one sees them against the background of these existing organisations with their specific ideologies. Via other rituals and other practices (a different explanation of the Law, other forms of prayer, of fasting and of charity, another way of acting with regard to prophetical activities) a new way of living arises, a way of living which wants to change the whole society. Different forms of possession, other forms of relationships and a new mentality - I am thinking specifically of the denial of all thoughts of vengeance - will bring God's covenant with Israel to reality: that is the message of the Sermon on the Mount. The proper organisation into an 'ecclesia as representative of the whole city' is its basis as well as its result.

3. ideology is not singular in class society

I have now to say a number of things simultaneously. Because any ideology is a specific material expression of the relation to the productive relationship, the ruling ideology will be the ideology of the ruling classes in a society where the class distinctions are based on oppression and domination. In such a society the ideology of the oppressed class will always have fewer possibilities, but it will not be completely absent. It will be there 'in principle', because it has little chance to find full expression without the necessary economic, political and social support. Its fragmentary character is in itself the expression of an oppression: it is prevented from reaching full development. This does not mean that the ruling ideology obtains its position through guile and deceit. An experience of 'self-evidence' develops which affects all members of a given society, because the ruling class agrees on what has to be done in the political, economical and ideological field. To make his point Althusser gives an historical example from the history of the emancipation of the bourgeois: 'In the ideology of freedom the bourgeois experiences its relationship to its own conditions of existence very precisely, i.e. its true relationship (the right of the liberal capitalistic economy), but embedded in an imaginary relationship (all people are free, including the free labourers)'(4). The freedom of the bourgeois is the model of the freedom for all people. An alternative ideology based on the unfree conditions of the labourer can only express itself in opposition to this.

It is clear that via the Jesus-movement people got a voice which otherwise would have remained unheard. The text of the Sermon on the Mount is in some way part of this. Its opposition to the ruling ideology comes through most forcefully in those sentences and expressions which explicitate this opposition:

-in the sentences dealing with persecution and oppression;
-in the abuses which characterise the opponents: that they are hypocrites, pagans, publicans and false prophets;
-in the metaphorical comparisons which have negative overtones: the evil eye, the dogs, the swine, the wolves, the bramble bushes and thistles, the house built on sand;
-in the way position is taken in the legal texts: your justice must be greater than that of the Pharisees and the scribes; you have heard how it was said to your fore fathers ... but I say to you; do not practise justice to obtain a reward; go away from me, breakers of the Law.

In this study, however, the emphasis is less on this opposition than on the continuity with the tradition. An opposing ideology can prove itself only if its opposition is expressed in the context of the ruling ideology. The latter's self-evidence is the constant point of friction and this has its influence. New rituals, practices and organisations are grafted onto existing forms and are in opposition to them:

- the new Law is based on the traditional Law and does not want to abolish it;
- the new forms of charity, praying and fasting are connected to the existing practices;
- the new economic order reacts to the economic structures of ancient times where the triune reality of hoarding, land possession and trade are rational from an ideological point of view;
- the new relationships of power connect with the old,

lost phantasies as the story of the Paradise and Israel of the Covenant.

Establishing this symbiotic reality continuously plays an important role in the reconstruction of meaning of the texts.

But the opposition is also a continuous part in one way or another. I would like to exclude all possibility of misunderstanding right from the beginning: this study will make clear that this opposition is not an opposition between Judaism and Christianity. Much of what is new and different links up with inner-Jewish discussions. That is, obviously, not always so - the Sermon on the Mount is a text which was written within the new organisation -, but in many more places than is accepted by the scientific exegesis, the beginning Jesus-movement connects with elements of ideological opposition, present in Jewish thought. I will elaborate, this in the explanation of the legal texts, also in what I have called the 'relecture of the legal texts' in chapter V on the mutual relations of the people. But the same phenomenon can be seen in the beatitudes, in the texts which deal with possessions and in the critique on the prophets. We find this connection all through the Sermon on the Mount: a reality which is not all that extraordinary, if one remains aware of the origin of the Jesus-movement.

4. every ideology has its specific tendency

Any society which is based on classes will show a configuration of ideologies which are mutually contradictory. The ideology of the ruling classes will be dominant until the system disintegrates. The 'tendency' of an ideology will be determined by its position vis-à-vis this reproduction of the system whether it maintains it or destroys it. The 'tendency' of an ideology is, therefore, a dynamic concept. It indicates how an ideology is connected with the dominant structures in a society. By showing a certain 'tendency' one can determine the specific class character of the ideology of the moment. Does this actual ideological statement fit into the existing productive relationships and into the ruling oppression of the time? Or does it resist them by trying to create the presuppositions which will make new productive relationships possible in a different societal organisation? These extremes keep hidden the innumerable in-between solutions, partial adjustments and changes and possible partnerships which can be resolved any time etc. As a living reality it expresses the continuing class war which is ultimately based on the economic substructure of society.

By showing the 'tendency' it becomes clear from which

class the ideology has been formulated. Applied hermeneutically to the texts this means that the question comes up in how far one can make clear which interests are pursued by whom and for what purpose and also what this concretely means for the people: a whole series of questions which in a general way has already be mentioned. This study defends the position that 'Matthew', notwithstanding the fact that he has progressed socially and economically, consistently takes the position in favour of the poor of his time. The beatitudes seen as declarations of solidarity with people who suffer under injustice and power, hunger and death, war and poverty are his opening sentences. This study will show that the author takes this opening seriously and that he is practically always consistent in his choices:

- in the legal texts in favour of women and slaves, in favour of peace and good relationships in absolute contradiction to all feelings of vengeance which lead to murder and manslaughter, to war and persecution;
- in the economic texts in favour of the have-nots in opposition to the rich;
- in the eschatological closing texts in favour of acting correctly in opposition to cheats and exploiters.

In the case of a few texts I will indicate my doubts: in the torah about the prohibition of divorce and taking an oath and in the argumentation on the torah on the need to love one's enemies: that the disciples should not act like the publicans and the pagans. I am not sure whether in those texts Matthew's basic option is consistently developed. But this does not diminish the clarity of the 'tendency' in the whole.

As I said already: the 'tendency' of an ideology is not static. The same sentences do not always have the same meaning in different circumstances. There is a good deal of difference whether a rich man calls a poor man blessed or whether this is done by a poor man. The same is true with the saying on the prayer for one's persecutors. If the persecutor says this, it would be close to blasphemy according to me. This change of meaning will demand our attention from time to time, though not always. To speak about peace and to call people to become peace-makers has a very different meaning before a war, during a war and after. And what do we think about texts which speak about the Temple after its destruction or which open the possibility to condemn to capital punishment to a court which probably does not have that juridical possibility? How should we judge the difference in meaning when agricultural practices are in opposition to city life? The command to pray in the inner room means something different for hearers who do not have access to the synagogue than for people who can go there every day or at least once a week. What changes in meaning occur in texts which originate from a beggar's culture - the pericope on the care for clothing and food; the prayer for the daily bread in the Our Father; the saying about asking, searching and knocking - when they are read and heard by people who are financially better off? This study will try to ask these questions and to find answers. Complete certainty will not be always possible. I believe it is good that these sorts of question are asked in exegesis.

5. ideology has a relative autonomy

The productive forces and the productive relationships based on them are 'ultimately' determinant for the totality of a given society-formation. This does not mean that everything is immediately and directly determined by economic factors. In any society the economy is the finally determining substructure, but it is not independent from other societal realities and it does not exclude the possibility of some kind of independence of the other levels of society. Politics and ideology are relatively autonomous and one had better to accept that.

To limit myself to ideology: because it has its own materiality and, therefore, its own mode of existence, existing oppositions can only be resolved within this ambitus. One should not try to find solutions by going to the other levels of society. If this happens nevertheless and with a certain amount of success (e.g. all supporters of a national liberation army are exterminated by the army; all activities of the unions are prevented by economic and legal shenanigans), it will have its repercussion on the other levels: the dictatorship becomes even more repressive, the economy becomes more exploitative, the ideology of the state becomes more unified and resistance grows.

Obviously this kind of horror is not always what is in question - but the Roman war against the Jews is a case in point! -, the pattern of reaction will always be the same. If one does not respect the relative autonomy of the different levels, the social confusion and opposition will become worse. This is especially true for the level of ideology. It has its own relative autonomy which is expressed in its own history, its own legality and its own sphere of influence. That must be respected. Work done within the sphere of ideology has its own importance, because important decisions are made within this sphere which influence the totality of man's life.

The importance of this observation is first of all negative. It should prevent us from a wrong conclusion: working with texts is neither politics nor economics. The texts are not political or economic realities. Not that they cannot infuence those realities or are irrelevant for them. Nothing could be less true. But one should never forget that they belong in the sphere of ideology: in that sphere of human life which expresses itself in phantasies, images and thoughts, which are expressed in any given society in language. Ideology is a relative reality which does not encompass the totality of man's life.

But there is also something positive to be said. However relative it is, the sphere of ideology has its own identity. Texts influence people and it is important to determine what kind of influence is exerted. This study wants to identify elements of this influence:

- the ideological direction of some texts: that they are directed to the totality of society. The Sermon on the Mount is a text which describes an ideal Israel in order to lure people from Israel and from the nations to stand behind the message: the beatitudes as texts which speak about the restoration of Israel-of-the-Covenant; the legal texts as the juridical stratum for this new society; the economic texts as part of the theologoumenon on the joy of the Law; the eschatological texts as texts which describe the reward and the punishment. The Sermon on the Mount has a political and social direction which no one will want to deny.
- But also elements of actual influence: the texts are written from the reality of a group of people ánd for the reality of a group of people who want to realise the consequences of their choice: the actual structure of this group and the problems they confront; its organisation, rituals and practices. Even if this reconstruction is beset with hypotheses, there are a number of things which can be said. And even if we must accept that not everything developed according to the ideal expressed in the text, the text itself remains as an ideological stumbling block for all the things which still have to be done because of human weakness and unwillingness.

6. the literary-historical point of departure

To accomplish this research project I have accepted some limitations. The most important one is the literary-historical point of departure. The study consistently asks how Matthew's text has been understood in Israel of the first century. Therefore, to reconstruct the meaning of the text I constantly refer to Jewish writings which, with some probability, are relevant for this time period and for this text; and to existing organisations, practices and rituals which appear important in the Palestinian reality. So not only Jewish customs but also non-Jewish realities are to be included. Writings of certain Hellenistic and Roman authors are not per se excluded but the emphasis is on the material which is relevant for first century Judaism.

I am well aware that this is only a partial reconstruction and that more research is still necessary(5). It is a possible readers' position which can stand next to other readers' positions. One could also give a reconstruction of meaning of the text as it existed in Rome or Athens or Alexandria. To determine the 'Wirkungsgeschichte' of the text this would be extremely important. If anything is to be clarified by this study, it should be the fact that 'meaning' is necessarily bound by history localised in time and space. A text cannot be read out of 'contexts': nor without the co-texts which determine the connotative meanings in a given culture of language; nor without the con-texts which determine the denotative meanings in the totality of that culture. In this study the emphasis is on the latter, an area which is still largely unexplored. From time to time the first will also come up but completeness is a dream which will never be realised.

This means by and large that this study will not take up position in the debate on the historical background of Matthew's gospel: is it a Jewish-Christian or a pagan-Christian document; has it been written in Alexandria, Caesarea or Antioch etc? The method I use starts from a literary-historical presupposition which helps to reach certain conclusions as to content but which does not answer those questions. The historical background of Matthew's gospel poses a complex of questions which this study does not clarify.

However, this does not mean that the results of this study are irrelevant for those questions. They can be easily fitted in. To limit myself to the most explicit proposal - to what J.P. Meier wrote in his study 'Antioch and Rome'(6), which mutatis mutandis is valid also for other proposals - one can read this study as an approximation of the manner in which the Jewish community of the Antioch church understood Matthew's gospel, inclusive of the absolute Israel-directedness which crops up in this study in every chapter. It is only an approximation because of the reservation that some adaptation may be needed to the Antioch background. However, in this supposition Matthew's name as author needs to be seen as 'the Jewish-Christian participants of the ekklesia in Antioch who see in Matthew their spokesman'. It is very interesting to refer to J.P. Meier's study because - to my surprise- these Jewish readers, hearers and interpreters are fairly regularly described by him as 'the conservative people of the right wing of the local church'. It is an indication which, unless it is meant to be anti-Jewish -, has at most an historical meaning, because these people lost their fight in the later church. That they were right-wing people, is not apparent from what follows according to me.

Chapter I
SUFFERING OF THE PEOPLE AND ITS RESTORATION
Mt 5, 3-16

The beatitudes touch only briefly on a number of problems, which are still unresolved if we look at the social realisation. That Israel be restored could be the quintessence of this whole pericope. From a negative reality, which shows poverty, physical violence, repression and oppression, the text looks at a reality in which the covenant with God is realised in fidelity to the Law in land ownership, in eating and drinking, in peace and justice.

The call of the beatitudes exists in the fact that the author thinks in reversals which have an inner coherence however unexpected they may be. The preface and conclusion of each sentence are always connected to each other. This cannot be said about the totality of the text. Other realities could have been mentioned with the same effect. The eight (resp. nine) suggest a totality and with that comes the end. That is not unsatisfactory because enough problems are taken up to call forth the image of a people which looks for change.

Jesus gives the promise that Israel will be restored so that it can shine as a light for the 'goyim'. Oppression and power, hunger and death, war and peace, poverty and land reform, injustice and justice are the evoked realities. The problem for the modern reader lies in the fact that this paradisaical Israel is still a long way off. When Marx, after the revolution in Paris in 1848, came to the conclusion that the time for the great change had not yet come, because in the centre of world trade, in England, the proletariat was not yet capable of taking over power, he wrote: 'It is with this generation as with the Jews whom Moses led through the desert. Not only must this generation conquer a new world, it must come to an end to make place for the people who are capable of carrying on a new world'(1). It seems that one must start from the beginning time and time again.

> Blessed are the people who are poor in their very spirit, because they possess the dominion of heavens.
>
> Mt 5,3

The opening sentence stays in the memory. That is not surprising, because it encapsulates a whole program which is still to be realised: the poor to whom dominion is promised which coincides with God's own kingship. It is laid on thickly. The deepest humiliation is connected with the highest honour, without intermediary as if they are two realities which are inherently connected: the people, who are poor in their very spirit, possess the power of God.

I need to say many things at the same time to expose the inner logic of this connection. That is to say: I have to start with the reproach to Matthew, because he watered down the extremely strong statement of Luke about the poor: he made the materially poor into the 'poor in spirit'! 'All traces of class hatred have been washed away in this clever revisionism of Matthew', wrote Kautsky in 1908, long before the end of the First World War, when he had not yet abandoned the concept of the dictatorship of the proletariat(2). This is a summary of what almost all exegetes have said before and after him. Matthew spiritualises the original saying of Jesus(3); he gives a pacifist, submissive interpretation of an original resistance text(4); he spiritualises the material reality of poverty and makes it an ethical imperative: in order to be allowed entrance into the kingdom of heaven, one must become poor in spirit, i.e. one must be humble, or at least one must become humble(5). These interpretations have not remained without effect. That the poor became 'poor in spirit' was seen as an enlargement in interpretation, which could even be used against the materially poor. However rich one is, however many possessions one enjoys, everyone can be poor in spirit as long as one is detached. And such inner freedom is a command also for the poor(6).

Firstly it has to be asked, therefore, what Matthew intends with his 'poor in spirit'. Is it possible to be poor in spirit without being poor? I do not think so. There is a strong argument in the immediate context. When Matthew explains how it is with people who are pure in heart - a beatitude which linguistically is parallel with the opening sentence, he speaks about a man who looks with desire at another man's wife and who, therefore, has already committed adultery in his heart(7). Whoever is pure of heart must also be pure in his desires. But in the same way as here the act of adultery is excluded primarily, so it is also with the saying of the poor: in any case poverty itself is presupposed.

This interpretation presupposes the following implication: in the same way as the 'pure in heart' are people who are pure in their very heart, the same with the 'poor in spirit': they are people who are poor in their very spirit. Matthew does not intend to spiritualise or to speak only about an inner reality, but he rather intensifies - if it is necessary to characterise this specific text. Matthew is not more mild but rather more strict in doctrine. He makes a distinction within the group of those who do not possess: only to those who are poor in their very spirit, is the possession of the dominion of the heavens promised. While one cannot be poor in spirit without being actually poor, one can be poor without being poor-in-spirit. I will, obviously, have to return to this 'extra'.

I have found in Blass-Debrunner, in his discussion of the dative of relation, a number of texts which use a similar extension in meaning as supposed in Mt 5,3 (8): Antiochus is angry as a wild animal unto his very ψυχή (9); Apollos, being instructed in the way of the Lord, is aglow unto his very πνεῦμα(10); Epaphroditus has been so carefree that he even puts his ψυχή (his life) in the balance(11); Jesus is humble unto his very heart(12). The dative of relation is the Hellenistic form of the classical accusative of relation which in this case stands for εἰς + accusative of direction. The τῷ πνεύματι of our Matthew text is a restrictive adjunct which on the one hand indicates the place where poverty is lived and on the other the direction to which poverty should extend.

That does not mean that according to the syntax this interpretation is necessary. The construction, in which an adjective is connected with a double dative, makes that clear: 'being taken away from you, in sight, not in heart'(13); 'I was indeed absent in body, but present in spirit'(14); 'Christ, being put to death indeed in the flesh, but enlivened in the spirit'(15). Matthew could have said: blessed are the people who, although they are rich in possessions, are nevertheless poor in spirit(16). But that this is not the meaning is absolutely clear from the use of the word πτωχός. In Greek there is a decisive distinction between people who do not have sufficient possessions to be able to live without working, people, in other words, who need to work to earn their bread(17) and the 'beggars' who are incapable or not in a position to work independently(18). Matthew makes Jesus talk about these beggars. That excludes that these 'poor-in-spirit' can have possessions. Blessed are those who in their very spirit, are willing and capable to be 'beggars'.

With this I have not said the final word about this

opening sentence of the saying. The concept πνεῦua also needs some explanation. There is no need to explain that it deals here with an anthropological reality(19) nor that it, parallel to words as heart, body, soul, mind, entrails, gives a total description of man under a specific aspect. Against the Jewish background of the word, 'pneuma' indicates the most fundamental life principle of all living creatures: breath, the flow of air as wind, the spirit which God blows into Adam and which man returns at the last breath of his life, noticeable but invisible. Breath is the beginning and origin of life. Whoever has no breath left is dead. Matthew knows this way of speaking as is evident in Mt 27,50: 'And Jesus cried in a loud voice, and breathed his 'pneuma''. The 'pneuma' is man as a living, breathing creature. Blessed are those who are poor in their very breath, i.e. blessed are those who are so poor that their very life is in the balance(20). It is not without reason that Matthew closes his list of beatitudes with those persecuted for the sake of justice: in their case too their life is (sometimes) in the balance and they also are promised to possess dominion of the heavens: an inclusion which only in this interpretation is fully explained(21).

According to the terminology of Baumgärtel, Bieder and Sjöberg(22), 'pneuma' functions as anthropological reality, also or even better connected with this, as the place of man's feelings, of his intellectual and voluntary actions: man decides and thinks in his 'pneuma'. As 'pneuma' he gets his insights, comes to understanding, makes decisions, gives up or perseveres in certain situations. 'Pneuma' is not only a vital principle; by his 'pneuma' man becomes a living creature distinct from all other living creatures.

Both aspects can be seen in Matthew: the cognitive aspect in the discussion about the Messiah - at least if here 'pneuma' is used in an anthropological sense - 'how is it then that David, speaking in his 'pneuma', calls him Lord?(23); and the voluntary aspect in the logion from the story in Gethsemani: 'because the 'pneuma' is πρόθυμον (willing, diligent, active), but the flesh is weak'(24).

It is time to make my point. My point of departure is that the Matthean addition τῷ πνεύματι has something to do with the changing sociological composition of his community. He is more directly involved with winning people from circles where money, land ownership and possessions play an important role. The arguments for this will be given in the course of this commentary. For the moment I will posit this as self-evident -anyway, it connects with the exegesis which explains the τῷ πνεύματι as a Matthean spiritualisation. We should understand this well. I am not saying that the original poverty option of the Jesus-movement has been abandoned by Matthew. For Matthew only those can enter the kingdom who are ready to leave all their possessions. The central story is and remains, also in Matthew, the story of the rich young man who, instructed in the Law, cannot fulfill the Law, because he cannot bring himself to the 'perfection' by leaving his possessions and giving them to the poor. Also in Matthew's vision the rich man who cannot leave his possessions, stands in opposition to the group of disciples who have left their families and their fields to receive eternal life in the coming aeon(25). Only the poor possess dominion of heavens(26).

What needs to be done in the 'pneuma' of those who are poor or who have made themselves poor? As I said, as parallel stands the expression 'pure in heart': in the 'pure in heart' even 'the desire to transgress the command' has ceased to exist. The heart is free of every desire to transgress the Law. For the expression 'poor-in-spirit' there is a similar explanatory sentence in Matthew. It is somewhat hidden but present in the allegorical explanation of the parable of the seed in Mt 13,22. This is a verse which deals precisely with the question. The third way of sowing - when the seed falls among the thistles -, is explained as: 'this is the man who hears the word, but the worries of the world and the lure of riches choke the word and the seed produces nothing'. Matthew has thought deeply about the problems of riches. He has discovered that being rich is a snare. The uncertainty of possession forces the rich man to strive for ever greater riches as the fata morgana where the end of all worries will be reached. The snare is the urge to have more, the lure of riches because the security will never be achieved. There is only one way to break out of this vicious circle: one must leave all possessions and entrust oneself totally to God. Blessed are those who, although they are poor as beggars, resist the snare of riches even in their very spirit: those who do not allow the worries of this world to take possession of them, because they have put all their trust in God - in his dominion and justice. Theirs is the dominion of the heavens.

I have not yet clearly demonstrated how there is an inner cohesion between the preface and the conclusion of the saying, between poverty and power. To understand this I need to explicitate the Jewish implications of the poverty-concept. In contradistinction to the Hellenistic society, Israel takes up the religious and political elements together with the economic elements. In a number of compressed sentences we can summarize this as follows: the poor are the oppressed who are incapable of resisting the oppression of the rich and the powerful. They are delivered to their arbitrary behaviour and they are humiliated by them and kept in a state of dependence. Therefore, they look for a deliverer, for someone who is willing and able to protect them against these god-less and law-less people. However poor and needy they are, in God's Torah, they find their support, because they will always know, against all injustice, that the God of Israel will not leave them in this misery(27).

In the course of Israel's history there are various emphases which cannot be brought under one common denominator. The phenomenon of poverty remains always central. This is clear from the constant factor that the concept in its totality includes elements from the economy (land ownership, division of property, gratification of needs), from religion (the law, the prophets, God as protector, defender and avenger) and from politics (suppression, liberation, the opposition between powerful and powerless). The opening saying of the Sermon on the Mount - this saying which indicates the connection between what is lacking in the (economically) poor and what will be given to them in (political) power from heaven as God's dominion - belongs in this tradition.

One finds the same constant factor in the Book of War, the only extant text where a Hebrew parallel is found for the 'poor in spirit'(28). The Book of War describes the definitive war of the sons of light against the sons of darkness. With God's help the fight is won and, even though the preparation demands close attention, in a language which is more than warlike, the fact remains that only God has given them victory. The word 'poor' is used several times as an indication of the group, always with the connotation 'the oppressed who have finally found justice': the poor are liberated by God and they will conquer the seven small nations(29); the enemies of all countries will be delivered unto them, unto the poor, the people who have been bowed down in the dust(30); the riches of the people will be brought to the needy; their kings will be their servants and the oppressors will sing a song of praise for them(31). There is a complete reversal. Where once poverty, oppression and subservience reigned, there is now abundance, power and dominion. The sons of darkness will never again have the chance to revolt against this decision of God(32).

Why do I bring in this Book of War which is so different in tone, content and design? The reason is that nowhere else are poverty, oppression and victory-with-God's-help so clearly brought together: precisely those categories which can serve to clarify the implicit meaning of our opening saying. The poor, whose life is endangered because of their poverty and, who, even then, are not willing to give in to the lure of riches, are promised the kingly power of God,- Matthew calls this the kingdom of heaven. It is essential to remember that the Greek word βασιλεία is not primarily local, but personal(33). It is not a geographical indication of the kingdom. It is a quality of person (the kingly power over against the power of the despot, the kingship which covers all free subjects etc.). All parables, which clarify this kingly power of God, deal with persons and events. Geography plays a minor role. God's kingly power is possessed by those who have no say and who, even in their very spirit, are unwilling to look for human power.

The first position has been taken. The area of the highest and definitive power is taken on from a position of oppression and of powerlessness. This works both ways: the weak are made strong, but also the kingly power of God can only be known in such an humiliating position. It is a support for the numberless millions who cry for justice, but it is also a critique on the moment that the position of power is taken. The presence of divine kingly power shifts - a historical dilemma for all liberation movements (34).

> Blessed are those who mourn, because they will be comforted

Mt 5,4

Every culture has its own mourning rituals. In the Middle East we find the large gesture, the loud lamentations, torn clothing, ashes on the head. One can see this in the representations which have been preserved: a group of people, usually women, although this is not necessary, but always a large group, because precisely at this moment one does not want to be alone, a group of people makes public the circumstances of this death with arms held high and drawn faces. In a mishnah we find: 'When somebody's wife dies, even the poor must pay at least for two flutes and one woman to lament'(35).

This public lamentation is a serious duty. According to Josephus it lasts seven days and brings serious obligations. About Herod's death he writes: 'After keeping seven days' mourning for his father (=Herod) and providing the usual funeral banquet for the populace on a sumptuous scale - a Jewish custom which reduces many to poverty, such entertainment of the people being considered obligatory and its omission an act of impiety -, he (= Archelaos) changed into white raiment and went forth to the Temple'(36). Archelaos' adversary will make political hay from the fact that Archelaos did not take this official mourning seriously enough(37). There are other texts which mention such a long mourning period(38), but it is not clear if the whole period was always completely respected. In any case certainly there was always a mourning parade, a meal of the deceased, seated on the floor, and an official condolence where people lined up to give comfort on the people concerned(39). Before that, the lamentation had been held in the house: the '^{c}inujim', the lamentations which were sung with clapping of hands, and the 'qinot', the lamentations with a female lead singer and a common chorus(40). In the Book of Biblical Antiquities contemporary models of such lamentations are probably preserved, in connection with what we know from Hellenistic culture(41). Normally the wake lasted the whole night and people were kept awake by the lamentations, the flutes and the drums.

To understand Matthew's saying, one has to keep in mind that there was a great difference between 'mourning' and 'being sad'. A text of Josephus is again very instructive. When Moses was absent for the second time for 40 days, rumors about his death made the rounds and they led to all kind of speculations. But even the people who liked Moses, could not evade the seriousness of the situation: 'Imagining themselves, however, to have been bereft of a patron and protector the like of whom they could never meet again, they continued in the deepest distress; and while their earnest expectation of some good news of their hero would not permit them to <u>mourn</u>, so neither could they restrain their <u>grief</u> and <u>dejection</u>'(42).

Mourning and sorrow go together, but are not the same thing. It is an added punishment when the public lamentation is not allowed, as in the case of people who have been condemned to death(43), or in the case of a tyrant out of cruelty(44). In such cases one can only be sad: one must keep the sorrow invisible in one's heart.

When one reads the scientific exegesis of this text, one would almost think that Matthew was writing a literary work. It seems important to know whether there was literary influence from a text from Isaiah(45): 'it is possible but not proved'(46); 'he connects with it but is not dependent on it'(47); 'it is a base text'(48), are some sentences of exegetes. Depending on the exegetical point of departure one will give more or less weight to the text from Isaiah: the description of the situation of a people suffering from the consequences of a war which has destroyed everything and has left so many people in despair and sorrow: the poor, the people who have been downtrodden in their heart, the captured and the blind, all of them people who lament. When God's anointed comes, the day of vengeance will be here, the year of God's grace. Instead of ashes on the head, there will then be a crown; instead of the dress of mourning, there will be a festive ointment; instead of being tired to death, there will be beautiful clothing. It is important to know whether Matthew recognises his own time and society in this description, for example in the supposition that he wrote after the great war of 70 AD, and/or after many people died in persecutions in his immediate vicinity.

Before entering into this question, I need to point out another narrative reality: the opening story in Matthew which gives the setting to the whole book and which refers directly to our saying, via the mention of the lamentations of the mothers from Rama, the daughters of Rachel(49). From the very first moment, Matthew starts his story from the point of view that violence, deceit and royal arbitrariness are matter-of-fact realities as are the sufferings of people: the necessity to leave the country, the inconsolable mourning of Bethlehem's mothers, the impossibility to ever return to one's own city of birth. No other evangelist begins his story with so much terror and dread(50).

I am well aware that this way of reading is not the ordinary way. Matthew is considered as an author who is far removed from the turmoil of people: as a Christian rabbi who peacefully explains the Law, as a teacher in a catechetical situation, as a Hellenistic scribe whose only concern are his books. Matthew as a leader of a 'School of Matthew', who begins his book with an exposition about who Jesus is and from where he comes, is an image well established since the sixties(51). The innumerable data from the Targums and the Midrash, which since then have been presented as parallels, have not changed this. To the contrary, the author of the Matthew-gospel has become more a person who is drowned in all kinds of literature.

The story is about the Magi, about people who know the course of the stars and planets and understand their meaning. They come from the East to Jerusalem and go from there to Bethlehem, to the house of the mother and the child. They bring royal gifts: gold, incense and myrrh; they adore the child with a royal salute, on their knees in adoration, completely unaware of the trail of hatred and sorrow they leave behind. They are presented as influential and powerful people who lack nothing. Their arrival creates turmoil in Jerusalem and immediately they are received at the court and by the highest Temple authorities(52).

The story breathes the social matter-of-fact reality which rules the relation between the powerful and the powerless: the quiet agreement of the powerful is indeed disturbed by the dream coming from God, but this is not true for the ruinous result of their unexpected visit: the flight into Egypt of mother and child, the slaughter of the children in Bethlehem and environs, the impossibility to ever return to the own native land. Various quotes from Scripture are brought in to explain at least a little of what is happening: God has seen the sorrow of Israel in Egypt from its infancy(53); Israel's exile: Rachel's lamentation over her children, whom she has lost, is still on-going(54); a new branch has grown on the dead trunk of Jesse to do justice to the poor and to judge the oppressors(55). This is more than a story of Christological origin. The whole of Jesus history is set against the background of Israel's liberation in which the exodus, the exile and the messianic liberation by David's son are used as 'leitmotiv' in order to overcome the evil of the experienced violence(56).

'Blessed are those who mourn because they will be conforted' are the words which Matthew makes Jesus say in his first major address. And all initial events of Jesus' life are brought together. Bethlehem's mothers were left inconsolable, but now that is over and done with. That their lamentations have been heard by God is the content of Jesus' words, making these mothers part of the long series of people who have been victimised by the brute force of the powerful and who possibly were forbidden to show their sorrow. Jesus is, for Matthew, someone who knows whereof he speaks, because he stands with them as a fugitive and exile himself. All his life Jesus experienced the misery of brutal force in his own person and his own family.

Matthew does not have our vision of an historical perspective. What happened happens. Israel's history happens in Jesus' life in the same way as Jesus' history is used to give a clearer picture of what is happening in his own time and situation. In this sense Jesus' listeners are part of the community in which Matthew lives: they are in a similar way actual victims of the violence of the present power structure. It seems that Matthew knows quite a few, because he returns several times to the concrete experiences of persecutions which end in death, in a future-form which for the actual readers of the gospel represents the past and the actuality. He uses a typical language not found in the other gospels: they are stoned and crucified(57); but also more general words: they have been killed(58). Matthew knows these persecutions in their most horrible form: when the relatives denounce each other and have each other killed: brother against brother, father against child, children against their parents(59). How these persecutions are brought in line with the events of the war of 70 AD will be further explained in the last beatitude about the 'persecuted for the sake of justice'. It will become clear that for Matthew Jew and Christian will find each other again in death, in striving for justice. The consolation Matthew gives his readers can be seen in the one sentence Jesus speaks: 'who perseveres till the end, will be saved'(60). In Matthew's community live people who know what it means: to be happy while mourning.

Because all indication of a natural death is practically absent(61), the impression is given - probably incorrectly -, that people die only through violence and oppression: a form of death which leaves the relatives in far greater sorrow. But it is precisely these people who will have been touched most deeply by Jesus' saying. Lack of justice is experienced more strongly when superior force is more manifestly present.

In the conclusion of the saying a promise is given of a consolation yet to come. As in the first beatitude we should not understand this in a meek sense. The use of the passive is a hidden indication of God. He guarantees the consolation. He will right the balance of injustice. He will restore all that has been lost through the violence of people. The eschatological perspective is clearly present in this promise as it was in the cause of mourning - the actual persecution for the sake of Jesus' name and God's justice. When the Son of Man comes, the elect will be gathered and the just will shine like the sun in the Father's dominion(62).

Blessed are those who are subjected, because they will inherit the land

Mt 5,5

When the Romans made Palestine into a satellite state, they changed not only the political structure of the country. The imposition of taxes to be remitted in money or in kind, the necessity to maintain an extensive system of civil servants and soldiers, and the possibility of extended international trade created changes in the economic substructure. The fact that the Jews lost the war against the Romans, intensified and accelerated this change. Because the impulse to all this came from outside, foreign juridical changes were introduced: ownership relations with regard to money, goods and land were reformulated, because they had to function in a new order.

They will inherit the land, says the text the Matthew. This was said at a time, when the traditional rules of inheritance were more and more abandoned(63). In ancient Israel the land could only be sold to other clan-members and then only according to strict rules of relationship. The owner could, in times of need, lease his parcel of land to a stranger. He found himself and his family then in a situation of dependency, which could take several forms, but the land remained his property. That legal protection disappeared: the land became an object for trade, not hindered by any previously determined inheritance rules. We read in a contract of sale: 'The buyers who are (mentioned) above and their heirs have the right over this site, to acquire (it) and to sell it, and to do in it everything that they please, and their heirs (as well), from this day (forward) and forever'(64). In this way the sale was guaranteed even against the juridical consequences of a jubilee.

This last fact has a certain importance, because in contemporary documents mention is made of returning properties to the original owners only in the context of the jubilee year. These are probably juridically fictional texts, because in reality the jubilee year was (no longer) celebrated(65). But by determining the differences with the text from Leviticus on the jubilee(66) we can get an indirect description of concrete situations.

Philo gives us the most extensive commentary(67). He connects in his ideology immediately with what the Torah has to say about land ownership. The land has been divided by lot over the different clans and this division must be preserved forever, but no one is owner in the strict sense of 'possessor of the land': 'the whole country is called God's property, and it is against religion to have anything that is God's property registered under other masters'(68). That is why a real sales contract is impossible for land. It is always only about the 'sale of the fruits'.

In the context of the text from Leviticus, Philo indicates that people can sometimes be forced to sell their land or even themselves, but the reflection he gives is typical for his own time and milieu. It brings him to remarks about the precariousness of fate(69), but also to the more realistic statement that these people lack the means necessary to stay alive(70). Most remarkable is that he does not say anything about the duty of the family and the clan to buy back the land and their own people. Whoever falls into debt and is thus forced to pawn and/or sell his land or himself has apparently lost the protection of the clan.

This is even more remarkable in the short juridical description which Josephus gives about such practices. The original legal protection of the land owner is vanished. According to him, one can only become a slave by trangressing the law(71), and he has surprising rules regarding the freeing of these slaves(72). Even more interesting is the fact that the sales contract of land has become a fantastic arithmetical problem which almost always is to the benefit of the buyer: 'When the Jôbêl comes round - the name denotes 'liberty' - the vendor and the purchaser of the site meet together and reckon up the products of the site and the outgoings expended upon it. Then, if the proceeds are found to exceed the outgoings, the vendor recovers the estate; but if the expenditure preponderates, he must pay a sufficient sum to cover the deficit or forfeit the property; if, lastly the figures for revenue and expenditure are equal, the legislator restores the land to its former possessors'(73).

Even if we accept a large amount of fiction in these texts, they show a juridical tendency to make persons directly responsible for the fact that they lose their land and their independence. This happened as an historically irreversible event after the war of 70 AD, when the Roman Emperor confiscated vast tracts of land, declared them as his personal property and/or gave them on loan to veterans and collaborators. Maybe Josephus generalised too much with his sweeping statement: 'Caesar sent instructions to Bassus and Laberius Maximus, the procurator, to farm out (or to lease) all Jewish property'(74), but from the stipulations of the Mishnah about the 'siqariqôn' - the laws dealing with the purchase of confiscated property -, it is clear that Jewish countermeasures were necessary. It is generally understood that these laws(75) were intended to get as much land as possible back into Jewish hands. They effected at least some results.

It is against this rather complicated juridical and socio-economic background that we must understand Matthew's saying. It will be clear that it is a plea for the restoration of ownership relationships which was unheard of in his time. It is a revolt against the increasing confiscation of Jewish land at the expense of the people who, out of dire necessity, have become malleable. Anyhow, for the interpretation of the saying it is important to see that there is a close relation between debt-dependency and loss of property. Loss of land and economically-dependent slavery belong together. Should we not then think of a relation in this sense between the opening and closing sentence of the saying?

In the exegesis of this text we find similar phenomena as in the previous saying: the almost literal similarity with Psalm 36,11 (LXX) is evaluated purely literarily and the subject of the beatitude is understood exclusively in a psychological-ethical way.

From the above, I believe that we should take for

granted that Matthew recognised in the psalm his own time and situation. Notwithstanding all differences in time, there are enough parallels: the cry for justice and righteousness, the struggle between good and evil which remains hidden, but will finally benefit the good because of God's help and fidelity; the identification of the good man with the poor man, the needy and peaceloving man; the identification of the evil man with the rich one, the warring man and the tyrant; the readiness of the just to loan money or goods and the deceit of the one who keeps the mortgage(76). It is a psalm which in many ways resonates as background, but that does not make Matthew's text a quotation in the literary sense of the word. The saying takes an independent position in the series of beatitudes which cannot be reduced to beautiful words: a need in Matthew to come to eight beatitudes or a necessity to express his own thoughts in parallel sentences(77).

The determining point in the interpretation of the saying is the meaning of πραΰς :who are the subjects of this beatitude? One can take many directions here. One comes to a positive evaluation of the concept, if one uncritically follows the Greek background of the word in the way this has been developed in the philosophical ethics. Aristotle is seen as the decisive spokesman: meekness as the golden median between short-temperedness and the lack of anger. The meekness is an attitude which is highly regarded by the Greek philosophers, because it organises mutual relations between people on the basis of humanity(78). Within the Hellenistic culture(79) the concept can, therefore, be used very well in the description of a 'good king'(80). However, for the interpretation of the saying this meaning of πραΰτης does not help much, because it does not explain how the inner logical relation between the preface and the conclusion of the saying should be interpreted. At least I cannot understand how this form of meekness and inheriting the land, can be brought together.

L. Schottroff(81) shows in her study on Christian non-violence, how much the ethical admonitions and basic concepts are tied to concrete social contexts. There is a great deal of difference to be modest and patient from a position of power rather than to show these virtues from a situation of subjection. Something like this is also the case with the meekness in our saying. Meekness becomes more attractive as one finds oneself in an ever more comfortable position. Returning to the psalm where the same sentence is used about the 'meek who inherit the land', it appears that the psalm speaks about the opposition between the law-abiding and the lawless. The evil ones beset the good with violence and cunning. They use sword and bow to hit the poor and needy, to kill them and to take their place. But their power will not last. God already sees the day that they will be put asunder and he laughs at them. For everyone who trusts in God the day of reversal will come. If one is prepared to suffer injustice just a little longer, not to give in to vengeance and anger a little longer, the light of justice will shine. The meekness in this psalm is, on the one hand, an attitude which one must make one's own by being ready not to give in to feelings of anger and vengeance, but, on the other hand, is also something which is imposed on these people. The element of injustice, of the wrong which is done to them, is very explicitly present.

I believe that this 'passive' reality of the concept, the result of what is done to a person, plays (at least a partial) role in Matthew. In Greek the word πραΰς is used also in relation to animals: it is said of horses, asses and bulls which are tamed to work on the land, to carry burdens, to be used in war(82). If this is done to people, it is no longer positive. The word is a description of people who have been made into beasts of burden(83), from whom all aggression is taken away, because they should be ready to be submissive and to give service docilely on the land and in war. 'The meek' are people who have been made subject. As a cluster of words this plays clearly a role in Matthew: indirectly, in a quote from Zachariah which he uses in the story of Jesus' entrance into Jerusalem: 'Look, your king comes to you, in a humble way he rides on a donkey and on a colt, the foal of a beast of burden'(84); and directly, in the words of praise Jesus applies to himself: 'Come to me all you who labor and are overburdened: I have been made humble and little to my very heart' (85). Submissiveness belongs to the animal world: to asses and beasts of burden which carry the yoke on their shoulder, which are exhausted and carry heavy burdens. As an additional argument, I could adduce that the Jewish parallel word is very close to this: the poor person who bows down into the dust, who is being subjected, and who is covered by injustice(86).

This cluster of words creates a bond between the forced expropriation of land and the promise of restoration. Meekness is a beautiful virtue for philosophers, judges, kings and governors. Sumbissiveness is for the common people, but this humiliation will come to an end. All relations of possession will be definitively restored.

Blessed are those who hunger and thirst in relation to justice, because they will eat their fill.

Mt 5,6

What can be nicer than to be able to state something with certainty? It looks like that in this text. 'The addition of the word justice is certainly from Matthew. The re-interpretation of hungering in 'desiring justice' answers the tendency in Matthew to make the beatitudes into ethical prescriptions', writes Schulz as one for all(87). For the exegetes it is crystal clear that Matthew remodelled an original text about hungry people to whom a meal is promised(88). By explicitating the object of their hunger, he has given the saying a different point and a different target group. Hunger has been changed into desire and the subject has been broadened to take in all people who long for justice.

Such unanimity is rare. One must have good arguments to go against this. Yet, I do have a number of questions.

If this idea were indeed so typical for Matthew, one would expect to see it more often. In fact, one puts words in Matthew's mouth as his own, which appear nowhere else in his book. Justice is something which must be fulfilled, must be done abundantly, must be practised; it is a road which one must walk, one must search for it(89). That it can be an object of desire is not be found anywhere.

Furthermore, what can one do with the unchanged use of 'eating one's fill'? To Greeks this sounds rather crude, because it refers to the eating of animals. In koinè and the Greek of the Septuagint the word underwent a social lift, because it is used also for eating and feasting of people, but it has not lost the material meaning that food is consumed. Matthew may have intended it metaphorically. Everything is possible even if there is no repetition of the object. But I am still not sure about the meaning of 'eating one's fill with justice' unless the text deals with the removal of real hunger and real thirst.

The real problem lies in the use of the accusative with the verbs 'hunger' and 'thirst'. This suggests an object-relation between hunger and thirst ánd justice, with all the metaphors that this calls forth. We can find parallels for this, but they are few and they do not really correspond(90). I would like to suggest whether it would not be better to read it as a so-called Greek accusative: blessed are those who hunger and thirst in relation to, or, in relation with justice. Obviously I cannot prove this, but it is a grammatical possibility which offers advantages for the understanding of this text.

Since in this interpretation the literal meaning of hungering and thirsting and of eating one's fill is kept, the saying functions then against the background of this existing reality. Hunger was a real problem in the Palestine of that time. In the course of the century people became poorer and poorer. The loss of the coastal towns and of the rich cities in the Decapolis from Pompeius to Antonius, the exploitation under Herod as a consequence of his building activities, his court in eastern style, and his obligations to Antonius and Augustus, the growing influence of Roman state power under the procurators and the Roman clients, all this was paid for by the people. And if the weather was inclement as in the time of Claudius, under the procurator Tiberius Alexander, the whole country suffered under a destructive famine, which also coincided with the beginning of the war(91).

However, I do not want to suggest that there was always hunger (and thirst) in Matthew's community. Rather the reverse. If we gather the texts which refer to this reality - and it is indicative that there are few -, it becomes clear that these texts call for people to 'give help' rather than that they show their own need. In the question 'what will I eat and what will I drink?',(92), one could still doubt the real meaning. Later on I will try to make clear that in Matthew these questions are not asked by poor people. In the other sentences even this kind of doubt would be improper. The gospel-readers are supposed to help people in need. To give a cup of cold water is praised as a good deed(93). As an example to follow, we have the statement that Jesus did not want to send the people home without food, when they followed him for three days 'because he is afraid that they will collapse on the way'(94). And more important: in the parable of the last judgment the hungry and the thirsty are seen as the living representations of the Son of Man: 'I had hunger and you fed me, I was thirsty and you gave me to drink'(95). The problem of hunger was for Matthew an actual reality, but he and his community are not suffering from it.

Let us return to the saying. The addition 'in relation to justice' changes the point of the saying. Something similar as in the first beatitude has happened and one could well ask whether this change is connected with a changing sociological composition of the group. Addressed are no longer the people who hunger and thirst from a situation of need, but those people who place themselves in that situation in relation to justice. In the same way as in the 'poor in spirit' poverty is presupposed in this saying 'hunger and thirst'. The group of those addressed is curtailed.

In support of this interpretation I think that in the totality of Matthew's gospel a double practice can be pointed out: first there are the people who fast in relation to justice, and secondly there are the people who hunger and thirst when they go out to announce God's kingly power in the vicinity.

The first group is described further on in the Sermon on the Mount, in a following chapter which opens with the programmatic sentence: remember that you will not do justice to be seen by people(96). The practices of justice are mentioned there: giving alms, praying and - that is what we discuss now - fasting. To abstain from food and drink willingly and consciously is, for Matthew, in relation to the practice of justice, i.e. with doing the Torah of God. It is a behaviour which is like Jesus' conduct: he is prepared to bring the totality of justice to fulfillment(97) and, immediately after his baptism, he is driven into the desert by the spirit to fast for 40 days and 40 nights. People who do this are blessed, because God himself will provide food in abundance: manna from heaven to make them aware that man lives from what comes from God's mouth.

The second group is described in the speech Jesus gives when he sends his disciples as royal heralds to announce God's kingly power: to heal the sick like the Messiah does; to raise the dead, to cleanse the lepers and to cast out the demons. They are sent out without anything, without a haversack, without a spare tunic, without sandals or even a staff. They are given the counsel not to accept gold or silver, but to depend on what people will give them to eat. They have received without charge, they should also give without charge. 'The labourer deserves his keep', Matthew adds as the only evangelist(98). In the form of an address to his twelve disciples by Jesus, Matthew describes the early Christian phenomenon of the itinerant preachers, of these homeless and shabby heralds of God who are poorer than the poorest beggar, because they consistently reject any possession. God's slaves, Israel's shepherds, the poor of the land, in search for the lost sheep, they hunger and thirst till they find a welcome in a house or a village (99). Those are the people Matthew thinks of, when he makes Jesus say: 'Blessed are those who hunger and thirst in relation to justice(100), because they will eat their fill'. They are given God's guarantee that he will never let them down.

The change in the original Jesus-saying does not have all that much to do with moralizing. There is a concretisation in practices which occur. There is a certain distance from the hunger people suffer from fate, but - and that is the new aspect - by taking up willingly the fast and by bringing oneself in a situation which carries with it hunger and thirst, this distance is bridged again. The practices mentioned open the possibility, without ideological flattery, to show up the religious implications of hunger: that people are totally dependent on God even to survive.

Blessed are the merciful, because they will experience God's mercy

Mt 5,7

It is a pity that one has to pin oneself on one interpretation in a translation. Matthew chooses his word on the boundary of Greek and Hebrew languages. Thus, he covers a multitude of meaning with one simple word. In translation one must choose one word, but the word will not effect the same associations. In an explanation the cluster can be laid out in its inner coherence.

First of all, it has to be noticed that 'the mercy' primarily refers to the biblical covenant-practices in which the partners bind themselves mutually in fidelity to help one another steadfastly and forever, to stand by one another, to assist the weaker partner in the covenant. This can deal with all kinds of contracts: kings who make peace with each other, but also a guest who is given guest-friendship or family members who want to settle their mutual relations. God entered into such a covenant with Israel and everything which fits into such a covenant is found here: the mutual obligations, the oath of fidelity, the punishment in case the covenant is violated. Mercy is the key word: the prohibition to abuse one's position of power, the obligation to strengthen the weaker partner. There is an element of dependency, but also the possibility of pointing out to the stronger partner that he has obligations. In this way a moment of equality is achieved through the covenant(101). For example, in the covenant between Jonathan and David, Jonathan states at the end: 'And the Lord will be with you as he was with my father. And if I live, you must be faithful (ἔλεος) to me; and if I die, you must not take away your fidelity (ἔλεος) from my house for all eternity'(102); or in the covenant between God and Israel: 'The Lord is a merciful and gracious (ἐλεήμων) God, slow to anger and great in love (πολυέλεος) and faithful; who does justice and creates mercy (ἔλεος); who forgives crime, violation and sin, but who will not let one go scott-free for certain'(103). It is unthinkable to have a Jewish covenant without love, mercy, compassion, pity, fidelity etc., the series now in question(104).

The element of compassion has been given an extra emphasis, because the Septuagint translates, fairly consistently, the Hebrew word with ἔλεος. That does not take it out of the context of the covenant. But there is more attention given to the psychological implications: because of the covenant which God made with his people, which states that God is always ready to overlook the errors of the people, people must also be merciful to one another. The mutual, human compassion becomes the touchstone for Israel regarding its fidelity to its covenant with God.

This is also an ever recurring theme in the literature which is more or less contemporaneous with the Matthew gospel(105). Two phenomena are important for our context: the reflections on God's mercy and those on the correlation between human mercy and divine reward. Without any claim of completeness I would like to point to the following.

In the text from Exodus which I quoted, the relation between the punishment for breaking the Law - as the violation of the covenant - and the mercy of God remained too vague for the interpreters. This became, therefore, the set place in Jewish literature to bring out the problem of the relation between divine justice and divine mercy. The point of departure is always: God is faithful notwithstanding Israel's sins. 'The measure of goodness is five hundred times greater than the measure of retribution' says the Tosephtah in which 'the mercy for thousands' is opposed to 'the punishment until the third and fourth generation'(106). This text can be seen as a later compendium of what has been taught here and there forever (107). In Moses' prayer, as recorded in the Book of Biblical Antiquities it says: 'I ask you, Lord, that your mercy (misericordia) may rest upon your people and your compassion (miseratio) on your inheritance and that your long suffering (longanimitas) may be confirmed in you, because you have loved them above all others'(108). God holds fast to his covenant and even though the sins of the Israelites will make him angry, he will remember his covenant and he will save them 'iuxta misericordiam'(109), when he sees the staff of Moses. God's mercy is a central topic widespread in the actual paranese of Matthew's time and long thereafter.

Similar, even though less widespread is the correlation between 'acts of mercy' and God's answer in mercy. This correlation is especially brought out in the Wisdom literature as elaboration of the principle 'measure for measure'(110). I will return to this in the explanation of Mt 7,1f. I can point especially to Zebulon's Testament

(111), apart from other possible texts(112), in the contemporary literature. Zebulon is presented as someone who, moved by deep pity for Joseph, did everything possible to prevent something bad from happening to Joseph. When his brothers throw Joseph into the well anyway, he does not eat or drink, for two days and two nights, out of pity for Joseph. This way of behaving gives him the right to teach his sons, that 'they have to show mercy to their neighbor, to have compassion on all'(113). Because he did this, the Lord preserved him from sickness and blessed him. God does what man does to his neighbor(114). Zebulon's life must be the great example, because he has always been merciful: 'you also, my children, have compassion toward every person with mercy, in order that the Lord may be compassionate and merciful to you'(115). It is a text which can be read as a very close commentary of the Matthean beatitude.

Matthew's saying is imbedded in the totality of this contextual reality: blessed are the people who know mercy because they will experience God's mercy. No other saying can claim more right to be seen as motto of the gospel: as a summary of content which can be found all through the book.

In the discussion with the Pharisees and scribes the battle is fought over ideology. Mercy is, for Matthew, the discriminating element in Israel's covenant with God - not the sacrifices, not the tithe, but mercy. Three times he returns to this. When Jesus is attacked, because he eats with publicans and sinners, and when Jesus has to defend his disciples, because they have collected ears of corn on a sabbath to eat them, a quote from Hosea serves: I want mercy rather than sacrifices(116); and in the long tirade against the Pharisees and scribes we read: you pay tithes on mint, anise and cummin, but the most important part of the Law - justice and mercy and fidelity - you forget(117). The Torah of God, which is the expression of the covenant which God made with his people, finds its core in mercy. The Law of the covenant and Mercy are identified as it were(118).

This may be sufficient as indication of a larger dispute. Of more immediate importance is the positive understanding of the concept. Jesus is the one who lived it before us. It deals with whole groups of people. In a concluding statement, after describing a series of healing and liberating procedures, it is summarised in a general way: 'and when Jesus saw the masses, he took pity on them because they were worn out as sheep without a shepherd'. Jesus' mercy is for the people who are sick; the blind people he meets on his journeys; the woman from Canaan who comes to plead for her daughter; the two blind men along the road to Jericho; the people who bring their sick; the people who are prepared to follow him and then become hungry; the publicans and sinners who need a doctor more than the healthy; the innocent who are condemned without reason. From the parable of the king and his servant who is unwilling to remit another a small debt, it is clear that mercy should cover also these areas of reality: remittance of debt belongs to the obligations of the Law(119).

Hunger, sickness and debt are the things which Jesus finds and which call forth his mercy. Not so that they stay in their misery, but so that by changing them people will be able to share again fully in the life of the people. Hunger, sickness and debt are the things which Matthew finds in Israel and which he wants to change via the Jesus-movement: also Jesus' disciples are being sent to heal the sick, to cast out demons, to forgive trespasses, to take care that financial debts are remitted, to pray that there will be enough bread for today. Mercy is the source which makes it possible to fulfill the Law of God, the obligations which flow from the covenant between God and his people(120).

More than with the other beatitudes the promise becomes here a reward. The relation between human mercy and the experience of God's mercy was given already in the text of the covenant: 'with the merciful you show mercy', is written in the psalm(121). The guarantee of divine fidelity makes sure that the still expected future can be experienced as already present at the moment that human acts of mercy take place.

Blessed are the people who are pure in heart, because they will see God

Mt 5,8

In Jewish anthropology - the theoretical concepts which in their connection determine the vision of man - the heart plays a central role. It is seen as a psychosomatic quality which represents the whole man. The heart is not a separate part. It is human existence taken as heart. All its characteristics are applicable to man himself. They are legion. The heart is the source of courage and bravery, but also of joy and sorrow, of care and pity, of excitement and desire, of lust and pride, and also of intelligence and foolishness, of trust in God and of conscience. The heart is the centre of man from where he opens himself as a living creature to his environment, reacting to it, giving himself up to it, capable of good and bad decisions, as his own accountable responsibility(122).

'Blessed are those who are pure even in their very heart' is, therefore, a beatitude in which purity is attributed to people, a purity which expands unto the very centre of their being. I have already stated that, for Matthew, this saying must be read in connection with his explanation of the law about the prohibition of adultery: 'it is said: do not commit adultery, but I say to you that whoever looks at another man's wife with desire, has already committed adultery in his heart'(123). The supposition is not that freedom from evil desire leaves the door open for actual adultery. Rather the contrary. The prohibition of adultery implies a heart, pure of all desire to break that law. Matthew is an absolutist who wants a form of Christianity which keeps the Law in its totality.

A number of exegetes see the saying as an ideological slogan in the dispute between Christianity and Judaism. They presuppose a connection with the discussion about ritual laws of cleanliness: a cup and a plate must be cleaned very well, because otherwise they make the person unclean, unfit to perform religious functions. That is meant against the Pharisees especially. They clean the outside of the utensils very well, but do not worry about their own inner reality, in opposition to Jesus(124). This background would then form the concrete content of the saying. Christians must take care to be pure in heart, because the inner, moral cleanliness is more important than ritual cleanliness. Ethics is superior to ritual. The saying would then be a step in the direction of abolishing all rules of cleanliness in Christianity, or, even stronger, it is a Christian criticism on these Jewish practices(125).

It is possible that the saying began to function in this way in later times, but in the Matthean gospel we find indications that this is not true for the time of the book's origin. The halachah i.e. the law-interpretation on adultery is an example in point. The saying does not intend to abolish this law on adultery. The dispute between Jesus and the Pharisees and scribes about their traditions is even clearer. It is a discussion about the ritual law of the washing of hands before meals. From Jesus' answer it is immediately obvious that the whole Law is in question. The command to honour father and mother is mentioned first, but this command stands for all. When the statement on man's uncleanness must be explained, mention of the whole Decalogue follows automatically: evil thoughts, murder, adultery, fornication, theft, false witnessing and blasphemy: what goes out of the mouth comes from the heart and makes man unclean(126). The heart is the place where man's decision is taken to hear and to keep the Law.

This presentation of facts can only be understood against the background of another Jewish theorema: the connection between the realities - Heart, Desire and Law. We find this train of thought in the Palestinian targums, the Aramaic translations which, in the form of additions to the text, give a running commentary. In a summary reconstruction it looks as follows. It began with Adam. God laid two desires in his heart: the desires for good and evil. He allowed him to live in the garden of Eden to keep the Law and to follow the commands. But the evil desire became stronger and made him break the Law. Since then is sin, the possibility to break the Law, at the door of man's heart. This does not take away his responsibility. On the contrary, man must take care that his desire for good becomes victorious by doing justice, i.e. by keeping the Law. Not as Cain did, who thought that there was no judgement, no judge and no future world and, therefore, murdered his brother Abel. Not as the generations after him, whose every desire was always directed to evil, but as Noah and Abraham, as Joseph who suppressed his evil desire when the wife of Potiphar tried to seduce him.

From the beginning the heart is the seat of desire, but this desire is ambiguous: it can lead either to respect the Law or to break the Law(127). That will determine whether a man is just or not. Only he who cleanses his heart from all evil desire, fulfills the Law and is faithful to the covenant which God made with his people. He fulfills the mission which was given to Adam: not to desire to eat from the tree(128). The background of the saying seen from the story of Adam - Adam in the garden of Eden - gives meaning to the promise made to the people who are pure in heart: they will see God. God will show himself in Paradise as he did to Adam: a theme which plays a role in the whole of the apocalyptic literature of the time. The book 'Apocalypse of Moses' puts it all together very clearly: 'Then to them (= all people belonging to the one holy people) shall be given every joy of Paradise and God shall be in their midst, and there shall not be any sinners before him, for the evil heart shall be removed from them and they shall be given a heart that understands the good and worships God alone' (129). The people who are pure in their heart, who do not break the Law even in the desires of their heart, are given the promise that they will be the elect inhabitants of Paradise. And God is in their midst. Paradise, the Law and the Covenant come together in the heart of man(130).

Blessed are the peacemakers, because they will be called children of God

Mt 5,9

Peace is brought in also, explicitating what was already implicit. God's kingly power, possession of the land, justice, mercy, the law and the covenant have been mentioned, as are their opposites - subjection, murder, exploitation, poverty, hunger, thirst and evil desire. Peace means that the struggle has been brought to a good end; that the forces of evil ultimately will be the weakest. Peace carriers are needed for this: Israel, the king, the Messiah, the just are indicated as the proper subjects in Jewish tradition, faithful in this way to its own origin that for Israel nothing can be thought of outside of the covenant. However much peace can be seen as a general situation of salvation, Jewish shalom will not abandon this religious, political and social dimension(131).

The war of 70 AD was (probably) already over, when Matthew wrote his gospel. People of his time looked back on a lost struggle for national independence. The Temple had been set on fire and was in ruins. Jerusalem had been plundered and destroyed. The population was decimated and suffered under a severe political pressure. The impression which one gets from Josephus' book about this war - that everything was lost -, is naturally not correct. Israel's national history did not end in 70 AD(132). The violence of the Roman war machine had put down the centres of Jewish resistance, but it did not put an end to Jewish national consciousness and the desire to live the Torah peacefully: one's own worship, one's own jurisdiction, one's own power structures, one's own culture in language, education and customs. Life went on under changed circumstances. The saying about peacemakers gets a very specific meaning in such a setting. It was heard by people, who knew what war was about and how destructive it could be for mutual relations.

But peace is important also in non-war situations. In his gospel, Matthew uses material from a much earlier period, from the pre-war period when the Temple, the city and the land still functioned normally. And the saying refers to this reality too, thus extending the task to bring peace to the totality of the social order. First of all, making peace is a mission prescribed in the Torah itself. Matthew elaborates on that in his explanation of the torah on murder and the torah on love for one's brother(133). Concrete mutual relations are discussed: if someone wants to bring a sacrifice and remembers that his brother has something against him, he must go to his brother and change him from an enemy into a friend; for anyone who wants to keep the Law, it is essential that he loves his enemies and prays for his persecutors(134). Making peace demands the restoration of mutual relations, which are disturbed by quarrels. It demands a concrete offer of peace to concrete enemies. It demands benevolence, spoken before God, for known persecutors. However difficult this is, whoever is prepared for it will make sure that the Torah retains the force of law notwithstanding everything.

Apart from this concrete behaviour which immediately affects ordinary daily life, Matthew knows another peace movement which is quite specific. In Jesus' address to the twelve he recommends it as a model behaviour. Jesus' followers must spread the message of peace all over the country: they should not go to the pagans or the Samaritans. First of all they must search for the lost sheep of the house of Israel from city to city, from village to village. And when they arrive and have entered a house, they shall speak the greeting of peace, - shalom -, which will function as a blessing or a curse. Woo to them who do not receive them. On the day of judgment it will go easier for Sodom and Gomorra than it will go for those inhospitable people(135). Magical practices are used which are effective, because these heralds of the nearness of divine kingly power will prove it with their lives. Peace is a prophetical reality, which becomes salvation or damnation depending on whether one is open to this urgent call. God's kingly power is near. The people of Israel will be restored in all its glory(136).

Then, finally, Jesus is himself a peacemaker for Matthew. I take the most central story when Jesus enters Jerusalem and the Temple as Messiah of Israel. From the quote from Zachariah it is clear that peace is here in question: 'see, your king is coming to you, humble, sitting on an ass'. Horses and chariots have disappeared. Peace will come because the Messiah-king, David's son, will take power. 'Hosanna for the son of David' shout the people of Jerusalem. And in the Temple he shows how he will use this kingly power. Buyers and vendors, all changers of money and vendors of doves are driven out. But he allows the blind and the lame to come in and heals them from their afflictions. This has not happened since David, since the prohibition that the blind and lame are not allowed to enter God's house(137). David's son restores justice. He prefers these outcasts above all owners, as he prefers the children who recognise Jesus as Messiah in a 'bat-qol', i.e. in a voice of which no one knows where it comes from, or how it is possible that anyone can say such things and which, therefore, is seen as an indication of God. Matthew gives this specific historical reconstruction to clarify that this peace offer is divinely guaranteed(138).

With this story Matthew connects polemically with a long political history, with all the stories about kings and those in power who occupied the Temple in Jerusalem: with the conquest of the Temple by Antiochus Epiphanes who had an altar erected for the slaughter of pigs(139); with the entrance of Pompeius into Jerusalem and his violation of the Temple, because he entered the holy of holies with his court(140); with the battles over the Temple by Herod the Great, at the beginning of his dominion, supported by the Roman army(141); with the final conquest by the Romans under Titus(142). When they had the Temple in their possession, city and country were open to them. It is the same as with Jesus who after his 'liberation of the Temple' leaves the city to spend the night outside, in Bethany, and who returns the next day to enter into his ideological battle with the Pharisees and scribes in long discourses, tirades and curses, and finally goes away and announces the destruction of the Temple, standing opposite it in the garden of Olives, and links this with his parousia: his coming in glory as lightning, unexpected as the downfall of Noah's generation(143). Therefore, be vigilant, because you do not know on which day he will come.

The connection with the great Jewish peace tradition will be clear. The just maintain the Law by making peace with their own brothers, with the enemy and the persecutor. Jesus' heralds appear as prophets of God who give peace or take it away. And Jesus, as David's royal son, realises peace in Israel from the Temple in Jerusalem. But his parousia - his appearance in glory - has still to come. Torah, Prophets and Messiah are the 'leitmotivs'. That all this does not function as an ideology appears from the preferential option which determines the target group: the sick, the possessed, the children, the persecuted and oppressed by enemies as opposed to the leaders of the people, the legal experts, the healthy who do not need healing. Shalom does not become a beautiful saying of salvation, but it is a reality which must be achieved, connected with and rooted in a society full of conflicts, injustice and imperfections.

Paul Billerbeck wrote, in 1926, that he did not know of any rabbinical text which made a connection between making peace and being called child of God. This is probably still true today notwithstanding all new discoveries(144), so that we must accept that Matthew constructed his own theologoumenon. But it is not all that difficult to understand how these two themes could be brought together, if one looks at the biblical background. Especially in the Wisdom literature David, David's son (the Messiah), and the just are those who are appointed as the proper carriers of peace as well as those who are called children of God(145). In Matthew, for whom these texts are verbalisations of experienced actuality, all this has become one single reality. Whoever makes peace will be adopted by God as his child. Or rather God is seen as the one to whom the fatherhood of peace in the final analysis belongs. The covenant, which the Lord made with Israel, is a covenant in which God himself guarantees peace - an eternal covenant of peace(146).

> Blessed are those who are persecuted for the sake of justice, because they possess the dominion of heavens

Mt 5,10 - 12

Matthew lives in a community where physical violence plays an important role, not only as a reality of war, but also on levels which are not so nation-wide, in the relations between groups of people, between an individual and a group and between individuals. If such violence starts from lawful authority or is fostered or supported by it, it is called persecution. That happens because a part of the population cannot tolerate a minority or, in more dictatorial societies, because such a minority takes up positions which are considered dangerous for the state. Blessed are the people who are persecuted for the sake of justice.

What is the reality which Matthew wanted to express? The Lucan imagery has always been determinant in the presentation, especially as the story develops in Acts. If one speaks about persecutions, one thinks about what Luke has to say: the imprisonment of Peter and John, their questioning before the High Court, Stephen's being stoned, Paul's presence there and his journey to Damascus: a historical image in which the growing opposition between Jews and Christians brings about the growth and flowering of the church in Greece and Rome.

Matthew does not know such vivid descriptions or this geographical extension. The reality of persecution is verbalised only indirectly, through Jesus' pronouncements. Geographically, his story is embedded in the Jewish milieu. Persecutions are described in the perlocutives: they will slander and ridicule you; they will drive you out from house and village, persecute you from city to city; scourge you in the synagogues, deliver you into the hands of kings and leaders, kill you, stone you, crucify you: a cluster which should be seen primarily in the context of Palestinian practices(147). This is not to say that is not an important reality for Matthew. He returns to it at the central points of his story(148). The fact that he repeats it six times indicates how much it is an experienced actuality.

The addition 'for the sake of justice' in the beatitude is most remarkable. There is no article: by being just, one attracts persecution. It touches every activity which has a relation to justice, keeping the Torah in all its aspects. It is not by change that the saying has been formulated in this manner. Whenever persecution is mentioned, Matthew places it in the context of 'justice'(149). But he does this in many different ways: as torah to pray for the persecutors; within the context of the desire of the just to see and hear what is given to the disciples; as 'the way of justice' as John walked it; as the blood of the just Abel, the innocent blood shed in the persecution; as lawlessness, finally, which will get worse till the love of many has cooled. Fidelity to the Law stands over against the lawlessness of the persecutor. It is about injustice which is accepted by the just man within God's law(150).

The persecution is always seen as a Christian reality. And there is no need to deny this as long as one also sees that it is embedded in a social reality which is much larger. The struggle for justice, the preservation of the Torah in all its aspects is a continuous political issue, which brings one persecution after another since the arrival of the Seleucides in the territory of Israel, one hundred years after Alexander the Great's death. We can read about this in the books of the Maccabees, in the Sibylline Oracles, in the Testament of Moses and especially in Josephus. In Matthew's time this struggle took on the special form of resistance of those faithful to the Law against the growing pressure from Rome to see the Temple in Jerusalem on the same level as all other temples in the Empire. One can see how the conflict grew from its origin at about the time of Herod the Great's death, when he wanted to place a golden eagle over the gate of the Temple, until the time under Pilate who through pacifist action was forced to remove the army standards with the image of the Emperor from Jerusalem, until the events under Caligula who wanted to place his own statue in the Temple. There were always Jews who resisted with an appeal to the Law, people for whom keeping the Law was more important than life itself, who were persecuted for their actions; slandered, ridiculed, scourged, killed, burned alive, crucified. A bitter history which ultimately led to war(151) and to the destruction of the Temple: 'when you will see the abominable sacrilege in the holy place'(152).

Against the background of this central issue there are many local actions: Jews who resisted the desecration of the Temple by a Roman soldier, the burning of a bible scroll(153), the desecration of the sabbath in Caesarea, and who, therefore, were scourged, murdered and crucified (154). There is mention also of a whole series of individuals who were killed because of their fidelity to the Law. Matthew mentions three of them: the just John the Baptist who accuses Herod of breaking the Law(155); the just Zechariah, the son of Barachiah who is murdered although innocent between temple and altar, when the Romans prepare to besiege the city(156), and, naturally, the just Jesus himself(157). In fact their number is legion: keeping the Law, doing justice was a dangerous business in Matthew's time.

The conclusion of the saying shows a repetition of the opening sentence: 'they possess the dominion of heavens'. The repetition has the effect of a closure. There is, also in content, a similarity between beginning and end, via the people who are being persecuted and the poor in spirit who are threatened in their survival. The series of beatitudes ends as it begins: the attribution of the highest power to people in whom all oppressive power is absent. By keeping the Law of the God of Israel, even if this brings persecution, one shows that one takes God's kingship seriously. It will not remain without effect.

In the form of a direct address to a listening public- 'blessed are you' - Matthew concretely applies the saying: 'blessed are you when people abuse you and persecute you and falsely charge you with evil for my sake'. Persecution is seen in the reality of ridicule and slander, and justice's place has been taken by an 'I': Jesus who now speaks, the Messiah who guarantees justice, Christ who has given his name to his followers(?). For Matthew, it is always clear that Jesus can only be the cause of persecution 'because his followers realise a justice whose norm is taken from Jesus' word and his practice'(158).

Against this background we see, in this further concretisation, a persecution which Jews begin against Jews, because they are in conflict about the question whether Jesus has the authority to test the justice content of living the Torah, to criticise it and to fulfill it. It is not a Christian dispute in which the value and existence of the Torah itself are in question: 'when you are ridiculed, persecuted and accused of all kinds of evil because of the Messiah who stands for justice, you will share in the history of suffering of the prophets of Israel'. Persecution, Justice, and Prophets are the structural codes which come together(159).

Is this the final word on this text? Strecker thinks not(160). The rather vague words - ridicule, persecution and slander, which could happen anywhere - indicate according to him that Matthew thinks of the ever recurring local quarrels, persecutions which are started not so much by Jews, but rather by arbitrary (pagan) citizens. This is not historical proof. At most one can say that Matthew uses a language which is open to interpretation in a Hellenistic milieu: a phenomenon which we have encountered time and again. A fallacy of misplaced concreteness avenges itself. By concentrating too much on one concrete text, one loses sight of the overall picture. The connection between the immediately foregoing and what follows must be maintained at all costs. If we read the text in a 'purely' Hellenistic milieu, it remains true that the persecuted should know that they are part of the history of suffering of the Prophets of Israel. According to Matthew, also in this 'pagan' milieu, the Christians are 'people of justice' who are persecuted as the prophets of Israel, because they keep the Torah. The messianic living of the Torah remains essential for Matthew.

the salt and the light

Mt 5,13 - 16

You are the salt of the earth. You are the light of the world. A combination of metaphors closes off the introduction in grand style. The perspective is directed to the whole world. That is not to say that the reach of Israel is exceeded(161). It goes the opposite way: the perspective is expanded from the hearers in Israel to the totality of the world.

It opens with the metaphor about salt. This is a typical comparison because it is the only place where salt is compared to man(162). Its implication is that salt is a treasure, a value important for survival. It belongs to the first needs of man, next to water and fire, to wheat and clothing(163): to cleanse newborn babes(164), to strenghten the fire for baking bread(165), to pickle meat and fish to preserve them(166). Salt was taxable from very early times, because it is such a necessity of life: one cannot live without it.

However, this aspect of the metaphor has not been developed. It is a silent presupposition which serves as point of departure for a threat: if salt loses its tang, it is good for nothing and can only be thrown out on the street to be trampled on. The point of comparison lies in the possible transition from valuable to useless(167). The metaphor wants to make the hearers aware of their special position: however valuable it may be, it is not to be taken for granted. The everyday expressions 'to throw out' and 'to be trampled on by people' allude to eschatological realities where people are thrown out, in darkness and cold where there is weeping and grinding of teeth. The real point is expressed in the fact that the salt can become 'senseless': a typical use of words, presupposing a Hebrew pun which plays on the meanings 'tasteless' and 'senseless'(168). In Greek only the 'tasteless' has been preserved so that the meaning of the metaphor is reduced. A strange literary effect results from this reduction. The saying is referring now to the closing part of the Sermon on the Mount, to the closing parable about the wise and unwise builder(169) with its message: whoever hears the words of Jesus and does not act accordingly will perish. It is a reference which gives the saying its meaning: the hearers are the salt of the earth when they act according to Jesus' words; if they do not, they will be thrown out of the house like useless salt.

Whether we may take the parable itself - that they are the salt of the earth - as a metaphor of Israel, is a difficult question to prove, although it sounds attractive. The unique answer by Rabbi Joshua in the Talmud, that salt cannot lose its tang (to make clear that Israel cannot lose its vocation?)(170), should be dated rather late, if it is seen as an anti-Christian point. And there are no other parallel texts(171), but the context in Matthew seems to indicate that a Israel-metaphor is intended.

I am alluding to the fact that the addressed are called the light of the world. Without any doubt this was still an Israel-metaphor in Matthew's time. As Israel, in its suffering servant, is the light for the peoples, to heal the blind, to liberate the captives, to bring salvation to the end of the earth(172); as Jesus is the light for the Galilee of the pagans, for those who sit in the region of the shadow of death(173), so are his hearers addressed now as the light of the world. Is this intended as a criticism of Israel: from now on it is no longer Israel, but Jesus and his Ecclesia, the people of God, who will bring light to the world?(174).

Against the background of the given interpretation of the beatitudes this would be a contradiction. Israel in its totality has always been the addressee. It has been stated that the promise of restoration for Israel remains in all the suffering, oppression and persecution. It is stated that God will not renege on his covenant with Israel, notwithstanding the evil of tyranny, injustice and war. In this saying about the light is added that this promise of

God is a light for the whole world. Those addressed stand for the restored Israel, shining as a light for the 'goyim', in the measure in which the beatitudes are applicable to them, whether they are the disciples alone or the whole of the people(175).

This is elaborated in a double parable: via the metaphors of the city on the hilltop and the light in the house. Two qualities are thematised in connection with the mission which 'being light' carries with it. Firstly an impossibility is emphasised: light cannot remain hidden. Just as a city on a hilltop cannot be invisible, the same is true for the light which shines out. The point of comparison is 'one cannot remain hidden'. In all its simplicity it underlines the reality of the diffusion, which Israel effectuates in the world through the addressed hearers: Israel exists as the elect partner in the covenant of God and concrete people are appointed as its bearers. This necessarily gives light to the whole world, in the same way as a city on a hilltop cannot remain hidden.

In a second instance this is amplified with the description of the oil-lamp: it does not belong under a tub, but on top of the standard. Presupposed is the situation of a simple Palestinian house in which there is one tub and one standard and in which all the people are together in the one room(176). The point of the parable is precisely the 'availability for everyone'. The lamp should not be hidden, but placed in such a position that it serves everyone. The hearers must do the same: they should be convinced of the universal value of their option - they are, after all, the representatives of Israel itself - to such an extent that they are ready to act before the eyes of the world so that the whole world will be enlightened.

The finality is expressed in the closing sentence: the fact that the good deeds become visible leads to homage for 'your father in heaven'. Emphasis is on doing, now as 'good deeds': i.e. deeds which flow from fidelity to the Law of the covenant. This will be further elaborated in the next passages for the content. The basic principles are expressed: in solidarity with the poor and the oppressed renounce all vengeance; accept hunger and thirst for the sake of justice; be directed to the good also in situations of persecution, war and injustice; do not give evil desire a chance to take over one's heart. The good deeds must serve to give honour to God himself, the father of the oppressed Israel, because he effects permanent justice in Law: a fidelity which is even willing and able to be compassionate.

Chapter II
THE LAWS FOR THE PEOPLE
Mt 5, 17-48

After the beatitudes we enter into a completely different world with these legal texts. With the former everything was in motion - there were grand sentences full of promises on the basis of endless injustice -, now we are confronted with everyday reality: quarrels, marriage problems, mutual trust and suspicion, evil as it enters one's own life. Peace and Righteousness form the main perspectives, but in fact it plays itself out on the level of the immediate, mutual relationships which are tested daily, affirmed or rejected. We find the behaviour of real people who enter into relationships in the city and in the countryside, mostly harmonious relationships but often in disharmony, if we see the factual legal problematic.

Judgments are made on social realities, not directly, but indirectly via the legal prescriptions which indicate a number of basic preconditions for a peaceful and just Israel. Evil must be eradicated at the root: mutual aggression, evil lust, the unfaithful word, the need to repay evil with evil. Society will be torn apart if aggression, the need to possess, the impulse to deceive and the vindictiveness are not brought under control and transformed. One will have to start working on this, if one wants to give the Torah force of law as the expression of the will of God. There is not much choice, because the alternative is a society of murderers, patriarchs, deceivers and people full of vindictiveness, a reality which no one in Israel wants.

Jesus is the giver of the Law who explicitates how the ideal Israel can be realised. Only if the laws are kept will Israel fulfill the conditions of the covenant which it took upon itself at Sinai. Therefore, each person's commitment is demanded. The whole of the people is addressed to give their cooperation: the 'ekklesiai' of the cities in the first place as the proper institutes to determine punishments, as also the judges, the priests and the men to act according to the Law; but also the slaves, the women and the persecuted to be strong so that they are the ones who will stand to gain. The text remains intriguing, because the whole plays itself out on the paper-thin division of law and ethics. There are many ethical judgments about what must be done, but the real intention is to be a legal text. What are the conditions to give force of law on Matthew's propositions. It is a problematic which is of vital importance for Christianity because its very identity depends on it.

Unless Israel succeeds in bringing about a society where the weak can win from the strong, because the weak have the protection of the Law, it defaults on its purpose: to make the 'goyim' into disciples of Jesus so that they can take part in the covenant which God made with Israel(1).

the prolegomenon

Mt 5,17 - 20

A prolegomenon is a text where a code of law is introduced by a preface. Here the general points of departure are formulated, positions which determined the choices which have been operative in the formulation of the law. Conflicts are resolved by placing together the conflicting tendencies. Even if a specific tendency wins out in the formulation of a certain law, the opposing party has played its role and finds itself in a minority position in the preface.

Law is not an indifferent matter. It stands at the focal point of opposites. This is true from the moment that the law is proclaimed. Whether it is a further elaboration of existing prescriptions or whether a completely new law is formulated, it is always a mirror-image of concrete power positions. Even if it seems that the final text of the law bypasses all opposed interests, these will appear again in the commentaries and the jurisprudence: the interested parties, the defenders of certain interests. Always, the law responds to a specific social struggle.

The history of the Jesus-movement is not different. Christianity profiled itself through the interpretation of the law. Jesus' followers based themselves on him who had given a quite special interpretation of the law. They made his interpretation their own: they developed it and finally concretised it in the gospels. Even if - according to Matthew - Jesus 'interpretation of the law does not play an essential role in the process against him - Jesus is condemned because he presented himself as the Son of Man who, seated at the right hand of the power, as Messiah-judge will appear on the clouds of heaven(2) - his legal practices and his teaching of the law have certainly given offence during the preparation of the case. Matthew presents Jesus in long and short stories as someone who initiated a legal interpretation which found a wide response among the people.

How far was Christianity already separated from Judaism when Matthew wrote his gospel? The choices one makes here determine the total interpretation of Matthew's gospel. They also determine the concrete interpretation of this legal passage in the Sermon on the Mount. It is clear that there were divisions, but the question is whether they existed in all the discussions on the law. Was it a division through the social strata or did the line run along the various groups of the populace? These are questions to which we do not know the answer, although there are some indications to which we need to be attentive. In my interpretation I will show, in any case, that the Jewish way of thinking and feeling is a living reality for Matthew. He is much closer to Judaism than is usually thought; if it is not a lived closeness, it is at least a hope that everything will still turn out for the good. In the introduction to this chapter I have formulated as a summary where this interpretation leads us; now I will have to show which arguments brought me to this view.

'Do not imagine that I have come to suspend the Law and the Prophets. I have not come to suspend but to give them force of law. I tell you solemnly: Amen. Till heaven and earth disappear not one dot, not one little stroke shall disappear from the Law until all things are achieved'. With this famous opening sentence Matthew has Jesus begin before he enters into the real explanation of the Law. Many decisions are at the basis of this translation, the most important of which is the supposition that the opposition between abolishing the Law and its fulfilment still connects completely to the contemporary legal discussions. A law is suspended when no one pays attention any more. It has force of law if it is maintained as a legal prescription. The distinction between suspending and giving force of law is a legal opposition where the very existence of the law is in play(3). According to Matthew, Jesus is a person who maintains the Law, the Torah and the Prophets, in word and deed, exactly in every respect. Notwithstanding the criticism leveled against Jesus, for Matthew he is the final arbiter of the Law, the final interpreter who pays attention to every little stroke.

The two sentences are not without inner connection. The metaphor, in which Jesus is presented as the lawyer who takes care that the law remains in force, is causally connected with the metaphor on the scrolls which will remain unblemished until apocalyptic times. Matthew uses visionary language(4), with words like 'amen', and 'till all things (written in the Law and the Prophets?)(5) have happened'. The holiness of the Law is paramount, its permanence and also the fidelity of Jesus to the Law: conservative attitudes which pose many questions. Does Jesus not say anything new. Are there not abolitions of a number of concrete laws and substitions of law in the following legal pronouncements?

The repeat of the introduction in the following concrete legal texts of Jesus creates the deepest opposition. Time and again(6) the difference between the Old Law and Jesus'-own pronouncements is emphasized: 'you have heard what was said to the elders ... but I say to you'. It looks as if Jesus is proposed as the new Moses; not as an interpreter of the Law, a lawyer, but as a law-giver who proposes for his followers a new, better and more perfect Law.

There is no need to deny that in these legal texts new things are said - I will, obviously, come back to that -, but D. Daube and E. Lohse(7) have produced long quotes from rabbinical bible commentaries which show that, also within rabbinical Jewry, certain legal discussions are formulated from the point of opposition between 'hear' and 'say', 'understand' and 'explain'. The rabbis in the second century treated the Law much the same as Jesus did. The point of departure is always the letter of the Law. After such a quote from scripture comes the commentary, sometimes anonymous, but most often as a pronouncement credited to a rabbi by name, often in the 'I' and 'you' form. The Law is then explained in an actualising application. Ordinary, worldly arguments are used, but also other quotes from the Law as well as discussions, comparisons, stories and parables.

The Law is holy and not a iota or stroke will be abolished, but in the meantime it is necessary to solve urgent problems of life. The rabbis want to commit their lives to the Torah and its fulfillment, because that is the will of God, but they are also faced with new questions and problems for which they must find a solution. The very urgency of the need makes them creative. Through this solution they have managed to give Judaism a chance to survive till the present day notwithstanding the crisis of two exhausting wars against the Romans.

Because they discuss - text after text - the whole of the Torah, all subjects of the mosaic law are scrutinized: that the Law must be fulfilled is taken also in this quantitative sense. It presents them with the opportunity to develop their ideas on a broad scale: marriage, legislation for foreigners, sacrifices and prayer, oath-taking, legislation on eating and drinking, commerce, sickness and health, the relation to authority, the judiciary, education. Who can manage all that? Not without reason do they have the tradition that the Talmud is like a sea of knowledge, an encyclopedia where everything is discussed.

Matthew's texts find their foothold in a living Jewish reality. I have to limit myself to show this. For historical reasons, especially, I have concentrated on the Mishnah itself, the first, complete Jewish legal compendium after the great wars against the Romans. No other contemporary book gives a better insight in the actual legal discussions. Obviously, one may not date every sentence to the time of Matthew's gospel back - the Mishnah was written as a book only about a century later - but, as a totality, it expresses certain models which do not change all that quickly. Furthermore, on the basis of critical Mishnah studies(8) we can distinguish between earlier and later traditions, based also on the way the rabbis used it, dating traditions by name(9). Add to this the fact that a number of legal texts have been preserved which date back to the time of Matthew and which can therefore be used as basis: Philo in his texts which give a literal interpretation of the Torah(10), and Flavius Josephus when he summarises the Law(11).

Six Torah pronouncements are in Matthew's text the point of departure for a longer or shorter halachah: an instruction about the way one must go, if one takes this or that command or prohibition as expressive of God's will and wants to bring it to realisation. Not only knowledge needs to be helped, but above all the doing of the Law. In the introductory sentences it says: 'who abolishes even one of these commandments, be it the most unimportant, and who teaches this to men, will be the least in the kingdom of heaven; who fulfills the Law and teaches it, will be called great in the kingdom of heaven; because I say to you: if your fidelity to the Law is not greater than that of the Pharisees and the scribes, you will not enter into the kingdom of heaven'.

Central is the kingdom of God: who will be considered great or small or who will be excluded completely. Oppositions are created which are of extreme importance, because well being or exclusion is at stake. In final analysis it is a question of the difference between saying and doing (words and deeds): a theme which is dear to Matthew and which he always links to his criticism of the Pharisees and scribes. They can say it so well, but they do not act accordingly(12). Jesus' followers must not make that mistake: a greater punishment and guilt will befall them(13).

Matthew deals with a controversy about the Law, but it is part of a much wider message. What Jesus imminently will be teaching about the Law, is so much tied up with Righteousness, the real intention of the Torah, that from now on no one can get around it. The closing sentence of this introduction is at the same time the opening sentence for the whole of the following.

> you must not kill; and if anyone does kill he must answer for it before the court

Mt 5,21 - 26

First comes the Law on murder. The text of the law as given by Matthew shows that there has been a change in the old practices of vengeance, where killing obliged the relations of the dead person to bring about a restoration of the balance. What is added is that he, who kills, must answer for it before the court. Between murder and the revenge-killing we now find the court has to pass judgment. The court will then also take the responsibility for the execution of the sentence(14).

Even if not everything is clear, we do have fairly good information on this contemporary legal organisation. Basically we have a two-tiered system present in every place of some importance(15). On market days, the second and the fifth day of the week(16), the 'court of three' sits: a tribunal of three men which dealt with monetary matters. It makes sure that debts are paid and that marriage contracts and buy-and-sell contracts are adhered to. If need be, it determines the taxes, fines, indemnifications and punishments. It oversees the payment of the tenth and other forms of taxes. Finally, it determines the date of the new moon and the new year: important for the beginning and the end of many religious, social and financial obligations(17). So this 'court of three' is an important institution.

That, at least, is the way the Mishnah sees it. According to Josephus, this 'lowest' court was organised in a slightly different way. According to him, Moses prescribed that seven virtuous men should be appointed judges in each city, men who were trained in zeal for the Law; they must be assisted by two servants from the tribe of Levi(18). When he himself was the leader of Galilee, at the start of the great war, he appointed seven men in each city to act as judges for 'simple' cases(19). Apparently the numbers fluctuated. In the Damascus Document there is mention of a court of ten(20) and the number 12 is also mentioned(21). It is impossible to prove a preference on historical grounds; most likely, different numbers functioned in different places. Common to all the sources, however, is that there existed a 'lower' organisation, competent in specific legal cases.

Apart from this there is another body, the 'court of

twenty-three', which handled all capital questions: all those matters in which the Torah demands the death sentence(22). They are quite numerous because the point of departure is the Decalogue: idolatry, blasphemy, black magic, conjuration of dead people, desecration of the sabbath, cursing one's parents, murder, death caused through the fault of man or animal, transgression of all manner of sexual codes, abduction, giving false witness in capital cases(23). There is an extensive casuistry, not only about the deed itself but also about the proofs, the procedure and the ways to come to a conclusion to prevent the court from acting without due care(24). The college is called the (small) sanhedrin to distinguish it from the large sanhedrin in Jerusalem which, however, had the same function apart from some local peculiarities. It acts as the gathering, the 'keneset' of the whole city-community (25). There are indications that in Hellenistic-Roman times it took over functions from the 'city council'(26): an institution which presented itself as the representative of the various groups in the community, as the (representative of the) 'ekklesia'(27). In any case the same people will often be present in these consultations in one or another capacity.

It is important to understand this in order to see how Matthew meant the extension of the torah about murder. Some read a crescendo in it: he who is angry with his brother will answer before the Sanhedrin (in Jerusalem?); he who calls him a fool will be punished with the fire of the gehenna. It is seen as a progressive procedure in which the gravest infraction calls for the most serious punishment(28). A number of things can be brought up against this interpretation. The sequence 'getting angry-saying raka-calling a fool' is not a climax. The expressions are more or less equivalent. The same can be said for the different courts mentioned: the sequence does not fit. Where the torah on murder is in question, one comes automatically before the small sanhedrin. For calling raka, which directs to the sanhedrin, one should then think of Jerusalem as a court of appeal. But this institute does not fulfill the function of a court of appeal(29), even though its jurisdiction is greater than that of other local sanhedrins because it had authority over the Temple and the palace and therefore enters into negotiations with the Roman occupation. The threat of punishment with fire, finally, is anyway outside this (supposed) sequence; this is not for a tribunal but speaks of a sentence of being guilty even unto the netherworld of fire(30).

Therefore, the halachah is not meant as a climax. The prescriptions are rather parallel sentences which repeat the same message(31): not only murder but even the aggressive expression is by itself under the law of murder. The aggressive instincts which form the origin of the act of murder are as divisive of the community as the act itself. It may seem that Jesus says something completely new, but in fact it is only a refinement of what the Torah already says. Actually, it is an explanation in rabbinical fashion of Num 35,20 - 21. This text states: 'If someone maliciously manhandles another or intentionally throws something so that he is killed, or when someone because of enmity hits another with his fist so that he dies, then he who has hit him, must die because he is a murderer'. In the same way as Hillel explains the text of the torah on divorce - 'érwat dabar' (something unbecoming) is read as 'érwat' ánd 'dabar' -, in the same way the text from Numbers has been separated in two possibilities: when someone kills another ánd when someone hates another or is his enemy, he must die. Jesus uses halachah to make sure that the torah on murder will be respected.

Not only the actual killer but everyone, who out of hatred or enmity divides the community, must be discussed in the 'ekklesia' of the city and must be condemned. He is answerable before the court, before the sanhedrin in order to undergo the sentence. This judgment will have force even in the netherworld where the fire of destruction burns. We need to remember Mt 18,15 - 17 which gives the procedure: if your brother has broken the Law, try to convince him privately. If that does not work, call in one or two others; if he still does not listen, call in the ekklesia: if he does not listen this popular assembly, consider him as a heathen and a publican, as someone who does not count anymore as a member of the people, but as a foreigner in the city(32).

Exegetes would rather wish that the saying of Jesus is a saying of Wisdom(33), because they cannot imagine that this radical way of saying things can be real. Even more, it is unimaginable that emotional outbursts are connected with politics via the Law: as with murder, so with anger; what is in question is the community itself. In the name of the people the balance of peace is reset time and again in the sanhedrin.

This is a strong opening. From the very beginning we see a community of brothers who make mutual love their strength. That this requires more than self-control is verbalised in the following halachah: if someone is on his way to the Temple and remembers that his brother has something against him, let him leave his offering before the altar and let him return to his brother to reconcile. This reconciliation is the centre of the saying. Διαλλάσσω is the exact word to indicate the transition from enmity to friendship. Wat is in question is an exchange of positions: the hostile brother is made into a friend again, because there is no access to God in a community which is divided by enmity(34).

It is a saying which in all its simplicity does not need much commentary. At its origin is a way of thinking in absolute oppositions: if the mutual bond has been hurt, enmity takes the place of the original relationship and enmity is opposed to access to God. And according to the rabbis, enmity already exists when someone refuses to speak to his brother out of hatred for three days(35). Is something like this intended? Anyhow, the mention of the Temple wants to make clear that mutual peace does not exist outside of God.

It seems that Matthew without much ado recommends practices which after the destruction of the Temple can have had very little meaning: a phenomenon which characterizes the whole of Jewish literature for centuries(36). This is often explained as a conservative tendency. The factual context in Matthew creates, however, a particular literary effect: as a reader one is placed in the time before 70 AD and this reinforces the literary illusion that we hear a word of Jesus himself. By presenting Temple practices as reality Matthew writes history without losing the inner meaning of the message.

A third saying is added: come to an agreement quickly with your adversary. It is a short parable which throws unexpected light on the immense oppositions which have arisen in Israel among the brothers because of the changed economic conditions. Notwithstanding the diminution in value of properties and services the circulation of money is increasing. Therefore, people live in serious debt without the possibility of redeeming themselves through other goods: lands, goods or personal services. The court holds that a contract must be honoured. This requires enforcement. Who has debts lives under the threat of a sentence which may put him in jail from which he can only be freed if a third person will pay his debt.

In this halachah it is a private debt, payment of which can be enforced by putting the debtor in prison in order to force the family to pay. In the parable of the merciless slave(37) the two principal possibilities are juxtaposed: the king can sell as a slave a state official together with his wife and children to pay his debt, if the man did not fulfill his fiscal obligations, and a private creditor can enforce the payment of a debt through imprisonment. Hard possibilities which make clear that the mutual relations have been severely disturbed(38).

After what we said above, it is not surprising that there is mention of the judge. More difficult to understand is that he seems to be able to function alone. We have seen that financial transactions belong to the 'court of three'. The proper name is 'court for financial matters'. Originally the three could be chosen by the parties themselves(39), even in a changing constitution of the court; but under the influence of the Pharisees this democratic openness had been more and more restricted. The members of the court must be 'experts in the Torah'. The president must at least be a 'wise man', an expert ('mufla'), fit ('mumcheh'), somone who by imposition of hands is accepted among the righteous: indications of the control which was progressively more exercised (led by the Pharisee members of the Jerusalem Sanhedrin?)(40). There is even a supposition that people are sent from Jerusalem to function as judges in other cities in the land(41). Whether this means that apart from the tribunal of three (or seven) and twenty three, there are also single judges is difficult to determine on the basis of available historical sources(42). More likely is the opinion that a judge as permanent president of the various colleges is seen as 'the judge' by the people, even though he himself as a legal expert will have taken care that the required number of judges was present(43).

Finally, the saying presupposes that the debtor has the possibility to come to an agreement with his creditor. This is probably based on fact. The fact that the punishment is not really adapted - a prison sentence does not guarantee the fulfillment of a contract sufficiently - gives the debtor an opening to negotiate. But he must act quickly, while he is still on the way with the adversary, because the punishment is terrible and he will not escape till he has paid the whole debt.

All in all it is a strange saying which is not easily explained. It must have been significant for the real situation that not the creditor but the debtor is addressed. The good counsel given is useful only for people who have debts. They know what it is all about and how true the insight is. However true to life the text is, it would be a mistake to regard it only as a concrete rule of behaviour. In the context the text functions as a basis for what has been said about the necessity of reconciliation. It adds that it must be done quickly, while the time is still there, because the punishment is close at hand and is terrible. Jesus uses a practical insight which his listeners recognise as sensible - come to an agreement quickly with your enemy -, in order to bring them to fulfill the law on manslaughter even to its most difficult consequence: the reconciliation with one's enemy. The need for speed reinforces the appeal not to postpone peace in the community even by a day.

you must not commit adultery

Mt 5,27 - 30

Just as in the Decalogue, the torah on adultery follows that on murder. There is no further explanation of intent or punishment. The fact that the texts in Exodus and Matthew are short and identical, suggests that they speak to the same reality through the centuries. But that is, obviously, not true. Adultery as an act is connected with marriage and marriage practices. These change under the influence of changing economic conditions. So does adultery. Therefore, I will have to deal with marriage and opinions on marriage, first of all the position of the man because the man is addressed in the following commentary.

The man is the absolute possessor of the woman. She is not without rights as we will see in the following halachah, but the man has an extremely dominant position which he never loses. I want to trace this shortly in the various phases which the Mishnah distinguishes in marriage.

entering into marriage:
'There are three ways a man can acquire a woman: by money, by a document or by sexual commerce'. This is the general point of departure(44). Even though there are historical developments in this, all three ways are in the nature of a sales contract in which the man is the buyer and the woman the merchandise. The man can open a court case on the basis of hidden defects(45), unknown promises made(46), a promised virginity which is non existent(47), wrong information on social and financial position(48). And he will win his case because he bought 'in error'(49). He is advised to enter into a marriage with a virgin on the fourth day of the week, so that he can bring his case to court on the fifth day when the court of three sits(50). It is clear, then, that the legal position of the man and the woman are not equal. Once a man enters into marriage with a woman through one of the three manners of acquisition, she becomes his possession: she is passed from the dominance of her father into the dominance of her 'baal', her husband. The woman is bound to her husband. For her this means that any other marriage relationship is an infringement of the rights of her husband: it is an act of stealing, a rupture of an existing marriage. A man is bound by the rights of another man. If these are not infringed upon, he is free. He can marry more than one woman. Each marriage is an

increase in property which gives him a greater social standing in the community(51).

obligations of the husband in the marriage:
A woman will never be completely self-sufficient. She is and remains in a position of dependence, more so when she marries because, then, she loses even the right over the 'products of her hands'(52). Before the marriage her father has control over these but he is not allowed to use them. After her marriage her husband can use them for the maintenance of the family. He can even impose the amount of work she is to do. That is not to say that the man has no obligations. He is responsible for her maintenance, for her eventual freedom from slavery, and for her burial: i.e. he must care for her till the end of life. This obligation for maintenance is expressed in ordinary things: minima are indicated(53) which, obviously, are time- and condition-bound. It does not look very generous: some barley, oil, dried figs, a bed, a hat, shoes, a dress for the year. It is proposed as the minimum for the poor(54).

the end of the marriage:
Let us leave aside for the moment the possibility of repudiation which is treated in the next halachah. Marriage ends with the death of the husband: a complex situation because there remain many financial obligations. The remaining wife (or wives), children and possible other relations have their own rights. The wife is given priority: she can claim the marriage payment, which is to give her a chance for survival (and a future marriage?)(55). If she remains in the house of the husband, she retains the right of sustenance which is guaranteed over the rights of the children(56). The laws of succession determine that the sons come before the daughters but, in case of a lack of means, the maintenance of the daughters comes before the share of the sons(57). Daughters are a possession which needs to be protected against loss. And that closes the circle(58).

Against this background we must see the law on adultery. The freedom of the husband and the unfreedom of the wife indicate the unequal position of both. A man cannot commit adultery against his own marriage. Only the woman can do that. Therefore, she is always the guilty party. A husband's adultery relates to the rights of possession of another husband. He commits adultery if he infringes on acquired rights: when he, either by money or by a document or sexual commerce acquires a woman who has an existing marriage relationship with another man. Adultery is a question of right of possession which begins when a man has laid claim to it(59).

Jesus' commentary on this law does not change anything, although it is a real radical explanation: whoever even looks at another man's wife with lust, has committed adultery in his heart. A lustful look infringes on the right of possession of the husband. The law is extended: not only money, contract or sexual commerce constitute an infringement in the marriage of a brother, desire is sufficient to commit adultery(60).

In the explanation on the beatitude on the pure of heart I have sufficiently explained the relation between heart, law and paradise. In this text the promise is concretised under a specific aspect. If someone is not master over his own heart, the locus of desire, he will be unable to live by the prohibition of adultery. The heart is as much a source of law-breaking as is money or sex. The accent here is not on the opposition 'inner' against 'outer' (the inner desire over against the external act) or on 'spiritual' against 'physical' (the intention of the act over against the act itself), but on the opposition between 'complete' and 'incomplete'. Only one who is free of desire in the depths of his heart, has fulfilled God's will and will receive the vision of God as his reward. The author probably wants to indicate an inner coherence between the two realities: one, who is free from desire, is perfect as God is perfect. However much this is in line with the stoic ideal of ἀπάθεια, against the background of Jewish thought it is a reference to Adam (and Eve) before desire entered the world through sin.

Although the main sentence does not express the punishment, the following sentences on the possibility of being thrown into gehenna after the 'scandals' of the eye and the hand, suggest this association. Adultery also calls for the sentence, because it breaks the peace between brothers: even if it is only a question of desire. Structurally there is a parallel with what is said in the earlier halachah on the infringement of the torah on murder.

The Mishnah treatise, 'The Sanhedrin', speaks about this quite openly: a man who has sex with a girl who is engaged, must be stoned(61); a man who commits adultery with a married woman, can expect to be strangled(62). I have already stated above that all infringements of the Decalogue are punishable by death.

Is this true also for Matthew's time?

Within historical research there has been a change of insight. More than in the past it is accepted that various, not uniform legal practices have existed in the Roman Empire. There are indications that on the local level-also contrary to the Roman legal system - the possibility to execute people remained for a long time(63). In that sense the general historical research supports the Sanhedrin treatise(64). But there remains a doubt regarding the time and situation for Matthew: why does he mention the gehenna, if one could execute the death sentence(65)? Why does he use as his last admonition that one must consider the lawbreaker 'as a heathen and a publican'(66)? Why is there no mention of the fact that such a person deserves the death sentence? Rather than of the death sentence these texts make us think of the sentence passed on an absent murderer: the exclusion from the community of Israel. The guilty one is handed over to the punishing hand of God which will come without fail: an early death, infertility, sickness, disaster etc.

People must have been become conscious of the fact that 'the exclusion' is a punishment which is not completely outside human interference. A social exclusion, which is decided upon in a people's meeting, does not remain ineffectual with regard to a person's well-being and functioning. It could even be used as punishment in situations where, for external reasons - e.g. the attempt of the Romans to obtain exclusive jurisdiction in capital cases - the death sentence became impossible. We find mention of this also in the Mishnah which dedicates a whole treatise to it: The Exclusions(67). This begins with a list of transgressions which the Torah punishes with 'expulsion from the people'. The list is generally the same as the transgressions for which the treatise 'The Sanhedrin' prescribes death(68). To make a long story short: the adultery of the husband is also mentioned here. The husband who has sexual intercourse with the wife of another, must be excluded from the 'ekklesia' of Israel. He is declared as a non-Jew, a goy who will have no part in the promises of Israel.

Against this background we can understand better the inner logic of the halachah in Matthew. Desire leading to adultery is punished by expulsion which will remain valid unto gehenna. The reward to remain part of Israel is opposed by the threat of expulsion which one calls upon oneself through desire, through the eye and hand: and it will be eternal in gehenna, in the underworld. Tearing out an eye and cutting off a hand are clearly prophetical practices which remind us of the desert ascetics. What is meant is that the fulfillment of the Law pertains to the whole person, the body included(69). If one strives for this perfection, one will not allow even eye or hand to bring one to the forbidden places(70).

anyone who divorces his wife, must give her a writ of dismissal

Mt 5,31 - 32

The man-woman relationship is intrinsically determined by the social and economic relationship of a given culture. Although there is no coincidence, social economics determine the concrete limits for the man-woman relationship. The innumerable variations which, nevertheless, exist in the various cultures, are like hopeful utopias. The position of the woman is not fate. Within limited contexts which cannot be immediately exceeded, there remains the possibility of new initiatives which will create a more equal balance between rights and duties, between likes and dislikes so that existing patriarchy will be limited and not yet existing matriarchy will be extended.

In the supposition that I have not overlooked important data for the time under discussion, there are three elements which influenced the man-woman relationship in Matthew's time: the barter on the basis of a sales contract, the dominant influence of agriculture, and the existence of slavery. Each has, in its own way, concretised the juridical and sociological position of the woman.
Let us consider this briefly:

the woman as a piece of merchandise:
I have already mentioned some elements. The point of departure that the future husband who acquires for himself a wife through either money or a document or sexual intercourse, is within the framework of buying something through a sales contract. This holds true specifically for the first two: acquisition through money or a document. Different from Greek, Latin and German customs, in Palestine it is neither the girl, nor the father of the girl who must take care of the dowry. Here it is the very opposite. The future husband must gather a sum of money, to be determined mutually, which is to guarantee that the marriage contract will be fulfilled. If the contract is broken, the woman can claim the money which was stipulated at the beginning of the marriage. From the times of Hillel and Shammai more primitive forms of acquiring a bride have disappeared. As a tradition to their names it is said that the acquisition sum is set at one peruta (say, a dime) by Hillel or at one denarius (a day's wage) by Shammai(71). Another model is developing in their time. The value of the bride is fictitiously determined in a document at (at least) 100 day's wages for a widow and 200 for a virgin. The husband needs to give that sum only when he divorces

his wife. In the meantime the document serves as a guarantee for the marriage: a mortgage on the property of the husband which must be paid in cash in case of divorce(72). Because of the lack of hard cash such a sum is not easily available. So it begins to function as a deterrence against quick and easy divorce(73).

the woman in rural culture:
How much the woman is linked to land property is clearest when it is said indirectly: after it becomes obvious that a woman did not enter marriage as a virgin and she is forced to say: 'after you got engaged to me, I was raped and your field has been flooded'(74). Juridically this is expressed in the obligation to acquire property for all the money which the woman brings into marriage. Even the fruits of her land must be used to buy new property. Even old slaves, old olive trees and vineyards, which she brings into the marriage, should be sold to buy new property, but this practice ran into great opposition(75).

the woman as slave:
Woman and slave are very closely connected. It cannot be without good reason that the description of a letter of dismissal is always followed by descriptions of obligations for slaves(76), and that the position of the slave alternates with that of the wife(77). However, the difference is also emphasised time and again. However much the wife's position can be compared to that of a slave, if she brings even one slave into the marriage she is freed from the obligation to bake, wash, or grind grain; if she brings two slaves, she does not have to cook or nurse the baby; for three slaves she is freed from the obligation to take care of the bed of her husband and to spin; for four she is allowed to sit the whole day on a chair - although not all the rabbis are happy with this last one(78).

To live in such a one-sidedly determined male culture is not easy for a woman unless there is a strong women's community: a solidarity among women softens the mechanisms of oppression. And that is what we see happening: the wife is directed to other women in her surroundings: to her immediate partner(s) in the marriage - her 'tsara', the woman who has been bound in marriage together with her if the man has more than one wife; to the house of her father, where she will find her mother and her sisters, her aunts and nieces; to her in-laws, her mother-in-law, sisters-in-law etc(79), to her female slaves(80), to the wives of neighbours with whom she shares the communal responsibility for the maintenance of her house(81). This female community becomes visible on the occasion of feastdays or days of mourning. We find it in Matthew's gospel when it says in the description of the death of Jesus: 'there were many women who looked on from a distance; they had followed Jesus from Galilee to serve him; among them was Mary Magdalen, Mary the mother of James and Joseph, and the mother of the sons of Zebedee'(82). We find it also in the story of the burial and the resurrection where Mary Magdalen and the other Mary support each other(83).

Men and women live in strictly separated worlds. Only in marriage are they together, but surrounded by a number of prohibitions and prescriptions which keep the total social system inviolate. The institute of dismissal needs to be understood in this context. In the Mishnah we read: 'Shammai's school says: a man is not allowed to dismiss his wife (to send her from his house) unless he has found something of nakedness in her because it is said: 'because he has found something of nakedness in her'. But Hillel's school says: (he must send her away) even if she has spoiled his food because it is said: 'because he has found something unbecoming in her'(84). The play on words of the Hebrew on which the different interpretation of the text of Deuteronomy is based, is not possible in English. The point is that Shammai's school sees only the reality of nakedness as a reason for dismissal, while in Hillel every way of acting of the wife which indicates a lack of submission, is a valid reason to banish her from the marriage. This discussion is found in the dispute between Jesus and the Pharisees. They ask whether a man may dismiss his wife for any reason. They take the point of view of Hillel's school to put Jesus to the test. Jesus does not answer directly, but from his answer he shows that he stands in the school of Shammai: a man is not allowed to dismiss his wife except in the case of adultery(85).

The mention of 'lewdness' as an exception - also in the Sermon on the Mount - is connected with the idea of obligation: a man must dismiss his wife if she has committed 'lewdness'. Adultery is obviously part of that, even though it is not so clear how it can happen in such a society. But the word 'lewdness' is broader which indicates that the author has had also other forms of misbehaving in mind. There are enough suggestions. In Matthew's community, the story of Mary and Joseph was known: because Joseph was a just man - i.e. because he wanted to follow the Law- Joseph thought he had to send Mary away(86). Using the word 'lewdness' brings in (at least) this possibility: a man must send the woman away, if she is pregnant by another man before the marriage(87). Bonsirven points in a different direction. According to him Matthew was thinking of the levitically invalid marriages when he spoke about 'lewdness'(88). It is now clear that his theory needs to be reformulated more stringently. We can see early traces of a caste-system in Palestine of that time: certain groups cannot marry certain other groups(89). If this happens nevertheless - something which is quite possible in a society where many adults die early in life and leave children unattended; where forced slavery exists and where many children are abandoned - a legally forbidden marriage must be corrected(90). Finally, the word 'lewdness' could mean (temple-)prostitution(91) in direct connection with fertility cults: the practice of entering a temple as being infertile in order to obtain children from the divinity cannot be excluded in first and second century Palestine (92).

Anyhow, the halachah about the right and the obligation to dismiss does not give a final decision about these 'exceptions'. In the principal sentence adultery is central: who dismisses his wife makes her into an adulteress, and who marries a dismissed wife commits adultery. This follows directly from the foregoing explanation of the law on adultery and amplifies it with a new statement: not only lusting after a woman falls under the prohibition of adultery but also dismissal(93).

All this is seen from the point of view of the man. He is responsible because he dismisses. He drives his wife to adultery and he commits adultery when he marries a dismissed wife. This explanation of the law should be seen as an amplification of what the Mishnah says about the seducer and the rapist. They are responsible for the consequences of their actions. The seducer of the girl must pay the damage, the loss of the value of the girl and the legal fine, unless he marries the girl; the rapist must marry the girl and furthermore he must pay a sum of money to recompensate for the pain inflicted(94). In the same way the man is bound to the marriage contract in Matthew: except in the case of lewdness he is not free to ban his wife from the house.

The formulation, however, is not that direct. It is stated in an indirect way that, via the indication of the effects of dismissal, it leads to adultery. As we said in the foregoing halachah, this means: it leads to expulsion from the people. The man effects the expulsion of his wife from the community of Israel in the same way as he places himself outside the community of Israel if he marries a dismissed wife. Matthew 19 gives the ideological argument: because of the hardness of their hearts Moses allowed a man to dismiss his wife, but that was not so in the beginning. The hardness of heart, which prevents Israel from keeping the Law of God, is a theologoumenon belonging to the covenant of the Sinai(95). This apostasy reached its height in the adoration of the golden calf. Moses had just received the ten commandments from God and found the people being unfaithful upon the return. Because of their stubborness he allowed them to dismiss a wife. The earlier infidelity to God continues till the present time. Whoever uses the permission given by Moses, participates in the events which followed the announcement of the ten commandments: he continues the infidelity to God's will(96). In the beginning this was not so. In the beginning God united man and woman into one flesh and what God has joined together, no man break asunder. The Covenant of Israel with God and the utopia of Eden belong together. A man who acts against this utopia of the paradise breaks the covenant, not only for himself but also for his wife(97).

I must add one thing more. To give an evaluation I would like to know how this prescription functions in reality. One could imagine that this anti-male character goes against the existing marriage culture which looks only at the needs of the man. It is really symptomatic in a society, which points to the woman as the one who breaks the marriage bond, that only the man is considered guilty for the divorce. Because the point of view of the man is maintained, however, an element of tutelage remains: the presupposition is that the woman needs protection against male arbitrariness. Apparently that was a necessary as well as the best possible solution. If we look at this from a different culture we can see its limitations. A lot of other conditions must be fulfilled if we are to realise the utopia of Eden in and through marriage: after all, the least one can say of that utopia is that it has to be good to be there.

you must not take an oath which you do not keep, but you must pay the debts of your oaths to the Lord

Mt 5,33 - 37

Coming from the Mishnah it is understandable that, after the halachah on murder, lust and dismissal, the oath is now the subject. Of the two treatises in the Mishnah on the oath, the first - on the judicial oath - is found in the seder on damage claims, among the treatises on civil law(98), the judges and the courts; while the second - on vows - is found in the middle of the seder on women, among the treatises on the rights and obligations of the woman in-and-outside marriage. Apparently it is the same in Matthew. After the court and marriage comes the oath: a remarkable indication that confirms how much this explanation of the law is rooted in Jewish thought and imagination patterns.

There is a double reality in the oath: the hard reality of the court where truth must be brought to light through the oath, and the reality of everyday life where vows are taken between man and woman and between friends, vows which say that the other will not be harmed by this special dependency. What binds these two worlds together is the solemn invocation of God's name (respectively a substitute of this name). This does not mean that the subject matter is the same(99).

For the court there are three possibilities: the oath of witness, the oath of mortgage and the oath of the judges. The point is always injustice: the breaking of the Law, debts which are unpaid, injustice done. The Jewish legal system is quite different from ours. Basic to it is the obligation to testify in a courtcase, if you have witnessed a crime. One must come to the court to tell about it and if two witnesses agree on their testimony, the verdict must be guilty. God's name is not used in this case, unless indirectly to make clear that someone has a good reason not to fulfill this obligation. Then, the 'oath of witness' is used: I swear that I have not seen or heard this crime personally(100). An oath of the truth of a fact is taken only when there is a conflict: in cases of loans, of theft and loss, of damage and injuries and of rape and seduction. The accused can prove his innocence through the 'oath of mortgage': he swears that he possesses nothing which belongs to the other; that he has not damaged the other etc(101). Not all conflicts can be resolved in this way. In case there is a quarrel over the amount, the judges can mediate by demanding an oath: the 'oath of the judges' (102). Social reliability is important: tax collectors, money changers, shopkeepers and dismissed wives are mentioned by name, because they are not loved by the people and are suspected of thinking only of their own interest.

This is only a superficial description of the Jewish legal system. It should be clear that an oath is used rarely, unlike our system. The Jewish court took God's injunction against taking his name in vain, as expressed in the third commandment, very seriously. I will come back to this.

According to contemporary writings the practices on oaths are quite different in the daily lives of family and among friends. There are so many rules on domestic matters that one must accept that it is a matter of daily occurence: vows to eat or not to eat, to drink, to sleep, to have sexual intercourse, to visit, to buy or sell, to lend or rent; there is a specification about the kinds of food, about cooking or frying, about fish, meat, vegetables and fruits; about drinking wine or milk or oil; about clothing, about adornments and anointments; about the precise time, its beginning and end; about the possibilities of defining boundaries and remissions: the father can undo the vow of his daughter, the husband of his wife, on the same day, with the extension of remission of vows which humiliate the wife; there are the possibilities of the scribes to undo vows and their conditions(103). It is a whole system of interdependence in which the frustrated and oppressed party can take recourse to the vow in order to force the other to do at least something: you have to believe me by God that I am not taking advantage of you; if you will do this for me now, I promise you by God that I will never again ask you for a favour(104).

It is easy to take an oath: God is the guarantee for what one promises to do. Right here the Torah steps in. As mentioned already, the third commandment of the Decalogue is about this: do not use God's name in vane(105). The Mishnah treatise on Oaths concretizes this forbidden oath. Two names are used(106): an empty oath and a meaningless oath(107), i.e. oaths which are impossible because they do not bring advantage or disadvantage to anyone or because they are beyond the truth. One swears that a stone pillar is made of gold; that one has seen a camel flying; that one has seen a serpent as thick as the beam of an olive press; that one will not keep certain commandments; that one will not testify even though one has witnessed the crime; that one will not build a booth(108). Because they are empty and worthless, one may not use God's name. What is impossible cannot be done: God cannot guarantee it.

I think that Matthew, in the legal text which he makes Jesus use, is saying nothing else than what I have just mentioned: you must not take an oath which you do not keep, but you must pay the debts of your oaths to the Lord. I have three arguments for this interpretation:

1. The first is general. On the redactional level of Matthew's text, we must presuppose that his text is to be taken as inherently coherent. Event though the two sentences come from a different context(109), they are in fact juxtaposed. The reader should understand the deeper unity. There are a number of reasons(110) for seeing the quote of Mt 5,21 as the closest parallel. As in that text the punishment is implied in the prohibition against breaking the Law, in the same way this will be the case in Mt 5,33: the demand to pay the oath to God implies that in the first part of the quote something is said about non-payment, non-

fulfillment.

2. So far, so good, but the problem is precisely here. It brings me to my second reason. The Greek word which Matthew uses to express the prohibition - normally translated as 'you shall not commit perjury' or 'you shall not take a false oath' - is in certain contexts not in opposition to 'take a true oath'(111), but rather to 'take an oath truly' or 'be true to the oath taken'(112). The oath which one takes, will either be fulfilled or not. Because there are no other conditions mentioned in our text, it remains doubtful whether the non-fulfillment is because of inability, impossibility, lack of understanding etc. In such a general statement this is not even good. In perfect Greek Matthew found the connection with the third commandment of the Decalogue: do not use the name of the Lord in vain (113).

3. In Mt 12,35 - 36 we see how Matthew himself saw this (114): 'a good person brings forth good things and a bad person bad things. For every unfulfilled word men utter, they will answer on Judgment day'. That unfulfilled word is the subject here. All words come from the fulness of heart. But, if they do not bring to action, one will have to answer on judgment day, because the action will show whether the word was good or bad, in the same way as the fruits show whether the tree is good or bad(115). Applied to the legal text this means: if you take an oath without being faithful to your own words, God himself will fulfill the oath. On judgment day you will have to answer for every unfulfilled word(116).

'I tell you, you shall not swear at all' is the new pronouncement which Matthew puts in Jesus' mouth: a going to the roots of the prohibition against using the name of God in vain. This is in line with has been said about the other legal prescriptions. The Law is truly fulfilled only when one is ready to attack evil at the root: anger, evil lust, vainly using God's name. This is a religious reality but one which will not remain without effect in society. When the use of oaths has become unnecessary because one can trust the simple yes or no of the other, society becomes more open and trustworthy: a society based on a fundamental truthfulness.

One must go to the root. Oaths which are used as substitute in a compromise - to swear by heaven or by earth, by Jerusalem or by your own head - are also rejected, because God's name is still present, though hidden: God's throne, his footstool, God's city. The spoken yes must be yes, the no must be no. Anything that is added is evil, i.e. comes from the evil desire which leads to breaking the Law. A simple theology is used. The lack of any compromise makes it unique(117).

It is an alternative society where God's name is no longer used to establish truth or reality. All in all, it is a surprising choice. Other solutions and prescriptions could be thought of, if we presuppose that in everyday life the frustrated and oppressed are precisely the ones who will have recourse to an oath to find at least some fulfillment of their desires: those who have less, but want to buy or sell something; the woman who wants something from her father of husband, the ones without hope who want to force God's hand through an oath. Sheer compassion would look to understanding or forgiveness. If one feels oneself above the ordinary people, one would think first of all of disapproval, irony or condescension(118). We do not find any of that here. The absolute prohibition has as its basis a real equality: no one is allowed to take an oath. Even though this equality is not found in reality, the prohibition brings it closer to reality. Once a simple 'yes' or 'no' is accepted as truth, it is necessary that everyone acts in this way (I am not absolutely certain of this)- the position of the frustrated and oppressed will improve. God's name will not be used anymore and little by little the dependence on priests, scribes, powerful friends and men will diminish.

It is not easy to discover whether the community of Matthew followed this halachah from the Sermon on the Mount. On the one hand, we must point to the tradition about oath-taking in the discourse against the Pharisees and scribes. There the text supposes that taking an oath can be justified. Its criticism is not against the taking of oaths itself, but against ideologically argued practices: the gold of the Temple, but not the Temple itself, the sacrifice, but not the altar, can be the object of an oath(119). On the other hand, the actual oaths mentioned in Matthew's story are always in a negative context. Three times it happens. Herod takes an oath that he will give his daughter whatever she will ask, which forces him to give her the head of John the Baptist(120). Caiphas forces Jesus to tell him whether he is the Messiah, the Son of God, invoking in this the name of God(121). Peter twice denies that he knows Jesus under oath(122). This seems to indicate that oath-taking is regarded negatively. The situation will have been much the same from what we know from Qumran. Outsiders notice that oath-taking is not used, but insiders do not always follow this decision-in-principle(123). Abuse is seen clearly and condemned; there is social pressure not to go along with the popular use of multiplying oaths, but faulty practices are not completely eradicated.

an eye for an eye, a tooth for a tooth

Mt 5,38 - 42

The need to maintain a balance of justice has brought about this judicial system: an eye for an eye, a tooth for a tooth. It is the first expression of a feeling for justice, starting from a sense of equality which must be preserved. Bodily harm, which cannot be undone, demands a reaction. Equality at least is served, if the perpetrator is given tit-for-tat: this brings about a moment of justice.

But already in the Torah and especially in Exodus(124) the text is part of a greater whole which transcends aggressive brawling in which eyes are torn out and teeth smashed. The subject is always the damage suffered, but it is much broader, taking in all sorts of damages inflicted under a variety of circumstances and responsibility: beating parents and slaves; a quarrel between men throwing stones; quarrels in which a pregnant woman is involved; maddened bulls who kill people; wells which remain open. The text deals with cattle rustling, robbery of people and valuables, meadows which are grazed by someone else's cattle, arson, goods given in custody which are lost or stolen, money which is lend usuriously. It is an array of facts which are regulated by the basic principle of 'an eye for an eye, a tooth for a tooth'. It is obvious that the same punishment is not always applicable.

From the way in which contemporary legal codifications speak about this, one can hear how this whole cluster is seen as the expression of a unique legal system. The lyrical names given to the treatises by the editor of the Mishnah are a testimony to this: The First Gate, The Middle Gate, The Last Gate, names which keep the memory alive of the time when civil cases were resolved at the gate of the city. So is the introduction by Josephus(125) and Philo (126) which are really short elogies on Moses because of his preeminence in providing rules for the πολιτεία: civil legislation as state law. Not much less is at stake at this time(127). While the starting point is the same, we see that the law now encompasses the whole civil order: legal regulations for conflict situations between Israel's citizens.

It is obvious that the juridical realities and solutions have changed. The influence of the court has increased. It is no longer necessary now to take the law into one's own hands. In money matters the court of three (or seven)(128) decides; in capital cases the college of twenty three convenes(129). Apparently they have discovered that a mediating body is useful to limit conflicts, a solution which is in harmony with the attempt from the pharisaical movement to broaden their influence over the people in 'doing the Torah'(130).

Slowly the insight has grown that redemption money is in many situations more just than parallel punishment. That practice became more and more common. Even though it is not clear when it began exactly(131), it is common practice in the first century AD. 'If someone has put out someone's eye, they should do the same to him unless the blind man is satisfied with the money as the law allows' writes Josephus(132), showing his ignorance because he mixes the original text of the law and contemporary practice(133).

Within the general principle that the damage must be compensated by the transference of (a piece of) the best field one possesses, money becomes the unifying factor which holds together the whole cluster as it were and which makes visible how such disparate matters are connected (134): damage done by men and animals arranged according to the biblical foursome: butting bull, uncovered well, grazing and arson; but also the damage in case of theft and the restitution; causing physical injury; a pledge according to the various possibilities of contractual obligation: keeping, borrowing, renting and hiring; finding lost goods and acquiring ownership. The law of restitution regulates everything that happens outside the sales contract in acquisition and transferring property(135). It has become a general law which deeply influences the lives of people.

This interpretation of the legal text determines how we should understand the text of Matthew. The samples given by Matthew fit all too well into this framework to look of other possible ways to read the text. It is not an enumeration of disparate things. These are real-life happenings which call forth the same legal principle within the framework of contemporary interpretation of the law: how to prevent the balance between injustice and revenge being lost(136). It opens with the general principle: do not defend yourself in a fight with the evil one(137). A manly word is used: if you fight do it as a soldier who stands fast in war. The adversary is shown as evil in the same way the Mishnah calls 'evil' one who beats a deaf-mute, an idiot, a minor, a woman and a slave(138). Evil is he who abuses his position of power. Do not fight with him.

This may sound submissive. G. Theissen calls this 'reject all resistance'(139) and he suggests that such an attitude is similar to the attitude of a defeated people after a war they have lost. But at least Germans should know that submissiveness is not typical of people who have lost the war. To base his position he points to the correlation with the saying of the peacemakers, the a-political character of Matthew's understanding of the Messiah, the rejection of the murder of Zachariah who was killed by Zealots in the Temple(140), and the address by Agrippa to the people just before the outbreak of the war against the Romans: 'one should try to win those in power and not antagonise them ... there is nothing which helps to stop Roman attacks as much as to undergo them patiently' (141). Over against the Pharisees and scribes who close themselves in their belonging to the chosen people so that they can act charitably to their own but are full of hate to those outside, Matthew teaches his people to overcome the defeat of the war by the inner realisation that one is better than the enemy.

All this does not look very historical(142). It follows rather what outsiders believe about love and hatred among Jews; so much so that Theissen feels justified in quoting Tacitus on the Jews. Internal national conflicts are at battle in which one can distinguish certain parties. In and after the war of 70 AD it is the same as in the war of 135 AD with its restoration of a reduced national 'independence' later on in the second century, under the leadership of Simon and Juda ha-Nasi, from the schools in Usha, Beth-Shearim and Sepphoris(143). The 'peace-party' within these movements, trying to maintain good relations with the Romans because the party represents the landowners and the powerful in the country, has interests which are completely different from the interests of the people Matthew is supposedly addressing. This is particularly clear in the war of 70 AD when these people are with their back against the wall. They are prepared to break any law then: treason, manslaughter, murder and extradiction are common(144). And, finally, however unpolitical Matthew's idea of the Messiah may be, an opinion which is based on misunderstanding, a confusing identification of the concepts of politics and war (old Clausewitz's order remains topical - the one who does not break the reed, does act politically -), if Matthew would have had the chance to preach his pacifist ideas to the rich and the powerful, they would have killed him just as they persecuted and killed Jesus. This would have been true even after the war of 70 AD which in no way interrupted the Jewish striving, full of conflict, towards national independence.

The idea of submissiveness can only arise if one isolates Matthew's text from its immediate context. It is not an independent sentence. It is an introduction which after the negation - in the fight with the evil one, one should not defend oneself - calls forth the affirmation: instead of defending oneself one should look out for a positive behaviour. The listeners are advised to act in a paradoxical way.

Four realities are mentioned which represent the totality of social order. The streetfight is presented in the saying about the turning the other cheek. The estimated monetary value of the phenomenon has been preserved for us in the Mishnah: if you beat someone, you must pay two days'pay; but if you give someone a blow or hit him with the back of the hand, if you pull his ear or his hair, if you pull down his coat or the veil of a woman, you have to pay four days'pay(145). The insult and the shame are the worst. The fines are the same for rich and poor. To be attacked in this way in a public place and to have to find the courage and strength not to retaliate ... anger is attacked at the root.

The next saying - about the undergarment over which they fight even in court - is more difficult to place because there is no real context. Luke's parallel text presupposes that it discusses a theft(146). This could only be thought of in a society which is so impoverished that tramps steal each other's clothes. The Mekilta on Exodus 22,25 speaks about the possibility of using a coat as a pledge for the day and an undergarment as a pledge for the night. Against this background the case is about this constant exchange of clothes and demonstrates something of the power a creditor has over a brother(147). Maybe the text is about a coat which is found and which is claimed by two people who then fight their case before the court(148). However, if someone takes off his uppergarment before the judge, he stands naked. That will make some impression and result in some shame.

The demand to go one mile brings us to the world of landowners and soldiers. The word used is the same as in the Passion narrative, when the soldiers force Simon of Cyrene to help when they meet him - laborers who are forced to work a day (or more) in the field, porters who must help in the harvest, forced labor requisitioned for the transport of goods and arms. Indicative of the kind of literature we are discussing is the fact that this word is used twice in this short text of Matthew, while we find it only once in all the writings of Josephus (and there in a text which says that it has been abolished)(149). The Mishnah knows the word very well. It is taken up in Hebrew as a word from the Greek(150), because it treats a reality which is completely unjewish and which has never been accepted. Matthew's saying calls for a doubling of forced labor on a voluntary basis. The unexpectedness of such an action and its freedom is an indictment against the evil of the oppressor. But, by increasing the injustice voluntary, one takes it upon oneself. It has something to do with carrying one's cross and following Jesus.

The problem with the saying about giving (money or food) and the willingness to lend something is not that it stands outside of the context. As we said above lending as well as depositing and renting belong in this series of civic realities(151). It is not so clear what is wrong with these things unless the author presupposes that those who ask for them, have evil intentions. The saying could then mean that even if one cannot expect to get back one's money or goods, one should nevertheless respond positively to the request: one would place fiercy coals on the other person's head (or is this interpretation to close to Lk 6,35?).

The remembrance of Ps 36 (LXX) probably plays a role in the background. This text is not without significance in Matthew's community as we saw in the beatitude on the meek. The 'lawbreaker' and the 'faithful observer of the law' are opposed to each other. The culprit will suffer because God shall annihilate him. He gets a short time in which he can torture and oppress God's merciful and faithful people, but God laughs at him. He will disappear like smoke and he will dry like the grass in the field. His own sword will hurt him and his arrows will be destroyed. Quite differently is the fate of the just one. He has God as his protector on all his travels. Even if he is poor and in need, the little he has will be for him more than the great riches of the sinner. His real strength lies in the fact that he does not become angry. He does not let wrath take over. He is not jealous of the evildoers. On the contrary, with him one finds goodness, kindness, gentleness, peacefulness and mercy.

In this context the psalm speaks twice about 'lending'. In Ps 36,21 it says: 'The wicked man borrows without meaning to repay, but the righteous man is generous and open-handed', and the presupposition is that the just man gives even before he lends, because he has pity on the man who is in such miserable circumstances. In 36,26 it is even clearer: 'he is compassionate every day and always lending and his children will be blessed'. Important is the merciful willingness to help another in his need without second thoughts about enriching oneself. It is clear how the oppositions fit into our passage of the Sermon on the Mount. The psalm in its totality is a demonstration of that which the halachah teaches: do not resist the lawbreaker. Even if the bad guy enters one's private life, one must show 'mercy' and 'willingness to forgive', if one wants to keep the torah on charity(152).

Matthew's halachah wants to give an answer to the problem of the infringement of the law: how do we deal with people who do not respect the Torah and who enter our lives with their evil. Quarreling, injustice, oppression and deceit are the underlying realities which influence even people who would like to stay away from this. The true answer is: do not return evil for evil.

Shaming the law-breaker by such paradoxical behaviour might hopefully bring him back from his wrong ways. Justice is realised anew by the voluntary acceptance of injustice. It is an attempt to break the vicious circle of rage and revenge(153).

you must love your neighbour and hate your enemy

Mt 5,43 - 48

All the searching of the exegetes to find a parallel text has been in vain(154). There is no text in Jewish literature which calls for hatred of enemies(155). It happens that one hates one's enemy, but it not something which can be demanded as a positive commandment. How, then, can Matthew say such a thing?

We do not have an answer to this question. But it forces us to examine the contemporary legal interpretation as broadly as the text itself suggests: we must take into consideration the torah on benevolence for one's brother as well the demands which regulate the way one should deal with one's enemies. That means we must look at the law on war. The humanness which is aimed at, shows how closely the two commands are linked.

It is the first time that Philo and Josephus on the one hand and the Mishnah on the other have widely differing versions. Philo, and especially Josephus, can still give a carefree comment on the torah on warfare: in case of siege of a city one should not try to arrange an armistice; it is not allowed to cut down fruit trees to make weapons(156); only combatants may be killed and it is not allowed to slaughter the city population; all the dead must be buried; a captured woman can be married only after 30 days and one may not then sell her or treat her as a slave. These are words of someone who knows what he is talking about(157). Notwithstanding the similarities with Dt(158) one can hear criticism of the Roman practices. Moses' law is better, in all aspects, than the Roman army's practice.

Nothing of this has survived in the Mishnah. The commentary on the Dt text stops exactly at the prescriptions for a city under siege(159) and there is no reference to a warlike situation anywhere. Even the mishnah on the duty to help an ass which has been overburdened speaks as if there is no explicit mention that this could apply to one's enemy's donkey(160). Could this be in line with the phenomenon that the later literature from the second century no longer reflects on 'questions of state', as we can see also in Epictetus, Marc Aurelius, Dio Chrysostomos and Lucian? It is a blank spot which speaks eloquently (161).

But even if the interest in state politics is lost, the Mishnah writers have given thought to enmities, and in depth. When capital punishment is discussed and a detailed description is given on how someone is to be stoned and then hanged and then to be buried before nightfall, it is followed by the mishnah: 'How does the Present (God) speak every time when a person suffers'? 'My head aches. My arm is heavy'. If God suffers because of the death of an evil person, how much more will he suffer for the death of a just man'(162). God is present even in cases of capital punishment. He suffers because it affects his own image. This is true in the case of each person however different persons are. When a man dies, a whole world is at stake. That is why no one's blood may be shed, because 'if someone kills another person, Scripture accuses him of having destroyed a whole world. And if someone saves another person, he saves a whole world'(163).

It shows the deep respect of the rabbis for man's life and it is completely in line with the torah on benevolence for one's brother: do not hate your brother in your heart; do not revenge yourself; do not become angry; love your brother as you love yourself(164). These sayings are accepted as individual laws(165). The torah on love forbids all destroying hatred.

Even if there is no real difference with that which Matthew makes Jesus say and propound as anti-law, even if one finds many variations in Greek and Jewish authors on the same theme, the paradox of the combination 'loving your enemy' is unique(166). This saying has determined the ideological presentation of Christianity even more than the demand to pray for one's enemies. Love of enemy has been abused as a slogan. At critical moments it is forgotten. It remains always as a demand. But I need to add a rider. As is true for many sayings of this sort, - the beatitude on the poor is the best example: only a poor man may bless poverty - it is also true here that only someone, who finds himself in the situation of being attacked, may invite someone to be peaceful. Only if one is being persecuted and pursued, only if one knows what it means to have powerful and everpresent enemies, can one rightfully say to someone else that an offer of peace is the only solution(167).

No one denies that Matthew's halachah must be understood in this way. Matthew writes against a background of real persecutions which also hit Christians because of their fidelity to the Law. This follows the suffering of Jesus as the just man at the hands of compatriots and foreigners. And it fits in with the persecutions of the many law-abiding people who try time and again to uphold the torah among the scattered sheep of Israel against all opposition. Enmity and persecution for the sake of justice are bitter truths up to Matthew's time and many groups of people suffer from it until the great war comes, when the whole people will suffer. I discussed this in the beatitude on the persecuted.

According to Matthew, 'Keeping the Law' goes together with Righteousness and Persecution. This halachah makes a specific connection. The text gives anti-examples, modes of behaviour of people, publicans and pagans which are themselves anti-types: do not act as they do. The association of words used in the saying creates a marvelous whole. There is a continuum in the concepts 'enemy - persecutor-evil one - unjust men-publican-pagan'. The publicans and pagans are put forward as people who cannot fulfill this. Jesus' followers must do better.

First of all comes the selfishness of the publicans. L. Schottroff and W. Stegemann have proved that the widespread Hellenistic and Jewish criticism of the publicans is a complex matter(168). Jurists and moralists condemn them only when they actually break the law. Merchants, who deal with them often, are in competition with them and have little good to say about them. The rich and the landowners speak about them from the background of their contempt for 'manual labor'. Matthew shares in this criticism of the publicans, but it is not clear on which level he should be put.

The reproach that they love only those who love them, reminds one of the classical saying on the equal exchange of good and evil: 'I will love who loves me and be an enemy to my enemy'(169). It is a moral stance based on a society which is divived into good and evil people and which gives a man a chance to remain standing notwithstanding life's changing friendships and enmities. Plato gives the most classical commentary on the saying. In his diatribes he returns to it time and again, because he wants to make clear to his audience that this 'popular idea' (the δόξα τῶν πολλῶν) is not very logical(170). The aggressive part of the saying especially - 'to be ἐχθρῷ ἐχθρός - places the perpetrator of the injustice in an evil position, because to do evil is worse than to have to suffer it(171).

Matthew's reproach of the publicans is limited to the first part of the saying: they are 'amicis amici'. The implication is that this way of acting is not the maximum of what the torah demands in love for the neighbour. He paints them as not fulfilling the law, and that is not just an insignificant accusation in Matthew.

Of the pagans he says that they only greet one another- an understandable custom among foreigners in a homogeneous society. In spite of their influence in government, trading and ownership they are excluded from the life of the city. They look for support among themselves, because they are dependent on one another. It sounds like a reproach: they only greet one another. It is a popular way of thinking and feeling. It appeals to the aversion felt by the people in the city and the country of being excluded no matter by whom; it appeals to the shame experienced in a Roman demonstration of superiority and to the frustrated anger of someone who has been despised publicly by a foreigner. Only asocial people do that.

But all this is not without political implications. By adding these sayings (or, maybe better, by leaving them in the text) Matthew has Jesus taking a stand in the arena of struggle between Jews and foreigners. The text has to be understood from actual experiences with these people in the city or in the village, in the same way as in the Mishnah the publicans, the tax collectors and the userers are the representatives of the great Injustice. Concrete people are the anti-type: the publicans and the pagans are not-fulfilling-the-law; they are the evil ones and the unjust; the people who - turning the saying around - are the object of the love for one's enemy.

Matthew's text does not go that far and that is its weakness. To make his people harbingers of peace he needs to make an appeal to enmity: something which is against that which is presented as the true intention of the Torah. The command to love one's enemy and to pray for one's persecutors presents an extreme pacifist ideal. Anyone who wants to fulfill this command on Jesus' authority, must promote shalom under all circumstances. No one can be excluded(172).

The saying, which is given as the argumentation of this law, speaks much more fundamentally: who loves his enemy belongs to God's family, to God who lets his sun rise over good and evil people and who showers his rain on the just and the unjust. This motivation is not without problems, because the train of thought is taken from Wisdom literature on the award for virtue and the punishment for evil. The world does not function very well, if it behaves differently. A God, who loves the good as well as the evildoer, does not fit in with our sense of justice. It presupposes a sort of indifference for injustice which cannot be reconciled with spontaneous reactions of revenge.

We should understand the saying from this offence. The saying is not trying to lay the basis for the universality of love - that all people must be loved - but rather for the totality of love: love must reach even the personal enemy. Love is only love if one is able to include even one's own enemy. In the foregoing interpretation this has been brought up several times. Here it is explicitly stated. One must be ready not only to forget all revenge, but even more one must wish well to one's enemy and persecutor. In spite of what they have done, one must wish for them the good gifts of the sun and the rain as one would for one's friends as a matter of course.

The last sentence verbalises the final utopia of paradise: be perfect as your father in heaven is perfect. Perfect is he who fulfills the Law to the very end; who does not allow an evil thought to enter his heart; who adheres to God with his whole being(173). That God himself is also called perfect is part of this reality. God represents Justice itself, expressed in his Law. Anger, evil desire, dishonesty, revenge and hatred are forces which threaten man in his perfection. They destroy his integrity, his solidarity with others, his sense of responsibility and his openness to God. The man who is perfect like God is perfect, will fulfill the Law to the very end. He is like Adam and Eve, walking under the sun of justice and peace, because there is no desire to murder or even hate one's brother.

Chapter III
THE PRACTICES OF JUSTICE
Mt 6, 1-18

the introduction

Mt 6,1

The opening sentence is quite extraordinary, really a connecting sentence. It returns to the prolegomenon of the legal texts in the renewed suggestion of an opposition between a justice which is already real and one which is still to be realised. Δικαιοσύνη has its own rules, which must be respected, if it is to come into being. One notices that there is no target audience. It will become clear that the different practices relate to different groups and that the connection of practices and specific groups is not as clear as it was with the legal texts. Precisely on the redactional level of this opening sentence we have a gap, which should not be filled.

At the same time the sentence introduces the next passage, which will describe three realities according to their content of 'righteousness'. It is a prior summary of the practices of alms giving, payer and fasting. In Jewish doctrine such a sentence is called 'kelal': a general principle which can be deduced from specific prescriptions of the Law(1). This is not only a rhetorical device, it is also an hermeneutical principle. This means: the sentence is an opening phrase as a rhetorical preparation for what is to come, but it is at the same time a generalisation transcending the individual prescriptions of the Law.

The content can be characterised as a negative command. It describes negatively how δικαιοσύνη does not happen. The actual wording comes from the theatre: before the people so that they can see. There is an implied opposition between a human and a divine audience. In the opening sentence this opposition is not expressed in placing 'hidden' against 'public', but in the following sentences it becomes clear that this opposition is the connecting link in the train of thought: who has received his reward from a human agency, cannot claim his reward from God. It is granted only once and wisdom demands that one acts accordingly.

It should be clear by now that this passage is not about

the opposition 'internal'/'external'. But it is not yet generally accepted that it does not oppose 'individual' to 'community'. I will try to prove this with arguments. The change from ὑμεῖς to the singular σύ is the real reason for this individualistic interpretation, but this happened at the cost of the insight that these pronouncements try to initiate a practice of disciples (plural!). It must be shown with texts that these new practices existed in the plural: in a Christian community, which made these sayings their own, in however stumbling a way.

The main sentence indicates that the real worry is about δικαιοσύνη. Justice is the framework in which the practices which are mentioned, must be realised. The giving of alms, prayer and fasting have their own relation to the Law as expressive of God's will; not from the point of view of the practices as such - as in the previous legal texts - but from the point of view of their realisation, of the manner in which they come or should come into being. I will handle all this as a hermeneutical principle and show time and again how the concrete practices are based on and part of the legal way of thinking of the time. How and where the sayings contradict concretely existing realities and how they can promote new practices, can also be clarified against this backdrop.

Finally, the introductory sentence is a general statement. No examples are mentioned. This creates its own literary effect: Jesus' diciples cannot be content with the practices which are mentioned: alms giving, prayer and fasting. Even if they do these things in the spirit of the speaker, the totality of their existence remains under the critical examination of the opening sentence.

the right way to give alms

Mt 6,2 - 4

Existing ideology does not promote almsgiving. Rather it construes an opposition between justice and charity. Inequality in the possessions of goods of this world demands a fundamental solution which is not sufficiently guaranteed by alms-giving. Justice must be the governing factor with equality as guide.

One should not construe this as an argument to place alms as an act of charity outside the economic field. As a human need it is part of the totality of economic relationships and is coloured by these. Giving alms has its own history notwithstanding a certain uniformity in all times and in all places. This history is determined by the way a current economic system operates, as a correction on the inequality which will always exist.

Charity is an economic sub-system of a much larger totality. It is very concretely organised with institutions, rules, regulations and executives. It is not just an individual task, even though it can sometimes appear as such. Most often it is part of a greater system which organises the giving, the receiving and the distribution. It is protected by legal rules, concrete presciptions, guarantees, executive organisations etc. Time and again we see new initiatives which try to fight injustices by organising the reception of gifts on a local, national and international level. Enormous sums of money are involved which sometimes do not reach their target, although often they do. No matter how individualistically it is perceived, charity is not an individual question. It is always embedded in the historical, economic, juridical and social realities of a given society.

The society, in which the saying of the Sermon on the Mount on alms-giving developed, was no exception. Also that charity was organised in a specific way, which we have to know about if we want to understand the proper context of the saying. It is not a general ethical statement where one can make abstraction of time and place. Only if we read it within its own context, can we get its true significance which - possibly - can then also have meaning for another time.

In Israel attention for the poor had a long history going back to Egyptian and Babylonian influences, which in the Torah have found a concrete expression. Bolkestein(2) has shown that this specific attention for the poor, the widows and orphans was a special phenomenon for which there were no parallels in the classical and Roman times. He may have placed a little too much emphasis on the oppositions-(3), - a little further on I will discuss the Hellenistic influences which reached Palestine -, it is certain that in Israel unique practices developed, which only at a much later time - under the influence of Christianity - reached the West.

It becomes clear how influential the rural culture was. First of all we see the prescriptions about the sharing in the harvest: one corner of the field was to be left for the poor and the stranger, and one should not check the field to make sure that nothing was left. Also the forgotten sheaf, the fallen grapes and the olives which were left on the branches belong to the widow and the orphan(4). In the Mishnah treatise 'The Corner of the Field' we can read how the rabbis of the second century saw these prescriptions as laws with a minimum and a maximum. Until that time it was accepted practice which was seen as a duty and a right:

during harvest time no one needed to suffer from hunger. He, who went with the mowers and the harvesters, could gather his own food. The economic value may not be important, but the yearly event of sharing in the fruits of the harvest gave it a real symbolic value. The owners of the land were reminded each year that their responsibility extended beyond the care for their own families(5).

Economically more important were the tithes, which must be given each year: an obligation which, where it dealt with the tithes for the levites, came close to a taxation. One tenth of the harvest from the field (corn and vegetables)(6) and of the fruits (grapes, olives, figs, dates etc) must be given yearly to the levites (and to the priests) (7). They were considered the poor because they did not receive a share in the land(8). They are, therefore, dependent on others for their sustenance(9). The story of Josephus about the events just before the destruction of the Temple shows us how dependent they were. The high priests decided to send soldiers to the threshing floors to confiscate the tithes: an action which resulted in famine and death for many poor priests in the rural areas(10). The tithe to be given to the levites was so important that, under stress, it could be sanctioned by military rule. The practice of the controllers, the Temple treasurers, to travel all over the country(11) shows clearly that a constant pressure was being exerted on the people which was apparently needed. Even the association of the Pharisees in which people claimed to have paid tithe on mint, anise and cummin, could not change that.

More immediately to the advantage of the poor was the second tithe(12) levied on the harvest. Every third and sixth year in the seven year cyclus that tenth part of the harvest, which in the other years was destined for a sacrificial meal in Jerusalem(13), was set apart for the poor: for the levites because they had no share in the land, but especially now, for the widows and the orphans, the poor in their midst. A minimum was set as an example: one litre wheat for two litres barley or three litres spelt; two litres dried figs for a quart of wine or one eighth of oil(14). These things were to be given in kind as in the other years they used to be eaten or drunk in Jerusalem, or were bought and then consumed. The texts seem to indicate that there was one festive meal of which small landholders took care. Big land owners probably had a popular mass meal at the conclusion of the harvest season. This tithe did not have the same impact as the tithe levied for the levites, because it had to be spread over so many more people. Large groups of the populace took advantage of this so that in final analysis it was a drop in the ocean.

If everything had been done according to regulations, a prayer was said in the Temple over the gifts: a profession before God that His commandments had been observed faithfully, praising His name for the gifts received, and a petition for future assistance(15). Alms and prayer went hand in hand.

Finally, the sabbath year can be seen as the most important economic institution. Land was left fallow for a whole year, primarily to give it rest - a practice which followed an old agricultural method to leave land fallow every other year or at least every few years -(16), but also to maintain the fiction that all were equal: the land belonged to all Israelites equally. At the time of Matthew's gospel, possible land reform was not longer considered as practicable(17), but the demand that the right of ownership over the produce growing on it and over the fruits of the trees, was suspended for a year, remained. This had great consequences because the law was observed nationwide. Many reports of famines and malnutrition, which are clearly related to a sequel of sabbath years, are known and reveal the disastrous effect of the practice(18). Ideologically it was a well intentioned practice, but practically it reduced the populace to poverty.

It is surprising that the practice was maintained. The rabbis were quite capable of finding juridical solutions for impossible situations in order to keep the law liveable. A famous example of this is the regulation of Hillel (from the beginning of our era) on the 'prosbol': the agreement between creditor and debtor(19). The Torah demanded that existing debts should be remitted during the sabbath year. Hillel realised that - to the detriment of the people - no one would give credit when the sabbath year came close, so he decided that one should make a clause in the contract. One should act as if the debt had been paid to a third part (to the judges of the financial court of justice who co-signed the agreement). These people could then stipulate that the debt had to be paid in the sabbath year or later. It was a first attempt to guarantee a contract juridically(20), a practice which quickly proved to be to the benefit of owners and creditors.

One can hardly overestimate the influence of agriculture on the daily lives of the people in Palestine at that time. Consequently, the majority of the people were, in one way or another, involved with the regulations regarding the care for the poor. Everyone was confronted with them, either each year or at least every sabbath year, when everyone was experiencing the consequences of the law. But, because it was a matter of clear rules under great social pressure, this abiding by the law did not bring much 'honour'. There was a continued appeal not to forget the poor, but it would not bring 'honour by the people'. These were laws which regulated life in rural areas, not rules which gave people a chance to be seen as 'benefactors'.

Life in the city opened much more possibilities for this. Hellenistic influences were also much greater here. Even though direct dependence might not be easy to prove (21), there were clear parallels between Palestinian and Hellenistic city life.

To begin with the most remarkable phenomenon - remarkable because it is so far removed from our own experience-, it was customary to appeal to the rich to fulfill their duty of 'leitourgia': to take care that the city was well built, that it could compete with other cities in the neighbourhood, that all conveniences were provided. Concretely this meant that the rich citizens - originally appointed by the city council, later on in the century imposed by the Roman government -(22), had to build, restore, maintain the common buildings: temple(s), market, theatre, gymnasium, bath houses, library, as well as the aquaduct, the city fountain and the highways. In short, they had to take care that the city would be esteemed and remain in esteem. It was an honour to the city, for which the citizens showed their gratitude by honouring the donor as a benefactor with a statue, a plaque, an inscription, a special place of honour in the theatre, a solemn coronation during a mass meeting of the people.

How this worked in a Jewish community becomes clear, when we read a text from the Mishnah which, by way of example, mentions as the property of a city the marketplace, the bath house, the synagogue, the book chest and the books themselves(23). It reminds us of the words of the city elders (!) who spoke to Jesus regarding the centurion who came to ask for the healing of his slave: 'He is worthy to have you do this for him, for he loves our nation and he built us our synagogue'(24). The greater the buildings, the greater the honour.

A famous example is Herod, who even dared to rebuild the Temple and who also financed numerous buildings throughout the country and even far away. The same can be said of his sons, his nephews and his grandchildren, who put up various buildings to obtain honour and fame from their contemporaries and from generations to come. We know of other examples on a more modest scale, sometimes even mentioning the reward(25). One could not dodge this care for the people, if one cared for the citizens and the city, and if one had the means to achieve it.

Apart from this, we know of other practices, which fit into this scheme of things. They overlap sometimes, because they have the same target group. There is mutual influence, but they are sufficiently distinct to mention them separately.

Building up funds for concrete projects seems to be something which happens in all ages. Typical of the time of Matthew were the funds for the sustenance of widows and orphans, funds for freeing slaves(26), and funds for the mass-people's meal(27). These were usually private initiatives - sometimes through legacies, but often given during the donor's life -, initiatives started in the name of a person, but in which others were expected to participate either as co-donors or as managers of the capital.

Early Christianity accepted these practices as a matter of course. The 'leitourgia' of Paul organising a collection in the churches founded by him to help the poor in Jerusalem, belongs to this category(28). So does the initiative of the church in Jerusalem to set up a fund for the widows. The Greek-speaking community objected to this fund, because they felt that their widows were being discriminated against in favour of the Hebrew-speaking widows. The institution of the deacons had its beginnings from this quarrel(29). We could mention also the practices of the agapè celebrations, the common meal of the Christians in which, if all went as it should, no distinction was made between the rich and poor, presupposed that the rich people would take care of the food(30). I believe that we should see the meals, which Jesus gave to the people, in the same light. I mention especially those in Matthew where they are an expression of 'compassion' for the people(31). Taking into account all differences with 'profane' people's meals, paid for by an individual(32), the similarity is still striking: Jesus gives them an abundant meal, because the people are hungry. Finally, early Christianity has probably known about the practice to take care of children who were left by their parents and to take them into the community and to accept responsibility for their sustenance, education and marriage(33): a special form of child care, which was necessary in those times.

So we have quite a cluster. Historically the question remains, whether there did not exist yet another institution in the first century: the typically Jewish custom of the collection for the poor. Two or three persons were appointed by the leaders of the synagogue (or the city council?) to collect money and food every day or every couple of days. This money or food was distributed by another committee of two or three to the poor of the place, whether they just happened to be there present or lived in the place. The Mishnah treatise 'The Corner of the Field' presupposes an organised institution and distinguishes between those who collected and those who distributed, between the purse (the money) and the dish (the food), between the poor of the place and the vagrant beggars(34). This treatise is usually dated in the second half of the second century after the war of Hadrian (135 AD), which caused a lot of poverty among the people(35). There are indications, however, that elements of it existed at an earlier time. Jesus himself with his disciples was given food and shelter, but also money, which Judas kept in the 'purse', money which was intended also for the poor. The institution of the collection for the poor probably had its origin in Jerusalem, where the money (and the food) placed in the offertory box overtly or in secret, was used for the maintenance of the Temple - a real unemployment relief -, but also for help to the impoverished rich(36). The only thing lacking to identify this with the institution of the collection for the poor is the provision to replenish the money regularly. In the Christian tradition we see that particular sub-groups were doing this already in the first century.

The saying in the Sermon on the Mount about the correct way to give alms should be understood against this background(37). In the language of Althusser, it is an intervention in an ideological debate, supported and kept alive by concrete practices. Important values are at stake. The care for the poor is connected with justice, seen as the keeping of the Law. 'Honour and glory from the people' is the compensation for financing specific projects by the rich(38). If we look at the similarity between the saying of Jesus and the concrete practices(39), there is no room for misunderstanding. The intervention precisely fits the practice. It states that the followers of Jesus should not imitate the practices of the rich, because that will not bring about justice.

If we see the saying against the background of the care for the poor in the first century, it becomes clear that we can identify the supposed adversaries much more aptly than usually is done. The reference to 'honour and glory from the people' as compensation for giving the gifts narrows them down clearly. It is not a general saying, which is applicable to any kind of charity. It introduces clearly a controversy in a culture of a specific socio-economic feature, where the rich had power and were ideologically supported in their power. The saying undermines this ideology: do not expect your recompense from man but from God who - as the Torah teaches - does not discriminate between people. The saying increases, thereby, the distance between the classes. It does not exclude that the rich can act righteously, but it does impose conditions which are culturally almost impossible to fulfill. Furthermore, the disciples of Jesus are warned not to fall into this trap. The paradox of the left hand, which is not to know what the right hand does, voices this contradiction in an incomparable way.

In a polemical summary the adversaries are described as ὑποκριταί. This is usually translated with 'hypocrites'. But it should be clear that such a translation is an anachronism: the use of the word in a time when the concept (the reality?) was not yet known(40). How then should we interpret the word? In connection with the Hellenistic meaning of the word we could think of actors who want to curry favour with the public (cf. vs 6,1). It speaks then about people who play the role of the rich man for the forum of the people, who look for publicity in the synagogue and the street - who literally or figuratively trumpet the donation -, people who, like fools, forget the divine forum.

Against the background of the Hebrew meaning of the word - which can be discovered through the Septuagint translations -, Matthew was thinking of 'transgressors of the Law', not without connotations with the yiddish word 'gannef'(41): through their practices the rich showed themselves as people who thought they kept the Law, but who did not really keep it (look again at verse 6,1 with the notation of δικαιοσύνη) The manner in which one gives alms has also to do with righteousness and with the Law(42). In the diatribe against the scribes and Pharisees we find a strong argument for this interpretation. When the tithe is mentioned - a reality which fits into this context as we said before - Jesus calls the scribes and Pharisees ὑποκριταί, because although they do indeed pay tithe on mint, anise and cummin, they do not respect the most important aspects of the Law: justice, compassion and fidelity(43). Here also we find a polemical confrontation between the Law, the explanation of the Law, and the care for the poor. The confrontation re-emphasises anew the interests of the people. The Law is not correctly explained and thus not rightly observed unless the poor are in the centre of interest.

One should not make a choice between these two meanings. Ὑποκριτής is a complicated word open to different interpretations, just as the opening sentence of this passage (v. 6,1) expresses righteousness as well as playing theatre. In Christian practice the implication of the Law on charity is concretised by the anonymity of the giver and the receiver(44) and by the collectivisation of the management of the money(45). Even if there is no direct connection between this behaviour and the saying itself, this way of doing things is supposed to give a better guarantee of the intention of the Law.

the right way to pray

Mt 6,4 - 6

Although in a different way as the giving of alms, also praying is intimately bound up with the totality of a given culture. As a human function it is part and parcel of the concrete setting of specific lives. It participates in and is part of the complicated interplay of every culture. Economic, political and social realities have an influence on it, never fully determined, but always present.

Most important is the fact that prayer is always somehow related to organised prayer. One learns to pray via received formulas which are determined in time and style. Existing groups take care of transmitting them: family, neighbourhood organisations if they are homogeneous, freely organised groups. One joins such a group or one reacts against it, but one cannot be totally free of them. The group determines how one will act, but the group itself is also determined from outside. To form a group implies that one will agree to certain arrangements, that some will act as leaders responsible for the way the group functions, that there is a place for prayer with all the architectural, juridical and administrative implications. Prayer occurs in an organised context which contains, as in a nutshell, the whole societal constellation.

That this is so with the saying of the Sermon on the Mount, should be clear from what I have said above. Again I see this saying as an intervention in an ideological debate. The speaker takes a position, which can only be understood in the context of the existing prayer organisation of the time. The meaning of the synagogue must then be mentioned in opposition to the 'inner room', which Jesus indicated as the place of preference.

To make that understandable and to make clear what precisely the change is, we must explain the meaning and function of the synagogue in the Jewish society of the first century. This is an immensely complicated question and I will limit myself to those elements, which have an immediate relation to the status questionis: the function of the synagogue as a community building and the actual procedure in the prayer services in as far as our text is involved.

The synagogue was the central building of (probably) every large town. Except in Jerusalem, where the Temple was obviously the most important place, if there was more than one synagogue as e.g. in the Jewish section of Alexandria, one would function as the main synagogue(46) and would be so called(47). The synagogue had the same function as the city temple(s) in the surrounding Greek cities. Next to the agora (and possibly the bath house) it was the most important public building in every city(48).

That did not make it the people's building, however,- one could almost say, not at all the people's building. The responsibility for the construction, the maintenance and the management belonged to the city council, respectively the sanhedrin, or the 'minjan' of the 'ten first', i.e. those people who were rich enought to find time for management functions(49): a rather aristocratic group on which the ordinary people has little or no influence.

The most important question for the managers was, as always, where to find the money to keep the building in a state of good repair. Sometimes one finds mention of small donations, which together formed the foundation capital (50), but this was not the normal thing. The inscriptions, which have survived, almost always list names of individual 'benefactors': people who paid for the whole building(51), or, more usual, considering the multitude of evidences, people who paid for a part of the building: such as a column, a threshold, marmor covering, staircases, the gilding of a chandelier etc(52). The real honour was to be able to add the ἐκ τῶν ἰδίων(53): he or she paid for this out of their own pocket. That is a permanent honour in stone: as already mentioned, it was sometimes supported by other honours: a golden shield, a wreath, a place of honour(54).

Every city had its policy-making body. They managed the synagogue. How strong this legal accountability was, appeared when there were problems: in situations where the synagogue functioned as a political centre. Josephus gives a number of these facts. When non-Jewish citizens of Dora placed a statue of the emperor in the synagogue, Agrippa, the king, felt he had to act (that is between 41 and 44 AD). Immediately he went to Petronius, the governor, who wrote to the 'first of Dora' telling them to undo the harm(55). Clearer still is the story of Josephus about the events in Caesarea at the outbreak of war. The 'most important of the Jews' had already given Florus eight (!) talents to convince him to act against the non-Jewish neighbour of the synagogue who started putting up a row of shops, right before the entrance of the synagogue. There were riots, when someone killed some birds before the entrance on the sabbath day. A commission of 'twelve important citizens' went to Florus to protest. They dared to mention the eight talents, but instead of being given justice they were imprisoned: the final motive for the great war(56).

'The leading men of the city' knew that they were responsible and they were held accountable for everything that happened in and near the synagogue. The city elders and the city synagogue had a symbiotic relation with one another.

The city council acted for the citizens: I would like to know how those who were not members of the council, the people themselves, the large group of people who used the synagogue, stood in relation to their nominal right of possession. It would have been a mixture of various forms of relation. Certainly, there would have been grateful pride, if we remember the widespread and deep-seated 'Heimat'-love of the ancients: the place of birth was important for the whole of one's life and created obligations(57). Josephus' stories, which I just mentioned, show how people reacted in tense situations with foreigners. The people were ready to defend their right of ownership. That is not to say that everyone felt free or could freely act in relation to the synagogue. There were enough contacts: the children went to school there; on the sabbath people went to the synagogue in great numbers, although we find a text, which says what to do if the minjan, the necessary ten people to begin the service, were not present(58). The prohibition not to use the synagogue as shelter against rain and cold or as a place to sleep, or to make a short-cut probably referred to existing practices(59); otherwise it would not have been necessary to treat of those things so extensively.

The experience of distance would have found its origin in the services, because once inside, the distinction between the 'professional' and the 'participant' would have been in force. Not everybody could understand Hebrew: what then was the situation of those who did not understand it? We wonder why it was necessary to use translators, or why there was a difficult discussion going on about the relation to the 'am ha ^{c}arez', the people who did not know the Law. A text from the Mishnah is particularly revealing: if a reader made a mistake in the words of a prayer, someone else was supposed to take over. Those present should not be 'refusers'(60). All indications are that the ideal of equality was realised in but a limited way.

A similar picture emerges, when we look at the contemporary descriptions of actual services. One can hardly expect anything else from Philo(61). He emphasizes peace and order. In Philo's view people sat silently. There was a separate place for men and women, for young and old. They kept their hands hidden in the folds of their dress, right hand on the breast, left hand at the side. One man who, in Philo's view, was a priest or an elder, read the words of the Law and another man explained the Law quietly. Everyone listened carefully and, at the end, the listeners showed their appreciation by nodding their heads in a friendly way. The assembly was meant to bring about virtue. The service resulted in philosophy, because the Law was explained in allegories. They sang hymns to praise God, old existing hymns as well as new: a cantor sang and the choir supported him(62) and the refrain was repeated by all. The assembly lasted until late in the afternoon.

In the Mishnah, things are a little different(63). In these texts the people who spoke, knew that they were responsible for the way things went, and who, therefore, set precise guidelines. There is a different presentation of facts because of the emphasis on those questions which related to rubrics: how the prayers were to be said, what the precise order was, who was responsible for what. The accent was on a way of doing things, where prayer became the most important element at the cost of the other liturgical activities. Because of their importance two prayers received special attention: the Shema, 'Hear Israel', the profession of faith in the one God, comprising Dt 6, 4 - 9; 11,13 - 21 and Num 15,37 - 41(64), and the Tefilla, the prayer par excellence, which was also called Amida, because it was said standing up, the Eighteen-prayer, which praises God for his deeds done for Israel (65). However, although less explicitated, the reading of the Law was also given some attention(66). In the Megilla treatise, the treatise on the reading of the scroll of the Book of Esther, we find the rules on the way the Law was to be read: how many readers were required; which reading should take place in feastdays; how one should treat the translation and which passages were not to be translated; who might not read and why(67). Everything was so completely organised that probably only the insiders could still find their way.

When Jesus told his followers that they did not have to go to the synagogue, but that they should pray at home and in secret, he really changed people's daily life. Only those, who were on the fringes of the synagogue, were capable of really hearing him: those who did not understand the spoken word, those who were not part of the leadership and those who were not au courant with the ritual. Only for those people the words were liberating, because it created the opportunity to express themselves in their own ritual.

This separation into different groups took place gradually. When Matthew wrote his Gospel, it was reality. He spoke consistently of Jesus going to <u>their</u> synagogue

(68). For the author of the Matthew gospel the synagogue was no longer a meetingplace(69). This separation did not happen without pain and trouble. In Acts we see the Lucan version of this history. From the point of view of Luke the synagogue functioned as the point of departure for the preaching of the good news, but also as the breakpoint until the programmed story of the definitive separation is told. Paul spoke for three years in the synagogue at Ephesus, but he separated himself with his disciples because of the constant quarrels. Then, for two years, he taught daily in the 'school of Tyrannus'(70). The Christians had found their own home.

I ask myself whether the prescription of the saying 'to close the door once one has arrived in the private room', should not be seen (also) against the background of the persecutions. I recall something, which we find in the stories of the resurrection, where the disciples 'out of fear for the Jews' stayed behind closed doors(71). Because the separation between synagogue and ecclesia took a couple of generations to become a reality, the saying would have functioned differently in, let us say, the 40s and 50s AD and much later. When Matthew wrote his gospel, people had already been scourged in 'their' synagogues(72), which made it impossible for them to go there. The 'private room' had already become the normal place for their own meeting. It was also their experience that this fact had not prevented lies and treachery. In the times of horror of the great war people said that the Messiah was in 'their private room' (73). The possibility of 'pseudo-people' existed also within their own circle.

Originally it was quite different. The saying started in the beginning of the Jesus-movement as a reaction to the aspiration of the 'pious' to impose rules about certain prayers as compulsery for everybody. There are proofs for this which, however, are difficult to place historically.

The saying is not only about 'praying standing up in the synagogue', but also about 'praying at the streetcorners', a custom which can best be compared to what we see nowadays with the orthodox moslems: at set hours they pray no matter and under what conditions. The treatise of the Mishnah on blessings gives the rules. The Shema, Hear Israel, must be prayed in the morning and evening. In the morning before the rising of the sun, although it could be done till the third hour; in the evening before the sun sets, although the time could be extended till the next morning. The school of Hillel maintained that one should say the prayer whereever one finds oneself at the moment, while the school of Shammai made a distinction between morning and evening prayer, because the text of the Scripture says: 'when you lay down and when you rise'(74). No day should pass without the prayer, because 'by saying the Shema one takes upon oneself the yoke of the kingdom of heaven'. Rabbi Gamaliel accepted the interpretation that a newly-wed husband was excused from the obligation, but when he was married himself, he said the prayer, 'because he did not want to be outside the kingdom of heaven, even for one day'(75).

The Tefilla, the Eighteen-prayer, was treated in much the same way(76). It must be said three times a day: in the morning, at midday and in the evening. If one was riding an ass, one should get off. If circumstances allowed, one should turn in the direction of the Temple in Jerusalem. One should do this at least in spirit. It was allowed to use a shorter version and this was considered obligatory, when one found oneself in a dangerous place(77). But if one knew the text by heart, one should say the whole text. If Berakot 5,1 is indeed speaking about the praying of the Tefilla, it is clear how much reverence was given to the prayer: 'one should pray standing up, but with bowed head. The old chassidim used to keep silence for an hour, before they began their prayer, because they wanted to direct their hearts to the Father in heaven. Even a king who passes by and says 'shalom', should not be answered. If a serpent crawls around your ankles, you should not interrupt your prayer'. The text makes clear that the real prayer experience was not neglected, notwithstanding the multitude of prescriptions(78).

If our saying, indeed, does speak about prayer, it must refer to these two prayers(79), but there are problems with both. There is no historical problem with the 'Hear Israel'. Some consider it to be of a very early date(80) and there are sufficient indications to place it as a unit before the year 70 AD(81). The first followers of Jesus and, maybe, Jesus himself knew it, and have prayed it out loud. The saying of the Sermon on the Mount presupposed, however, that the prayer would be said standing up in the synagogue or in the street, and that is certainly not according to the prescriptions of the Mishnah. Also the prescribed time - morning and evening - make it less believable, that people could so lose themselves in the prayer that it could be seen as a demonstration.

These could be sufficient arguments by itself to forget any relationship between the saying and the Shema, if there were not the complication of other facts. The Shema was intimately connected with the use of the 'tefillin', as they are called in the time of the Tannaim; the φυλακτηρία of the Septuagint and of Matthew(82), the leather amulets, which were worn during the day on the forehead and the left upperarm.

We know, now, how they looked thanks to the discoveries at Qumran(83). They were small round leather capsules containing papyri/parchments; they were held in place on the head or the forearm by a leather band. They must have created a macho image: a third eye and a band around your arm(84). The parchments gave the contact with the Shema, because they were covered, in miniscule writing, with usually at least the first two parts of the Shema(85). J. Milik distinguishes two types: the - so called - essene type, smaller in form but with a greater latitude in the use of the texts, and the Pharisee type, which was slightly bigger and more strict in the choice of the texts(86).

I should come back to Matthew's saying. He has Jesus say in his diatribe against the Pharisees and scribes: 'whatever they do, they do because they want attention. They enlarge the prayer-amulets and make the tresses longer'. This must refer to the same people as in our text. They wanted to wear the words of the Shema in an even more striking manner than other strict interpreters of the Law, because they wanted to be absolutely faithful to the letter of the Law. Looked at from the point of view of prayer, it was a form of hypocrisy, which cannot stand up under Jesus' criticism(87).

As to the Tefilla: we could say that the saying of the Sermon probably refers more to the public praying of the Eighteen-prayer than to the Shema. The rubrics, as far as we know them, can serve as an argument. This was the only prayer where 'standing up' was prescribed. Just for this reason, it was called 'amida'(88). Furthermore, it was to be said three times a day, which made it more probable that people would say it in the street. Even the posture was prescribed: in the direction of the Temple in Jerusalem, head bowed. All this certainly attracted attention(89).

The problem is that it is difficult to prove that it was known before the year 70 AD. Elbogen proved a close relation between a number of sentences of the prayer and certain texts from Ecclesiasticus(90), but that does not say much about the time of its composition. The texts, as we have them now, presuppose the destruction of the Temple and the end of the sacrificial cult, but this does not exclude the possibility of a shorter earlier version(91). The rules and the stories in the Mishnah about the Tefilla are connected with the names of rabbis from the first generation of the second century: Rabbi Gamaliel, Aqiba, Joshua and Eliezer were the authorities who put together a whole set of rules especially about this prayer; and that presupposes at least a certain period of time for its existence. All this brings the authors of the English version of Schürer to date the origin of the Tefilla between 70 and 100 AD.

If this is true, the Tefilla cannot be intended in our saying. I am not really convinced. To get a rule that a given prayer must be said three times a day, one must have a group of people who have made this a practice over a period of time and who publicize it. Only when the people have seen its value, can it be imagined that it becomes a popular custom. And it is certain that just a short time after the war the prayer got its eminent position in popular religion. It seems to me that the willingness to take over the custom of the Pharisees which before that was practised only by them, can only be explained by the fact that the people saw that the pharisaical movement was the one succesful movement to survive the war. As in the text about the use of the broad prayer-amulets, we are given here a glimpse of a practice of a small group of people who have a great future ahead of them.

Different from the previous saying, our attention here is focused more directly on the Pharisees. Other groups do not stand out so clearly historically; so, even if this interpretation is not absolutely certain, we will have to be content with this exclusive view: as if the Pharisees were the only practitioners of this custom. This is not unimportant, because the accusation is (again) summarized in the one word ὑποκριταί. The implicit reference to Mt 23 is thus given a broader background.

The meaning of the abusive word is here concretised by the contrast between 'public' and 'private'. The emphasis is on the difference between the appearance for people who act as public and who look at this public prayer with joy and approval, and the hidden Christian prayer praxis, which does not have onlookers. Jesus' followers should consider public applause as unimportant, because more fundamental values are at stake in prayer, values which are better guaranteed before the divine forum.

This emphasis on the 'theatrical' in ὑποκριταί does not mean that 'the Law' does not play a role in the background. Mt 23,5 ff suggests an opposition between the teaching of the Law and its fulfillment. In our saying on prayer a slightly different legal discussion comes to the fore. The Law not only tells us that we must pray, but prescribes also the mode. The Law is explained in the practice of praying standing up, and so a legal practice begins to grow as we saw. The saying resists this budding practice. A different interpretation of the Law is given by the fact that a different practice is prescribed. The intended adversaries are called ὑποκριταί, because they interpreted the Law badly(92): Law as the expression of the will of God was endangered by their practices. People in Matthew's community will also have found slowly and regretfully that the rule of Jesus was no real guarantee against abuses.

the prayer of the pagans

Mt 6,7 - 8

The sentence which denounces the prayer of the pagans does not fit into the simple literary structure of the passage on alms-giving, prayer and fasting. Probably the saying is more to be seen as an introduction to the Our Father than as an added commentary on the previous saying: one should not pray as the pagans do but as Jesus did. His followers should not only distance themselves from the Jewish practices in prayer, but they should also take a stand in opposition to the pagan culture in prayer. This opens up a whole new world with lots of questions: what was this 'pagan' religious culture in Palestine in the first century? What experience did the Jews have of this? Can anything be discovered with sufficient certainty so that this pronouncement can be better understood? Or rather, how should we interpret the saying against such a background? The saying was an actual pronouncement which presupposed existing practices, even though it was written in the context of a long literary tradition(93).

Notwithstanding the rather limited geographical background of the gospel, we can start with the observation that Matthew pays a lot of attention to places which, precisely under this aspect, can be considered 'pagan': places and regions where the Hellenistic religion is clearly demonstrable. It begins with the Matthean description of the residence of Jesus: Capharnaum as his own city from where Jesus makes his trips. A text of Isaiah, which Matthew uses as a proof of prophetical fulfilment, gives the ideological content: 'It is the land of Zebulon and the land of Naphtali, on the road by the sea, across the Jordan, the Galilee of the pagans'(94). The description has obviously nothing to do with Capharnaum but, as an indication of what is intended, it is very interesting indeed. Especially the 'Trans-Jordan' will become important. Time and again Jesus goes 'to the other side'(95), from north to south, from Caesarea Philippi(96) to 'the area of Judea at the other side of the Jordan'(97). One way or the other 'the territory of the Gadarenes' and 'the territory of Magadan'(98) must also be located at the other side, even though they are unidentified on the geographical map. Also important is the trip Jesus makes to the territory of Tyre and Sidon(99) and the mention of the result of this trip: his teaching reaches all over Syria (!) and attracts masses of people, not only from Galilee and Judaea, but also from the Decapolis and Transjordania(100). Maybe we should even mention that Matthew has Jesus pass his youth in Egypt (101).

An enormous amount of detailed research gives us nowadays(102) a fairly accurate understanding of the complicated reality of the territory. It is possible to give a correct description on the basis of archeological finds - buildings, statues, inscriptions, coins etc -, together with the literary documents. Even if not everything is certain(103), we do have a number of things clearly established. In the coastal area from Gaza to Sidon, in Samaria, in the Decapolis and in Transjordania- i.e. in all those areas where the Jews were in the minority - Hellenistic religion was abundantly present. There was the adoration of the whole Greek pantheon but also of Syrian, Nabatese and Egyptian gods and goddesses. Even the Roman emperor cult had found its adherents under the influence of Herod the Great. It would be wrong, however, to think that we find all this in all places: it is only a global overview we give here. There are differences between times and places, but we can safely assume that a combination of cultic temples existed in every πόλις. The great ruins of Baalbek, Gerasa and Palmyra make it clear, even today, how we should visualize temples in smaller places (104).

Furthermore, we should see this in connection with the phenomenon of the yearly or four yearly games, which precisely during this time expanded enormously(105). These games were intrinsically connected with the Hellenistic religious practice. Remember the processions, in which the statues of the deities were solemnly carried along with their attributes and their own music, and which were held under the responsibility of the local colleges of priests and priestesses. Remember the slaves dressed and masked like Mercurius (Hermes?) and Charon, who dragged away the corpses after the gladiator games, the games with wild animals and the realistically-presented battles. Remember the presentation of the mythological stories in the theatres; the public function of the priests in the organisation of the Greek games, the athletic games and the musical presentations under the auspices of the emperor-cult(106). Games and religion went hand in hand.

This brings us right back to the Jewish country. There are indications that Tiberias possessed an arena. Jericho had a theatre from the time of Herod, as well as an amphitheatre and a hippodrome. We must presuppose that even Jerusalem possessed a gymnasium, a theatre, an amphitheatre, a stadium and a hippodrome(107). The games created the opportunity for all Jews to come into contact with the world around them. Negative proof of this we find in the events after the defeat in the great Roman war. Titus was the organiser. It started in Caesarea Philippi (! cfr. Mt 16,13 ff). He produced all kinds of games with the Jewish prisoners: 'Here many of the prisoners perished, some being thrown to wild beasts, others compelled in opposing masses to engage one another in combat'(108). Later on, he continued these games in Caesarea on the coast, on the occasion of the birthday celebration of his brother Domitian. With all the pump of the occasion he used 1500 Jews as torches and had them killed in games and fights. It was even worse, when he celebrated his father's birthday in Berytus(109). From there he marched through Syria 'where he exhibited costly spectacles in all the cities through which he passed'(110). The closing ceremony was the enormous triumphal march in Rome together with his father and his brother, with as the finale the public execution of Simon, son of Gioras(111). So we see that the Jews were also the 'object' of the religious significance of the games.

Obviously these were exceptions. To get an idea how mutual contact and the possibility for contact functioned in daily life, we need to look at other texts. A unique document is the Mishnah treatise on idolatry(112). There is a problem, however. Considering the actuality of the problem with the pagans, it is most probably a very 'modern' document, i.e. a reflection on the practices of the second half of the second or the beginning of the third century. Hellenistic influence in Palestine was then much greater than it was in the first century. Without contemporary data, it can at most be used as a limit: it is not possible to assume that there was more contact.

Partly they are concrete examples of what is implied above: the presence of the many temples presupposes a cult. We should distinguish between the Greek and the Egyptian cults(113). The Greek celebrated in big yearly feasts with at most some periodical celebrations of initiates either monthly, or every nine or ten days. The Egyptians - as incidentally also the JHWH-cult -(114) had a daily practice supported by seasonal feasts.

Where the Mishnah forbad trading for three days before a feast, it was in the context of such a yearly feast of a city temple(115). The real spectacle was the procession led by the priests and priestesses, followed by the wagons with the statues of the gods and their attributes, accompanied by the men and women who were dedicated to the divinity. There was music. There were the sacrificial animals. The city was decorated with flowers, wreaths and torches. A popular mass meal was prepared for all the citizens. A special committee was responsible for the organisation, for the decorum, and for law and order. It was a popular festival, which attracted many people from outside the city(116). The shopkeepers decorated their stores(117) and there were extra bath facilities and a special market(118). The whole city was involved in the celebration of the divinity.

Because the city might have more divinities with their own temples, the festivities would take place several times a year. We know also of festivities on a smaller scale, depending on the number of initiates. Demeter, Astarte, Dionysos, Isis had their own followers: their cult did not always become a city affair. But the celebrations were held with as much pomp as possible(119). The Mishnah mentions several by name(120): we can document at least the κράτησις: the rememberance of the Augustus' assumption of power at Actium; and the γενέσια: the celebration of the emperor's birthday(121). The organisation of the circus games(122) and the popular meal at these feasts tried to popularize the emperor's cult.

The veneration of the Egyptian divinities - in our case we have to think only of Isis and Sarapis -(123) was differently organised. There were special feastdays which might seem to be more or less the same as the Hellenistic memorials(124), but the specificly proper feature was that the temple was used every day: after the ritual opening of the temple doors at dawn the statue was covered with precious ornaments. A fire was lit and water was poured out in libation. There was singing accompanied by flute and sistra. The whole day long, people came to venerate the deity till the evening when the temple was closed again at sundown. In the Mishnah we find a text which describes the ritual: 'it is forbidden to embrace the statue, to kiss it, to honour it, to sprinkle it, to wash it or embalm it, to dress it up or to put shoes on it'(125). As far as I know, this is an exact description(126).

Two things we have not yet mentioned. First of all the cluster of practices regarding the veneration of high places and the great green trees. There is a good bit of confusion in the texts. It is not always clear whether the high place itself and the green tree, or rather a statue placed there, was the object of veneration(127). Maybe this confusion was also felt by the worshippers themselves. Connected with this cult, although not entirely, is the cult of Mercurius. It probably originated with the veneration of small dolmen. At the time of the Mishnah, it was connected with the 'Mercurius standing at the crossroads'. The practice was to donate small offerings: coins, clothes, vines, ears of corn, wine, oil or flour which could be taken by those who passed by(128). We may suppose that they existed also in the land of the Jews in the first century, although they were probably venerated as Hermes.

Secondly, the inhabitants of Palestine may well have come into contact with pagan religion in as far as it imposed private obligations: when the foreigners of the country venerated their own gods; when they celebrated their 'eucharists': on return from a voyage, on the occasion of a healing, or in the case of sickness; on the occasion of marriages, birthdays, memorials of deaths and at other family occasions as for example the offering of the first hair of the beard; in connection with the use of amulets, rings and bracelets etc. with the image of the deity; when they gave donations on more important feastdays like fir cones, figs and dates which were used on the feastdays of specific deities(129). Even if the inhabitants of Palestine did not come too close, these pagan practices could have been clearly visible.

It will be clear that the mentioned practices represent indeed a mixed bag. If we knew what Matthew said precisely in his text, we might be able also to find his true meaning. But that is not possible. The βατταλογέω is a hapax in the New Testament. Most probably it does not occur anywhere else(130), so that we have a real puzzle. Three possibilities are given, but non is without its problems.

1) One can deduce the meaning of the unknown word from the context, from the πολυλογία which the pagans thought they needed, but which was not necessary for Jesus' followers, because their Fater knows what they need, even before they have asked. It is not a very neat solution, because the nuances are lost. Furthermore, it does not solve the question about what Matthew could have meant by this verbosity. From what we know of the prayers of the pagans, it can not refer to these(131), because sometimes they were not any longer than the example Jesus gave and they were certainly not longer than some psalms. If it refers to a reality, it must be to the dull length of some processions (132) or to the slow procedures of the Isis cult in which people were kept busy with the ritual for hours on end (133).

2) Blass-Debrunner(134) proposes something completely different. He presupposes that the Hebrew/Aramaic word 'btl' (use idle, empty words) has become Greek. If the question is how people in Irael might have understood Matthew's text, G. Delling's objection that Greeks were not supposed to guess the meaning of such a half-Aramaic word, falls(135). Maybe we can even go further. In the gemarrahon

Aboda Zara(136), the advice was given to make pagan expressions into terms of abuse: 'when they say 'face of God', the Jews should say 'face of a dog'; when they say 'eye of a cup', the Jews must say 'eye of a thorn'; if they say 'god of fortune', the Jews must say 'dunghill''. These are puns where the change of a vowel or a consonant makes the differences. This could be possible also in the text of Matthew. Originally the pagans used the word 'bs^{c}' (to bless) or 'b^{c}y' (pray, supplicate) for their own prayers. Outsiders then made this into 'btl'. It would place the saying in the context of the literary tradition of the religion critique of which the Book of Wisdom and Philo are the most verbose representatives. However, it is clear that this idea places hypothesis upon hypothesis and truth is not best served that way.

3) The third proposal(137) calls to mind either the stuttering and stammering, which occured in mystery cults, or the continuous repetitions of the names of deities in the magical practices. The mysteries of Demeter and Dionysos are possible as far as the time is concerned, but the places where these mysteries were held, do not fit at all(138). The mysteries of Isis should not even be thought of(139). Furthermore, what would outsiders have known about these mysteries? Up to now it is almost impossible to reconstruct them and we do not know anything about this ecstatic stuttering(140). If we accept that the real initiation was open only to people who had the money(141), the saying becomes a well hidden critique which could have been integrated much more simply in the previous aphorisms. As to the magical practices: if we take the Aboda Zara as a limit in the description of the historical possibilities (142), it is clear that they were unknown to outsiders in first century Palestine. The accumulation of epitheta - the main point of this idea - is documented only from the fourth century on(143).

What remains is the positive part of the saying: your father knows what you need before you have asked him. It is the real introduction to the text of the Our Father, in which the religious community itself is speaking.

Prayer in Matthew's community

Mt 6,9 - 15

The Our Father has been interpreted in many different ways in exegesis. There is agreement more or less on several main points: an interpretation which is extremely eschatological has been judged impossible(144); it is only partially possible to reconstruct the history of the text(145); nothing new can be said about the meaning of ἐπιούσιος unless some new texts are discovered(146). The Our Father is a text which has been used in prayer in Matthew's community and, therefore, it must be understood primarily as a Matthean text. In the superabundance of the literature on the subject these two aspects can reasonably looked at to advance some new ways of understanding.

I. Matthew's community as a prayer community

Matthew's gospel is, in its totality, a narrative text which by itself does not provide an insight in its milieu of origin. By telling a story, the author opts to bring his hearers to another time and place, to other personages and modalities fundamentally different from the time and place of the actual hearers (resp. readers) of the text. Literarily and theoretically one should accept a fundamental break between the actuality of a story as told and the actuality of the telling of a story. In the narrative literature of the New Testament this break is not always respected by its authors. The actuality within which the story of the life of Jesus is told to actual hearers has left its own traces in the text: components which we can use to reconstruct the milieu of origin. Relevant for this reconstruction are all those sentences, fragments of stories and stories which can be traced to have meaning still in the actuality of Matthew's time. They are the sentences which address the actual hearer and which, for some reason or other, break through the narrated communication between Jesus and his disciples (and/or) the people: as e.g. general pronouncements and statements which try to bring the actual hearer to change his behaviour over the heads of the immediate textual hearers as it were. Practically the whole of the Sermon on the Mount can be seen as an example of this. But the fulfilment quotations also belong in this category as the Matthean explanations of the parables and even, in a more convoluted way, the parables themselves. No text, and certainly not Matthew's gospel, can deny its origin.

Confining myself to the 'prayer'-context(147) it is possible to determine a number of questions:

- the organisation of prayer

Explaining the saying on public prayer(148) I already mentioned that Matthew's community almost certainly no longer visits the synagogue for prayer. People gather in the 'inner room', i.e. they meet in private houses. One could ask oneself whether the further determination that it should be done 'behind closed doors and in secret' has any connection with the fear of what they experience in the synagogues: the scourging which Jesus predicts in the context of future persecutions(149). The most important indication of the separation of the two groups is the fact that Matthew consistently speaks of 'their' synagogues. The synagogue is no longer 'their own' but belongs to 'another' group.

According to the text of Matthew, the synagogue has never been a 'place of prayer'. The words he uses to describe Jesus' actions in the synagogues are 'teach', 'proclaim' and 'heal'(150). Only the ὑποκριταί come to pray (151). It is the same as with the Temple. It should be a 'house of prayer', but the leaders of the people have made that impossible. In the long story about Jesus in the Temple we see that he is not doing anything else than what is told about his behaviour in the synagogues. He heals the sick, preaches his doctrine and attacks the scribes and the Pharisees. It is probably an indirect indication of the fact that the synagogues and the Temple have been historically the places for doctrinal expositions.

In the circumstances of the community of Matthew this conflict is a past reality. People now gather in their own houses. Can anything be said about the number of people taking part? Mt 18,15 - 20 has to be discussed then. According to the intention of the text the mentioned ἐκκλησία is the whole community of the city(152), but whether that ever happened in reality is doubtful. I think that it is important now to distinguish the literary level of the communication between 'Jesus and the disciples' from that of the communication between 'Matthew and his hearers'. On the level of the story as told, a gathering of the city community is envisaged as determining whether someone is a heathen or a pagan - i.e. whether someone is allowed to participate in the gathering. On the level of the telling of the story this is not necessarily so: the ecclesia should comprise more than two or three persons- required in the first round of enquiry - but it remains open how many more can be there. The group, which has actually gathered, considers itself as representative of the city: a special way of speaking which is symptomatic of the high level of self awareness of the first Christians.

One could even question whether the following saying, on 'two or three who gather in Jesus' name', has something to say about the number in the group gatherings. In itself obviously not. It could well be an indication of an absolute minimum. But the question is whether this does justice to all data. The Jewish parallel texts, which speak about gatherings in the synagogue(153) or about gatherings to discuss the Law(154), mention the diminishing number 10, 5, 3, 2 or 1(155). Point of departure is the minjan of ten persons which, however, is not necessary for the presence of the Shekinah. The Shekinah will not be absent when there are fewer persons present. The question is why precisely in Matthew have the higher numbers disappeared? Is it because there are seldom that many? Is it as a consolation that even in very small groups divine presence will not be absent? We cannot go much beyond such questions. But, if there had always been large numbers, the saying would not have been necessary in this form.

- the composition of the group
As J. Blank has shown(156), Matthew speaks of Christians almost exclusively in masculine terms. The 'disciples' are called 'brothers'(157) and most probably one should not think that in the plural an a-sexual terminology is intended. When Matthew uses ἀδελφοί he probably thinks only of 'brothers'(158). This is not absolutely necessary because in a number of places the text does not demand an exclusively masculine denotation(159). And in the Nazaret-passage(160) as in the scene in Bethany(161) there is even an explicit distinction between men and women. But these texts of Matthew follow precisely the text of Mark and they probably cannot be used to grasp his self-understanding. Therefore, one can say that Matthew's text, is certainly mainly directed to men, even if not exclusively. This does not say a lot about the actual participation of women, but it does say something about the position of women in the group.

One can only hope that the egalitarian attitude of Matthew did create resistance against this masculine tendency. It is expressly stated that no names of honour may be used in the community: the titles of rabbi, father and teacher(162) are anathema, because they could obscure the fact that the Messiah and the Father in heaven are the sole source of the community. As is clear from modern experience these admonitions have had little effect in the course of the reception of the gospel. For me it is even a question whether they were not already too late in Mat-thew's time. One must be aware again of the distinction between the actuality of the story as told and the telling of the story. There would be no need to actually mention the titles if there had been no actual practice.

There is an allusion to very concrete tasks which we cannot completely recapture(163). What is meant in the title 'father' or 'teacher'? The combination rabbi-teacher, however, points towards teaching activity in the context of the interpretation of the Law. If we accept that this use of words is connected with Jewish practices at the end of the first century, one should suppose that Matthew knows of a multiplicity of local communities. Apart from a few places where the Torah is taught (Jabne, Ushna, Tiberias) and where probably more rabbis lived together, the supposition for all other places is that only one rabbi would be available and competent in each place. One cannot make oneself into a rabbi. It is a title which is given by imposition of hands by another rabbi and in the course of history ever more stringent hierarchical rules are introduced.

Anyway, from several texts(164), it is clear that in Matthew's community specific people hold specific functions. He speaks in such an explicit way about scribes, prophets and the just that one must suppose that such people were actually part of his community(165). It cannot obviously be established whether these are also 'ministries'. It does indicate that there are distinctions in his group and that the school orientation, which so many exegetes want to read into Matthew, should be at least mitigated. Prophets and the just belong there only in a very limited fashion(166).

Finally, while there is a fundamentally egalitarian option, the presentation of the group around Jesus is clearly hierarchical. Opposed to the mass of people around Jesus stands the group of disciples, several times identified as the 'twelve disciples'(167). In thát group Peter is the undisputed leader(168), the first called and the first named(169), who is addressed by the authorities as the first one responsible(170). Matthew participates in the historical development in which the 'twelve apostles' as a group play an ever more important ideological role. His own contribution to this development is the greater isolation of Peter in the group. But, for Matthew himself, all this is not (yet) a reason to think of the founding of a hierarchical community. It is not used to strenghten the position of elders, leaders or episkopoi. Instead Matthew states that the twelve and also Peter are models for every follower of Jesus in whose life good and evil go together, but where the good can win victory via brotherly correction(171).

- demonstrable rituals

One should not expect a complete description of all the rituals which take place in Matthew's community. There are a number of allusions which can be used to provide a minimal description. One can safely accept that these rituals at least have existed in Matthew's community. There is no way to determine whether these are all the rituals in practice or that everything relevant for these people has been conveyed.

Notwithstanding this limitation we can provide a substantial historical reconstruction:

baptism:
Matthew is the only one among the synoptics who has an explicit baptismal formula which, as known, has been of great influence in the 'Wirkungsgeschichte' of baptism. Jesus' command in the last sentences of the gospel to make the pagans into disciples is amplified by the instruction to baptise them in the name of the Father, of the Son and of the Holy Spirit(172). A number of things can be said about this text.
1. Matthew sees baptism as an initiation rite which makes people enter in the school of Jesus, the Kyrios to whom all power is given and who has explained the Law of Israel according to God's will. It brings the nations under the covenant which God has made with Israel: a kind of theology which we will further substantiate in this study(173).
2. Striking is the use of a trinitarian text, which indicates that the theological reflection has developed beyond what one would expect a priori from the preceding text. The absolute equalization of Father, Son and Holy Spirit forces us to take the foregoing pronouncements in Matthew about the Holy Spirit seriously(174). The almost complete parallel with the texts of Mark and Luke has apparently not prevented a proper theological reflection from developing.
3. The group addressed is the goyim, the non-Jewish peoples. In this phase of the story only the mission to the pagans is mentioned. We already clarified that this does not mean that, therefore, Israel has been lost sight of. Does it mean that there is no more Israel-mission? At least as far as the ideological aspects go this question must be answered in the negative, but I will return to this later on(175). Anyway, it should be noted that for pagans there is no more circumcision. This thorny problem dating from the beginning of the Jesus-movement, of which we catch a glimpse in the story in the Acts, is for Matthew's community a resolved problem. Baptism is the only initiation rite. There is no longer any competition with the biblical command of circumcision.

From the story of John the Baptist, who introduces Jesus as the one who baptises in the Holy Spirit and in fire (176), we can add at least that baptism is, still in Matthew's time, seen as an eschatological event. From the parallels between the saying of John the Baptist about Jesus as the one who gathers the wheat and burns the chaff in never-ending fire, and Matthew's own parable about the wheat and the weeds(177), one may suppose that, for Matthew, baptism anticipates the last judgment in promise and in threat. It shows how serious baptism was taken in his community.

the memorial meals:
Matthew's text does not give a comprehensive term for the Christian communal meals, so that we do not know how they were called in his community: agapè, the supper of the Lord or paschal meal. We cannot even really speak about 'words of institution' in Matthew, because he does not mention a command to 'repeat' (as we find it in Luke: 'do this in memory of me'). According to Matthew's story nothing is inaugurated. Only the quote-like formulation of Mt 26,26 indicates that we may, nevertheless, suppose that they had communal meals. It has already been mentioned 'when they finished eating' (in 26,21), and is repeated when the story tells that Jesus took bread and broke it. Does this mean that in Matthew's community the separation of the ordinary meal from the ritual meal has already taken place? What is being remembered: the last paschal meal of Jesus, the meals of Jesus with the people? When did this happen: only at the festivity of Passover, on the eve of Passover? Only with larger groups of people? All questions which we cannot answer(178).

In the story of the last Passover meal of Jesus we deal, theologically, with loaded sentences which have been reflected upon innumerable times. Taking into consideration that exploitation leads to loss of meaning, we still need to mention some things:

1. In the communication Jesus-disciples there is an equivalent reality between on the one hand the 'breaking of the bread' and the 'body of Jesus', and on the other hand between the 'drinking from the one cup' and the 'shedding of Jesus' blood'. Activities which are of normal use at table - breaking the bread and drinking of the wine, - are being transformed by Jesus' words as somatic activities which are equivalent to his own body and the shedding of his own blood. During this paschal meal in which the treason of the disciples is a central element, from Judas to Peter to all the disciples, Jesus himself introduces the effect of this treason in the meal: the separation of his body from his blood.

2. The sentence about the wine is the most instructive in Matthew. Immediately following the Mark text there is mention of 'the blood of the covenant' and of 'for many'. Jesus' death is proposed as the slaughter of an animal, the blood of which seals the covenant, a covenant which is open

to 'many', the many pagan peoples who, via Jesus' death, will participate in the Covenant which God made with Israel(179).
3. More typical of Matthew is the remark that all this happens 'for the forgiveness of sins'. Probably we should not read into this a 'once and for all'. Through the obedience of Jesus to his Father's will through which all power has been given to him from God, this possibility for sins to be forgiven is given to 'man'. Forgiveness of sins has a broad ecclesiological effect for Matthew as we will see below.
4. In the closing sentence about 'eating anew in the dominion of the Father' the emphasis in Matthew's text is on the addition 'together with you'. The communal meals do not only look back, but are also a looking forward to a renewed togetherness with the Lord, when the dominion of the Father has come(180). It is a promise which runs parallel with the eschatological expectations surrounding baptism, but which in this case expresses only the positive side.

The emphasis in these sentences is undoubtedly on this theological progression of thought. Indirectly some ritual practices may possibly have been mentioned. This is true for the breaking of the bread. In the gathering someone breaks the bread and hands it around. If we are allowed to draw into this the stories about the meals Jesus shared with the people, it is not improbably that in the Matthean presentation of facts - Jesus gives the bread to his disciples and they hand it to the people(181) - a liturgical use of the story sneaked in: one person breaks the bread and gives it to several others who share it around.

As for the cup, we should take it for granted that one cup passes around from which all drink. The descriptive sentence in Mark has been turned into an explicit command: all must drink from the one cup.

Separate blessings are spoken over the bread and the cup. It is probably, although not verifiable, that these blessings were more than the sentences mentioned with the bread and the wine. In Jewish meals, nothing is eaten or drunk without blessing.

The closing mention of 'the singing of hymns' belongs to the level of the story as told. But Matthew has, maybe not completely without success, taken care that this Jewish paschal custom has found a place in the New Testament.

marriage and divorce:

Marriage and divorce were known to Matthew's community. A lot has been said already about the juridical and theological positions. Once one is married, the marriage is protected by the Law, but, in the case of 'porneia', divorce is obligatory.

Typical of Matthew in this context of marriage and divorce is his mention of 'eunuchs for the sake of the kingdom of heaven'(182). Even after A. Sand's recent study(183) we must hold that it is unhistorical to say that eunuchs are not capable of marriage. There is doubt about their sexual potency(184) which manifests itself in sterility: the absence of children in a marriage (!) of 'a eunuch who is so from birth'(185). If this is the basic point of departure in Matthew's logia on eunuchs, then 'eunuchs for the sake of the kingdom of heaven' refers to 'sterile marrieds': i.e. either about childless marriages in which the husband does not send his wife away because of the kingdom of heaven, or about married couples where the husband because of his commitment to the preaching of the nearness of the kingdom leaves his wife, who, therefore, will remain childless, but without sending her away.

These juridical positions do not say much about the question of the ceremonials used in marriage and divorce. Probably it all happens in the family circle. In cases of divorce they probably follow Jewish custom: writing the letter and handing it over, signed by at least two witnesses: a procedure which, in Matthew's opinion can also be done 'in secret'(186).

The customs surrounding marriage are less well known. We can perhaps suppose that Matthew's parables about marriage festivities indicate existing practices: a feast is given which will be more elaborate according to the social standing of the partners. The father of the groom pays for the expenses. There are invited guests who know beforehand when the feast will take place. On the eve of the day there is a procession of lights with girls who accompany the groom (to the house of the bride?). During the feast itself the 'friends of the groom' have a special place. Guests are supposed to wear a 'marriage dress'(187). Matthew does not mention any religious ceremony. We can take it for granted that a marriage contract is concluded and that a 'blessing over the couple' is said. It is not clear who speaks this blessing-at least during the first century after Christ. Later this will be one of the privileges of the rabbi; in a marriage between Christians a presbyter will have been present.

the forgiveness of sins:

No other NT author speaks about the forgiveness of sins in such a concrete way. It is clear that the Matthean community has been actively involved in this. As always in Matthew, there is a close connection between his theological and his practical concerns. In three observations I will put these together:

1. Point of departure is his more or less theoretical exposition about Jesus as the one who has brought the forgiveness of sins on this earth to reality. This idea is repeated three times. In the nativity story it is connected to the name Jesus. Joseph must give the child the name Jesus 'because this child will save the people from sin'(188). In the story of the healing of the lame person, Jesus proves by his healing 'that the Son of Man has power to forgive sin on earth'(189). As mentioned already, in the story of the last paschal meal, Jesus says that 'his blood is shed for the forgiveness of sins'(190). The inclusion of birth and death is striking: Jesus' life is, in its totality, the basis for his power to forgive. It is also striking that there is no reference to God and his exclusive right to forgive(191). This does not mean that Matthew would not have known this theologoumenon(192) but in this, as in other theological pronouncements, the Kyrios is identified with the Shekinah(193).
2. G. Strecker showed that Mt 9,8 has been formulated from the concrete ecclesial practice of the forgiveness of sins(194): once Jesus has proved that the Son of Man on earth has power to forgive sins, the masses glorify God 'because he gave such power to 'man''. In this practice of the forgiveness the community of Jesus' followers already participates here on earth in the Son of Man's power to forgive sins. Unlike the other NT authors Matthew has also written down the 'rite' of this practice as a command given by Jesus(195): firstly one must tell one's brother of his sins in private; if he is unwilling one should call on one or two others; after that one must tell the ekklesia which has the possibility to declare him a publican and a pagan. It is a well-developed procedure which is in direct relation to the Jewish system of 'the brotherly correction'(196).

The clarity of the description does not take away the fact that little is said about the real course of events. Is it a kind of process with an accusation and the right to defense? Is the accused present? How is the judgment rendered and what happens if the accused is acquitted? It is certain that people in Matthew's community had an explicit awareness of sins with clearly defined limits. The last criterion is the pronouncement by the community. The community has the last word which has value as the word of God: what they bind on earth or loosen is valid for the heavenly forum. Even if the emphasis in the sentence is on the negative aspect in this context, in reality the possible condemnation or acquittal is completely parallel in the formulation. Matthew has only one exception: 'whoever says against the spirit, i.e. whoever speaks against the Holy Spirit, cannot be forgiven either here or in the world to come'(197). Matthew's own emphasis is on 'either here or in the world to come'. By adding this he has taken this sin - which we cannot easily understand- out of the church's discipline of forgiveness.

3. The seriousness and the possibility for abuse of this procedure is softened by those commands of Jesus which point to the other side of the 'brotherly correction'. Before one accuses one's brother, one must be ready to forgive and to be self critical. I will come back to the latter. How important the command to forgive is for Matthew is shown by the fact that his only comment on the text of the Our Father is: 'if you forgive people their trespasses, your heavenly Father will forgive you, but if you do not forgive people, your heavenly Father will also not forgive your trespasses'(198). In the same way he ends chapter 18, where he describes the church order on the erring brother, with the parable of the slave who forgives and the one who refuses to do so. Whoever is not ready to remit a small matter to his brother, while so much has been remitted to him, should not think he will escape divine anger(199). One should not dare to bring a brother back from his error unless one is ready to forgive.

II An Analysis of the Text of the Lord's Prayer

It is in the totality of this context that the Lord's Prayer has been spoken as a prayer (sometimes? often?). We know nothing about its actual usage. The Didachè states that one should pray it three times a day(200), parallel to what the Mishnah says about the Amida prayer. But, notwithstanding the reference to the 'gospel', this does not say much about the concrete dependence(201). In Matthew's community the Our Father has been prayed in the form in which he wrote it. Beyond that we know nothing.

In the following analysis I do not pretend to give a total-analysis of this loaded text. Unlike the rest of the text of the Sermon on the Mount, I want to provide a modest first step to a more structurally oriented approach. There are several reasons for this. The text of the Our Father is a strongly coherent text which must be seen as one unit: a verse by verse analysis will not do justice to the text in its totality. Such a more traditional approach has been worked out often enough already and the danger of repetition is not imaginary as anyone who has read some of those analyses knows. But I will gratefully use them when necessary. As far as I know, a structural approach of the

Lord's Prayer has not been tried yet in the exegetical literature. This is a pity, because it opens the way to understand the connection of mythology and ideology as understood by Matthew. That connection, anyhow, is central to the following analysis.

- the reading problems:

The text provides a couple of reading problems which we need to determine a priori as a basis for the analysis. They are not all equally important, but in their own way they do influence the understanding of the text. The result will be a first reading structure:

our father who art in heaven:

It is the only person who is addressed. Grammatically this is expressed in the use of the imperatives which follow- which should be understood as request - imperatives(202). It stands as 'titlos' over the rest of the text.

on earth as in heaven:

Notwithstanding the fact that most exegetes connect this only to the immediately preceding prayer on the Father's will being done, it may be better to take this comparison as a conclusion to all three preceding prayers. Nothing in the content opposes this. One respects the inclusion of the first part of the Our Father in which the heavenly realities are mentioned(203).

the daily bread:

It is a well known crux which in the relevant literature has been treated extensively(204). Because the explicitly eschatological explanation - the future bread - does not actually fit in the context, one can fix oneself to the levels of meaning of 'the bread which needs to be prepared every day' to 'the bread which is needed today to stay alive' - the daily bread, or, the bread necessary for today.

forgive us our trespasses:

The basic metaphor is about real monetary debts as is clear from the correspondence with the parable of the king who remits debts and from the difference in the use of words in Mt 6,14.15: debt against trespass.

as we forgive those who trespass against us:

The comparison does not fit into the series of imperatives: it connects grammatically and semantically with the forego- ing prayer. The perfect has a present meaning, i.e. the debts which existed before, are supposed to have been remitted in the actuality of the saying of this prayer.

and lead us not into temptation:
Instead of an imperative we see here the negation of the conjunctive. The result of this is that, also grammatically - apart from the semantic differences - the fourth and fifth prayer are separated from the last two.

but deliver us from the evil one:
Considering Mt 13,9, where evil is personified as someone who steals the word of God's dominion from man's heart, the personal interpretation (the evil one) is not excluded, but this is not in opposition to the material interpretation (evil). Evil manifests itself in people and in actions and threatens the faithful. Because of the use of the conjunction ἀλλά and the semantic connection of 'evil' and 'temptation', this last sentence should be seen as an explicitation added to the foregoing prayer. It is not an inclusion of the three foregoing prayers as with 'on earth as in heaven', but neither is it a comparison as 6,12b. It is an independent prayer which is essentially parallel with the others.

Finally, taking into consideration the semantic distinction between the first three prayers - which treat of the heavenly realities - and the last four - which talk about the earthly ones - I come to the following reading model:

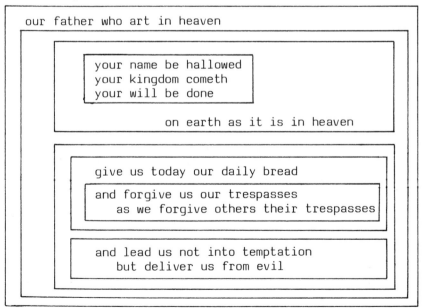

our father who art in heaven

your name be hallowed
your kingdom cometh
your will be done

on earth as it is in heaven

give us today our daily bread

and forgive us our trespasses
as we forgive others their trespasses

and lead us not into temptation
but deliver us from evil

- the narrative structures:
The text of the Our Father is a prayer text, but prayer texts exist in many different forms. Typical of the Our Father is that it is completely built up from requests in the form of imperatives. It is, therefore, not a complete text which in content comes to its end. The devotee is presented as someone who asks and that is it: i.e. one is introduced into a congealed communication system in which the one, who asks as a speaking dynamic subject, wants to bring another subject, by way of his requests, to behave actively in a process of transformation of the object and to bring about a change in reality. Reduced to a simpler form (in the actual context of the gospel it is an even more complicated communication system: Matthew tells his own hearers that Jesus has commanded that 'we' ... etc), it means that 'we' ask God to act. Because nothing is said about the compliance with the request, the narrative system is present only in nucleus: a flower in the bud. All elements are present, but not one comes to reality. This reservation applies to what follows.

That does not mean that the text does not imply very complicated activities. The Object, about which changes are requested, is not simple: there are seven separate prayers which, however, are mutually related, determined by the elementary narrative structures of place, time and persons. I want to follow this through step by step:

place:
In the mode of address there is already a geographical code: our father 'who art in the heavens'. It is a name which creates an opposition between two areas: the heavens as the place of God and earth as the place where men live who will say this prayer. However Jewish the use of the plural 'heavens' is, it works in the text as magnifying the distance: it does not remain without effect that the totality of the cosmos is brought in. While the one earth is filled with a multitude of people, the many heavens are filled with the oneness of God.

In the proposed reading model, in which 'on earth as in heaven' is seen as an adjunct to the first three prayers, this geographic code is further developed. The supposition is that in heaven the name of the father is hallowed, his dominion is exercised and his will is done, but that this realised situation is still to be brought down to earth. Heaven and earth are proposed as places where different power relationships operate. Heaven is the place of God, the place where God is recognised in his name, dominion and will; earth is the place of man where this does not happen. The first three prayers of the Our Father are a request for local transformation: the fullness of the heavently situation must resolve the earthly situation of defectiveness.

The geographical code is not followed through in the rest of the prayer. Earthly problems are mentioned, but the concept of 'heaven' does not appear again. Is not this a threat to the unity of the text? It is a problem which will come back soon in another context. Should one presuppose that if the request for daily bread and remittance of debt is complied with, and if one is freed from temptation and protected against evil, things will happen on earth as they are in heaven? Or, in other words, is it possible to interchange the first and the second part of the Our Father? I cannot give an answer to that question for now.

time:
With regard to the time perspective the same problems appear, but in reverse. The second part of the Our Father is now far more important and explicit. In the first part the time element does play a role, but remains less obvious. The heavenly situation is an actual situation, which is desired for in the future, but, when the heavenly situation comes to reality on earth, nothing changes in heaven. That means that the time perspective is subject to the geographical code.

In the second part this is different. Time is determinant. That is not to say that time functions exactly in the same way in the four prayers. There is a distinction between prayers 4 and 5, and prayers 6 and 7. That is because of the semantic content of what is being asked for. In the prayer for daily bread and for remittance of debt, there is a situation of need, which has to be transformed into one of fulfillment: there is no bread and no money to pay the debt and one asks for the debt to be remitted. About what is absent the prayer asks that it will be present 'now'. In the prayer for freedom from temptation and liberation from evil we deal with present threats. The danger is actual and one asks to be freed. About what is present, the prayer asks that it will be, if not absent, at least that it will be no longer present a threat.

Again one could ask oneself whether, in case the future perspective of the second part of the Our Father becoming reality, the perspective of the first part would still be open: i.e. once the requests of the second part are fulfilled, is there any meaning left for the fulfillment of the prayers of the first part? I think that the answer here must be negative, if we remember that the Subject of the fulfillment of the prayers - also those of the first three - is God himself. At the very least one will have to say that the text itself does not indicate time differences between the various prayers: the Subject is not supposed to make choices which can be valid for different times. In connection with the other two main passages of the Sermon on the Mount (the beatitudes and the passage on 'not to worry') I think that, in the experience of the fulfillment of the prayer for bread when people experience that the Father in heaven has taken care of the bread, one will know how the fulfillment of the other prayers is to be understood: whoever is poor in the very spirit, possesses the basileia, because such a person entrusts himself completely to God; whoever seeks God's dominion and his justice, will be given all the other things and has no need to worry about food, drink and clothing.

the persons:
As we said already, the communication structure of the prayer is in principle about two personages both of whom are the subject: those who pray are the primary dynamic subjects who ask that another subject will manifest himself for them as a dynamic subject. Remaining at the surface of the text, this means the distinction between the Father and 'we'. Secondarily - in the supposition of a possible reading of the text - the 'evil one' can be taken as a person -, a third personage is mentioned.

we:
In order to know whom Matthew wants to address as 'we', it is relevant to realise that Matthew strictly distinguishes between 'your father in heaven' and 'my father in heaven'. He never makes Jesus say 'our father' except in this text(205). Therefore, it is improbable that the 'we' is inclusive of Jesus. That is also clear in the introductory sentence of the prayer: 'this is how you should pray: our father ...'. 'We' refers to a group of which Jesus is not part.

Which group this is appears only in the second part of the text: give us our bread; remit us our debt as we remit our debtors; do not lead us into temptation; liberate us. Everything is personified and this indicates the most decisive determination of the passage: the local determination is not important; the time determination is important up to a certain point; primary is the personal determination. 'We' is the subject of the situation of need and the target group of the threats; it is the subject of the requests and the recipient of the Subject addressed: i.e. on the various levels of the text 'we' takes different narrative positions which in a complete analysis need to be clearly distinguished.

our father:
Only this: as the person addressed who is being asked to become active, i.e. as the intended dynamic Subject, appears in the 'titlos' of the prayer the name 'our father who is in heaven'. The unity of the text is guaranteed primarily by this Subject, because in the imperatives the same subject is always addressed. However great the differences between the first and second part of the Lord's Prayer, the unity of the communicative situation is not broken because the same Subject is addressed.

the evil one:
In the supposition that in the last prayer 'the evil one' should be taken in a personal sense, an Opponent is mentioned: the counter force which, on the level of being-able to do, exerts itself to prevent transformation. Not the whole transformation of the Object is threatened. The area of influence of the evil one is limited, expressed here in the close relationship between prayer 6 and 7. The semantic relation between 'temptation' and 'the evil one' is meant here (as in the story of the temptation where the evil one is identified as 'the devil who tempts'). 'Temptation' points primarily to the temptation at the terrible end of time, when there is a great danger of defection, because there will be many messiahs confusing people; this temptation is the time of the evil one who uses people and world to get the faithful in his power. But one could think also of a situation as in Gethsemani where Jesus says, as a commentary: 'pray that you will not fall into temptation'. That is a temptation in which man is confronted with God's will which threatens to go beyond man's forces.

In the text of the Our Father all this is only indicated so that the last two prayers have their own place.

All this put together, we can graphically describe the requested transformation of the Object as:

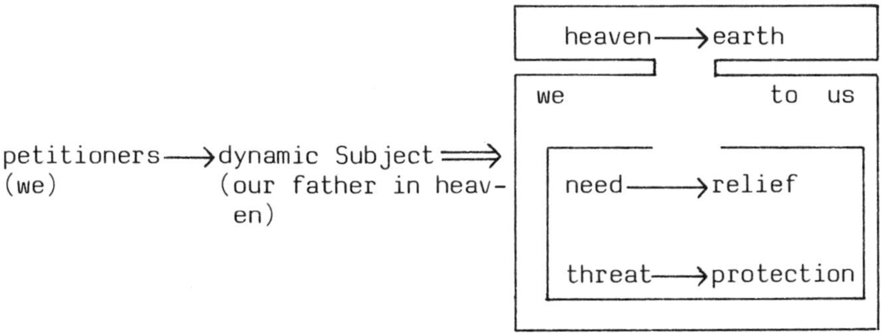

- the meaning of the used metaphors:
The text of the Lord's Prayer is part of a mythological language game to which we cannot easily find access. A succession of metaphors runs off in all directions and can maybe only be understood in their relationship with some reduction of meaning. At least I want to try this, because I see it as the only way to deepen our understanding of this text.

To clarify the argument I will give an analysis of the content.

our father in the heavens:
The expression is a combination of two more or less mutually exclusive formulations. In the lexeme 'our father' we find a combination of the two main personages of the text. The addressed subject is personified in the concept 'father', i.e. a family relationship is posited; and it is personified by the possessive adjective 'our', i.e. this father belongs to this group in opposition to other possible groups. Next to this is the combination of 'our father' and 'in the heavens': the nearness of the family relationship is combined wih the distance in place: heaven as all that is not of this earth. Nearness and distance, presence and transcendence, group determinant and group excluding: these are the relevant discursive words which can be used to described the 'titlos' in its function.

in heaven as on earth:
As I already have mentioned, the opposition heaven-earth covers the three first prayers. Therefore, we must start first from the fact that the text wants to describe a realised situation: in heaven God's name is hallowed, his dominion is reality and his will is being done. To understand what Matthew wanted to say we must concretize these sentences: God's name, his dominion and his will are not separate realities. He speaks about God as a person of power. In heaven God is respected in his name, in his power and in his will: i.e. one should think of the heavenly 'leitourgia', where the angels are thought of as adorers of God, as his subjects and servants - a way of thinking which is best known to us from the book of Revelation, but which plays an important role in all pseudepigraphic literature of this era: in heaven God is served and respected by his angels as a king. The metaphor comes directly from the oriental courts which, in their abundance of servants and in their emphasis on hierarchy and ritual, were perfect models for this description of the Transcendent.

However indirect - because in Matthew's text there is obviously no direct dependency - his presentation participates clearly in this king-ideology which gave the opportunity to see in the life of the court and the palace a metaphor to say something about 'the greatness' of God himself.

The prayer asks that the 'our father in heaven' will create this situation also on earth. Presupposed is that such a translocation is good for the petitioners. If 'the dominion of heaven' is realised on earth, Jesus' followers will be better off. In the second part of the whole prayer is indicated how we can imagine this concretely.

the daily bread:
The real opposition exists in the juxta-position of 'the daily bread' and 'today'. The uncertainty about the meaning of the word ἐπιούσιος - 'the daily bread' or 'the bread which is necessary for each day' - creates uncertainty about the urgency with which the prayer is imbued. The second interpretation indicates the greater urgency, because we must then suppose that the petitioners are dependent for their chances of survival on the fulfillment of their request: our father must give this very day the bread which is necessary to stay alive. In the first interpretation the petitioners know that they are dependent, but there is less urgency. It seems to me that this first interpretation is the more likely from the total context of the gospel which, as we will see, speaks from the viewpoint of a more advanced level of well being.

The request in its totality is taken from the ordinary human reality of children, who ask their father for bread. Later on in the Sermon on the Mount, Matthew will express this reality in its totality: 'Is there a man among you who would hand his son a stone when he asks for bread? ... If you, then, although you live in poverty, know how to give your children good things, how much more will your father in heaven give good things'(206).

I have already indicated that this does not prevent the king-ideology from playing its role. One should read this passage in conjunction with the beatitudes and the passage about 'do not worry'. Whoever is poor in his very spirit, whoever renounces his possessions, whoever accepts his complete dependence on God, whoever entrusts himself completely to God, will not be fearful because 'to them the kingdom of heaven belongs'; because not even Solomon in all his glory was taken care of like this. Do not worry about tomorrow. The presence of the bread for today is more than enough for those who believe.

the remittance of debt:
The addition 'as we remit our own debtors' is most typical

in this prayer. As in the main sentence, the basic metaphor in this comparative sentence is taken from the financial reality of remitting debts. That connects it to the other texts in the Sermon on the Mount, which deal with loans and repayment(207). It prevents us from taking refuge too quickly in the spiritual sense of forgiveness. I do not want to deny this aspect - I have made it clear above how deeply Matthew's community was involved in it -, but one should not present the text as if the financial fundamental condition were irrelevant for Matthew. Whoever is not prepared to remit his neighbour's debt cannot expect that God will remit his. In the parable of the king who remits debts, Matthew said it most clearly in his own inimitable way: it seems that also in this case 'a king-context' is not far away.

do not lead us into temptation but deliver us from evil:
These last prayers give the counter point: the anti-forces which in this world fight God's dominion. Whether 'temptation' only refers to the end of time with all its terrors of war, famine, pest and persecution, or every situation where man is painfully confronted with God's will; whether one takes evil in a personal or a more objective way, the presentation is always dualistic. The world is divided in two camps: the power for good and the power for evil and it is not self-evident that 'the good' will win victory as far as individuals are concerned.

Evil, in Matthew personified in the devil, exercises its power by keeping men away from Jesus' word and by making them disloyal to it. In the last judgment the account will be presented: a definitive separation between good and evil will take place. The good will be rewarded with light, glory and acceptance in God's dominion, the evil will be punished with fire, cries and gnashing of teeth. Now good and evil are present at the same time and in the same place, but they are in opposition to one another as divine and demoniac realities.

In these prayers Matthew uses cosmic-anthropological metaphors, taken from ancient mythological presentations about the fight between good and evil. In the text of the Lord's Prayer only elements are used: the threat of the danger to be lost; the test-situation which goes beyond one's own powers; the fear for the power of an enemy which might be too strong. The help of 'our father' is invoked in order not to be delivered into this crisis.

The relationship in all this cannot be denied. 'Our father in heaven' is asked to bring the heavenly 'leitourgia' on earth and to make it possible for his people to live without worries, without debts, without danger and without enemies.

Summarizing we can say that essentially two fundamental codes determine the meaning of the 'Our Father'. On the one hand, the code of fatherhood: God in heaven who as a father is responsible that his children will stay alive; and on the other hand, the code of kingship: God in heaven who as king is responsible that his subjects can live without trouble. In content the second code is more explicit, but there is no real opposition. God is addressed as Father-King, because man hopes for security in life which otherwise is impossible. It is because of this that the Our Father is called a hopeful prayer.

Graphically we can put it together in its essential elements, still remaining close to the surface of the text:

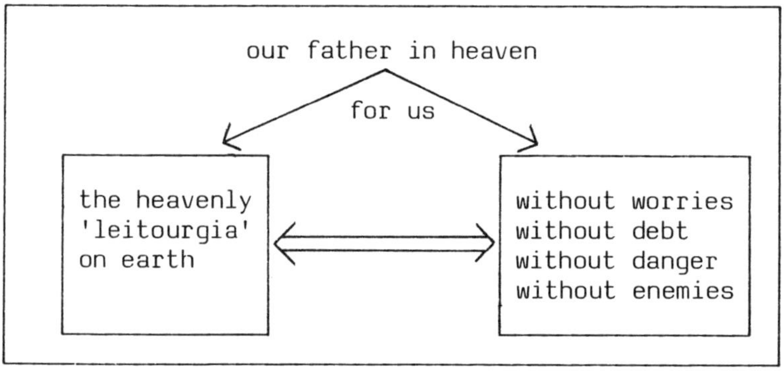

the right way of fasting

Mt 6,16 - 18

In the series on giving alms, prayer and fasting the latter presents the most radical material change in reality. An old Jewish tradition says: 'fasting is heavier than almsgiving, because it affects one's own body, while the latter is done with money'(208). Fasting means that one does not eat and that one does not drink. Bodiliness is affected, one's own body as the medium of expression of unfulfilled aspirations. There are motives aplenty. It is man's last way to protest. Even if someone is silenced and has no way to make himself heard, he can get publicity by a hunger-strike. Fasting is a signal, because whoever stops eating and drinking, is beyond human order.

One fasts, not only because one is full of sorrow, but also to strengthen oneself for the fight. It is a personal matter, but it also binds people together: with the suffering of others, with hidden cosmic powers, with mother earth itself which gives us life.

It is clear that fasting also is part and parcel of an actual existing culture. It is a reaction, which cannot bypass social realities, simply because it is a reaction. It happens in a social context: the economic, social and religious reality of a given society. This is true also for our saying in the Sermon on the Mount. It is an intervention against the background of a cluster of existing practices(209). To understand the real significance one must be aware of these realities.

Let us start with the most important: the practice of popular fasting, the special days which were imposed on everyone through mutual social pressure. First of all we have the Day of Atonement. The 'feast of the fast' it was called in the Jewish tradition(210), because it was connected with the Atonement rituals in Jerusalem: the sacrifice of incense in the Holy of Holies, the reading of the Torah by the high priest, the sacrifice of innumerable sheep and goats, the sending of the sacrificial goat into the desert, the dance of the daughters of Jerusalem in their white dresses(211). The Day of Atonement restored the relationship between Israel and God. The exceptional character of the feast attracted innumerable visitors, even though the day did not have the status of the three pilgrim feasts - Pass-over, Pentecost and the Feast of the Tabernacles - when the Jews were supposed to go to Jerusalem (212). It was a feastday for Israel and everyone participated through fasting. The longest possible time period was used: from sundown till sundown the next day(213). Shops were closed, no work was done, nobody ate or drank. The most one could eat was a dried date, the most one could drink was one mouthful. The only exception were pregnant women and those who sucked a baby, the sick and small children. Bathhouses were closed, because one was not supposed to wash or to anoint oneself. People walked barefoot and they were not supposed to sleep together(214). It was a yearly national feastday, which effected unity and symbolised it because of its special character.

We can be fairly certain that this fastday had been practised in the time before the destruction of the Temple. Although with less certainty, the same can be said of the seasonal fastday in time of long-lasting droughts. In the Mishnah texts on the fast we find a description of the practices as they existed definitely in the second century. The earliest starting-point is the Feast of the Tabernacles. Thereafter a prayer for a rain was added within the Eighteen-prayer(215). This prayer fitted in with the beginning of the early rains ('môreh') in October and November. These months were called 'fertile', because they prepared the ground for the new seed(216). If there was no rain in the beginning of November, the time had come for the fast. Individuals took it upon themselves to fast so that rain might come. It was still a limited fast: no food or drink for three days which were not consecutive and the day was reckoned from midnight till the next sundown. Work, washing and anointing, wearing sandals and sexual relations were allowed. But if there was still no rain by mid-November, the court announced the popular decision that the whole city must fast for three days under the same conditions as above. It worked towards a climax: the longer the rains stayed away, the more severe the fast became. First, there were three days which now were reckoned from sundown till sundown and the bathhouse was closed. One behaved oneself as on the Day of Atonement. Then it became really grim, because the time for sowing had passed. New fastdays were prescribed, up to seven: always on Mondays and Thursdays. All shops must close. The shofar was sounded. The arc was brought outside. People put ashes on their heads, especially the leaders. Public prayer meetings were organised, led by an old, poor, single man, because such a man would belong to God with all his heart. If the rain still did not come, the period of mourning began. There were restrictions on all activities, trade, building, planting, marriage and even greetings till the rain hopefully came: the late rains (the 'malqôsh'), which belonged in Nisan (middle of March-April)(217).

Whether we can prove that this practice, at least essentially existed before the second century, depends on the dating of the Scroll of Fasting, the Megillat Taanit, which mentions days during which Israel was not allowed to fast or mourn, because they were feastdays. It is a unique document, which most probably originates in the year 66 AD(218) and which can serve as proof. The coming of the rain is mentioned twice in Adar (half February-half March): 'on the eighth and ninth of Adar: the day of blowing the trumpet for rain (no fast); on the twentieth of Adar, the people fasted for rain and it came down upon them (no fast)'. Because the mentioned dates were supposed to be feastdays on which fasting was prohibited, we must presuppose that the blowing of the shofar on 8 and 9 Adar was successful. And besides, the Hebrew commentator on these texts indicates that the Scroll cannot mean to speak about two successive days, because the halachah prescribed that two fastdays should be separated by two ordinary days(219): i.e. the Scroll of Fasting wants to retain the memory of three successful fast campaigns. We cannot localise them any further. But Josephus(220) tells the story of the rainmaker Onias who was so just and so loved by God, that he obtained rain from God in a time of severe drought. This same story we find in the Mishnah with lots of additional facts about place, circumstances and practices(221). These practices and events have a long history.

Fasting because of disaster (plague, earthquake, storm, locusts etc) is sometimes put together with fasting because of drought(222). But there is a difference. In case of disaster, the mourning was more important, because it was 'post factum'. The impact was not the same as when the disaster had not yet happened. Individuals would also have experienced it differently and, therefore, it did not bind people together as much. I mention this, because in this series 'the sword' is mentioned: the danger from the enemy from outside(223). In that case a similar situation developed: fasting could prevent a future disaster. We have three texts which document this last practice. But it is not too clear, whether they speak about facts, because the stories themselves are legendary. The texts are primarily from the time of the Maccabees: in the story of Judith(224) to make clear how hopeless the people were, because of the threat of Holofernes to destroy the Temple in Jerusalem; and in the story of Antiochus Eupator(225), because the people were in danger of losing not only the Law, but also their fatherland and the Temple. Finally, there is a text from Josephus about a certain Izates, a king of Adiabene who converted to Judaism and who won a victory over the king of the Parths, because he began a fast at the decisive moment, put on ashes and prayed to the God of Israel for help(226). I believe that we should not deduce that Josephus speaks about factual truth, because this is the only place where he makes a connection between popular fast and war. The only other place which one could interpret as a fast but which was in fact a hunger strike, is the story about the cave in Jotapata, where Josephus retreated with forty warriors who were ready to die from hunger rather than surrender to the Romans: something which Josephus was not ready to do(227).

This brings us to a last question in relation to the occurrence of a popular fast: when did the practice of considering the ninth Ab as a general fasting day begin? There is no doubt about the time after the destruction of the Temple. The Mishnah makes this clear in its regulations, which are to be found all over the place: how to act when 9 Ab fell on a sabbath; that one was allowed to work, if one lived in a place where people did not follow the custom to stop working on that day; that one should not have a haircut or have his clothes washed during that week(228). As starting-point we can assume that 9 Ab is the day of the five disasters: to celebrate the remembrance of the fact that the Israelites were forbidden to enter the land, of the first and the second destruction of the Temple, of the surrender of Bethar and the total destruction of the city(229). When this text was written, the 9th Ab had become the focal point for a number of other disasters. The origin lies in the coincidence of the first and the second destruction of the Temple(230). Around this fact they gathered other historical data. All this makes it difficult to reason backwards from this series.

But there are a few other data, which could indicate that 9 Ab was possibly celebrated before the destruction of the Temple. First of all, we have the tradition of Eleazar ben Zadok in the Talmud(231) who taught as halachah that he remembered the 9th Ab to have fallen on a sabbath and that they fasted nevertheless. Because Eleazar ben Zadok is cited elsewhere as an authority, dating from before the destruction of the Temple(232), it would seem possible to do that here also. Furthermore, we have the much discussed texts of Josephus about the capture of the City by Pompeius and Herod (Sosius). He mentions(233) that this happened on 'the day/the feast of the fast'. In the literature on this text(234) it is thought that Josephus talks about the Day of Atonement. However, there are a number of problems with this, which are difficult to solve. If we could assume that it was the 9th Ab, one could situate the events in July-August, a time which is indicated by many other data(235).

Before we enter into a discussion of the practices in relation to the individual fast, I would like to call to mind the saying itself. Notwithstanding the existing exegesis the saying has to be understood against this background. It is clear that the text fits partly into existing practices, although partly it does not fit. The prescription not to leave washing and anointing is in agreement with the practice of people to take upon themselves the obligation to fast, when the drought begins. It agrees also with what happens during the first days of a popular fast, which are decreed when the drought continues. This means that no new practices were started from scratch.

But partly it does not fit. People who kept this saying were the exception on the Day of Atonement and on fast days which were prescribed on other occasions. It would even have been considered as a transgression(236), as a violation of the force of the Atonement, which came from these days of fast(237). People placed themselves outside of the social order, when they followed Jesus' saying. This would not have been taken kindly. It is even worse, when we remember that washing and anointing were socially connected with a visit to the bathhouse. These people needed courage.

We have seen already that there was a practice of

individual fasting together with the popular fast. When drought began, individuals could take the personal initiative to fast. The individual form of fasting is also presupposed in the parable of the Pharisee and the publican. The Pharisee boasts that he fasts twice a week(238): this practice seems to be so accepted that the Didachè prescribes that the Christians should not keep the same days as the ὑποκριταί(239). We find many of such prescriptions in the Pseudepigrapha with numbers, which often defy imagination(240). Such literary hyperboles presuppose a practice, but they do not describe it realistically. They try to astound the reader and glorify the hero or heroine disproportionately in order to proclaim the message more forcefully and effectively.

Fasting was admired at that time, as were the motivations and the results connected with it. These realities need to be described more clearly.

The more accessible form was the fast because of sorrow, loss or guilt. The Megillat Taanit describes the connection and the difference between fasting and mourning. Of these two, the fast was the most severe form, and it was, therefore, forbidden on all feast days. The prohibition to mourn was given only for the more important feastdays(241). If one felt that one should fast because of sorrow, the public holiday should not be used for it. The debate between the followers of John and Jesus(242) shows that Matthew knew this form of fast. Without any problem he puts together πενθέω and νηστεύω: a fast which cannot happen in the presence of the bridegroom, but which can be practised in his absence (while Jesus has been taken away?).

The Pseudepigrapha concretise this form of fast. One could fast because of infertility(243), or because a loved one did not want to stay(244). One abstained from wine, drink and meat to expiate for past sins(245). Especially, one fasted because of the destruction of the Temple in Jerusalem(246). Apparently there were many reasons for sorrow which people tried to express in a fast. I have already mentioned that this could become a popular fast in case of real disasters. The transition from individual to group fasting was gradual.

A very special form of fast is where it was used almost as a technique. We find this in the apocalyptic literature (247). The visionary prepared himself to receive God's mysteries by fasting for days, either by not eating or drinking at all, or at least by abstaining from meat and wine. Sometimes all that was taken, were plants(248). The visionary went into trance, his heart beat accelerated and he heard the voice of God(249). He began to pray and God answered him in his prayers, regarding the mysteries. He received insight and understanding, because God revealed to him the times of the world and the things to come. This fast had a very specific purpose. Its reality is difficult to gauge, but the very concrete descriptions seem to indicate that it had been practised at least in apocalyptic circles. In view of the story of Jesus in the desert, it is certain that Matthew knew of it. Several themes return: the extraordinary long time of 40 days, the retreat to a lonely place, the revelation which brings insight into his own mission. Jesus prepared himself by his fast to announce the kingship of God.

The place of the devil is special to this story and it brings me to a final consideration. Fasting was often seen in a context, in which devils and demons played an important role. The reason for this is that fasting was related to the forgiveness of sins. One could obtain God's mercy by a fast of repentance and, thus, one could hope that God would not destroy his vineyard. In a comprehensive description, all these themes are put together in the Apocalypse of Elia: 'But a pure fast is what I created, with a pure heart and pure hands. It releases sin. It heals diseases. It casts out demons. It is effective up to the throne of God for an ointment and for a release of sin by means of a pure prayer'(250). This text calls to mind the mission of the twelve disciples, when Jesus sent them to the cities of Israel to announce God's kingship: cure the sick, raise the dead to life, cleanse the lepers and cast out the devils (251). They were not allowed to accept anything except food while they travelled, because the worker deserves his food. He placed them in the situation of those who fast and who, through their abstinence, have the power to fight against demons and sickness. This is related to the synoptic tradition about the mighty demons who can be overcome only by prayer and fasting(252). It is a valid question, whether there is any connection between this and the prohibition to be σκυθρωπός while one fasts, as is mentioned in the saying in the Sermon on the Mount. Plutarch says that these beings in the world around us are 'big and forceful but also surly and gloomy'(253). 'Gloominess' is apparently a characteristic which is proper to demons and the prohibition to put on a gloomy air would then mean that one should not be under the influence of the demons while fasting. On the contrary, one must wash and anoint oneself, because this drives out the devil(254). Matthew's text cannot be read without this social context.

Different from the previous saying about almsgiving and prayer, it is not possible to point here to a specific group who practised extensive fasting as a group. Prohibition to anoint and wash oneself was a general prescription for the fast which was kept by everyone. Based on a text of Luke regarding the fast, the Didachè puts the Pharisees and the ὑποκριταί on a par. Even today this idea has its adherents(255). However, from the above it is clear that the Pharisees were not alone in this practice of this special form of fasting. Everyone was supposed to fast and everyone would, therefore, add extra abstinences to some forms of fast or to some special days of fasting.

The motivation that some people put on a gloomy air 'so that people can see that they fast', explains the ὑποκριτής - character. The theatre background of the word becomes clear again: it is wrong to change a private act into a public affair. In that way people become like actors who receive their reward from the adulation of the public. The low social standing of actors also plays a role in the depreciative use of the word.

But this meaning is not all, in the same way as it was not all in the other sayings where the word ὑποκριτής is used. There is clearly also a legal background, a reaction to a discussion on how the Law on fasting was to be explained and which practices best expressed this(256). In a certain sense, there is less controversy here, because the saying connects with existing practices. The author of the saying extends concrete practices of fasting, which do not forbid washing and anointing, to all forms of fasting so that the possibility of exhibitionism is taken away. He reacts against the actual admiration for the practice of the fast and against the tendency towards asceticism, which can flow from this. But he bases it on existing interpretations of the Law. By calling those who are 'more severe in the Law' ὑποκριταί, he makes clear that these cannot rightly appeal to the Law. On the contrary: while they think that they fulfill God's will, they remain prisoners in the world of the demons from which they wanted to escape through their fast.

Chapter IV
THE PROBLEMS OF THE RICH AND THEIR SOLUTION
Mt 6, 19-34

The community where Matthew lives, is sociologically different from the rank and file where the first messianic groups are recruited. There is more, and in a more directive way, attention for the people from classes where money, landownership and possessions play an important role. From Matthew's language it appears, that his community has climbed the social ladder. When money is mentioned, it is in large capitals and in treasures. Slavery is spoken off matter of factly and is mostly in the plural. When the subject is agriculture, one thinks of the larger landholdings.

This does not mean that Matthew has lost the preferential option for the poor of the original Jesus-movement. For Matthew only those can enter into the Kingdom of heaven who are prepared to give away all their wordly goods. In the following passage all of this enters: do not amass treasures; your eye must be integer and generous; one cannot serve God and the mammon; one should not worry about tomorrow but rather entrust oneself to the caring God. The solution of the problem of riches is: renounce them. The rich are promised as a reward, that they will be freed of their tormenting worries. God will take care that they can live: with more reason than that he cares for the birds. God himself will give them splendour and magnificence: with more reason than that he gives it to the lilies in the field.

By placing all this under the auspices of God's dominion and his justice - search first for God's dominion and his justice: then all this will be given to you -, it is clear that this passage must also be understood as a reflection on the Torah. This does not happen directly but in an indirect way. The one who, as a rich man makes the right choice, will experience that all the promises given to a person who keeps the Law, will be his: a treasure in heaven, a good eye, a faithful servant of God, life in its fullness and superabundance. Keeping the Torah is a joy for him who does it.

However difficult it may be to act according to Jesus' word, one should remember that Matthew started the Sermon on the Mount with the sentence: happy are those who are poor in spirit, because to them belongs the kingdom of heaven. The snare of riches must be eradicated from the very spirit. Only then entry into the basileia is guaranteed. Whoever is capable of doing it, will experience the Joy of the Law.

storing up treasures

Mt 6,19 - 21

With the saying about storing up treasures a new passage opens. The literary structure which binds the three logia on prayer, almsgiving and fasting together, is not continued here. This is a new series which treats a different set of problems. The train of thought, however, goes on: the presentation of the two realms and the two fora is maintained. Heaven with its own laws is opposed to the world with its treasures, possessions and troubles. He who commits himself to heaven builds on God: the faithful one and the safe one.

More cogently than ever before, we are confronted with a reality which is almost impossible to compare with our own experiences. It is a confrontation of two different worlds with two opposing points of view. There is talk about treasures which are stored away; buried in the ground; kept away in urns, leather pouches or iron-plated chests; hidden in closed-off niches or safely put away together with other people's treasures in underground cellars, in strong-rooms with reinforced walls where access is limited to doors with special locks, while the keys are kept by several people in order to prevent intruders to enter. How can we understand these practices as an economically reasonable behaviour?

Treasures used to be stored in antiquity in all kind of places, sometimes hidden so well that they are only now being found, treasures big and small, hidden in cellars, tombs or even in oillamps. Hoards, from the time about which our texts speak, have been found also in Israel: in Beth-Sachur, in En-Gedi, in Isfija (Carmel)(1). The last one is of special interest, because it is a real treasure: 3850 tetradrachma from Tyre, 1100 didrachma, 275 Roman denarii: silver money, worth some 3 talents, i.e. exactly 178.75 mna. One can see that they kept a careful account in that family.

The hoarding of money and valuables is, however, not the main point. The underlying reality is more important in order to understand Matthew's text. Matthew lived in a time, which considered it self-evident and for this reason sensible to keep valuables and money stored away, even though it would not accrue interest, as we would say today.

His society did not know 'capital' in our capitalistic sense of the word. There was an (enormous) piling up of cash, which was seen as an improvement of one's wealth and not as a separate source of income(2). I am aware that I take a specific position in the discussion on the understanding of the economy of antiquity by saying this(3). Is it possible to use a modern economic terminology, which has its origin in capitalistic realities, to describe the relationships of production and consumption in antiquity? Should we reformulate concepts like industry, export, trade, factory and banking, in a non-capitalistic sense? Were the same economic laws in force in antiquity as exist in our time? Can we speak of exploitation, added value, increase in interest, inflation?(4) These are not exactly questions for exegetes. Yet studying them might prevent us from taking the saying as a wisdom adage, which warns us of the 'spiritual danger involved in concern for the material things of life'(5), while it is clear that the passage clearly affects the economic way of life. The author of the saying was not trying to avert spiritual danger, he wanted to change economic behaviour.

The saying is formulated in a general way and wants to influence all forms of 'hoarding'. In the context of the actual culture of Matthew's time, we should think first of all of the Temple, even if that connection is not explicitated by exegetes. The fact that the Temple treasure was not far from the author's mind, is evidenced by his mention of the 'gold of the Temple' and the κορβανᾶς(6). The Temple treasure was the only treasure of note, which gathered in the greatest part of the surplus of the country. But, more importantly, the inhabitants of the country brought it together themselves. Every male Jew had to pay his yearly tax of half a shekel(7). On the 15th Adar (the beginning of March) the tax collectors of the didrachme went out to the province(8) to give everyone the chance to fulfill his duty. It is noteworthy to see that Matthew has a special story about this(9): the collectors of the Temple tax came to Peter and asked, whether Jesus was perhaps not paying this tax. To prevent a scandal Jesus let Peter pay, but he made it clear that he considered this a form of subjection and not freedom: it was comparable to what certain kings did to the people they had subjected.

The Temple treasure was not only a very important economic reality, but it was also the expression of national unity and national pride. Jews from the diaspora contributed to it. Delegations from Syria, Babylon and Egypt came yearly to Jerusalem to pay(10). Imperial edicts protected their passage(11). This was in the interest of the Romans, because it brought the gold and silver from the

Parths to the realm of the empire(12). There was a continuing flow of money to Jerusalem.

The treasure was complemented by innumerable free donations. The most impressive votive offerings are mentioned in the texts: the gold crown of Sosius(13), the gold handles of Augustus and Livia(14), the gold and silver inlaid of Alexander, the Egyptian alabarch(15), the gold staff of Queen Helena(16), the gold handle of king Monobazos(17), the gold chain of Agrippa I(18), the gold utensils of the high priests Ben Kalin and Joshua ben Gamla(19). The less fortunate could donate a grape, a leaf, a bunch of grapes for the gold vinestock in the Temple entrance(20).

The Temple was a safe place, not only because it was a holy place, but also because the walls were high and wide and there was a constant guard. As everywhere in antiquity the Temple was the place for the safekeeping of treasurers and valuables: gold, clothes and ornaments of the rich were kept there(21). They were deposited in care to the Temple treasurers who stored them up in the treasure rooms of the Temple. It is probable that the treasurers asked a compensation for this banking service(22). It is not certain whether the Temple owned houses and land, but the Torah provided for the possibility that someone would donate a house or land to the Temple: so the treasury was enriched at least by the monetary value(23).

But not all the money was kept as treasure: out of this capital the prescribed offerings had to be paid: the tamid and the musaf, the offerings for the community, the libations, the loaves of offering, the scapegoat and the red cow(24). From the rest(25) - in Jerusalem the major part - all other expenses were paid: the maintenance and beautification of the Temple, in building and personnel (26), as well as the improvements of the city, roads, walls, towers, aquaducts and all other things needed for the city(27).

Josephus dated a number of these things historically: the renewal of the Temple under Herod, the building of an aquaduct under Pilate, the provision for marble pavements under Agrippa II(28). So the money did circulate, even if it remained in Jerusalem.

But the main sum stayed untouched. Partly it was invested in gold and silver utensils, incense, cinnamon and other expensive spices, and especially in the vestments of the priests and the high priest(29), but the main sum stayed untouched as an enormous hoard. We have some figures: in the time of Seleukus IV (187-175 BC) it was estimated as 400 talents of silver and 200 of gold(30); Pompeius saw during his visit to the Temple (63 BC) 2000 talents, but did not touch them(31). Crassus (55 BC) did not suffer from such scruples and took away the 2000 talents plus another 8000 talents in gold coins and a bar of gold weighing 300 mna(32). When Titus finally sacked the Temple, talents were not mentioned anymore. The plunder had already taken place: Johannes smelted the cups(33), while the enormous fire did not leave the treasury untouched(34). In his triumphal march, Titus brought only the gold table and the candelabra: the only showpieces which survived(35).

Who was capable to gather a treasure in those days? We think generally of the rich, but we should really nuance that. The court was on a par with the Temple and its riches played a central role in this area. There were many connections between palace and Temple in the care both had for the well-being of the city of Jerusalem. With all the quarrels this entailed, there was a good deal of interplay and the Temple usually lost out. If Matthew's saying implies a criticism on the heaping up of treasures, because the people then put their trust in money and not in God, it just as much criticises the economic way of the kings, tetrarchs, princes and leaders. They, more than anybody else, were in a position to enrich themselves and their families.

The historical sources do not give more than a glimpse of this. It is all very indirect, in descriptions which speak about the effects of riches rather than about wealth itself. Then we have the confusion between private wealth and state wealth(36), in the same way as we find with the traders, bankers and leaders of the ἐργαστήρια. The leaders of the country presented their balance by subtracting expenses from income(37). There was no distinction between private needs and public funds. They considered themselves as public personalities who gave their lives for their work.

We have three kinds of texts which give an indication of what amount of money was involved in the court. This is not enough to draw up the balance-sheet, but it does give an impression of the immense amounts of money in circulation. First we have the texts which speak about the 'donations' to the Roman authorities: Aristobolos gave Pompeius a gold vineyard, a work of art, worth about 500 talents(38); Antonius donated to Cleopatra the coastal towns of Palestine, and also Arabia which was supposed to produce 200 talents yearly through the good offices of Herod, and he added the date palms and balsam plants in Jericho, a famous source of income for the Roman bureau of revenue in later times(39); Herod gave Augustus 800 talents after the battle of Actium(40), and 300 talents when he visited him, because he had troubles with his own sons(41); Salome donated to Julia, Augustus' wife, her possessions after her death: the cities of Jamnia, Phasaelis and Archelais which yearly brought in 60 talents(42). They knew that money could help to get into the good graces of someone.

Other texts describe inheritances: the texts about Herod's will give details about the content, though the numbers are not completely uniform: the income from Galilee was 200 talents yearly; the territory of Philip brought 100 talents and Archelaos' 400 (respectively 600). Then there was an additional 1000 (respectively 1500) in coins(43). Even though Herod had been on the point of bankruptcy several times, he seemed to have had enough wealth.

Finally a last text about the attitude towards money of the Herodians: the loans of Agrippa I before he had won the emperor's favour. It is a kind of rogue's story. He seems to find a way out every time at the last moment. He needed money to go to Rome, but he did not dare to claim his inheritance from his mother. He sent his own freedman to negociate with a freedman of his mother, but even then he was unable to get more than 17.500 drachma on a IOU for 20.000. The same thing happened in Alexandria. He asked Alexander for 200.000 drachma, but that was too much. On condition that Agrippa's wife answered for him, Alexander gave him 30.000 (5 talents). And when he finally reached Rome, the revenue people went after him. With difficulty he escaped Tiberius' anger. A princess paid his debt of 300.000 drachma(44). It is a beautiful story which makes clear that the rich also have their money problems.

Obviously, the people did not know about these amounts. Also, it is not all that clear, how much truth there is in these figures, but it does give us an impression of richness and a carefree lifestyle, which must have had its influence. We find it, moreover, expressed in Matthew. In his parables of the king he mentions talents in the plural in the same carefree manner: a slave owes his master 10.000 talents; a king gives his slaves one, two and five talents, which they manage to double without much trouble. The story of the γενέσια of Herod Antipas must be seen against the same background. Herod lets his daughter ask what she wishes, and confirms it with an oath. It will not make a dent in his wealth(45). Kings live luxuriously and always have money. That we find no critical remarks - different from the Temple money - may well be connected with history: the kings in Israel become more and more marginalised during the first century.

Palace and Temple were the places, although not the only places, where treasure was kept. It was reasonable to keep money: so individuals would also have done it, if they had the chance. If we can find out who was able to become 'rich' in that society, and how they managed it, it will become clear how deeply our saying cuts into the fabric of the economic system, at least if people are willing to follow the command given.

In the first place we should think of the 'professions' which were intimately connected with the big capital in the palace and the Temple: high priests, money changers and tax collectors. Without having a complete insight into everything, we know some facts.

the high priests:
They belonged to the class of priests but, in the same way as in republican Rome where the consulate determined a person for life, so also were the high priests in Jerusalem. Once a high priest, a person was marked for life(46). The high priests functioned progressively more like an aristocracy within the class of priests. This growing power also indicated a differentiation between poor and rich. This becomes very clear, when in Jerusalem the tithe of the harvest was safeguarded in the uncertain times before the destruction of the Temple: the high priests sent soldiers to seize the harvest, which for the poor country-priests meant death. Even in the City, there was then a distinction between the ordinary priest and the high priests(47).

J. Jeremias showed the historical background to this differentiation(48): the nomination procedure with all the political overtones this carried; the limitation to about four families which held all the power; the tendency of nepotism which created a growing isolation. It placed the supervision for the Temple and especially the treasury in the hands of a few families. The last high priests especially demonstrated that all control over the greed of the family was lost: Ananias brought gifts to the high priests daily (!) and also to the procurator; on his own initiative he took the tithes of the harvest, using his own slaves as a military gang of ruffians(49); Ismael did the same thing while in office(50), and Joshua ben Gamla was so rich that he could donate a gold votive offering to the Temple(51).

These examples make clear how the class of high priests became rich. The office was the main source of income. While in office, they lead the congregation far more often than an ordinary priest(52). But, more importantly, they probably had the first responsibility for the division of the Temple revenues(53); almost certainly they measured with a double standard. It was not without reason that the Zealots, when they were in power, killed several high priests and tried to start afresh with the selection by lot.

This truth about the high priests can be found indirectly in the gospel. Matthew speaks about them twice in connection with money: in the story of Judas whom they urged to betray Jesus for 30 silver pieces, and they did not know what to do when he returned the money. Again, in the story of the soldiers at the tomb who had to be bribed: with 'a lot of silver' they managed to present their story as true. In his sermon against the Pharisees and scribes, Jesus gave the ideological argument: who sets his heart on the gold of the Temple or on the offerings of the altar, cannot understand that God and mammon do not mix(54): where your treasure is, there your heart will be.

the money changers:
It is not all that clear, whether they could be characterised as 'rich bankers' already in the first century. After all, this is a quantitative difference: how far did their activities reach. The few names we know are from a later era(55). For the first century we have to be content with the professional names κολλυβισταί and κερματισταί, which is an indication that they were not upper-class.

The Temple is their real breadwinner. Lambert showed that we can distinguish five functions(56):

- the Temple tax. The yearly half shekel had to be paid in Tyrian silver, which could be bought from the money changers. A half ma^{c}a (according to Rabbi Meir, one ma^{c}a) was the κόλλυβος (agio) for half a shekel, i.e. 1/24th (or 1/12th) of the amount = 4,16% (or 8,33%)(57). This was quite a sum of money and must have brought in a respectable profit.
- the payment on the property given to the Temple. One tetradrachma had to be paid in Tyrian silver for each parcel of land which brought a harvest of what an ass could carry (= ± 380 litres). The money changer could accept 1/48th of that, as an agio (= 2,04%)(58).
- the payment of the Temple personnel. There were two forms: the money changer lent the treasurer current money needed for the payment of the salaries, or, alternatively, the treasurer used Temple money, which then was changed into current money by the moneychanger(59).
- the changing of money. Every city including Jerusalem had its own coin to buy and pay for services and goods. The money changer was the intermediary between the foreign coin and the city coin. In spending the money of the 'second tithe' (to buy the sacrificial meal in Jerusalem every first, second, fourth and fifth year of the seven year cycle), his intermediary function would sometimes have been necessary, but he was indispensable for the foreigners who came to the City. The real profit was made from the difference between the intrinsic, the nominal and the trade values of the coins(60).

- the acceptance of deposits. The Mishnah speaks about this as about an existing practice, whether they were open or close deposits. If one gave sealed up his money (or possessions) before going into safekeeping, one expected it back sealed. But it was also possible to give the money as a kind of loan. The money changer (the banker really) could use it either for short-term loans to others or for money changing purposes. He would make profit and the owner would share in the profit(61). That such was an existing practice in the first century, is clear from Matthew's parable about the king and the talents: the last slave is reproached, because he could have given the money to the money changers for profit(62).

It is a pity that we do not have enough evidence to qualify these activities. The Jewish sources do not give much more than this juridical framework which, surprisingly, is completely in line with the Greek monetary system. How the gospel looks at this, is known. The one time the money changers are mentioned, is in a negative context: the traders had made the Temple into a robber's den. To cleanse the Temple, Jesus overthrew the tables laden with coins (63). The scene is a new episode in Matthew's continuing story of critical remarks about the Temple treasure.

the publicans:

The heyday of the publicans' power and wealth as managers of public funds was over in the first century. Beginning with Pompeius and Gabinius the state collected its own taxes and used the system for its own purposes. In the time of Augustus, the system of direct taxation was completely taken over by the state - at least in Asia Minor and Syria - and the publicans were no longer used. Money and goods went directly to the state treasury respectively the emperor's treasury through 'pactiones' with cities and kings in cooperation with the procurators(64). In the first century the publicans collected only the indirect taxes (65): custom duties at the frontier for import and export; taxes on entering and leaving the city; tolls on roads, bridges and mountain passes; the tax levied on the sale of goods(66). Israel was not a frontier country(67) and the tax on sales contracts was under constant pressure(68). Therefore, the publicans in Palestine were really only responsible for the collection of the city taxes and the tolls.

We know little about the actual organisation. There were no big offices responsible for large areas. Everything took place on the local level. Literary sources and excavations have revealed some names of places: Gaza, Ascalon, Joppe, Caesarea (ports with a toll on the harbour facilities),

Jerusalem (market), Jericho (toll on dates and balsam, gathering place for Jerusalem-pilgrims) and Capharnaum (fisheries?)(69). Probably there were lease contracts(70), but we do not know who got the money which was collected: the king, the tetrarch, respectively the procurator or the city government. But it is clear that the income - the difference between the contract and the real proceeds- became less and less because of growing state interference(71).

Little can be said about the social position of the publicans. De Laet thinks that the many τελῶναι, about which the gospel speaks, were underlings. The publican Matthaios (respectively Levi) had his own house. But, even with rich Zacchaeus we do not know whether he was the owner. He could have been head of an association of publicans: the (pro)magister who was paid to accept the responsibility for the collection of actual taxes, and who was responsible for the official reports on the business. In that case, his wealth could not have made up for his financial dependency(72). The publican Johannes, mentioned by Josephus, was the only one belonging to the πρῶτοι of the city: an indication that he was a free man(73).

Matthew's gospel is rather ambiguous in its dealing with the publicans. We find texts indicating the negative social evaluation of the publicans. They are described as excluded from the community life, placed in a parallel position with the ἐθνικοί, the pagans who do not share in the existence of Israel. On the other hand the publicans are precisely the people who become members of the Jesus-movement: Jesus is the friend of publicans and sinners. He sits with them at their tables to make God's mercy true: the restoration of God's covenant with Israel. We should think also of the parable of the father with his two sons. Publicans and whores are proposed as the antitypes, in opposition with the high priests and the Pharisees. They do not say 'yes' to God, only to neglect to do his will. They are like the second son of this parable who originally said 'no', but who nevertheless went to his father's vineyard to work. Finally, the author of the gospel found in the publican who followed Jesus, his namesake (or respectively made him a namesake). He is mentioned as 'the publican' in the list of apostles, one of those whom Jesus sent out without the possession of gold, silver or copper (!), in order that they might live from what the people offered them: near to the kingdom of God. Matthaios realised the saying from the Sermon of the Mount in his own life(74).

landowners and traders:
There were not too many trades, apart from those connected

with the Temple and the palace. Rabbi Isaac's saying that everyone must divide his money into three parts: one third in property, one third outstanding with traders, and one third (as treasure) close at hand(75) characterises the economic thinking in antiquity(76). Either one could keep the cash in a safe place, or one should use it to buy land, or one should participate as a trader, using the money for short-term and seasonal loans. It is clear that this advice was only for the well-to-do.

We have the better information about the landowners. We know some names of people connected with land possession (77). The sales contract of a '^{c}ir' that we find in a text of the Mishnah, makes clear that something like a Roman villa must have been in existence in Palestine: 'if someone sells a '^{c}ir', he has sold also the houses, wells, ditches, winecellars, bathhouses, columbaria and the barns for the olive-press and for the hides'(78). Archeological finds indicate that a double system was already operating in the first century: isolated villas have taken over smaller combination housing units, while at the same time isolated villas grow into housing agglomerates(79). Roman occupation, after 70 AD, brought enormous property confiscations and contributed to the fantastic growth of big landownership.

There is much less information about large-scale trade practices, probably because they did not really exist. The economic condition in the country did not encourage large internal or external transactions. Josephus gives us by chance an example, which shows how it operated. When war problems began, Johannes of Gischala used his position of monopoly: it was forbidden for the Syrian Jews to buy oil from pagan salesmen. Johannes bought oil wholesale in Galilee for the price of one tetradrachma for four amphora (= 104 litres), and sold it in Syria for the price of one tetradrachma for one half amphora (= 13 litres), gaining eight times the value(80). The most profitable investment, although also the riskiest, was an investment in ships. We have no knowledge of actual transactions; but there are the innumerable representations of ships and ships' attributes on Jewish coins(81), the constant reference to ships in the Mishnah(82), and the flourishing fishery on the lake of Galilee which all indicate the probability that this sort of trade took place also in Palestine.

Later on we look in greater detail at what the gospel of Matthew says about (large) landowners. For now, it is sufficient that we realise that Matthew evaluates the reality of landownership and trade. He does so in a couple of parables. In the parable of the king, who invites the guests for the marriage of his son, the guests are unwilling to come even though repeatedly invited. They do not care: one goes to his 'farm', another to his 'trade'. 'Αγρός and ἐμπορία are more important than the wedding feast: it is a behaviour that results in their exclusion from the festivities.

In contrast, we have the parable of the hidden treasure and the precious jewel: a double parable which also speaks about ἀγρός and ἐμπορία. The buyer of the field and the tradesman in jewels sell everything they possess, to buy the treasure and obtain the jewel.

The story of the rich young man shows that these parables are not just interesting fiction. The young man could have amassed a treasure in heaven, if he had been willing to sell his possessions and give the money to the poor. In this way the two treasures are placed in opposition. Following Jesus is not compatible with wealth(83).

the threat of darkness

Mt 6,22 - 23

The mashal about the eye as the lamp of the body is a general saying, which can be embodied in many ways. This has led to a multiplicity of exegetical discussions. If one uses a valid literary theory, not all of them are really necessary. Because the meaning of a given text results from the interplay between connotation and denotation, one should explicitate only those denotations, which have a function in the given context. But, even if this limits the direction of the search, the real problems remain: how to make the connection between speaking about eyes, light and darkness with the gathering of treasures and the rejection of mammon? We need to search in Matthew, and sometimes even in other contemporary literature, to understand the saying in its intended concreteness.

To find out what we need to examine, we must take the saying in its own inherent structure. It begins very simply. After the opening sentence, which is a key sentence, - the eye is the lamp of the body (a slightly different anthropological presentation than we are used to) - follows a double ἐάν - sentence with its consequence: if the eye is ἁπλοῦς, the body is well lit; if the eye is πονηρός, the body is darkness. The problem is found in the closing sentence. Even if we presuppose thet 'the light in you' is identical with the 'eye' from the foregoing sentences(84), we have two options. The sentence can either be seen as a final conclusion, which does not add to what has already been said: there are two kinds of eyes and it is terrible if your eye is darkened(85); or, which seems to me to be more probable, the conclusion adds something: if your eye is σκότος, i.e. not only murky but really blind, the lamp is completely extinghuised, how dark that will be! The saying is a climax leading from good to bad to worse and then adds the final threat.

So we have three realities. They are not all that different, but each gives a specific emphasis. It begins with the ἁπλοτής: a concept which breaks down immediately the literalness of the mashal. Physically one cannot call the eye ἁπλοῦς, at least not in Greek. People have looked everywhere in the literature to find the single Hebrew/Aramaic equivalent of the word(86), but without result. Obviously it is a word which has a complex meaning.

I see three conceptual components here. I base my opinion on contemporary literature(87), which is unavoidable because in Matthew this is a hapax. But I have always in the back of my mind the actual way the word is used in the Sermon on the Mount.

1. The total adherence to one simple view of reality is obviously the most significant factor. When someone is called ἁπλοῦς, the intention is to show that this person is completely and totally dedicated, heart and soul. It is positively intended, because the reality is seen as positive.

But the reality has many aspects. One should say that there are two categories. Mostly all-encompassing words are used: God, Law, Christ, the good(88), but sometimes there is mention of more human realities: the man who wants to know only his own wife(89), the worker who dedicates himself to hard work, the farmer who limits himself to farming(90), the slave who without serving to the eye is dedicated to his master(91). The connecting thought is always the total dedication. A 'dedicated' person has his priorities right. It will be clear that there is a danger of real ideological nonsense in the combination of all-encompassing realities and human subjectivity.

This component of the concept is very significative to the understanding of Matthew. The 'concentrated dedication' relates to the context of the mashal: the 'dedicated' will dedicate himself to God and heaven without any distraction, because he does not look at the worldly realities with their passing treasures and mammon. The person who 'concentrates' his eye, shines out this concentration in his own life.

2. The 'economic' component is important, if we are to understand Matthew correctly. This connonation is most obvious in contemporary literature, because it is worked

out extensively. The ἁπλότης should then be seen as liberality, connected with the command to love one's neighbour, especially when he is in need. Whoever has something, must share. Paul develops this theme, where he tries to convince the Corinthians to take part in his 'leitourgia' for the poor in Israel(92). But this idea returns again and again in the literature. Issachar boasts that he has helped the poor in need: he shared his own bread, he never ate alone, he had compassion with every person in pain(93). It is the same in the Shepherd of Hermas. The author uses one whole mandatum to give these prescriptions, finishing it with the general phrase: give freely without hesitation to whom you should give and to whom you should not give(94). The giver should not have respect for persons.

In the context of handling one's possessions this connection is not restricted to liberality; that would anyway be impossible, given the idea of totality of the concept. The readiness to give expands, in several texts, to renounce any kind of (superfluous) possession: gold, wealth, excessive meals and superfluous dresses(95) cannot be combined with 'simplicity', because they stimulate desire and satisfy lust. A generous person is willing to share his goods with others(96) as an antithesis of the greedy person who will try to enrich himself at the expense of others(97). For the generous it is more than liberality: he wants to be free of his possessions and lets everyone share, so that the passing things will not fire his passions(98).

Again, it is clear that, against this background, Matthew could insert his saying logically, precisely where he did: between the exhortation not to gather treasure on earth and the saying about the choice between God and Mammon. If the eye is 'generous', man can realise these sayings in his life: to seek God by maintaining freedom with regard to worldly possessions.

3. Really surprising and also enlightening is the opposition between ἁπλότης and ὑπόκρισις, in which the latter refers to the divided person who does not take the Law seriously. A simple man does not have a double tongue, a double face or a double hearing. He is not divided in himself, uncertain and tossed about as the waves of the sea, without rest in all his doings(99). There is no deceit and no lie in a simple man(100). There is no jealousy or envy in him(101). He does not use slander nor will he speak evil against anyone: in short, he does not act as a censor against his neighbour(102).

Apparently it is easier to think in negatives than to

find positive concepts. In this multiplicity of virtues and vices we have the image of a man who is integrated in himself and with his neighbours, because he respects the Law as it applies to himself and to others.

The relation between the mashal and the context is reinforced again by the specific use of the word. The saying speaks about the eye, which shines with one light only, because it is not open to transgression of the Law: the ἁπλοῦς opposed to the ὑποκριτής. In this way we have a connection with the foregoing sayings on alms-giving, prayer and fasting. The wrong interpretation of the Law is rejected, because this leads to unacceptable practices. The good eye knows what is good and ensures that man walks in the light of the Law.

To do justice to the references, we should accept that this threefold meaning of ἁπλότης plays a role in the saying. It is some kind of praise for the ἁπλοῦς who is respectively dedicated, generous and integrated or, even better, who realises all three in toto: a person who can live in peace, because he is dedicated to God, because he can freely handle his possessions and because he is integrated with himself and his neighbours.

If we can show that these references - to God, to Economy, to the Law - play a role in the two other central ideas of the saying, we have found a homogeneous interpretation.

This is not too difficult. I do not think that it is at all necessary to show, via other texts, that 'the evilness' - the next central concept of the saying - has to do with God and the Law(103). These are the proper connotations of the concept, which in this saying are indicated by the physical reality of a murky eye. This sick eye, which causes the darkness, is a metaphor for the evil person who cannot see God and his Law and who is, therefore, at the mercy of the darkness of evil, the evil spirit and life in lawlessness(104).

Whether 'evil' also points at an economic reality, is not generally accepted(105), but seems nevertheless indicated by the author in view of the context(106). This would be definitively true, if we connect it with the only other text where Matthew speaks of an 'evil eye'. In the parable of the workers of the eleventh hour, we hear, at the end, the questioning reproach of the owner of the vineyard, why will the workers not allow him to give a minimum wage to all of them: is your eye 'evil', because I am good?(107). There is no injustice towards them if he, as owner, gives to every labourer a full day's wage. The liberality of this rich man who wishes the minimum of existence to everyone, is opposed to the social envy. The man with a 'greedy' eye hates to see another man's satisfaction. The saying in the Sermon on the Mount says that his own light will be darkened by this.

This parable is a story which reminds us of the saying from Abot about the four ways to give alms: 'he who wants to give, but will not allow others to give: his eye is evil in relation to those others; he who wants others to give, but refuses to do so himself: his eye is evil in relation to himself; he who gives and wants others to do the same: he is a just man (someone who respects the Law); he who does not give and will not allow others to give: he is an unjust person (he transgresses the Law)'(108).

This is a perfect commentary on the saying from the Sermon on the Mount as far as we have seen it. The good and the evil eye represent two types of people who are diametrically opposed. The man with the evil eye does not see that he transgresses the Torah of God because of his greed and his jealousy. He cannot bring himself to give, but he cannot even allow that others should give; even if he can bring himself to give, he will not allow others to give, because it would injure his pride.

The last sentence, the conclusion of the saying, in which the author explicitates the further consequences of extinguishing the light, is still to be treated. We still have to show that the associations which we mentioned, fit into this last sentence. The darkness, which is the consequence of total blindness, is the metaphor par excellence of the evil things in life.

With regard to Matthew's gospel I want to point out the following: In a number of texts the 'outer darkness' is presented as the decisive and the last threat(109). It is always followed by 'there will be weeping and gnashing of teeth', the same sentence as is used in the context of 'being thrown into the oven'(110). This makes it clear that the gnashing of teeth is connected with the fear and the perplexity of the punishment of being excluded. The threat of darkness is used in opposition to the presence in the house where a feast meal is prepared: the sharing of the table with Abraham, Isaac and Jacob; the invitation to share in the marriage feast of the son of the king; the entrance into the joy of the Lord(111). They are all metaphors taken from the city festivities where slaves and citizens are glad of the honour to be invited. They express the privilege of the elected to be allowed in God's presence. The 'outer darkness' is its antithesis: who has been thrown out, lives outside of God.

But Matthew speaks about darkness also in a very concrete way, by way of its effect, the blindness which makes it impossible to distinguish anything. In the discussions with the scribes and Pharisees he determines his ideological point of view: the blindness makes them incapable to be leaders of the people. They cannot prove their contentions, because they live in darkness. Worse, they deceive the people because they are not even aware of their blindness.

These discussions are important for our text, because they show that in the case of 'darkness' the same connotations are operative as in the case of πονήρια and ἁπλότης. Wherever the text speaks of darkness, there is not only a negative reference to God but there is also - and these discussions prove that - a relation with the keeping of the Law as well as with the economy.

Obviously, the non-observance of the Law is mostly in discussion(112). All texts treat the same problem in principle: the Pharisees and scribes do not have a good understanding of the Law and are, therefore, blind. If they think that they are leaders of the people, they make things worse. In their blindness they lead people astray. This legal discussion is really about the opposition between human rules and the divine Torah: the laws of purification are less important than God's Law. Whoever does not observe God's Law, but emphasizes the laws of purification is ὑποκριτής: he has changed God's forum for the forum of the people. Do not act according to their deeds.

If one looks a little more closely at the content of the texts, it becomes clear that the economic side also plays a role, be it a modest one. In the critique on the practice of taking oaths, the opposition between the gold of the Temple and the offering brought to the altar, is opened up(113). It is important to remember what we have said before, that this pronouncement should be seen in connection with the critique of the Temple treasury. Matthew thinks that the Pharisees and scribes implicate themselves too readily with the Temple treasury, at the cost of the one for whom the treasury exists in the first place: God himself. In the pronouncement on the inner and outer side of the cup and the dish, the blindness of the Pharisees is connected to theft and the inability-to-control-oneself (114): a combination of concepts, which indicates the connexion between wealth, lust, theft and the blindness of people to see these things. It is a theme, which is broadly treated in contemporary literature, sometimes in unexpected places(115).

the slave of God and the slave of possessions

Mt 6,24

In this saying we find something quite remarkable. There is a basic assumption which is simply not true: it is not true that a person cannot be a slave to two masters at the same time. We have a number of mishnayot, which bring into discussion precisely the consequences of such a double 'belonging-ness' and which, therefore, obviously presuppose its existence. The most complicated is the case of someone who is half slave, half free, because his master does not possess full mastery over him, but neither does he have full mastery over himself in action or decisions. The marriage rights of such a person become a point of debate between the Hillel and Shammai schools. It is one of the few situations where Shammai takes the milder position in favour of the oppressed person: because everyone has the right to marry, the half-slave should be given this freedom by his master(116). Hillel, later on, accepted this point of view. But we have also the situation of the slave who belonged to two trading partners: two (or more) brothers or two (or more) associates own one single slave in common-(117). That can be the result of inheritance, but more often it is an indication that someone is rather poor. In an economy, which is based on slavery and which knows the situation of tens and hundreds of slaves(118), the possession of one slave held communely is obviously a ridiculous fact.

It does not give the slave a cause for laughter, however. We should never forget that. I say this, because the saying is particular for yet another reason. This may become clear, if we listen to present day exegesis. The case of a slave with two masters is well known(119) and is occasionally mentioned(120), but no conclusions were drawn from it. Everyone seems to act as if the saying expresses a reality, i.e. one lets oneself be deceived by the rhetoric of the words, or rather one allows the point of view of the narrator to coincide with one's own.

That is a fallacy. What is said is true only from the perspective of the owner. Only a (possible) kyrios can have the view that a slave, who must be shared with someone else, is an insecure possession, because the emotional ties create confusion and that is bad for productivity. We must start from the supposition that the saying is originated in circles where this institution was known and where the difficulties were experienced; in other words, in circles of (small) owners, where the house slave had become the property of several people by way of inheritance, or, where through difficult contracts(121), the one slave was finally bought to take care of the worst jobs. The saying speaks about slaves, but not from their point of view.

To prove this point, I am obliged to cover a lot of material. It is necessary to consult the Latin agronomists Varro and Columella who - together with their description of the work to be done in a Roman villa - also explicitate the way the dominus should act towards his slaves(122). These texts describe the ideal behaviour of a slaveholder from the viewpoint of the owner, and they show forth a mentality, which in many ways runs parallel with the supposition of the saying of the Sermon on the Mount.

Varro (115 - 27 BC) writes in the time after Sulla, after the suppression of the slave revolt under Spartacus, when large tracts of agricultural land have been changed into pasture lands. We see certain benevolence towards the slaves, greater than Cato showed, but this benevolence never loses sight of the owner's interest. It is a dominium, which tries to find ways and means to bring the slave to greater productivity. A rather long quote may elucidate this: 'You must get labourers (operarios) who can stand hard work, who are not less than twenty-two years old, and who will be quick to learn the work of a farm. You may form an opinion about this from the way they have performed other tasks, or by asking those of them who are new to farm work what they have been accustomed to do when with their former master. The slaves should not be timid, nor yet of too high spirit. Those set over them ought to know how to read and write and should have received some slight education; they should be of good character and older than the labourers mentioned above - for the latter obey them more readily than they do younger men. In addition to this, the one quality necessary in an overseer (vilicus) is practical skill in farm work; for his duty is not merely to give orders, but to set an example, that those under him may imitate him as he works, and realize that his superior position is not without cause, but is the result of superior knowledge. Nor must an overseer be allowed to enforce his orders by the whip rather than by words, provided that the same result can be obtained equally well by the latter. It is well, too, not to have too many slaves of the same tribe, for this is a principal cause of quarrels in the household.

You should quicken the interest of the overseers in their work by means of rewards, and should see that they have something of their own, and women slaves to live with them and bear them children. For this makes them steadier and more attached to the estate. The slaves from Epirus are a case in point, for owing to these family ties they are of better repute and fetch greater price than others. The goodwill of the overseers you should win by an occasional mark of esteem, and you ought to discuss, too, with the best of the labourers the farmwork that is to be done, for where this is the case their sense of inferiority is lessened, and they feel that they are held in some account by their master. Their enthusiasm for work is increased by treatment more generous than usual, by better food and clothing, by occasional exemption from work, or the permission to graze a beast of their own on the farm, and by other privileges of the same kind, so that any who have been given too hard a task, or too severe a punishment, may thus be consoled, and their goodwill and kindly feeling towards the master be restored.'(123)

The last couple of sentences are important, but one must understand them against the background of their application to the system of productivity: goodwill and benevolence are necessary in order to increase productivity.

Columella (1 - 70 AD) is even more explicit. He gives parallel advice for the vilicus, the mandated slave-overseer of the villa as well as for the dominus. It is a broad scale of advice which Varro had only put together briefly. I will quote some selected texts which are important for our research:

'After all these arrangements have been acquired or contrived, especial care is demanded of the master not only in other matters, but most of all in the matter of the persons in his service; and these are either tenant-farmers (colonos) or slaves, whether unfettered or in chains. He should be civil in dealing with his tenants, should show himself affable, and should be more exacting in the matter of work than of payments, as this gives less offence yet is, generally speaking, more profitable. For when land is carefully tilled it usually brings profit, and never a loss, except when it is assailed by unusually severe weather or by robbers; and for that reason the tenant does not venture to ask for reduction of his rent. But the master should not be insistent of his rights in every particular to which he has bound his tenant, such as the exact day for payment, or the matter of demanding firewood and other trifling expense; in fact, we should not lay claim to all that law allows, for the ancients regarded the extreme of the law as the extreme of oppression. On the other hand, we must not neglect our claims altogether ...'
'The next point is with regard to slaves - over what duty it is proper to place each and to what tasks to assign them. So my advice at the start is not to appoint an overseer (vilicus) from the sort of slaves who are physically attractive ...'

He should be of a certain age, strong, knowledgeable about farming; there is no need that he can write or read (it prevents fraud); he should have a woman to keep him company; he should take care of the tools and of the clothing and food of the slaves.
'He should be not only skilled in the tasks of husbandry, but should also be endowed, as far as the servile disposition allows, with such qualities of feeling that he may exercise authority without laxness and without cruelty, and always humour some of the better hands, at the same time forbearing even with those of lesser worth, so that they may rather fear his sternness than detest his cruelty ...'
We find the same system in the description of the obligation of the dominus:
'In the case of other slaves, the following are, in general, the precepts to be observed, and I do not regret having held to them myself: to talk rather familiarly with the country slaves, provided only that they have not conducted themselves unbecomingly, more frequently than I would with the town slaves; and when I perceived that their unending toil was lightened by such friendliness on the part of the master, I would even jest with them at times and allow them to jest more freely. Nowadays I make it a practice to call them into consultation on any new work, as if they were more experienced, and to discover by this means what sort of ability is possessed by each of them and how intelligent he is. Furthermore, I observe that they are more willing to set about a piece of work on which they think that their opinions have been asked and their advice followed ...'
Then he must inspect whether everything is done according to the rules he set: whether the chained slaves are indeed in chains and why one or another is set free of his chains or not ...
'Accordingly, a careful master inquires not only of them, but also of those who are not in bonds, as being more worthy of belief, whether they are receiving what is due to them under his instructions: he also tests the quality of their food and drink by tasting it himself, and examines their clothing, their mittens, and their footcovering. In addition he should give them frequent opportunities for making complaints against those persons who treat him cruelly or dishonestly. In fact, I now and then avenge those who have just cause for grievance, as well punish those who incite the slaves to revolt, or who slander their taskmasters; and, on the other hand, I reward those who conduct themselves with energy and diligence ...'
Female slaves who can still bear children, are given gifts: the more children, the more freedom ...

'Such justice and consideration on the part of the master contributes greatly to the increase of his estate ... And whatever his age, he will never be so wasted with years as to be despised by his slaves'(124)

I completely understand that we cannot use this material directly, as if they originated in their totality from the same background as the saying in the Sermon on the Mount. They do give a lot of information. But my main concern is that they make visible, that the possible hatred and aversion of the slave influence the way the dominus acts in anticipation. Love and devotion are not mentioned in Roman authors, with the exception of the expression in Varro, where he speaks of the 'benevolentia in dominum'. This is, probably, a consequence of the system being enlarged, and of the greater exploitation, to which the slaves in a Roman villa were exposed. Fear for the opposite plays a role in their considerations and as such it illustrates the manner which slave owners should adopt with regard to their slaves.

I need to make one last observation to place the saying of the Sermon on the Mount in the perspective in which it functioned in Matthew's community. It is noteworthy that the number of slaves is multiplied in several of Matthew's parables. Where Luke and Mark speak of 'a' slave, Matthew has a multitude of them. In the parable of the evil winegrowers it is a complicated question, because Mark also speaks about 'many other slaves', yet Matthew presents a different story. The landowner possesses many slaves from the beginning and he sends them as a group to his vineyard 'to get his fruits'; later on he sends even more than he did the first time(125). The recounting of the parable of the festive meal is clearer. Luke lets one slave do everything, but Matthew speaks of 'his slaves' and 'other slaves'(126). In the parable of the talents the difference is not in the number of slaves, but in the amount of money given to them. Where it speaks about slaves, we should compare this parable to Matthew's parable about the merciless slave: this presupposes also enormous amounts of money and a multitude of slaves as ficticious reality(127). Finally, we have the parable of the weeds: at the start it seems that the man himself sowed the seed, but later on it becomes clear that 'his slaves' are responsible. They are really so unimportant that they not hinder the allegorical explanation(128). Matthew accentuates the normality of a situation where people own many slaves. It is all ficticious but it clearly presupposes an actual experienced reality. The supposition of many slaves is obviously a literary device, which, however, can be understood sociologically, if we accept the multitude of slaves as a normal reality in the social situation in which Matthew writes. In the context of this situation people have understood the saying from the Sermon on the Mount about the slave who belongs to two kyrioi as a saying about something really impossible(129).

It is interesting that in this saying the position of the free man is maintained until the very end. The slave cannot really serve two masters: in the same way you will not be able to serve God and the Mammon. But the slave does not have the freedom to choose, which you have. The actual choice, which is a compromise between God and money, will cause trouble as you can see from these slaves. It will lead to annoyance on the master's part. The saying is an invitation and a challenge to the owners, but there is also some threat.

It has already been sufficiently argued that 'mammon' is not in itself something purely negative(130). Only from the additions can we know whether honest or dishonest money is intended. In itself, it only indicates possession, goods, money etc. It is a neutral concept which needs to be evaluated in the context. In this saying the mammon is the absolute opposite of God, attracting in its own interests love or hatred, devotion or hatred. It is a power which is incompatible with God, once it takes hold of people.

It is right what has been said: Matthew does not develop the poverty - wealth problem in the same way as Luke does(131). That does not mean that Matthew does not have a message for the 'rich'. I have mentioned this already several times in this chapter. One can find a number of texts in Matthew, which - by way of narration or by way of discourse - should be interpreted as concrete elaborations of our saying.

The central story remains the story of the rich young man who, even though well instructed in the Law, is nevertheless prevented from striving for perfection because of his possessions. He cannot bring himself to sell them and give them to the poor. Jesus' followers are the opposite: they have renounced their families, their brothers and sisters, their fathers and mothers, their children and their land. A hundredfold reward is promised to them, but not in this life. They will possess eternal life as their inheritance.

In Matthew's story the rich young man, who cannot renounce his wealth, is contrasted with those who have left their families and their land to follow Jesus in their joy of discovering God's dominance(132).

From the way Matthew treats the allegorical explanation of the parable of the seed, it is clear that this contrast between rich and non-rich is important to him. He does not just follow Mark's option. In his last two allegorical explanations, he makes his point in his own way: the seed which falls among thorns, is the man who hears the word but the care for the aeon (more about this in the following passage of the Sermon on the Mount) and the snare of wealth chokes the word and it remains fruitless; but the seed which falls on good soil, is he who hears the word and understands it: he will bear fruit(133). The accent is on the contrast between the rich who does not bear fruit and Jesus' follower who hears and understands what he must do. The rich are incapable of bringing forth fruits and for this reason they will be excluded, in contrast to the real followers of Jesus. It is a contrast which implies that the followers of Jesus no longer dispose of wealth.

The extent to which Matthew is moved by the problem of the response of the 'rich', is most obvious, finally, from two of his own parables: the one about the treasure in the field and the one about the precious jewel(134). I mentioned the twins 'landownership' - 'trade' earlier(135), in connection with the negative answer of the people in the parable of the son of the king: people who are not ready to accept the invitation to sit at the marriage feast of the son. In the parables of the treasure and the precious jewel they take the right decision: they sell everything they have, the landowner to buy the piece of land with the hidden treasure, the pearl merchant to gain possession of the precious jewel. The treasure and the pearl signify the dominance of God. There is joy: it should tempt all other rich people to act in the same way. Remember that Matthew opened the Sermon on the Mount with 'How happy are the poor of spirit, theirs is the kingdom of heaven'. The snare of wealth must be eradicated even from the πνεῦμα. Only then entry to the βασιλεία is guaranteed.

God's lordship and his justice instead of worry for tomorrow

Mt 6,25 - 34

The text which contains the reference to 'worry', raises the question about the subject who is addressed here: who is told that they should not worry about what they will eat or drink and how they will clothe themselves? This study makes it clear that such generalisations as 'the people' (136), 'the listeners(137), 'the disciples'(138) remain too indeterminate to help us understand the origins or the sphere of influence of these sayings. Because the worries relate to the basic needs of food, drink and clothing, which are of prime importance to survive, it has been said that they deal with 'die nackte Angst ums Existenzminimum' (139). The fear of the simple people would be the theme of this important text, the fear of people who live at the edge of the poverty line, as paupers who daily face the fearful question whether they will survive the day in the rat race for existence(140). Is this also true for our text in this concrete context? 'Therefore I say to you' in the opening sentence connects the saying with what went before. There the subjects addressed were people who, to say the least, had some surplus income, as became clear above: they could hoard this surplus income as treasure, or donate it as gift and give it away for the sake of God's sole dominion over them. The context indicates people who possess money and goods which are an obstacle to enter into 'life'. It would be strange, if suddenly we were confronted with a totally different audience.

Obviously, it is not just this formal argument which brings me to this conclusion. There are a number of other indications, if we may presuppose that the imagary which is used, points to the milieu of origin. The descriptions of the non-activity of the lilies and the birds are important. Of the birds it says that 'they do not sow or reap or gather into barns': a series of things which belongs to the farm and describes in a global way the farming cycle from the start of sowing until the pride of the farmer who has gathered his yearly income into the barns. The very fact that Matthew mentions 'barns' seems indicative, in comparison with Luke's text which uses the singular. Apparently, Matthew presupposes that the farmers have their own barns, while Luke seems to have in mind a smaller operation when he speaks of ταμεῖον, a supply room and a simple single barn. Of the lilies Matthew says that 'they never have to work or spin': activities descriptive of the woman's part of a farmlife, indicating the work needed to make cloths from wool, washing, drying, dyeing, spinning and weaving (141). The industrious farmer's wife carries her responsibility for her part of the work, together with her husband: her pride is cloths for herself, her husband and her children. The imaqary makes us think of a flourishing industrious farmer's existence where security can be achieved through hard work.

Let us try to indicate a little more clearly the sort of people Matthew thinks about. In the literature on the subject(142) we find a treasure trove of data about the organisation of a farmer's life, even though the material has been preserved rather accidentally. The extremes have most clearly left their traces in history. So we are rather well informed of the enormous latifundia belonging to Herod and his family, which, later on, were taken over by the

Roman emperors: their size, their structure and the produce(143). Comparatively, this applies also to the private big landowners. Varro's and Columella's texts, which we quoted above, do not need much explanation, because they so clearly describe the structure of a Roman villa. They are instructive also for Palestine. The 'dominus' (οἰκοδεσπότης) has the use of a 'vilicus' (ἐπιτρόπος respectively οἰκονόμος) as overseer of the affairs and as taskmaster of the slaves. Most often the vilicus is a slave himself. If the dominus lives in the house, he will personally act as overseer. Depending on the size of his landholdings, he will appoint someone responsible on his properties which are further away, so that the work can be organised(144). There is a tendency towards the colonate: the landowners rents out small parcels of land or gives them in lease-hold to 'free' farmers who, bound to the land must do everything in order to pay the rent(145). It is an agricultural policy which is more and more preferred above the simple use of slaves. The 'coloni' probably do not own slaves for themselves. Until the time of the Mishnah, we know that two forms of lease contracts existed in Palestine: the 'aris'-contract which obliges the leaseholder to hand over part of the harvest, half or one third so that the leaseholder and the owner are in the same position as far as the produce of the land is concerned (146), and the 'choker'-contract which obliges the leaseholder to hand over a set amount of goods. In case of a bad harvest this, obviously, is disadvantageous for the leaseholder(147). Finally, we know that the system of small free holdings existed extensively in Palestine(148). Ben-David tried to calculate what the income of these poor people was and he came to the conclusion that they were living at the edge of the poverty line(149). To sum up, all possible forms of agrarian organisation existed in first century Palestine.

Matthew's Gospel mirrors this reality, however globally. That all forms appear is especially clear, when one uses the parables as informative material. The οἰκοδεσπότης who appoints slaves but is absent himself, appears in the parable of the faithful slave. The kyrios appoints a slave for his οἰκετεία to make sure that people get to eat on time. Opposite to that we have the bad slave who mistreats and beats his co-slaves at the same time as he eats and gets drunk(150). In this parable the absence of the kyrios is of short duration. In the parable of the evil winegrowers we find a real absentee landowner. The οἰκοδεσπότης has a vineyard, which he leases on the basis of a share in the harvest. He sends his slaves to collect 'his produce'. This seems to be an indication of a 'choker'-contract where the amount to be handed over, is predetermined independently from the actual harvest(151).

There are other texts where the οἰκοδεσπότης is present and, therefore, personally involved in the work. Not that he does the work, the slaves do that, but he acts as overseer. We see this in the parable of the sowers, where the farmer uses labourers to sow, to weed and to harvest. Probably they are hired labourers, because the text distinguishes between the sowers and the harvesters and different words are used for them(152). We see the same thing in the parable of the workers of the eleventh hour. The οἰκοδεσπότης uses an ἐπιτρόπος who takes care of the money, but he himself contracts the μισθῶται and tells them what to do(153).

On a still lower level, we find those farmers who do have their own parcel of land, but who have to work it themselves. It remains an open question whether the buyer of the parcel of land, which contains the hidden treasure is supposed to labour on it himself, but this is clearly not the case with the man who uses it as an excuse to reject the invitation to sit at the feast of the son of the king(154). He thinks that the 'work on his own parcel of land' is more important. The parable of the mustard seed also presupposes that the farmer himself sows the seed 'in his own field'(155). That does not necessarily mean that there are no slaves around. John the Baptist's mashal clarifies this. His imagary comes from the reality of house slaves. He considers himself as the least of them, lower than the slaves who are to 'carry away the shoes'. Jesus is placed in opposition to them as the farmer who winnows himself to separate chaff from the wheat to gather it into his barn(156).

This brings us to the last group but one: those texts which imply that the farmer does all the work himself alone. We can think of the farmer who is sowing the seed on his Palestinian stony field, full of thorns - at least if he owns this field, it is not certain from the text -(157), but also of the parable of the mustard seed which is parallel to the parable of the leaven, where the wife of the farmer bakes her own bread(158). Maybe the same financial situation is presupposed in the parable of the father who has two sons. But this is not necessarily so, because the possessive is lacking with 'vineyard', indicating that it might be a leased vineyard(159). The shepherd with the hundred sheep definitely belongs in this series: the independent shepherd is a typical phenomenon of these regions and has important ideological implications(160).

Finally we come to the texts which speak about the people at the lowest financial and social scale: those who are wage-earners, the slaves who work on the farm, those who rent and lease parcels of land, and who must work hard for small wages. They were included in what we said above: the labourers in the parable of the weeds and that of the workers of the eleventh hour; the leaseholders of the vineyard in the parable of the wicked husbandmen; the slaves in the parable of the faithful slave, in the parable of the talents and of the merciless slave. We can add two texts from the eschatological discourse: the man who works in the field should not go home to get his cloths, and the two men who work in the field and the two women who work in the mill of whom one will be taken, the other left behind (161). Even though it is not explicated further, it paints a picture of people who have to earn their living by working with their own hands. In the last text is, most probably, spoken of slaves or wage-earners.

To return to our question: what kind of people did Matthew think of, when he has Jesus say that they should not worry about what they eat, what they drink and what they wear? It is possible now to add some nuances. As said above, the beginning of this section 'therefore I say to you' connects this passage with the sayings on the riches and wealth, i.e. in the pericope the 'rich' are also the addressed ones. This means: Matthew certainly did not think of the lowest group: the slaves and wage earners. At closer view it is possible to prove - or at least, it is in all probability to show -, that Matthew did not think of the impoverished 'free' farmers either. He did not think (any more?) that the sayings of Jesus were addressed to the poor, be it slaves, wage earners or farmers with their miserable little field in lease or in ownership.

During my research I have noticed a strange phenomenon in Matthew. It is an observation which runs parallel to what has been said about the ownership of slaves. If one selects the specific characteristics of Matthew's text by comparing his text with the synoptic parallels, it becomes clear that the degree of ownership has been shifted. Matthew seems to have in mind a group of people who are better of than the parallel synoptic texts seem to indicate.

I will give the data without further comment: the farmer in the parable of the weeds uses wage earners who sow, weed and harvest for him. The man in the parable of the hidden treasure is capable of buying the field acting on the same financial level as the buyer of pearls. The man in the parable of the workers of the eleventh hour is obviously well off, considering that he uses an ἐπιτρόπος and hires in wage earners. The parable of the man with the two sons is the only parable in this series of specific Matthean parables which is not clear. One can ask quite reasonably why the fact that one obeys or not, does not have financial consequences. This is slightly more easily comprehensible, if there is a situation of a man who is better off.

It is already a remarkable series of texts. But it does not finish here. There is also a set of particular Matthean text variations. In the parable of the mustard seed only Matthew speaks of 'his own field', while Mark lets the man sow 'in the soil' and Luke 'in the garden'(162). In the parable of the wicked husbandmen Matthew indicates a 'choker'-contract as we said above, while Mark and Luke seem to speak of an 'aris'-contract(163). In the parable of the feast there is a really different story. It may not be correct to state that different levels of possession are represented, because Luke also speaks about the acquisition of a field and five pairs of oxen, but we have indicated several times already that the pair - ownership of a field and trade - is symptomatic for the community of Matthew-(164). A reduction, respectively enlargement, comes to force only in the parable of the faithful and the unfaithful slave. Matthew still speaks about a large οἰκία with many slaves, but in Luke it is still larger: there is a division of goods much greater than what Matthew has to say about the sharing of food(165).

This multiplicity of data brings to the conclusion that Matthew thinks of the somewhat richer farmers and wives of farmers, when he has Jesus say that they should not worry.

What kind of worry does he have in mind? Obviously, the μέριμναι can concern anything(166), but a relation to the financial, economic condition is clearly presupposed in this text. It must be something like the saying of Rabbi Gamaliel: 'the more one's possession, the more one's worries'(167). I do not think there is an essential difference between Matthew and Luke who uses as a preliminary text the parable of the foolish rich man. He worked hard to bring in the harvest. He pulled down his granaries to put up new, bigger ones so that he could enjoy his well-earned rest. He did not realise that all his troubles were useless, because he would die that very night(168). Matthew makes his point at the end of the text, where he says: so do not worry about tomorrow: tomorrow will take care of itself. Each day has enough trouble of its own(169). The rich worry because they think about a future, which they do not know. They keep busy with their toil and slave in endless works, because they want to safeguard their lives: acquire wealth so that you do not have to worry about food, drink and clothing. But the story will never end, because man has never enough.

This way of thinking appears again in Matthew in the

allegorical explanation of the parable of the seed, where the third part, the seed falling among the thorns, is explained as 'the man who hears the word, but the worries of this world and the lure of riches choke the work and so he produces nothing'(170). 'The worries of this world and the lure of riches' is in Matthew a 'hendiaduoin': one concept explains the other. The worries of the world are the trick of riches and vice versa. That is the worry of which this aeon is full, worry about all that belongs to this world and which is seemingly solved by the possessions of wealth. But that is a lure, a temptation, because one will never acquire such wealth. In the meantime the word of the gospel is not heard and does not get the chance to bear fruit(171).

The text of the Sermon on the Mount adds two arguments in support of this train of thought. First there is the actual helplessness of the rich. Who do they think they are? With all their worry about tomorrow they cannot lengthen their lives or - as it is said in an other possible translation - they cannot add a single cubit to their span of life(172). The first translation follows more closely from the intended meaning of the text. All their worry for an unknown future is useless, because in no way can it help to lengthen their lifespan. Nobody knows what tomorrow will bring. They will die like the grass and their worry will not help them. The other possibility accentuates the helplessness of man: however rich they are, God has determined how tall they will be and no one can change that.

The second argument is taken from Solomon as prototype of the 'doxa', which determines the striving of the rich. Even Solomon cannot compete with the 'doxa' given by God to the lilies of the field. Seeing the relativity of the greatest human glory is connected with the argument of the brevity of life. Σήμερον and αὔριον are again put in opposition. In the saying of the 'grass of the field', this 'today' and 'tomorrow' can be grasped, because it all happens in one day. The saying points to the futility of the 'doxa', which does not guarantee its permanence and the rich should understand that.

The sentence ends with ὀλιγόπιστοι: a concept which, if understood against the Jewish background, connects perfectly with the intention of the whole series of sayings. The reproach of being 'men of little faith' plays an important role in the rabbinical literature of the manna-story. 'Men of little faith' are the people who, against the command of Moses, keep the manna till the next day; they are the people who look for manna on the sabbath or who gather the quails the whole day and the whole night long(173). As an actual paranaesis it all comes together in the saying of Rabbi Eleazar ben Hyrcanus: 'Whoever carries a piece of bread in his basket and says: 'what shall I eat tomorrow', is a man of little faith'. This corresponds with the manner in which Jesus speaks to his disciples, when they find out that they have not taken enough bread for their trip to the other side of the lake: 'Men of little faith, why are you talking among yourselves about having no bread'(174). Men of little faith are they who are not content with the security of today but always want to look ahead.

The alternative to wealth and its never ending worry is to look for the basileia of God and his justice. There is no need to say much about this, even though it is the central point of this pericope, because we now have general agreement on the meaning of this expression(175). The point is the fulfillment of God's will so that he can rule over all peoples. The rich have till now not (sufficiently?) entered the Jesus-movement in which God's dominion is being realised. If they want to do that, they will have to divest themselves of their possessions. Their reward will be that they become free of all their worries. God will guarantee that they will have life: much more so than he does for the birds. God will give them honour and beauty: much more so than he does for the lilies in the field. They hand over to God's faithfulness by giving away their wealth. Life will be better than they have ever known. Not without reason is the 'search' a pointer to the parable of the treasure in the field, which is 'found' and the parable of the pearl which must be 'sought'. Search is the first requirement, not because there are other things which need to be searched for, but because the basileia and its justice is the only reality(176). The one who searches, will find; to him who finds the pearl, all other things will be given.

A last remark: this central sentence has an important function against the background of the totality of the Sermon on the Mount. It ensures that the 'solution of the problem of the riches' is placed within the context of the Law and the keeping of the Law. The mention of δικαιοσύνη points to the other places in the Sermon on the Mount where 'justice' is brought in: to the people who suffer hunger and thirst in connection with justice; to the people who are persecuted because they do the Law; to the people who approach the Law with more respect than do the Pharisees and scribes; to the people who in keeping the Law, do not pay attention to the forum of men, but who act solely for God. The keeping of the Torah is demanding but it also gives great satisfaction. Abandoning worldly treasure, rejecting the 'evil eye', preferring God above the mammon, not worrying about food and clothing, are only possible, when first one seeks God's dominion and his justice. The keeping of the Law guarantees the realisation of God's dominion which gives fullness of life and, therefore, puts an end to the seduction of riches. Doing God's justice- i.e. keeping the Torah - opens the possibility even for the rich to make a good choice. Because, he who does the Law, is gathering treasure in heaven, illumines with his light his whole body, is a faithful servant of God and will be provided for by God. To him who seeks justice and does it, are promised great rewards. Matthew proposes a theology of the Torah which connects directly with everything that we find about the Joy of the Law in Jewish theology.

Chapter V
THE LAWS FOR THE PEOPLE: MUTUAL RELATIONS
Mt 7, 1-12

The variety of exegetical opinions shows that Matthew did not succeed in putting together the Sermon on the Mount as a well structured whole(1). Confronted with the dilemma-content vs. structure - he opted for content rather than structure, resulting in a text which is missing an obvious and unambiguous structure. It seems impossible to structure the text and not to admit some redundancy of content. Verse 7,6 'the prohibition to give what is holy to dogs and to throw pearls in front of pigs' especially, is difficult to place.

It is clear to me that 7,1 begins a new series of prescriptions. Having treated the special problem of handling money and goods, attention is focused again on the people as a whole: how should the people act in accordance with the Law. The word δικαιοσύνη no longer appears. But the concluding sentence 'for this is the Law and the prophets' shows clearly which point of view the author proposes to his readers: the Torah regulates also the mutual relations among people. These mutual relations are the real topic. That is clear from the similarity in content of the opening sentences on judgment and the prohibition of mutual criticism, and the concluding sentence on how one should act in relation to other people. Even though the text does not always say the same thing, the inner coherence is guaranteed by this similarity. Notwithstanding the changing point of view, mutual relations among people are brought to our attention again and again. The saying on giving and receiving as a metaphor of divine giving links up with that, as we shall see. Is this also true for the mashal about dogs and pigs?

We can say, in any case, that the whole of the passage uses a metaphorically homogeneous language. All images are taken from the life of a small town: the 'judge'/'reviewer' who passes judgment or not; the merchant who has a 'measure' to judge his wares; the 'brothers' who judge each other and muddle up splinter and plank like bad craftsman; the owners of dogs and swine who should know how to handle these animals; the beggars who find food by asking, searching and knocking on doors, parallel to the 'sons' who ask their fathers for bread and fish. As you want to be treated by others, so you must treat them, because that is the Law and the prophets. Selected elements from the life of a small town are used to inculcate the general Law.

Without too much insistence I would like to make a suggestion. There are a number of parallels in this passage to the foregoing pericope on the Law. They are so consistent that one feels inclined to see Mt 7,1 - 12 as a repetition of Mt 5,21 - 48. This becomes even clearer when I place the parallels together:

7,1 - 2: the logia treat the way one should act in a κρίσις. One should not judge because such a judgment will turn against you; κρίσις is the central word

   5,21 - 26: the legal saying is about ἔνοχος εἶναι τῇ κρίσει as part of the mutual relations among brothers. This explanation of the law is further elucidated in two meshalim on 'disagreement' and 'jurisprudence'. Κρίσις is the central topic as it is in Mt 7,1 - 2

7,3 - 5: the saying is about brothers who unjustly condemn each other. The central point of reference is always 'the eye' as the place where it all happens

   5,27 - 30 (31): the content is on adultery and sending the wife away, but here too it all happens via 'the eye' as the locus of desire and scandal

7,6: the saying on τὸ ἅγιον and οἱ μαργαρῖται

   5,33 - 37: there is not so much similarity here, but yet ... can we not compare τὸ ἅγιον with the 'oath' and with all the sacred things which are then enumerated?

7,7 - 11: a double saying where asking and giving are central

   5,38 - 42: this treats the law of the whole of civil order which is obviously more elaborate than 7,7 - 11. Yet the pericope ends with the statement on asking and giving (5,42)

7,12: the last logion has become well known as the golden rule because it regulates mutual relations:

   5,43 - 48: the content comes closest. The closing statement says nothing else than the golden rule. From the parallel text in Luke (Lc 6,27 - 30 and 6,31) it is clear that there has been also a textual connection.

With this list I do not want to say more than it is worth. Sometimes the similarity is more striking than at other times. As to content, the legal passages in 5,17 ff treat many more questions than 7,1 - 12. But that does not negate the real parallels. Probably it means that the thought patterns of Matthew are more cyclical than we think. It certainly means that there are relations and connections which give a certain direction to this pericope.

the threat of condemnation by God

Mt 7,1 - 2

Because this saying is so closely connected to the next saying, which limits itself in its imagary to the criticism of people among themselves, one can understand the tendency to explain also this first saying in an 'individualistic' way: as a pronouncement against a purely personal background(2). People should not condemn one another because this would call forth God's condemnation of them. Even though this is obviously implied, Matthew seems also to talk in a broader sense about a rejection of all concrete legal practices: no one should act as a judge over another. Or, at the very least, after all Matthew accepts the functioning of existing legal practices in other texts(3), by his μη κρίνετε, the prohibition to judge other people, he has placed all human judgments in a legal framework. Whoever condemns his brother breaks the law of the Torah and will be punished by God in the same manner according to that same Torah.

The first interpretation is supported in the parallel text in Luke(4) which mentions 'condemnation' and 'acquittal' next to κρίνω. The whole legal procedure is mentioned in a nutshell: from the accusation one comes either to condemnation or to acquittal. κρίνω is the comprehensive word which divides in καταδικάζω (condemn) and ἀπολύω (acquit)(5). If we are allowed to read the text in this way(6) we must of necessity understand κρίνω as an absolute prohibition to exercise any judicial function. This presupposes an anti-legal attitude which can only be explained in a situation where people have had very bad experiences with the courts. In this interpretation, Matthew's text is part of the criticism of the courts, the judges and the jurisprudence which we find in many reflections of contemporary literature.

For the second interpretation, we can point to two texts. The closest parallel is James 4,11 - 12. The relation with the law and, from there, with the lawgiver, are clearly enunciated. Because κρίνω goes with καταλαλέω (rail at), it is clear that the author deals with micro ethics here. Leave the other be and do not act as his 'critic'. The argument then uses the big words like law, lawgiver and judge. Acting on this micro level is part of the Law which comes from God. If you do not respect your neighbour and slander him, you break the Law and act against God(7).

The parallel text in Romans(8) is important because it deals very extensively with God's judgment as can be expected. While Rom 2,1 lists the enormous catalogue of sins describing all that went wrong with the pagans because of which they earn death, Rom 14 deals with the little misunderstandings which hurt mutual love. But little or great, whoever believes that he may accuse concrete persons without self examination or respect, detracts from God's 'sole dominion': God is the only judge who passes judgment. If one is not ready to leave the judgment to God alone, one will find oneself judged ἀναπολόγητος, i.e. without defense(9).

From the inclusion in Mt 7,12 'this is the Law and the prophets', it is clear that this same legal context is necessary to understand Matthew's μὴ κρίνετε. Even if only the micro ethic of brotherly relations is in question, as stated in 7,3 - 5, this larger context plays a role. Furthermore, from the addition of the sentences about the judgment with which one will be judged and the measure by which one will be measured, it is obvious that a lot more is involved.

The possibility to interpret the text in two ways makes it more difficult than usual to search for the place of the text in the contemporary contexts, especially if we see the text as an ideological intervention in an existing polemical debate. We have to follow two lines of thought which partly interact with one another but which also exist independently. I will start with the opinion that Matthew's μὴ κρίνετε has to be interpreted as an absolute prohibition to deal with judicial activities: do not act as judge so that you will not be judged. The saying must then be understood against the background of criticism on judges and courts within the Jewish tradition. The text takes an extreme position which is extraordinary but not unique.

The coordinates of the discussion on the way the judicial system has to function, are set down in the Torah. Ex 18,21 and Deut 1,17 give the concrete prescriptions. The context is the story of Jethro's visit to Moses. Jethro sees that Moses has too much work and advises him to seek helpers in the daily work of judging. It is an aetiological story presenting the existing order as something introduced by Moses. In this context we find a critique which functions as a correction on beginning (or existing) abuses. The simplest expression is given in Ex 18,21: the men who are to become judges must be people who already have power. They should fear God. They should be trustworthy and should not accept gifts(10). The parallel text Dt 1,17(11) proposes different conditions: 'You must be impartial in judgment and give an equal hearing to small and great alike. Do not be afraid of any man, for the judgment is God's'(12). Even if the formulation makes clear that the two texts presuppose different social contexts, the 'Wirkungsgeschichte' brings them together in a coherent critique.

The power of the judges, their behaviour towards 'small and great' which could well make violations of the law a real possibility, the enticement of money, and God as ultimate judge are the parameters within which the Jewish critique of the Law plays itself out. There is no need for me to describe the whole history, but it should be clear that, via prophets and wisdom teachers, the actual legal practice in Israel is kept within bounds by a constant critical undercurrent(13). In our context, Eccl 7,6 is interesting as a close parallel for Matthew: 'Do not scheme to be appointed judge, in case you are not strong enough to stamp out injustice, in case you let yourself be swayed by an influential man, and so risk the loss of your integrity'(14). To be a judge can be a danger for a man who is faithful to the Law because he may not be strong enough to stand up to the powerful in the community. Consequent violation of the Law is laid at his door. The saying presupposes a practice whereby the faithful person renounces a possible position of power out of respect for the Law: to be a judge is beyond his social status(15). The argument is not completely in accord with the presupposed interpretation of the text in Matthew which starts indeed from abuses of the court but not out of fear for the 'powerful'. The judge is capable of sentencing but the measure of the sentence will make him suffer.

The contemporary authors, who discuss this question, do not show this basic critique any more apart from some exceptions. That is understandable because these people realise they are closely connected to the problem of the organisation of the legal system itself. Philo gives the most elaborate story. In view of his platonic background it is not surprising that he tries to find in the judge the personification of what Plato wishes for the citizens: that they have acquired insight in the truth, that they be just, manly and strong(16). According to Philo it is necessary that these characteristics are combined with freedom from all unreasonable passions and from all manner of evil. Only perfect people are good enough to become judges. Only then can a person not only impose Moses' Law, but also set an example of how to live it: a person is only fit to become judge if he can judge and be judged at the same time. Even in his elaboration of the more concrete prescriptions, Philo makes his typical choices. A judge is not allowed to base himself on rumours and use them as a proof. He can rely only on eye-witnesses(17). A judge is not allowed to accept gifts, even if his sentence is fair and just in itself, because the danger of greed must be avoided at all costs(18). A judge should be able to remain objective and should be able to separate persons from things(19). And finally, very typical, he should not take pity on the poor because pity has no place in matters of the Law(20). All in all, it is clear that Philo is embedded in the critical stream of thought which the Torah has indicated. Nevertheless, his exposition represents an idealistic viewpoint as a consequence of his apologetic and didactic intentions. Notwithstanding critical remarks about functionaries who do not operate too well, it looks ideal.

Josephus shows a different picture. He was involved in the appointment of judges in the time that he defended Galilee against the Romans(21). He is aware, therefore, that judges can only do justice from a position of power. He emphasizes that judges should be given honour in the city because that is the only way for people to speak as κύριοι in freedom, unless they are accused of bribery or some other violation of the Law. A weak judge is an insult and injury to God's power. If a judge falls for the temptation to be prejudiced in favour of the powerful in the city, he makes them more important and powerful than God himself because justice ís the power of God(22).

In the Abot also we find people speaking who know that they are directly responsible for the whole procedure, people who often act as judges themselves. We should not see these sayings as a unit. It is a collection of sayinqs originatinq in different times and under different circumstances. On the whole, we see three positions. First of all, we have the prescriptions which refer directly to the administration of justice, as an instruction for the people who will have to act as judges. We have a very old saying on this which is attributed to Juda ben Tabai: 'one should not (being a judge) act as an advocate(23), and when the parties stand before you, they must be considered in your eyes as guilty, but once they have left they must be considered in your eyes as innocent because they have accepted the judgment'. And with that goes the saying of Rabbi Ismael ben Jose: 'one should not judge alone because no one can judge alone except The One'(24), a saying which we should understand aqainst the background of the tribunal of three. These sayings give concrete indications. They presuppose wrongdoinq but it is simple to rectify that if one accepts good counsel.

The second position is expressed in the sayings which are on the borderline between judicial procedure and ethics. The words are derived from tribunal proceedings but the content points in the direction of a 'way-of-life' which is important for many more people than just for judges(25). Two sayings are especially important. First Josue ben Perachja's: 'Judge every person according to the scale of (his) merits; (= base your judgment on the good you find in man)(26). Then, Hillel's, the mild one: 'Do not judge your neighbour without having placed yourself in his situation'(27). These are sayings from Wisdom literature which show great psychological insight and which would change the world if we only lived by them.

The last position, which is closest to our supposed interpretation of the text of Matthew, is also attributed to Ismael ben Jose(28): 'Whoever stays away from the tribunal, liberates himself from hatred, larcency and idle oaths'. It shows the negative in judicial proceedings very clearly and honestly. In its conciseness the saying shows forth certain practices which we can surmise, but which are not so clearly mentioned elsewhere. It is good to compare the saying with the text from Eccl 7,6. The one who is faithful to the Law does not need the tribunal. He will find little justice and many transgressions of the Law. The judge's responsibility is not mentioned in Ismael's saying. The others transgress the Torah. But the close contact can be a temptation and a danger for the man who wants to be faithful.

In conclusion, we must say at least that in the first and second century criticism of the existing judicial system was widespread(29). We find various opinions which cannot be reduced simply to one common reality. This is due partly to the fact that different authors represent different interests. In this choir Mt 7,1 plays its own modest role, always presupposing that the text can be interpreted as 'anti-law'. This background information makes this at least more plausible, I think. However much Matthew's sound is his own, it is by no means an exception.

What is so special and proper about Matthew's saying? The absolute prohibition to act as judge presupposes, as we mentioned already, a community which has had bad experiences with the courts. One should see this from the point of view of experienced courtprocedures. Matthew returns to this theme twice: in Jesus' address to the Twelve, where Jesus warns his disciples against people because they will deliver them up to the courts, but there is no need for fear because they will be strengthened in words and deeds; and later on, in the discourse about the end pains where this same experience is placed against the background of the end time. The persecutions, which will lead to court-cases and to much suffering, are the beginning of the pains(30). Both times the closing sentence is that whoever perseveres till the end will be saved. The disciple is not higher than the master. What happened to the Baptist and to

Jesus is likely to happen also to the disciples. In the descriptions of the death of the Baptist and the suffering and death of Jesus, the whole legal procedure enters lexically: the handing over, the taking prisoner, the binding, the taking away, the being thrown into prison and the accusation. They are (probably) realities which the people have experienced wholly or partially. A (small) number of more indirect indications point in the same direction: 'if you only knew what it means: I want mercy, not sacrifice, you would not condemn the innocent'(31), and, 'I was in prison and you did not visit me'(32). Prison and condemnation of the innocent are real experiences which are not easily forgotten.

I may be allowed to remind you that the text preceding this saying - the passage on 'not to worry' - must be understood in Matthew as spoken to those who are (a little more) rich, i.e. to those from whose numbers the judges are selected. The well-to-do are the only people from which judges can come because a judge needs to have ample free time and because social standing is a prerequisite if the judge is to function reasonably well. In the beginning of the Jesus-movement these services were (probably) not very highly regarded by the followers of Jesus. The situation in Matthew (and Luke) seems different from the situation in the text of Sirach. Sirach dismisses social climbing(33). Matthew rather rejects judges as members of the community: one should not allow oneself to be selected for the function of judge(34). It is the same kind of barrier which exists for the rich when they are asked to give up their possessions or not to look for honour.

Really typical is the argumentation which Matthew uses: do not function as a judge so that you will not be judged (as a culprit), because you will be judged in the same way as you judge, and you will be measured in the same measure you use for others. Something goes wrong with the judgment and God will pay you in that measure. I will come back to this 'measure for measure'. In this context it is more important that the only other time Matthew speaks about this measure, in his attack of the persecution and murder of the prophets, precisely those realities are mentioned that make it rather difficult to think beningly of judges: 'you filled the measure of your fathers, vipers, how will you escape the judgment of gehenna?'(35). Jesus is speaking there against the Pharisees and scribes in his tirade against these leaders of the people. It is not without relevance to remember that these people put themselves forward in the first century as the defenders of the Law and placed themselves as judges in many towns.
As I indicated, this is a possible explanation of the text.

But it is not the only possible explanation. The actual context, where the saying is followed by the mashal on the brother who sees the splinter in the other's eye makes it more than probable that Matthew is not really thinking about a criticism of the courts any more. One should argue that the saying has been formulated as a text against judges and has been interpreted later on in a much broader way, applicable to other people and circumstances. In any case Matthew's community knew an institution where the brothers judged the 'accused'. If one cannot prove this from 5,21 - 22, it is clear from the procedure in 18,15-17(36). I have already said that this does not mean that all reference to the Torah has disappeared. But I want to make this clear from close up.

I will use for this the interpretation of the saying 'measure for measure' as it developed in the Jewish community. B. Couroyer(37) showed from Egyptian and Hellenistic papyri that the expression was in a certain sense a normal business expression by which contracting partners bound themselves for rent, buying and mortgaging-purposes. You will receive back in the same measure as you gave. That may be the measure of the one who received but also of the one who makes the loan, or one could stipulate an official measure guaranteed by imperial officials. The point is that one receives back what one has given. It is the only way to ensure justice: the balance of the same measure.

However clarifying this background information is, it is not really relevant to understand the saying of Matthew. In the concrete context in Matthew, it touches at most the figurative level of understanding, i.e. the way of thinking comes from the world of business but the saying is not about how to do business(38). The history of the Jewish interpretation of the saying 'measure for measure' will make clear that something far more important is involved (39).

In the Mishnah treatise on the woman who has committed adultery (the Sota-treatise) we find as mishmah(40): 'with the kind of measure that a man measures they will mete to him'(41). It is interesting to find an immediate parallel, but it is far more important to see how this saying is interpreted. The Sota text determines in a way the frame-work for all other texts. The point of departure is the change which awaits the adulterous woman. It is portrayed quite graphically. She has beautified herself, God will make her dirty; she has unclothed herself, God will make her naked; she started with the hip and then the belly, God will hit her hip and then the belly and the other parts of her body will not escape punishment. It is a rather rigorous example which, however, is completed with historical happenings where the rabbis have recognised this 'measure for measure'. In this mishnah Samson and Absolom are pointed out. From our concern they are not so relevant. More important now is what follows. The saying is extended with 'and so it will be regarding the good'(42). This seems to say that the good will be honoured in the same way as the bad is punished(43). But that is not the case. The reward is several times bigger than the good deed, as is shown in the examples: Miriam waited for one hour for Moses (on the Nile) and, therefore, the people waited for seven days for her (at the Red Sea). Joseph buried his father and was thus recognised as the greatest among his brothers. And so it goes on with Moses and with the just who have such merits that they will be buried by God himself(44).

In the Tosephtah on this text(45) no new conceptual structures are added, but the expansion of the text is not unimportant, if we are to understand how the saying functions in the gospel of Matthew. We see that not only the events around the adulterous woman are more broadly painted, but also the examples from history are much more numerous. As a text of punishment the saying is applicable to the generation of the Flood, the generation of the Tower (of Babel), the people of Sodom, the Egyptians, Sisera, Samson, Absolom, Sennacherib and Nebuchadnezar(46). If we look at the rewards, these also are much more explicit. Based on Ex 20,5 - 6 it is stated that the measure of the good is 500 times that of the bad. And then this is worked out on the hand of examples from the lives of Abraham, Joseph and Moses(47).

Leaving aside the data which are irrelevant in view of Matthew's text, we may summarize: the expression 'measure for measure' speaks of the generation of the Flood and of the people of Sodom; the measure for evil calls forth the measure for good which is many times greater; the measure for good is applicable to the just.

Also the midrashim use the texts from the Mishnah and the Tosephtah time and again. Sometimes they quote them literally(48), sometimes a special emphasis is given because only the 'measure for good' is applied(49). The Mekilta on Exodus, where we find a unique development, may be a case in point. The mishnah on the measures is apparently a saying which is much loved by its authors because they return to it time and again. It should be no surprise that the events surrounding the Exodus are commented upon in the usual manner: the Egyptians are punished in the same measure as they have sinned. But sometimes the commentary is very ingenuous, via puns which look like cryptograms (50). Israel has experienced in the exodus that God uses 'measure for measure'. It is a torah which is to be found in many places in scripture. The long list of parallel texts(51) wants to clarify that the saying explicates a framework of thought of scripture which keeps turning up and which has kept its force till this day.

Finally, in the targums(52) the saying is placed in the context of the story of Judah and Tamar. Tamar receives back the proof of her innocence because she is not guilty and Judah admits his guilt. He knows that 'measure for measure' will be applied to him. Because he lied to his father by showing him the blood-covered dress of Joseph with the question whether his father recognised it, he deserves punishment: measure for measure, judgment for judgment. Tamar is innocent. The haggadah in which guilt and innocence, condemnation and acquittal are the heart of the matter, makes clear how these realities are the framework of our saying. God does not allow the innocent to be punished or the guilty to go free. The bat-qol, at the end where Judah is also freed from his guilt, shows that God's measure is not man's measure. Whoever wants to convert himself will find a merciful God facing him(53).

If one places these data against the background of the gospel of Matthew, the two great clusters which are envisaged in the saying 'measure for measure' appear to have been spon out in large measure.

As far as punishment is concerned we can look at all the material which is used within the framework of threat, judgment, condemnation in the case of non-conversion:

23,37 - 39: the generation of the Flood: till the Flood comes they remain ignorant. As it was in the days of Noah so it will be when the Son of Man returns;

10,15: the land of Sodom and Gomorrah: the idea of punishment is more clearly expressed in this saying. If a house or city is not ready to accept the message of peace of Jesus' apostles, they will fare worse 'on judgment day' than the land of Sodom and Gomorrah.

11,23 - 24: the land of Sodom. The fate of Sodom is compared with what awaits Capharnaum. Opposed to raised up to heaven stands the being thrown down into hell.

11,20 - 22: the curse of Chorazin and Bethsaida. If in Tyre and Sidon the same miracles had happened as in Chorazin and Bethsaida, they would have converted. Therefore, they will fare better 'on judgment day'.
11,20 - 24 are in Mt the concrete execution of the rule from 10,5. In this passage it is said by Jesus himself and carries thus greater threat.

12,38 - 42: the condemnation of the inhabitants of Niniveh and the queen of the South. The present generation is evil and adulterous. They will receive the sign of Jonah as a last chance. If they do not convert, their condemnation is certain, because 'here' is someone greater than Jonah, greater than Solomon.

5,29.30; 18,8.9: the hand, the foot which become a scandal are better taken away, rather than that they become an instrument of total destruction.

3,12; 7,19; 23,33: the people who do not 'bear fruit', the evil ones, the lawless will not escape punishment.
How far the act conforms to the punishment is most impressively developed in the story of the judgment of the Son of Man(54).

the parables: I could quote just about all the parables in Matthew. There is always some conformity: the parable of the sower is literally explained (οὗτός ἐστιν); the parable of the weeds and the fishing net (13,40.42; 13,50: as the weeds are burnt now, so it will be at the end of time); the parable of the slave who is not willing to condone the debt (18,35: so my father in heaven will act, if you do not forgive your brother wholeheartedly); the parable of the workers of the eleventh hour (20,16: thus the last will be the first and the first will be the last); the parable of the two sons (21,32 with an application to the publicans, whores and high priests); the parable of the evil wine growers (21,43: therefore, the kingdom of heaven will be taken away from you); the parable of the marriage feast (22,7: the destruction of the city; 22,11 ff: the man without a wedding garment); the parable of the ten virgins (half of them are not allowed in); the parable of the ten talents (from 25,24 on the development of the unprofitable slave).
The negative aspect is developed time and again: punishment comes when one judges reality wrongly.

It has become a long list but the comparison with the Mishnah and Toshtah texts is clear. The 'measure for measure' must also be taken in that larger context in Matthew. The whole of human history, from the generation of the Flood to the coming of the Son of Man, from an individual ethic to the mode of behaviour of whole cities and generations, is guided by this torah(55).

The second cluster on which the 'measure for measure' saying is applicable is the award. Measure for measure is true for punishment but also for reward. The difference is that here there is no reference to social events and facts. This is true also in the Jewish texts where concrete persons are referred to, never whole generations or cities.

The accent on ἔλεος reality is typical of Matthew(56). I referred to that already in the discussion on the beatitude on compassion. It became clear there that sickness, hunger, and (financial) debt are the basic realities for Matthew to which the ἔλεος refers, because the ἔλεος is seen in the context of God's convenant with Israel. The corresponding aspect of the reward is the all-surpassing ἔλεος from God: the healing of all diseases, the elimination of all evil, the condoning of all debts, the unbelievable reward for people who created that ἔλεος: to shine like the sun; to be allowed to enter in the happiness of the Lord. Again the most graphic words are used in the story of the Son of Man where the sheep and goats are separated at the right and the left, depending on whether one has recognised the Son of Man in the hungry, the thirsty, the foreigners, the naked, the sick and prisoners. As we know, in the parables which follow this tendency, the negative is stressed more than the positive. The positive is not absent but apparently Matthew finds the threat of punishment more important. This reality is also present in the saying of the Sermon on the Mount - the threat of judgment is the real point - who judges will be judged with the measure with which he judges.

the brotherly correction

Mt 7,3 - 5

Ww have mentioned several times that the mashal on the splinter and the plank refers to the micro-ethic of mutual relations of the brethern. The imagary is, in all its absurdity, so clear that its meaning tends to cover the whole context. I have explained this in the former saying. I believe that I have sufficiently resisted the temptation. So let us now look at the saying on the relation between the brothers.

It is of decisive importance to understand the three step structure: a phenomenon which we have encountered several times already. In the first sentence, the emphasis is on the 'seeing'. Two kinds of seeing are distinguished: seeing the splinter in the eye of your brother, and not seeing the plank in your own eye. The second sentence gives the sequential action. After the 'seeing' comes the 'speaking'. One would like to take out the splinter from the eye of the other, but there is not a word about the plank in one's own eye. The final sentence give the sound advice which describes the right way to act: in order to be able to see how the splinter can be removed, one's own eye must be clear.

This description of the procedure shows that in first instance the ὑποκριτής is addressed, who is always ready to point the finger at another but will not let himself be criticised. A subtle way of formulating causes that at the same time something else is also alluded to. One should notice the sequential way in which is said 'in the eye' and 'out of the eye'. The saying begins with stating the fact that the splinter is 'in the eye' of the observed as well as of the observer. In the second sentence, the speaker wants to remove the splinter 'out of the eye' of the other but the plank is still 'in (his own) eye'. The final sentence only mentions 'remove out of the eye'. This means that the real point of the saying is to remove all dirt, not only from the ὑποκριτής but also from the brother who has but a small splinter in his eye. In final analysis, this means that there is no fundamental opposition between this saying and the mutual court procedure which is described in chapter 18. The saying gives the condition but is not opposed to it. I will return to this later on.

The use of the saying in Jewish literature - not so much the saying itself but rather the imagary - illustrates again a number of aspects of the function and meaning of the mashal. We find a couple of surprising connotations which definitely when taken cumulatively cannot be accidental.

Two texts are important.

In b Baba Batra (15b)(57) the problem is the question whether and when Job existed. The point of departure of a whole series of positions is the statement of a disciple of Rabbi Samuel ben Nachmani(58) that Job never actually existed. The book Job is a mashal as is the story of Nathan as told to David about the poor and the rich sheepfarmer. This leads to the defense of all kinds of ideas about the historicity of Job, a.o. Rabbi Jochanan's who says: 'It is written: 'and it was in the days that the judges judged: the generation which judges the judges'(59); when one says: take the splinter out of your eye, the other will say: remove the plank from your own; when one says: your silver has become dross, the other will say: your wine has been diluted with water'(60).

Leaving aside for the moment the difference with Matthew's text, it is striking that the saying is embedded in a 'court'-context. It begins with a quote from Ruth which is explained as dealing with an evil time in which the judges accuse each other of abuse of the Law. One accusation follows another and it goes from bad to worse. It ends with a quote from Isaiah and the accusations fly thick and fast again. If we may bring in the context of the Isaiah text, it becomes even clearer what criticism of the court process is in the mind of the author. It is a time when the leaders are rebellious, robbers, coveting bribes and gifts without doing justice to the widows and the orphans. This context is, obviously, too well known from the story so far.

The second text from the Talmud (b Arakin 16b) is structurally somewhat more complicated but more interesting. The point of departure is a mishnah from the treatise on estimations, the explanation of the contents, values and prices of the punishments as stated by the Torah(61): whoever - having married a woman - gives her a bad name (by saying without justification, that she was not a virgin) must pay one hundred sela(62). Slander deserves a worse punishment than an evil act. Thus it was in Israel's case. Because they had an evil tongue, they were not allowed to enter the promised land because it has been said: ten times they tempted me and they have not listened to me(63). The gemarah on this mishnah text begins with the question why Israel was punished so late. Rabbi Hamnuna(64) knows the answer. God punishes when the measure is full(65), an answer which brings reminiscences of Matthew's text. After a whole series of other questions we read: 'our rabbis taught: do not hate your brother'(66). The explanation for this Leviticus text is the immediate starting point for our saying, relating to the problem of brotherly correction. If you want to follow the torah, you must correct your brother, even more than once if necessary, but not in a shaming manner because then one becomes guilty oneself. In connection with this explanation, Rabbi Tarfon says(67): 'I would be surprised if in this generation there is still a person to be found who accepts a correction; when one person says take away the splinter from your eye, then the other will say 'remove the plank from your own eye'. This brings Rabbi Eleazar to second him with the words 'I would be surprised if there is still a person in this generation who knows how to give a correction'. Rabbi Jochanan objects to this because he has corrected Rabbi Aqiba several times and nevertheless, or maybe just because of that, Rabbi Aqiba loved him more. The tannaim see in this the demonstration of what is said in the Book of Proverbs: 'do not correct a fool(68) because he will hate you; correct a wise man and he will love you'(69).

So it is clear that the text is full of references. If seen against the background of the Matthew text one is surprised over the parallelism of thought. To start with we have the fact that the point of departure of the gemarah is tied to the torah on man-woman relation when they get married. I may be allowed to remind the reader that Mt 7,3 - 5 could well be a 'relecture' of Mt 5,27 - 31. Does this show that not only the eye is the common ground as the organ of good and evil in these texts but that there are also inherent similarities between the torah on marriage and the torah on brotherly correction? I cannot really go beyond this suggestive question. It is certain that in the Talmud this mishnah has been seen in the context of a 'measure' which is filled or not. And this brings Matthew 7,1 - 2 to mind. From the immediate context in which the imagary of the splinter and the plank is used, we can point also the reference to the Leviticus text and to the quote from Proverbs which give the point of the Talmud text. Brotherly correction is a fruit of wisdom. It will make the wise man wiser but one should not expect this to happen with the fool. If there is a direct connection between these 'fools' and the ὑποκριτής the Sermon on the Mount (70), one would almost think that the Talmud text is a reaction to what Jesus said in the Sermon on the Mount (71).

Not without reason I want to end this rather extended discussion of the text with the supposition of a connection between the Talmud text and the saying from the Sermon on the Mount. Commentaries sometimes use this connection, obviously in an interpretation which is prejorative for the Jews(72). This seems to me quite wrong. Rabbi Tarfon separates the two sentences on the splinter and the plank not just for fun. He expresses bitterness, or pain if one wishes, because in his time the torah of brotherly correction is no longer practised. People are no longer willing to listen to each other if there is correction involved. Rabbi Jochanan reacts by clarifying that one should not only look at the other but also at oneself. The manner of correction is of the essence. The tannaim find one another in Rabbi Aqiba. His way of acting is praised because he was capable of accepting corrections - and they were not even always just - and because he was a 'chakam': a model for all. The real point of view of this Talmud text is about 'reception': how difficult it is and how it shows real wisdom. Matthew's text precedes this, if not chronologically then at least psychologically. It gives the conditions necessary to correct one's brother.

This round-about way on the use of the saying in Jewish literature has given us the insight that the torah on brotherly correction is the real background of the saying (73). It seems obvious to explain the central evaluative concept of the saying that the one addressed is ὑποκριτής in this same sense: the obligation of brotherly correction is not fulfilled because the ὑποκριτής has developed a wrong understanding of this torah. Looked at from the three steps expressed in the saying, this means that he lacks a perception of self because he fails to see the difference between what is wrong with his brother and what is wrong with himself. He lacks self-improvement because he is ready to correct his brother but is not capable of seeing the consequences for himself. He has no insight in the most fundamental condition for every brotherly correction: to accept oneself as the one more guilty and to get rid of one's faults. The imagary where splinter and plank are central shows that the ὑποκριτής makes a basic mistake in interpretation. The judgment on the other's reality is faulted by the lack of an objective self-judgment in seeing, speaking and judging(74). The prohibition to judge of the foregoing verses is somewhat weakened here in our mashal. But that is to some extent only partly true, because the command to be self-critical puts the listener in such a humble position that he will hardly ever think of judging his brother.

Because the saying remains in the cadre of a mashal it is almost impossible to judge its reality. The imagary used presupposes a practice but it is without enough references to point to concrete persons who practise this. The same is true for the use of ὑποκριτής. Even though this word is linked to specific persons in the gospels - the scribes and the Pharisees -(75), this does not allow us to reason that, therefore, this mashal envisages the scribes and Pharisees. This is even more stringent because the gospel does not refer to this further on. One could think of certain accusations in the diatribe against the Pharisees and scribes: that they do not touch the more difficult obligations of the Law and put more emphasis on the easier ones; that they accuse their fathers of being the murderers of prophets, but do not recognise that they themselves are doing just the same(76). One can admit that these accusations are implied in what is meant in this mashal, but one can hardly claim that they refer directly to the saying. The saying wants to encourage a manner of acting which affects far more people than just this group(77).

The returning use of the word ἀδελφός, in connection with the narrative context of the saying, is decisive for this interpretation. The saying is part of the Sermon on the Mount to which the disciples and the people are listening. Three times an opposition is expressed in the saying between one's own eye and the eye of one's brother. The person addressed is confronted with his 'brother' whom he judges wrongly as the text presupposes, and to whom he appears as ὑποκριτής. The mashal of Matthew must be interpreted against the background of his ideas on brotherhood.

In the study of Matthew this is not a simple question. Everyone agrees that Matthew speaks significantly more often about ἀδελφοί than the other synoptics. But beyond this point the ideas are very divergent. In question is the interpretation of the totality of Matthew's Gospel: is Mt as text oriented towards Israel, towards the Ecclesia as a self-sufficient entity, towards the goyim either excluding or including Israel? It may be clear that several opposing alternatives are proposed.

There are a couple of things we can state.
In the Sermon on the Mount, Matthew does not go beyond the framework of Israel. There is no need now to repeat all the separate arguments which in the totality of this commentary are stated in the context of each separate saying. Jesus is presented in the Sermon on the Mount as someone who wants to reform and restore Israel. In the beatitudes, Jesus pronounces his promises to liberate and restore the people from their sufferings. In the law-texts Jesus gives his interpretation and explanation of the Torah. He shows how God's righteousness is connected to his dominion and how this consequently is connected to almsgiving, prayer and fasting. He shows the rich how they can solve their problems and thus experience the joy of the Law. He indicates how the doing ultimately determines access to the basileia of the end-time. The narrative character of the Sermon on the Mount is determined by the peoples who belong to Jesus and who are addressed as Israel and asked to convert and to gain access to God's basileia. This means that the texts of the Sermon on the Mount, where the word ἀδελφός, is used(78), do not go beyond this framework of Israel as people.

But this does not mean that Matthew writes his gospel in a situation where the contact with Israel is unbroken. I have pointed several times to texts where this brokenness is expressed. It appears fundamentally in those texts which treat of the persecutions as result of or as cause of the separation from the synagogue. The very negative judgments on Israel are perhaps also part of it: the guilt over the death of Jesus and the blood of the murderers of the prophets which cries to heaven.

Does this mean that Matthew has definitively broken the relation with Israel? I do not think so. The way one looks at Mt 28,16 - 20 is decisive here: the mission of the eleven disciples to the ἔθνη. 'The brothers' of the risen Lord are the subject here(79) who are sent to make disciples of all peoples(80). It seems as if Israel is not important any more but that is not the case. One should read the text carefully. The mission of the eleven apart from baptism is precisely to teach the 'goyim' to keep all those things which Jesus taught his disciples. The totality of all the previous events is part and parcel of the mission that Jesus gives the eleven. The commandment of Jesus to his disciples, i.e. the Torah of God as explained by Jesus, is the 'didachè' for the peoples as the will of God that has to be done. With the mission of the eleven to the 'goyim', Israel becomes the model and the light for the peoples(81).

Jesus has set the example of what the commission of the disciples will be. As Israel's Messiah he settled in Capharnaum 'in the midst of pagan territory so that the people who walked in darkness would see a great light'(82). That does not mean that with this settlement in pagan territory Jesus abandoned 'Israel'. Matthew develops this in chapters 8 and 9. A whole series of events is concluded with the exclamation 'never before has something like this been seen in Israel'(83). Even though there is this reference to the peoples - and there are many instances where Jesus leaves Israel in the literal sense of the word as we have shown above(84) -, this does not mean that he has left 'Israel', i.e. that the presence of Israel has been diminished. Where Jesus is, there is Israel. Either in the literal sense of the word because, being in Israel, Jesus speaks to Israel (as e.g. in the Sermon on the Mount, but also in the mission-sermon in chapter 10, where Jesus forbids the apostles to go the road of the peoples or to enter a Samaritan city), or in the symbolical sense of the word as a representative symbol of Israel, as e.g. when Jesus spends time in pagan country, or when the disciples are told that they should go to the pagans(85).

The remaining texts which treat of the 'brotherhood' fit easily into the background of this double perspective. Jesus' brothers and sisters - finally the 'sisters' are mentioned, be it only once - are those who do the will of the father, i.e. those who keep the Torah of God as explained by Jesus(86). Jesus, the Messiah as teacher, warns that Israel will split up again when some people want to be called rabbi i.e. teacher(87). As the Son of Man, Jesus identifies with the least of his brothers because he recognises in them the persecuted and exploited people in Israel(88). The brothers, of whom the parable of the unforgiving slave speaks, give us the nearest parallel(89). The parable is about a king who has slaves who should act as brothers. It comes up after Peter's question about how often one should forgive one's brother. The context shows that the problem of the ἁμαρτία of the brother is in mind. The Torah demands that one should correct him, first of all in private, then with two or three witnesses and, finally, in the presence of the whole ekklesia (of the city). The parable tells us that something else should happen first: one should forgive one's brother not seven times, but seventy times seven - the opposite to what Lamech had in mind with his vengeance(90). Self-improvement and forgiveness are for Matthew the necessary steps which precede the doing of the torah on brotherly correction. The brothers in Israel know what they should do.

the holy for the dogs and the pearls for the pigs

Mt 7,6

Everyone tries his best to find the meaning of this saying. The multitude of suggestions - and I will add to that-proves that it is a difficult text and that we cannot say much about it and come to a definite decision. Not without reason, it was suggested quite early in the history of scientific research of the gospels(91) that we have a Greek mistake in translation. Instead of τὸ ἅγιον which presupposes the Aramaic 'qudsa' one should have read 'qedasha': 'do not give the dogs a valuable ring'(92). The most recent suggestion(93) gives as reconstruction of the Aramaic text: 'do not put your rings on dogs and do not hang your pearls on your pigs'. The meaning of this proverb would be: do not use your valuables in a senseless way; do not abuse them. It is clear that only part of the text is accepted as original. Furthermore, and this is the more important difficulty, I cannot see much advantage in this reconstruction. We have a saying which I cannot fit in with the Wisdom sayings of Jesus or the early Jesus-movement. Finally, - but this will true also for all the other explanations - what kind of practice would be the basis for this saying? Did dogs wear rings? Did one put pearls on pigs? The argument would gain in force if one could show contemporary archeological and/or literary indications. For the moment it seems wiser to try to understand the given Greek text.

Most exegetes presuppose that it is a double saying where the first part is completely parallel with the second. That is probably true for the given text in Matthew, but it is far from necessary for the supposed original sayings. Searching for the origin of the saying, from which situation or from which mode of thinking, it is necessary to separate the two. Giving what is holy to dogs does not seem to presuppose the same background as throwing pearls before pigs. At least I would like to introduce in the research this sugggestion.

Following the proposition of a number of exegetes(94), I start with the suggestion that the saying not to give to dogs what is holy determines a position within the halachah on the first-born. The torah that the first-born must be offered or bought free is not passed on unequivocally. Num 18,15 ff prescribes that children and unclean animals need to be redeemed, while the first-born male of a clean animal (sheep, goats and oxen) must be offered in sacrifice. Ex 34,20 gives a special rule for asses which are unclean. For the first-born male ass a lamb needs to be offered as ransom or one should break the animal's neck. This differentiation has given rise to all manner of discussion(95) which in this context is of no concern. Of importance now is the question what should be done if the first-born animal dies: does it still need to be redeemed? The question arises because one wants to know what one is allowed to do with the dead animal. Should it be buried or can it be given as food for the dogs? As first-born animal it belongs to God and is thus holy. When it is redeemed-in the case of unclean animals - it is free for ordinary profane use, or when it is offered - in the case of clean animals - this sacrifice redeems the other animals which are born thereafter. If the animal is stillborn(96) or when the animal dies before the obligation is fulfilled, the halachah should point the way. We find the decisive answer in Sifre on Num(97). Rabbi Tarfon determined in Jabne that dead animals follow the same rule as clean ones. They cannot be redeemed, i.e. they must be buried because one cannot give to the dogs what is holy(98).

To state it correctly: this formula cannot be found as such in the midrash. It is an implied presupposition which makes understandable how, from the question 'if a first-born animal has died, should the owner redeem it or throw it to the dogs?' the given answer follows ' you must redeem live animals but you cannot redeem dead ones. You must redeem unclean animals but you cannot redeem clean ones'. God's judgment has been given over the dead animal. It belongs to God and may not be profaned.

If we must understand the saying in Matthew against this background, it is clear once again how, also in this passage of the Sermon on the Mount, halachah is done which is not less than the halachah in the first series of legal explanations. From the supposition that Mt 7,6 connects with the torah on oaths, we may emphasize that the same halachah of the first born animals is valid also in case of animals which are destined for sacrifice by vow(99). If the animal dies between the time the vow is made and the time the vow is to be fulfilled, the dead animal cannot be redeemed so that it could be used as food for dogs. It is to be buried because one should not give to dogs what is holy. Notice that the death of the animal places human judgment in opposition to God's judgment: a way of thinking which fits in quite well with Mt 7,6.

It cannot be completely excluded that another, similar halachah has also served as background for our saying. Dt

23,19 gives as torah: 'if you are fulfilling your vow, you must not bring to the house of the Lord, your God, the wages of a prostitute or the earnings of a dog, for both are detestable to Him'. What is meant by the wages of the prostitute is reasonably clear(100), but the same cannot be said for the wages of the dog. Josephus understands it as the money earned by using the dog as stud: the money earned may not be used as offering to God(101). The Mishnah gives a completely different explanation. The 'earnings of the dog' is part of a long series of animals where something went wrong - an animal used for intercourse with man of woman, an animal used for idolatry, set aside for sacrifice or to be venerated as an idol in a pagan procession; an animal which is used in a prohibited manner as stud or an animal killed without ritual ceremony; an animal, finally, which is delivered by operation(102). 'The earnings of the dog' is then the animal which has been exchanged in some way for a dog. It is an animal which has taken the place of a dog and which, therefore, may not be used anymore for the service in the Temple.(103)

If we may read the saying against this background, its meaning goes in the direction of 'do not change what is holy for a dog'. This may seem somewhat strange but it has a great advantage. It can explain the train of thought which is the base for the story of the Canaanite woman (104). Jesus is in the region of Tyre and Sidon and a Canaanite woman runs after him to ask his help for her daughter. The disciples do not like it and Jesus is also unwilling. His reasoning presupposes precisely the opposition which we just described. He cannot exchange the sheep of Israel for dogs(105). He may not use the bread of the children 'to throw it to the dogs'. The woman's answer, that dogs run around during the meal and get something to eat, is accepted in a positive sense. There is no need for a real exchange because dogs and sheep can live together without damage to Jesus' mission to Israel. The saying in the Sermon on the Mount starts from an absolute: Israel may not be exchanged for the pagans(106). The story of the Canaanite woman shows that the community of Matthew did not draw the conclusion from this that all access should be prohibited to the pagans. It is possible to find a way of living together which, although respecting the content of the saying, opens the possibility for the pagans to share in the 'bread of the children'.

However hypothetical these suggestions may seem, compared with the hypotheses on the saying of the pearls and the pigs, it looks as if there is no solid ground left to stand on. Literally understood one cannot think of an instance that someone would feed pearls to pigs. Therefore, the saying must be formulated, from the first, as an allegorical sentence. One or another concept - it may even be true for all the concepts - is, from the origin, not to be seen as figurative language but as denotative language. It can be compared with the absurd imagary in the mashal of the splinter and the plank. A plank in the eye is absurd. Therefore, the hearer knows that by this plank a denotative reality is meant which does not coincide with the used imagary.

It is more complicated in the case of the pearls and the pigs, because the pearls and/or the pigs are figuratively to be interpreted differently from the beginning. We must, therefore, search for all the possibilities as in a jigsaw puzzle. A scale of meanings offers itself which all carry some probability. But it is not possible that the author intended them all. So the result is rather doubtful. The only real possibility is to look at each possible explanation.

One possibility is that 'your pearls' is meant literally, while 'pigs' is meant figuratively. Two realities might be intended.

To start with the least probable: 'pigs' means 'idols' and 'your pearls' indicate the showpieces and ornaments which are offered to idols. The advantage of this interpretation is that it offers a connection with an existing abuse. One could think of the letter of Jeremiah repeating as in refrain how people donate gold and silver to idols (107). They receive gold crowns and purple vestments(108). They carry a sceptre, a sword or an axe(109), and gifts and food are given to them(110), but they serve no purpose. Or one could think of a text which is even closer to Matthew's formulation, a mishnah from Aboda Zara: 'no one must make ornaments for idols: chains or nose rings or signet rings'(111).

Obviously, this is not all. It would be necessary to prove that idols are seen as 'pigs'. I do not know of any literal text, but it is well known in Jewish tradition to see a connection between the eating of pigs and the sacrificial cults of idols. One could think of the stories from 2 Macc about the martyrs under Antiochus; or of the custom of the suovetaurilia: pigs are the accepted sacrificial offerings in Hellenism(112). One should recall the evangelical tradition that pigs are the proper place for demons from the story of the Gadarene swine(113), or the series in the Mishnah where pigs are mentioned together with idols and the skins of animals slaughtered for pagan cults(114). Pigs function in the pagan ritual. Apart from the legal uncleanness, they get, therefore, a ritual ticket of uncleanness because of the Jewish criticism against polytheism.

However, even if it is clear that this interpretation is understandable together with statements from the Sermon on the Mount which speak negatively about pagans and their cult(115), the closing sentences about trampling and tearing to pieces attributed to the pigs cannot be applied to 'idols'. Rather the opposite. In Jewish religious criticism idols are impotent and incapable of doing anything. It is an old Wisdom tradition which is still strong in the contemporary situation of Mt's gospel. Compared to Israel's God all other gods are nothing(116): a train of thought which is absolutely contrary to the possibility of ruin which the 'pigs' can cause the donors of valuable gifts.

Therefore, it may be better to look at a second possibility. 'Your pearls' is again taken literally; 'pigs' then means a figurative indication of 'whores, male and female temple slaves, hierodouloi'. The meaning is not that far removed from the one explained just now, because 'idolatry' and 'prostitution' are closely connected. Gifts play an important role here. Even though Jewish literature does not speak about it directly(117), it is expressed indirectly in the description of the effects of dealing with these people. It is one of the most important arguments against this practice which we find in Wisdom literature: do not deal with the 'foreign' woman because she will suck you empty(118). The man who deals with adulterous women throws away his money(119); do not come close to a 'hetaere' because she will catch you in her nets; the harlot will make you loose your inheritance(120). If one deals with πόρναι, ruin is threatened, physical, financial and moral. The prophetic threat of divine punishment(121) takes on an anthropological form in the Wisdom literature: the punishment will come in this life through those who are connected with the act. In one's old age one will regret not having listened to the advice of the Wisdom teachers.

This interpretation would be perfect if we could find in literature the equivalence 'pig' = πόρνη. I did find one(122), but that is probably not sufficient to carry this interpretation.

So I come to the conclusion that the mashal in its totality should be taken as an allegorical saying. Every concept is equivalent to a denotative reality. In the proposals made by the exegetes the saying of the holy and the dogs is included, so that one single interpretation of the saying becomes possible. Basically we have again two possibilities.

The first fits in with S. Brandon's suggestion(123). It could be more acceptable than is usually thought. In short, the dogs and the pigs stand for the Romans, the holy and the pearls stand for Israel/Jerusalem(124). The force of this interpretation is in the possibility of its use for the trampling and the tearing. If this points to the events of 70 AD, either post factum, or as a warning before the event, we finally find something literal as truth. The way the Romans acted could well be described as the work of a troop of wild pigs which attack innocent people in blind rage and tear them apart because they do not get what they had hoped for.

It is relatively certain that the image of pigs and dogs can be used to describe the Romans(125). It is not so clear that we can prove the equivalence of 'the holy' and 'your pearls' with Israel/Jerusalem. Is it wrong to point to the Apocalypse texts which describe the heavenly Jerusalem as an abundance of gold, precious stones and pearls(126), following the Merkabah literature where God's heavenly throne is described in similar terms(127); or to point to the vision of Esra where Lady Sion changes into a beautiful city with mighty foundations(128)? It would be more convincing if 'pearls' had been in the singular. As for the 'holy' we can point to the typically Matthean description of Jerusalem as the 'holy city'(129) and of the Temple as the 'holy place'(130).

There is no good reason why this warning of the mashal, understood in this sense, could not have its place in the passage of the Sermon on the Mount where it is found. The threat of 'measure for measure' which expresses the ruin of cities and generations and the halachah on the conditions for brotherly correction could very well have been followed by the warning addressed to Israel's citizens that they should beware of the danger from abroad: a warning which, after the events of 70 AD, is seen as prophecy of Jesus in which the sad fate of Israel functions as a warning for his actual listeners.

The second possibility, based on the supposition that the whole saying is allegorical, can be found in the commentaries, usually as the only possibility(131). There is no need, therefore, to spend much time on it. The supposition is that 'pigs' and 'dogs' are equivalent to 'pagans', and that 'the holy' and 'the pearls' stand for the (Christian) message. This follows Jewish texts where an especially beautiful explanation of a torah text is called 'pearl'(132). The saying then means: one should not bring the gospel to the pagans because the message is in danger of being profaned and the life of the messenger is threatened.

Such an interpretation is difficult to maintain within the context of Matthew's gospel which is so clearly positive to the mission to the pagans. Therefore, it is stated that, in Matthew, the saying refers to 'renegade brothers': the brothers who have refused to accept brotherly correction and who now are a danger for the community (133).

The advantage of this interpretation is undoubtedly that we can stay within the context of Matthew. But, on the other hand, persecution of Christians by (renegade) Christians is not well documented, to say the least. The use of the saying in the Didachè(134) - but without mentioning the 'pigs' - shows that at least this author sees the saying as directed to non-Christians and we may then suppose that those were mainly pagans. All in all it means that this reading is no more than a possibility. Certainly it is not without problems. I do not think I am saying something which even its promoters would not agree with. The extreme metaphorical character of the mashal, outside of any context, makes it practically impossible to propose a definite interpretation.

the promise of God's generosity in relation to the norm for mutual relations

Mt 7,7 - 12

The problem of the structure of the closing passage of the Sermon on the Mount is the most urgent problem in this passage. A loose structure seems best because, after the statements on measure for measure, the brotherly correction and the mashal on dogs and pigs, two new topics are brought in: a series of sayings which in content deal with prayer and a statement on love of neighbour. There seems to be no coherence any more in this so-called 'miscellaneous series of instructions'(135).

I propose that we should make a clear distinction between the 'Traditionsgeschichte' of the sayings and Matthew's use of the sayings in the context of the Sermon on the Mount. Considering the parallels in Luke(136) where the sayings are discontinuous, and seeing the diversity in content, one can think that they have functioned independently from one another. Exegetes treat the passage usually in this way. One starts with a caesura between 7,11 and 7,12 and one reads the clusters as independent units. However true this may have been in the context of the 'Traditionsgeschichte', it is not valid in the text of Matthew. Even though it is a simple observation, the use of the particle οὖν in 7,12 proves that Matthew saw the golden rule as a conclusion of the preceding sentences. For him it is a consequence from what has been said before: a last conclusion which expresses the implications of what has remained unsaid(137).

This has real consequences for a good understanding of the pericope. In a way one could say that there are two statements. It begins with a long, intricately constructed question, connected via a γάρ-construction (in vs 7,8) and an ἤ-construction (in vs 7,9 and 7,10), which is concluded with a 'qal wachomer'-reasoning: if you know how to give each other good gifts, how much more will your father in heaven. It ends with a concluding sentence on mutual relations which via the γάρ-construction about the Law and the prophets, makes a final inclusion with the beginning of the legal text in 5,17.

Putting this together as far as the content is concerned, it means that, in opposition to the series of statements on acquiring and receiving, there is a statement on giving, i.e. the willingness to do unto others what one hopes they will do to you. The passive indication of God in 'it will be given to you, it will be opened to you' and the promise of the abundance of God's generosity are in a consecutive relation to the task for 'people' to act likewise. Mutual relations among people are determined by the divine norm of the abundant generosity because this is the Law and the prophets. The conclusion is not really logical. But that is precisely the striking force of the text and the reason why the connection is often not seen. Summed up precisely the text says: as God gives you good gifts, therefore you must act in the same way towards each other.

Basic to this interpretation are a number of steps which we need to explicitate further. For that we must go back to the beginning, with the sayings about asking, searching and knocking. We should see these as 'beggars's wisdom'(138). That is immediately clear for asking and knocking on doors. The beggar insists in order to receive his part and if he insists long enough it will be given to him and the door will be opened. The train of thought behind this can be supposed to be expressed in the introductory commentary of Luke's text: 'if the friend does not get up to give bread to the nocturnal visitor because he is a friend, he will do so because of his 'impertinence''(139). The beggar is out of necessity beyond all shame which in a culture based on shame will have results.

The real problem in understanding the trio ask-search-knock in the context of a beggar lies in the 'searching'. What has 'searching' to do with begging? The exegetes are silent(140). Yet, that is not necessary. Discussing the saying on almsgiving I have tried to clarify that within the existing culture the 'alms' largely function via the halachot on agriculture. The Mishnah treatise on 'The corner of the field' deals with this. And as a refrain we find mentioned there the 'gleaning' (of cornfields, vineyards and olive trees); the 'corner of the field' which must remain untouched and which is not allowed to be harvested, and the 'forgotten' - the forgotten sheaf, grapes and olives(141). All this is placed in the context of the poor who, in time harvest, get the chance to obtain a share of the harvest through the 'inattention' of the owner. Against this background it is not so difficult to explain why 'search' comes after 'asking': the beggar must know when the harvest is by asking so that he can come and 'search' for the 'forgotten'.

Ask, search and knock belong together contextually as a trio. The sentences speak from a situation of people who know that they are dependent on others and who, therefore, understand the promises connected with it: to receive, to find and to have the door opened. Their lack of possessions gives them an awareness of the largesse of the promised riches.

Somewhat further on in the text we have another indication that the opening sentences originate in a poverty-culture. The problem here is that the concept is ideologically occupied. It is the description of the 'fathers', who will not give a stone but bread, who will not give a serpent but a fish: they are presented as πονηροί. I do not know any translator who does not translate this as 'evil' with all the moral and religious connotations of 'evil' (142). The multifarious interpretations, going from a strict lutheranism in which all people are evil, to an interpretation speaking of the lack of charity of such people, prove too well that the content does not allow this idea of 'evil'. The 'fathers' from the mashal do not do anything evil. On the contrary, they give their children the best possible.

Why not simply take the first meaning of the word: that these fathers 'although they find themselves in a sorry plight', do know how to give good gifts(143). The concept πονηρία contains, as I explained in vs 6,23, a 'physical-economic' component which fits in too well in this context.

This exegesis is supported by the opposition between bread-and-fish and stone-and-serpent. W. Ott(144) showed that the imagary of the mashal discursively represents the opposition use-uselessness. Maybe it is possible to think a little more concretely of the opposition eatable-uneatable. Instead of uneatable things like a stone or a serpent, a father gives his children something which helps them: bread and fish. How the mashal-narrator thinks of a stone is clear. For the serpent we will have to think of something similar to what we are told about in the parable of the fishnet. If one goes fishing with a trawl-net one brings up all kind of fishes: some are good and will be kept in baskets, others are σαπρά and are thrown away because they are 'uneatable'(145). The serpent in our mashal is like that kind of fish. The uneatable stone runs parallel with the uneatable serpent. If fathers, however poor, will not give these to their children but give them good gifts, how much more will your father in heaven give good gifts to those who ask him.

The last sentence 'to those who ask him' forms an inclusion with the opening imperative 'ask'. This indicates that in Matthew's context the meshalim are taken up in the prayer parenesis, but we should not take this in a limited religious sense. 'Prayer' is seen as all activity of people who lack everything. The exegetical question circles again around the question in how far imagary and reality interfere with each other. That the origin is situated in a poverty culture does not mean that it is directed necessarily to the have-nots. A rich man could also understand what is meant here. Even if he does not feel the need to ask for food or drink or for whatever material thing, he can still use the meshalim in a setting which fits his situation better: to keep clear that only through insistent asking and searching all kinds of still lacking things, like faith, truth, the light of Christ etc, will be found. The history of the exegesis of these verses(146) makes clear that Mt 7,7 - 11 has been used in this sense.

Is this true also for Matthew himself and his community? Till now I have tried to clarify that the poverty-riches problem has a meaning also in Matthew's gospel. Not because Matthew would know only poor people but because he tells the rich that they will be capable of being part of the Jesus-movement only if they are ready to renounce all their possessions. Jesus' followers must abandon themselves to God as he did. They should not be afraid because they will not lack anything. I think that the 'prayer sentences' in 7,7 - 11 must be explained against this background. There is an immediate connection with what has been said in the preceding pericope about the μέριμναι of the rich. If they give away everything for the sake of God's dominion, they do not have to worry because their father in heaven knows what they need. In our text we find precisely the opposite: ask and you will be given. The content of the Our Father is summed up here: access to God's kingdom is not in opposition to the prayer for daily bread.

This interpretation does mean that 'what is asked' is something material for Matthew and his community. There is still the literal sense that in the mashal about the father and his children mention is made of the basic necessities: bread and fish. The wisdom of the beggar about the insistent demand, search and knocking is (still) understood in its elementary sense. The dependence on God is experienced as the very fact of survival. The promises expressed in the passive as indicative of God and the statement 'how much more will your father in heaven' need this divine guarantee because otherwise the whole Sermon on the Mount is untrue(147). He who entrusts himself completely to God, hopes to be heard by God if need forces him to ask for something.

In exegesis it is sometimes seen as a problem that 7,12 concludes with 'this is the Law and the prophets' while there has been no mention of the first commandment: love of God. Kl. Berger writes: 'The two main commandments - to love God and the neighbour - can be replaced by the golden rule and the first of the two can then be left out(!)'-(148). From our interpretation above it should be clear that this statement is true only under very special conditions. The love of God is not literally stated but trust in God is put in such an absolute way that the first commandment is certainly there: you must love the Lord, your God with your whole heart, your whole mind and all your soul. He who understands that and acts accordingly, will have had the experience of God's generosity in his life.

Matthew connects this, in his factual text, consecutively with the golden rule: 'you must, therefore, act in the same manner'. Even if it does not exhaust the meaning of the logion on mutual relations, the use of the consecutive 'therefore', points to a mode of behaviour which has something of 'generosity'. A (limited) number of texts in Matthew proves that this is a train of thought which is not alien to Matthew, to say the least.

First of all one should think of the statement directed to the rich young man. If he wants to be perfect, he must sell his possessions to give to the poor(149): a behaviour which is basic for what has just been said. More typical and closer to our text are the statements which have a wider application.

Three texts are important:

In the Sermon on the Mount we have encountered one - in the explanation of the legal text on 'an eye for an eye, a tooth for a tooth'. The series of examples how civil order can be maintained notwithstanding the abuses of the law breakers ends with the sentence: give to the person who asks you for something and do not turn away from the person who wants to borrow something(150). The other's evil may not become an excuse to abandon your willingness to give and to lend. I may be allowed to remind the reader of the suggestion that Mt 7,7 - 11 is a re-lecture of Mt 5,38-42. This connection would give it an extra emphasis.

The second text can be found in the mission sermon of Jesus: 'freely you have received, freely you must give' (151). It is a typical addition in Matthew, relating here to the possibility of healing the sick, of raising the dead, of cleansing the lepers and of driving out demons. The coming of God's dominion is accompanied by messianic activities which bring about the well-being of the people. It is a concrete example of the abundance of 'good things' with which the father in heaven surpasses all earthly fathers.

As a third text, we can point to a surprising parallel. In the stories about the meals which Jesus offers the people the ingredients are bread and fish. Typically Matthean is the emphasis on the mediation of the disciples. Jesus gives thanks and hands the broken pieces of bread and the fish to his disciples(152) and they give it to the masses. Can we see here a reference to the mashal about the father and his children - via the mention of the bread and the fish - as an example which is fulfilled in the meals Jesus offers the people and which should keep alive the memory of the still greater generosity of the heavenly father? We cannot go beyond this simple suggestion(153).

Generosity towards one another is the presupposed concrete expression of the logion which we call the golden rule. A. Dihle(154) has shown that the meaning of the saying is wider than that. The saying is the formulation of an ethical stance which represents the temporary end result of the historical struggle of classical humankind to live with experienced feelings of revenge. He sees the logion as part of a series of stances which starts with the statement on the equivalent reparation of injustice - an eye for an eye, a tooth for a tooth -; which then begins to see the possibility of an equal exchange of benefits and injuries- inimicis inimicus et amicis amicus -; and finally comes to the statement on the most rational behaviour to act benevolently toward one's neighbour in order to prevent him from doing anything against you. The golden rule expresses an ethic of behaviour which presupposes a certain rationality to provide a chance to escape the vicious circle of revenge and retaliation(155).

Our reflections on this whole chapter make clear that, with his Sermon on the Mount and especially with this short passage from the Sermon on the Mount, Matthew fits in very well with the larger 'discussion' of his time. Time and again it appears that Matthew wants to prevent his listeners from taking the law into their own hands and to return evil for evil. Not an eye for an eye; not to love only those who love you; not to judge others but rather leave the measure for measure to God; one should entrust oneself completely to God. It is a real struggle to curb human aggressiveness. The concluding statement gives the final limit: prevent the other's aggression by putting yourself in his place and look from there to yourself. It really means to opt for the good in an absolute sense because no one wants to get hurt. Do good to another and it will go well with yourself.

There are two interdependent observations to be made on Matthew's text with regard to Dihle's reflections on the logion. Matthew places the golden rule in the context of a legal system by adding the reason 'for this is the Law and the prophets'. This addition indicates that the totality of God's obligatory Law is involved(156). Matthew is not proposing human truth. However human the saying sounds- and the number of times we find it back in Hellenistic, Jewish and Roman literature(157) is enormous and shows that it corresponds to a deep seated human desire - Matthew sees it as a summing up of God's Torah.

He returns to this later on in his gospel when he makes the Pharisees ask Jesus which is the greatest commandment. The Law and the prophets depend on the love for God and neighbour(158). As we already stated, the commandment of love for God plays a role also in this passage of the Sermon on the Mount. This is not to deny that the link of the commandment of the love for neighbour with 'the Law and the prophets' is not more explicit. With this Matthew is in good company. Paul also thinks he can state that whoever loves his neighbour has fulfilled the Law: love is, therefore, the fulfillment of the Law(159). In the letter to the Galatians we read 'for the whole Law is fulfilled in this one word: love your neighbour as yourself(160). James also speaks about this commandment as 'the regal law'(161). The torah on the love for the other which has found its expression in the golden rule, is the Law and the prophets i.e. is the Torah of God. As the most near parallel, therefore, the targum of Jerusalem on Lev 19,18 can be quoted: 'love your brother as yourself so that you will not do to him what you reject for yourself'(162). The torah on brotherly love and the formulation of the golden rule come together here. Matthew wanted to say exactly the same.

One last remark. The conclusion 'for this is the Law and the prophets' has a special literary effect which is worth mentioning. As conclusion it refers to the opening passage on 'Law and prophets': the introductory sentences which introduce the legal texts in the Sermon on the Mount: 'do not think that I have come to suspend the Law and the prophets'(163). The inclusion, which is developed in this way, gives an extra emphasis to the legal character of this passage. What in the prolegomenon on the explanation of the Law is stated as an adage, appears to retain its force till the end. It is the last indication of the suggestion that 7,1 - 12 should be seen as a re-lecture of the first group of legal texts. In his laws for the people Jesus does not go beyond the Torah of God.

The point in Matthew is, therefore, not only ethics, it is (also) a juridical principle or rather, more correctly, the ethics are contained in a legal order which is society-oriented. This brings me to the second observation on Dihle's reflections. Notwithstanding all the things which all kinds of people have said in many different ways, the golden rule is not limited to the micro level of the immediate mutual relations. They certainly speak about those too but they are only one aspect of a much broader way of thinking(164).

This is true from the first time the saying appears as an historically provable reality. Herodotus uses the saying twice(165). In his first instance he speaks about changing the tyrant Polycrates with Maiandraios. The latter addresses the people and says that, since the death of Polycrates, he has the possibility of ruling as a tyrant but, 'as far as possible I will not do what I abhor in others'. The other case deals with the murder of the ambassadors of Darius by the Spartans. This murder has brought them great trouble because they do not receive any more good omens. So they send ambassadors to Xerxes hoping that he will murder them in vengeance, but Xerxes answers that he will not do what he held against the Spartans. It is clear. The saying is placed in Herodotus in a context of a tyrannical system and in a context of the respect for foreign customs among peoples.

Isocrates is the other early author where the saying is found. It is used again in the context of matters of state. In Ad Nicocles he treats the duties of a good king, who should exercise his authority over the masses but who should, at the same time, be aware that he has to preserve their good will. A good king must look for the well-being of the πόλις. He will take care of things in the same way as he takes care of his fatherly inheritance. He treats the weaker cities as he wishes that the stronger cities will treat him(166). In the treatise Nicocles, the same problem of the 'good king' is treated with similar advice. The golden rule refers of the way of caring for one's own possessions and for those of others(167). Finally, in the Panegyricus the reasoning is about the great merits of Athens and Sparta for the freedom of Greece. Their citizens are praised because they were doing their best for the states as if they were involved in a contest, not to come out as victors but in the interest of their own πόλις. They did not want tyranny or despotism but real leadership. They could be taken on their word 'demanding in themselves the same attitude towards inferiors as they received from superiors, since they thought of the individual towns as their own abode, but of Greece as the fatherland of all'(168). Again, it is clear: the golden rule is used in a context which deals with the well-being of the state.

There is no need to look at all the texts. The principle is clear: the context determines how the golden rule must be interpreted. For Matthew this means that we should read his text in the context of what is said before: the encompassing cadre which is indicated by 'measure for measure', the emphasis on the legal character of all his statements, the special connection with generosity: they are all indications of the fact that Matthew understood his saying much more in a social way than the micro-ethical observations of exegetes give rise to. As halachah speaking the torah of God - even though obviously the immediate mutual relational level is not excluded - it is meant as a guideline open for many more explicitations.

Chapter VI
NOT WORDS BUT DEEDS
Mt 7, 13-27

It has been said that after the impressive torah about mutual love, there is an anti-climax: a series of sayings which are totally unrelated. At first sight it is not too clear how we could see a relation in these sayings. The mashal about the two roads and the two gates, the pronouncement against the pseudo-prophets, the condemnation of Christian prophets, and the mashal about the two houses: their content is indeed without much relation, but this does not mean that there are no mutual connections.

V. Fusco showed(1) that there are three reasons why this whole passage should be seen as a unity:
1) In each of the four pericopes there is the idea of a contrary opposition, which does not leave room for an alternative middle ground: the narrow road and gate are opposed to the broad road and gate; the good tree is opposed to the bad one; doing the will of the Father is opposed to saying it, but not doing it; the house on the rock is opposed to the house on sand.
2) This opposition is about doing and not doing. The verb 'to do' appears in three of the four pericopes: to do the will of the Father; to do the words of Jesus or not to do. It is only the first pericope which does not have this verb, but there it has been replaced by the imperative 'enter into the narrow gate'.
3) In all the pericopes the background is forensic-eschatological: the alternative do/not to do is systematically given the meaning of the alternative salvation/non-salvation. The broad gate leads to downfall, the narrow one to life; the bad tree will be cut down and thrown into the fire; whoever says Lord, Lord, but does not do the will of the Father, will be excluded from his presence; the house on the rock will stand and the house on the sand will perish.

The passage wants to bring the hearers to make the right choice. A lot is at stake, but that will only become clear at the end of time. To do is the final criterion: people will be judged by their deeds, not their words. This deals again with a Jewish theologoumenon which refers to the Law. The Torah should not just be heard, it needs to be done. Only then is God's will fulfilled and only then will the promises of the Law become reality.

The opening and closing sayings indicate reward and threat. The opening saying deals with the degree of difficulty: to reach the city on the narrow road and through the narrow gate. Many are led astray. They think they can enter on the broad road and through the broad gate, but they do not understand the times in which they live. There is danger on all sides as there is in a war. Whoever does not keep hidden but seeks to get into the city on a difficult road and through a narrow, unguarded gate, will perish before he has even reached the city. The closing saying shows the result of the choice: whoever hears and does is as a man who builds his house on rock which will stand forever; whoever hears and does not do it lives in a house built on sand which will fall down at the first downpour.

In the main part of the passage, Matthew makes Jesus speak about the danger of pseudo-prophets in whom we see the opposition between saying and doing in an examplary way. Again, there are 'many', all sorts of people, who sometimes by accident, sometimes permanently, sometimes consciously, sometimes unconsciously are in contact with supernatural and preternatural forces, which enable them with the help of Jesus' name to make predictions, to drive out demons, and to heal the sick. One should think of some kind of magic by which people, who are living in (small) places and in (restricted) milieus, can do rather extraordinary things. Matthew warns his people to be alert. If they accept money, if they do not act according to their words, if they lead people astray, one should not listen to them. Determinant is that one can recognise them from the fact that they do either the will of the Father or not. Moses' Law, as the will of the Father as made known by Jesus, is again the last criterion to test Jesus' disciples.

the two gates and the two roads

Mt 7,13 - 14

The mashal about the two gates and the two roads has known an important 'Wirkungsgeschichte' from the beginning. Prepared and supported by parallel texts, it has been taken up in the eschatological imagary of humanity as a description of the non-apocalyptic last judgment. The difficult, dangerous and lonely road is opposed to the easy, broad and joyful highway. Each individual is responsible for what he does. At the end of his life-road it will become clear whether he made the right choice. Whoever enters by the narrow gate will come into the beautiful light but he who chooses the broad gate will fall into a terrible pool.

In the 'Testament of Abraham'(2) we probably find the first indication of this interpretation of Matthew's text. It has been taken up narratively in the description of a journey to heaven by Abraham, who is accompanied by the 'angelus interpres' Michael. When Abraham arrives at the first gate of heaven, he sees the two roads and the two gates as described in Matthew(3). The gates are described quite explicitly: indirectly via the description of the behaviour of a man who sits on a golden throne before the gates, and directly via the explanation of the angel, who reveals to Abraham what happens at these gates. The man on the golden throne is Adam. He is sad when he sees how many souls are lost. He is happy when many (still relatively few) are saved(4): 'And when he (= Adam) sees many souls entering through the strait gate, then he arises and sits on his throne rejoicing and exulting cheerfully, because this strait gate is (the gate) of the righteous, which leads to life, and those who enter through it come into Paradise. And on account of this, the first-formed Adam rejoices, since he sees the souls being saved. And when he sees many souls entering through the broad gate, he pulls the hair of his head and casts himself on the ground crying and wailing bitterly; for the broad gate is (the gate) of the sinners, which leads to destruction and eternal punishment'(5). One can see how the interpretation is made. The Matthean expression 'the strait gate which leads to life' is surrounded by a double formulation: by 'it is the gate of the righteous' and by 'those who enter through it come into Paradise'; in the same way 'the broad gate which leads to destruction' is introduced by 'it is the gate of the sinners' and is explained with 'to eternal punishment'.

The metaphor of the two roads, whether in combination with the two gates or not, can be found all through classical literature. There are Greek, Hellenistic, Hebrew and Roman authors who, in one way or another, use this metaphor to urge their readers to make the right choice. In as far as I can get an overview of this varied situation, I can see four types(6)

1) In its most general form, which is also the most widely used, there are two roads which lead to opposed destinations. The destination can be described in different ways, but includes always the basic contrary concepts: light or darkness, life or death, good or evil, justice or injustice, virtue (ἀρετή) or vice, truth or untruth, reward or punishment(7). It is not always clear whether the metaphor of the road is seen as a description of reality, because the moralising aspect sometimes takes the upper hand. The

road, so to say, is overgrown with a multitude of commands and prohibitions which try to indicate the concrete fundamental option(8). It seems that in other cases there is no real alternative because it deals more with a form of anthropology: 'God has granted two ways to the sons of men, two mind-sets, two lines of action, two models and goals. Accordingly, everything is in pairs, the one over against the other. The two ways are good and evil; concerning them are two dispositions within our breasts that chooses between them'(9). The metaphor of the double road is retained as metaphor only when there is a choice: 'Thus says the Lord: I give you a choice between the road to life and the road to death'(10). The author obviously does not see this as a real alternative, but that is the way it is presented in order to lead the reader to the good road.

2) More effectively, or at least more explicitely, we see this in the second type. The roads are given their own special attributes which correspond to the destination. In accordance with a special persuasive technique - one wants to lure the reader to agree - the road, which leads to the good destination, gets positive qualities ascribed to it. The rejection follows the opposite argument. The road of the 'law abiders' is broad and easy to walk, but the road of the lawless is difficult and narrow. One can find this way of presenting things in various places in Proverbs. The roads of the wise are straight, those of the foolish twisted and winding(11); the roads of the just shine as a light till it is daylight, but those of the godless are dark: they do not know over what they fall(12); their road is full of thorns, but those of the strong are well trodden(13) - on which one can walk easily. It is a train of thought which Philo has also made his own. The road of the ἀρετή is one which carries people(14), a highway which is safe, broad and dry(15), but the road of the κακία should rather be called a non-road(16), because it is so muddy and narrow(17). Because of his Egyptian background, Philo sees this on the plain, on sandy roads which are metalled or not and which lead straight to their destination or not. Dio Chrysostomos has a similar image, but he thinks from the background of rocky country(18): 'Then, taking him (= Herakles) in charge, he (= Hermes) led him over a secret path untrodden of man till he came to a conspicuous and very lofty mountain peak whose sides were dreadfully steep with sheer precipices and with the deep gorge of a river that encompassed it, whence issued a mighty rumbling and roaring. Now to anyone looking up from below the crest above seemed single; but it was in fact double, rising from a single base; and the two peaks were

far indeed from each other. The one of them bore the name Peak Royal and was sacred to Zeus; the other, Peak Tyrannous, was named after the giant Tryphon. There were two approaches to them from without, each having one. The path that led to Peak Royal was safe and broad, so that a person mounted on a car might enter thereby without peril or mishap, if he had the permission of the greatest of the gods. The other was narrow, crooked and difficult, so that most of those who attempted it were lost over the cliffs and in the flood below, the reason being, methinks, that they transgressed justice in taking the path'(19).

3) In a number of places one finds the types of thinking in combination: good and evil are presented in a more complicated way. About the road leading to evil it is said that it is more easily passable. But the road to good is more complicated: in the beginning it is difficult and onerous, but there is a point where it becomes easy and enjoyable. This presentation is among the oldest in our culture. It is already present in Hesiodos:

I say important things for you to hear,
O foolish Perses: Badness can be caught
In great abundance, easily: the road
To her is level, and she lives nearby.
But Good is harder, for the gods have placed
In front of her much sweat; the road is steep
And long and rocky at the first, but when
You reach the top, she is not hard to find,
For the difficulties are done away(20).

In the contemporaneity of the Matthew text, one can indicate really only one text which presents a similar picture(21): the philosophical treatise 'Pinax of Cebes' (22). About the road to real Paideia (Education) it is said at a certain moment that it is initially very difficult, narrow and rocky; then one comes to a high hill where a narrow lane with steep abysses runs and then one arrives at an impassable rock, which can be climbed only with the help of the women, Self-Control and Perseverance. From that moment the path to Paideia is beautiful, even, easily passable and clean(23). The road to good is initially difficult but there is a reward. Whoever dares to walk it will arive in a better situation which makes it easy to go on. I will come back to this treatise because of a number of parallels with the Matthew text.

4) The fourth and last type connects immediately with the Matthew text: the road to good is difficult and the road to evil is easy. It is remarkable that there are only few parallel texts. The metaphor used is apparently more

extraordinary than one thinks because one is so used to it. In this case, there is a double Philo text in which he explains Gen 49,17 (LXX)(24): 'Let Dan become a serpent in the way, seated on the beaten track, biting the horse's heel. By 'track' is meant the road for the horses and carriages trodden by men and by beasts of burden. They say that pleasure is very like this road; for almost from birth to late age this road is traversed and used as a promenade and a place of recreation in which to spend leisure hours not by men only but by every other kind of living creatures. For there is no single thing that does not yield to the enticement of pleasure, and get caught and dragged along in her entangling nets, through which it is difficult to slip and make your escape. But the roads of sound-sense and self-mastery and of the other virtues, if not untrodden, are at all events unworn; for scanty is the number of those that tread them'(25). Philo puts this as an adage in his 'Allegorical Interpretation': 'the path of virtue is unworn for few tread it, while that of vice is well-worn'(26).

We find a number of elements from Matthew here: the road to good is difficult and the road to evil is easy and enjoyable; there is a disproportion between the few who choose the difficult road and the many who look for their own pleasure. Notwithstanding that, there are differences even in the use of the metaphor let alone the application. There is no mention of gates which provide access to something and the element of 'finding' the narrow road and gate is absent too.

One finds all this back in the Pinax of Cebes. On the narrative level of the story, it is said that a number of people are on a visit to the temple of Kronos, where they admire the votive offerings. They come to an image on a 'pinax', the meaning of which they cannot discover. They see some kind of fence within which there are two other fences, one larger than the other. According to them it looks like an army barracks or a city. Because of their interest in the painting an old man is willing to explain, and it becomes clear that there is even more to see than they had thought as simple tourists.

It is an allegorical painting. The high fence represents life. To enter one must pass through a gate where a woman lets men drink from Error and Ignorance and the women, Honour, Desire and Pleasure, lead them on. Because of the Snare some people are 'saved' and others are 'lost'(27). Lady Fortune is also present, sitting on a shaky stone which makes some happy and some sad. If people have received something from Lady Fortune, they are surrounded by women who look like hetaerae: Immoderateness, Dissipation, Greed and Flattery. They deceive people. They lead them on to the larger fence, one of the two which are found within the large one representing life. They take care to keep them under their protection till they hand them over to Punishment who brings them through a narrow gate to a dark place. There the Ladies Punishment, Sadness, Pain and Despondency, receive them. With the help of Lady Sorrow they manage to escape from this fenced-in area(28).

One then arrives at a second fence where True Education is found who, once she is found, will bring 'salvation' (29) and make people happy and blessed. One always has to pass Pseudo-Education and 'many' as well as the hasty(30) are content with that, because they believe they have found True Education. But they are in error because the road to True Paideia is a lonely road: there is a small gate and a road in front of the gate which is not much frequented, but quite a few go into it as if there were some obstruction, for it seems rough and stony(31). We have arrived now at the place (and the text) which I quoted before. Initially the road to Education is very difficult: first there is a high hill with a steep path and abysses on all sides, then there is the large and high rock which goes straight up and where one is drawn up by the Ladies Self-Control and Endurance. After a rest, one can go on one's own along the beautiful, even, easily passable and clean road(32). One then arrives at a holy forest in which there is a beautiful grassy place filled with light. In there we find a new fence: the home of the blessed. Near the gate sits Lady Paideia on a square stone, surrounded by Truth and Persuasion. Inside this fence is another road which leads to the acropolis and on its gate sits Lady Bliss. However nice it is there one cannot stay. The Virtues bring one back so that one can see how badly off are the other people who have not been able to 'find' the road there(33).

As one can see, there is much ado about fences, roads and gates which all fit into one another as the 'matrushkas' of a Russian egg. It is good to see in how many details the metaphor used is similar to the one Matthew uses: the roads and the gates, the differences between degrees of ease and difficulty, the distinction between error and truth, the downfall and the salvation, and, finally, the remark that it is not self-evident that people find the right road. Many are led astray and only few have found the proper access. Notwithstanding that, the Cebes text, in the final analysis, attempts a totally different application. In metaphors things are never easy.

Following some authors(34), J.D.M. Derrett recently raised the question for exegesis in Matthew research that there is a need to investigate more accurately to what situation in real life this metaphor alludes. He correctly accepts that, unlike the Cebes text where on each level a construction is fashioned, Matthew's text is much closer to reality. He made some interesting suggestions himself. Matthew's mashal deals with a city which next to the large gate possesses a small one. The large gate is on the πλατεῖα: the main street which leads to the market place and where publicans naturally keep their business(35). Everything, which enters or leaves the city, is taxable. Every merchant will try to evade paying; he will try to prevent (part of) his merchandise from being lost (the 'downfall' which is part of the broad road and gate). However well the city is guarded, there is always an unguarded entrance, a narrow gate, a hole in the wall where one can try to enter safely. But one needs to know how to find it.

The problem with this explanation is that the author must presuppose that the merchants, or even the people who carry their wares on their head, will have managed only very rarely to enter along this by-pass, normally speaking. Also the authorities know how people enter. Entering by the narrow gate the furtive intruder is in danger of losing all his merchandise. True, they have escaped with their 'lives', but that would be the same, if they had entered through the main gate.

So it remains an open question of which real situation Matthew was thinking in this mashal: what should we imagine in this strange opposition between 'life' and 'downfall' in combination with the trouble one must take to find the narrow road and entrance to the preservation of life? It is clear that what is at stake is some kind of mountainous place, because in the plain no road can remain hidden and there would be no need for a narrow and dangerous access road(36). One could check with some geographers. In any case, we find in Josephus a number of descriptions of places, with topographical and historical particulars, which would fit in quite nicely with what this mashal presupposes as reality. They are cities and fortresses which in his description of war play an important role. I think that three of them should be considered.

1) Jotapata is described in the following way: 'The town of Jotapata is almost entirely built on precipitous cliffs, being surrounded on three sides by ravines so deep that sight fails in the attempt to fathom the abyss. On the north side alone, where the town has straggled sideways up a descending spur of mountains, it is accessible'(37). In the rest of the text this 'not-north-side' plays an important role. 'Josephus devised another stratagem to procure himself supplies in abundance. There was, leading

down to the ravine on the west side, a gully so difficult to traverse that it had been neglected by the enemy's outposts'(38). Josephus sends letters via this gully and gets answers. Mainly, he succeeds in bringing provisions into the city by letting his people crawl through like dogs, with vats on their back till the Romans discover the ruse and block the access.

2) Gamala is one of the last cities which surrendered, because it thought itself impregnable because of its situation. 'From a lofty mountain there descends a rugged spur rising in the middle to a hump, the declivity from the summit of which is of the same length before as behind, so that in form the ridge resembles a camel; whence it derives its name, the natives pronouncing the sharp sound of that word inaccurately. Its sides and face are cleft all round by inaccessible ravines, but at the tail end where it hangs on the mountain, it is somewhat easier of approach'(39). It is from this side that the Roman army eventually conquers the city fairly easily. Before the attack proper 'the people began to run from the town, down trackless ravines where no sentries were posted, or through the underground passages'(40); those are 'the more adventurous of the population who stealthily escape'(41).

3) Massada is most extensively described. There is no need to describe once again all the rocks. Important is the fact that there is a second entrance. 'Of these tracks one leads from the Lake Asphaltitis on the east, the other by which the approach is easier, from the west. The former they call the snake, seeing a resemblance to that reptile in its narrowness and continual windings; for its course is broken in skirting the jutting crags and, returning frequently upon itself and gradually lengthening out again, it makes painful headway. One traversing this route must firmly plant each foot alternately. Destruction faces him; for on either side yawn chasms so terrific as to daunt the hardiest'(42). The road on the West side, which is much more easy to traverse, has been made difficult because Herod placed a large tower there: 'this tower it was neither possible to pass nor easy to capture; exit being rendered difficult even for passengers who had no cause for alarm'(43).

Reading the mashal against the background of these geographically-oriented war descriptions, Matthew's text deals with a city as a place of refuge. People flee there, because their life is in danger. 'Many' cannot make it because they take the broad road and gate which lead to destruction. Only 'few' find the good but narrow and dangerous road. It is a time of danger and distress and the city on the mountain promises preservation of life. Downfall threatens on all sides as the many who choose the easy road find out to their sorrow.

This interpretation presupposes that the participium-construction: πολλοί οἱ εἰσερχόμενοι δι' αὐτῆς is seen as a 'participium de conatu': Many try to enter the city through this road (resp. through this gate)(44), but they do not succeed(45). The city represents life, not a combination of life and downfall. It is, in this mashal, no different from the imagary of the meal: the man, who managed to enter without the proper dress, is thrown out before he can become a participant(46), in the same way as the five foolish girls are not allowed to enter(47). Under the dominion of heaven there is a separation of reward and punishment, but it does not happen in the same place: there is fire, the Gehenna of fire, an oven of fire, and next to that there is the light of the dominion of the Father, life itself. They are two realities which in locality are separate: within or without, above or beneath(48).

If the mashal about the roads and the gates indicates a city - as in the Pinax of Cebes - and not a combination of roads which come from nowhere and lead to nowhere, whose gates are only access to salvation or damnation - as in Abraham's Testament - then the logic of the image demands that the access through the narrow gate, which promises life, will function differently from the access through the broad gate. The place itself, as a city, guarantees the finding of life and its preservation. All the things which represent downfall are without. Josephus' texts indicate how in war situations precisely the difference between narrow and broad, between hidden and overt in combination with difficult and easy, means the difference between life and death.

I would not have the right to present this interpretation, if there was not a text in Matthew which corresponds with this train of thought. I think I have found it in his eschatological address. He talks there about war situations, wars and rumours of war, about earthquakes and famines, in a mixture of prophecy and realised events. It is also important that he always speaks about 'many' who lead 'many' astray - to be led astray is not to be taken only in an intellectual context -, many will say in Jesus' name that they are the Christ and they will lead many astray. They are pseudo-prophets and pseudo-christs who, if that were possible, would lead even the elect astray. The love of many will cool through the abundance of lawlessness. Where the corpse is, the vultures will gather(49). Matthew lived at a time in which apocalyptic events had happened and were still expected.

Apart from the history of the origin of the mashal, the saying functions actually in a time in which this apocalyptic situation is experienced as reality. The road of the 'many' is the wrong track. They will lead many astray through their actions. The only road, which leads within, is narrow and filled with θλῖφις: it calls forth the hatred and persecution of the others. Whoever perseveres till the end will be saved. It seems to me that the fact that Matthew immediately after this saying says: 'look out for the pseudo-prophets', is a not negligible argument in favour of this train of thought.

We must add two observations so that we can understand the mashal in the total context of Matthew. First of all, the opposition between Peter (and the disciples) over against the Pharisees and scribes, in relation to 'admission policy', is important. Peter is promised that 'the ekklesia will be built on this rock and that the keys of the dominion of heaven will be given to him, which he can open and close'(50). There is mention again of a city on a rock, defended by a gate which can give access or deny it. Peter's choice is decisive. Over against this are the Pharisees and scribes, presented as people who close off the dominion of heaven, because they themselves will not enter, but they will also not allow others to enter, even though they want to(51) - see also the connection with the parable of the two sons and the road of justice along which John went(52). The mashal of Mt 7,13.14 is given in a context in which there is a discussion about letting people enter and going in. New leaders are opposed to old: internally the new christs are rejected as pseudo-christs, externally the discussion between Jesus and the Pharisees goes on.

Secondly, as far as content is concerned, the mashal is concretised only once in the whole of Matthew's gospel. The narrow and difficult road has as parallel image only the camel which has to go through the needle's eye(53): the difficult, if not impossible, condition for the rich to enter. Whoever wants to enter the dominion of heaven must be ready to renounce his riches and give them to the poor. The message may, by now, be known, but apparently it is not without reason that it keeps returning.

the rejection of the pseudo-prophets

Mt 7,15 - 20

The many, who try to enter through the broad gate, are under the influence of the 'many' pseudo-prophets who lead people astray. The mashal about the two gates is followed by a number of sayings, which bring to the fore a very special reality: there are pseudo-prophets in Matthew's community who are dangerous for the group and who are not aware that they themselves are in danger. There is a concern here which expresses itself in a warning: look out for the pseudo-prophets; not everyone who says 'Lord, Lord', will enter into the dominion of heaven.

This is a very special reality and the question is sometimes asked whether Matthew does not end his Sermon on the Mount with an anti-climax(54). After his broad-side is it possible that he thinks only of a small particular group? The answer is 'no'. There are probably 'many' for Matthew(55), and one should imagine this group as varied as possible: a collection of all those people who have something to do with predicting the future, with casting out demons, with healing the sick, gazing at stars, announcing disasters, pointing out the messiah etc. I will come back to this. But, a priori, we must accept that 'prophetism' is, for Matthew, an all-encompassing reality which existentially touches the lives of all people.

This is clear first of all and mainly(56) from the way in which Matthew deals with the main personage in his βίβλος. 'The life of Jesus' according to Matthew is seen from the contemporary ideology about the appearance of a prophet. Notwithstanding the fact that Matthew calls Jesus a prophet only a couple of times(57) and then only in passing - as a quote from what the masses say about Him -, his story about Jesus is embedded in an extensive cluster of 'prophetic realities'. From the very beginning till the final end Jesus' life stands under the inspiration of the divine spirit and can only be understood in that light.

I do not want to deal with this extensively, but it deserves to be concretised.

1) The first and most remarkable phenomenon is the numberless prophetical quotes which Matthew, in or (especially for the modern reader) out of season, adds to his story. They are absolutely typical of the Matthew gospel(58). There exists an extensive literature about this, which accentuates the 'fulfillment-character' in Jesus: in Jesus is fulfilled what the prophets have foretold. According to this vision they are Christologically-oriented pronouncements, using the authority of the biblical prophets to express and affirm Jesus' identity. But there is another aspect which is even more important in our context. This 'fulfillment' touches the prophets themselves. In the life, actions and words of Jesus, prophecies are fulfilled, which till that moment were still open. I think of something similar to that which Josephus writes about the prophecies

of Balaam: 'he foretold what calamities were to come for kings and what for cities of the highest celebrity (of which some had not yet so much as been inhabited at all), along with other events which have already befallen men in bygone ages, by land or sea, down to times within my memory. And from all these prophecies having received the fulfillment which he predicted, one may infer what the future also has in store'(59). A prophecy is only true when it is fulfilled. Because Matthew sees the prophecies of the biblical prophets fulfilled, he strengthens the trust in their credibility and reliability. Trustworthy prophets have foreseen how it would go with Jesus.

2) Very typical of Matthew is that he is the only evangelist who mentions dreams which determine the course of events in his story. Especially in the opening stories we find many dreams: Joseph hears in a dream that Mary's child is from the Holy Spirit; the Magi hear in a dream the oracle not to return to Herod; an angel of the Lord reveals to Joseph in a dream that he must flee from Herod and, later, that he must return to Israel and once again that he must retire to Galilee(60). Jesus' life is protected by truthful and holy 'dreams of oracle'(61). That is also the motive, when Pilate's wife lets him know, at the moment that he is already seated on the justice bench, that she has had a dream this night and suffered much for the sake of this just man(62). In the dream there is a struggle about Jesus' life, but the story does not go on to say that the dream is listened to.

3) The way Matthew elaborates on the miraculous phenomena after Jesus' death is quite remarkable. The 'tearing of the curtain' hanging in the Temple, mentioned also in Mark, is expanded with a whole series of τέρατα: the earthquake, the splitting of the rocks, the opening of the tombs, the resurrection of many people and their appearance in the holy city. Other cosmic events are related in the story of the resurrection: a strong earthquake, an angel who comes down from heaven whose face looks like lightning and whose clothes are like snow(63). It is a kind of ὅραμα parallel to what happens on the high mountain where Jesus changes in appearance before his disciples Peter, James and John.

4) Not so typical of Matthew, but nevertheless it is necessary to mention the 'miracles and signs' which Jesus performs as 'indicia' of the presence and the coming of God's dominion. Mt 11,5 sums them up as 'the works of the Messiah': the blind can see again, the lame can walk, the lepers are cleansed, the deaf can hear and dead are

resurrected, the good news is given to the poor(64). Forces of nature are not excluded: the wind and the storm, walking on the water, the withering of the fig tree. It is typical of Matthew to bring his stories together in groups which have a closing sentence which explicitates the 'prophetical' air(65); also typical is that Matthew makes Jesus' adversaries ask twice for a sign from heaven and that both times they are referred to the sign of Jonah, the prophet (66).

5) A similar remark can be made about the exorcisms which Jesus practises. Matthew relates a number of situations where the devils are cast out by Jesus(67). Jesus overpowers the demons with divine power. By casting him out, Satan's power is diminished, and God's dominion is extended. It is typical of Matthew that he refers to the last judgment as the final victory. Now, at this moment, good and evil are still co-existent as are the good seed and the weeds, and as the good and the evil are both invited for the festive dinner. The separation will take place at the last judgment(68).

6) Jesus as the one who predicts future events.
All through the gospel we see Jesus as a person who knows what the future will bring. This is true for his own life: he predicts what will happen to him(69) - one cannot apply to him what in the critique on the prophets occasionally is used as a counter-argument(70) - he predicts also the suffering and persecution which his disciples will have to suffer(71). Jesus is presented in Matthew as a forecaster, an announcer of disasters and adversity. He foresees the downfall of cities(72), the ruin of the Temple and the destruction of the world in wars, famine and cosmic confusion in connection with the coming of the Son of Man(73). Salvation is often indicated in one single sentence.

7) Matthew presents Jesus occasionally as someone who has ecstatic experiences. One should think of the temptation story in which the Devil talks to Jesus and takes him along to the Holy City and to a high mountain(74); of the events which happen on the high mountain in the presence of John, James and Peter; of the revelation-saying, put in his mouth, about what has been revealed to him by the Father (75); more typical of Matthew, one should think of the 'bat qol' from the mouths of children who shout 'Hosanna to the Son of David' in the Temple(76). Matthew presents it as if it has been revealed to Jesus that 'access to God is given to small children'(77).

8) Finally, the assignment to Jesus' disciples(78): a number of these realities are handed on by Jesus as an assignment for his disciples. We find them together as a cluster in chapter 10: the task to heal and to bring peace, but also to curse; the promise that, even in the dangerous situation of persecutions, they will be able to speak freely because of the Spirit from the Father; the prediction that they also will be accused of being possessed by the Devil; the safety with God and, finally, the promise that whoever will be hospitable to these prophets will be richly rewarded. In the chapter of parables is added that the disciples are initiated in the 'secrets': an initiation which fits in with a prophetical fulfillment of a text from Isaiah about understanding and not understanding, and with the fulfillment of the desire of many prophets and just people. Matthew's point is that one will 'understand' this because whoever accepts the word and understands it will bear fruit(79). Jesus' disciples are prophets: therefore, the fate of the prophets in Israel will also be theirs(80).

We must read the passage about the prophets in the Sermon on the Mount against this whole broad background. Matthew sees prophecy as an all-encompassing reality under all aspects. Not only does it encompass more realities than one could easily imagine, but it is also an extended phenomenon in this sense that in Matthew's community probably more people participate in it than one would think if one looks at it from one's own experience(81). The fact that Matthew foresees many pseudo-prophets in the future suggests, anyway, that he is not thinking about an end to prophecy. To the contrary, a real battle will be fought about prophetical activity. The saying against the false prophets in the Sermon of the Mount is one aspect of this battle.

Before we enter into the text itself, we should determine how far this passage extends. There are some advantages in reading the text without caesura between 7,20 and 7,21 ff. The content in 7,22, prophecy, casting out devils and performing miracles in Jesus' name, gives some concretisation so that we have at least some way of imagining something in connection with the pseudo-prophets. Combining this with 'coming in sheep's clothes', they are wandering Christian prophets who preach one thing and do something else. Their 'lawlessness' proves that they are charlatans, or, as said by D.E. Aune, 'the norms of Christian behaviour, represented by Matthew and his circle, are not completely accepted by these itinerant prophets'(82). An argument in favour of this combined reading is that, apart from the overflow of meaning from one passage to the next, (both deal with prophets and the abuses to be denounced), in Mt 24,11.12 the pseudo-prophets are associated with 'lawlessness'; this would then be true also in reverse for Mt 7,23.

I am not sure whether this argument is valid. The concept 'lawlessness' belongs to the 'Wortfeld' of a pseudo-prophet, but this cannot be said vice versa, at least not for Matthew(83). Would it not be better to forget a combined reading of the two passages? They do not deal with entirely different realities obviously, but they do have their own individual option. Mt 7,15 - 20 functions on the level of ideology, in this case the contemporary critique on prophets. It presupposes certain practices, but we cannot find out much about them. Mt 7,21 - 23 speaks in a much clearer language in this respect. It is a text which is embedded in a describable concrete reality of prophecy (in the broad sense of the word). Against this background the text takes an explicit Christian stand.

the wolves in sheep's clothing

The text opens with a description which, even though more explicit than all the following sentences, still gives us difficulty in interpretation. Are the sheep's clothes literal or metaphorical? O. Böcher(84) makes a strong case, in a rather impressive study, for the view that Matthew may have thought, with these sheep's clothes, of something similar to the dress which biblical prophets used and which was, therefore, also used by John the Baptist. The text would then allude to people who enter the community disguised as prophets, dressed only in sheepskin. They pretend to be prophets by their dress, but in reality, they are rapacious wolves. This suggestion is attractive(85), but the argument is weak. One would have to accept that animal skins, clothes from animal wool, camel's hair, sheep's wool and the 'saq' all have the same meaning as the typical clothing of the prophet(86) and that is asking too much.

Matthew probably did not intend to speak so explicitly. Enough content remains in the imagary. It is typical of Matthew, anyway, that he sees the opposition between sheep and wolf as an opposition between the exterior and the interior. This brings his pronouncement in line with his critique on the Pharisees and scribes, especially with his reproach that they (too) are filled inside with rapacity (and love of pleasure)(87). Therefore, what is in question are evaluative differences. The pseudo-prophets think that they are doing something which is allowed, while Matthew rejects it as improper. It is generally accepted that this means that these people probably accepted money in some form or other for their services. They would see nothing strange in that, but it is sharply criticised by Matthew: they present themselves as innocent sheep but, in fact, they are only after money.

Matthew's text does not give much ground for this interpretation, but one could connect the text with the image of the rapacious wolf(88), as is demonstrated in two other texts.

1) In Ezek 22, which speaks about corruption in Israel-kings, priests, leaders, prophets and the people themselves are guilty of all kinds of evil - it says in 22,27 (LXX): 'The leaders in their midst are wolves who go out plundering to shed blood so that they can enrich themselves in their avarice, and their prophets will fall because they silence them, see worthless things, prophesy in deceit by saying: 'Thus speaks the Lord', and the Lord has not spoken'(89). Presupposed is here some kind of evil covenant between the prophets and the leaders of the people so that they can enrich themselves through the services of the prophets. It is not stated that the prophets accept money, but they are in close contact with the leaders of the people, who like rapacious wolves, enrich themselves in their avarice.

2) Acts 20,29 is without doubt closer to Matthew. Luke lets Paul give a farewell speech in his discourse in Ephesus to the elders: after his departure wild wolves will come who will not spare the flock; from their midst people will come forward who will draw away the disciples with their twisted doctrine. Two dangers are envisaged: wolves coming from outside, false teachers from within. Can we identify these two groups as one? The wolves could also be the persecutors who will not spare the flock, who will attack the flock in the future. But the rest of the text does not suggest this. Rather the reverse, because there is talk only about the unpaid working activities of Paul as a model for all the leaders in the church. That this is the aim of the address becomes clear in the closing sentence: it is better to give than to receive. It is clear, anyway, that Luke rejects the idea that people will accept money for their services in the community

This prohibition to accept money is discussed also in Matthew in an important place - the mission address to the disciples - and in a remarkable way(90). After the apostles have been given the mission to go out to be heralds of the dominion of heaven, to heal the sick and to cast out demons, i.e. after they have been sent out as prophets, it reads: 'for nothing you have received, for nothing you will give. Do not acquire gold or silver or copper in your belts'. Even keeping possessions is made impossible: they are not allowed to take along a sack. This means, anyway, that the prohibition to accept money is of importance to Matthew too. The labourer is worthy of his keep, but this should not take the form of a salary.

With this criticism Matthew connects with a topos from the critique on the prophets which is fairly widespread from classical ancient times until far in Hellenistic times(91). In Christianity one finds it especially in the later documents: in Acts via the discussion between Peter and Simon Magus in Samaria, who believes that he can buy the Holy Spirit with money(92); in the story about the prophesying slave-woman who brings in a lot of money for her masters and who shouts after Paul and his companions that they are the servants of the most high God(93); in the rejection of the trade in statuettes of Artemis in Ephesus (94); and as already mentioned in the farewell address of Paul. The author of Acts seems to connect immediately with the advice from Didachè that a prophet who prophesies for his own pocket must be rejected. The good prophet pleads the cause of others(95). One's own interest and the interest of others must be clearly distinct. Paul did this according to Luke, but of the prophet Agabus a similar story is told(96). In the early post-apostolic Church the problem clearly exists. The rather frequent admonitions against it(97) speak clearly.

From texts of Josephus and Philo(98) it appears that this criticism was uttered also within Judaism. Philo is interesting because he connects this criticism with the Balaam story: the preferred place of the Jewish criticism of prophets in this era. The gifts, which the emissaries from Balak carry - also according to the scripture text- to persuade Balaam to come with them, have become in Philo 'gifts at once and to follow'(99), a presentation which is repeated with the second group of emissaries 'who brought more money and promised more abundant gifts to entice Balaam'(100). When Balaam departs after all the unwanted blessings of Israel, he hears the reproach from Balak at the end: 'Most foolish of men, of what story of wealth and presents, of what fame and glory, hast thou robbed thyself by thy madness'(101). Balaam takes this to heart and advises Balak via the women of Moab to seduce the men from Israel to apostasy. Balaam is the prototype of the reprehensible prophet. He does not know how to withstand the temptation which the office of prophet carries with it. He is an easy touch for the money. It is interesting that the story of Balaam is told twice for the same reason in the post-apostolic literature of the New Testament: in Jude 11 against the people who have 'dreams' because they give themselves completely to Balaam's error 'because of the money'; and in 2 Peter 2,15 against the pseudo-prophets who follow the road of Balaam, the lover of unjust wages(102). If prophecy becomes connected with money, something is fundamentally wrong.

you will know them from their fruits

The mashal about the fruits and the trees is rather complicated, when we look at it more closely. There are a number of pronouncements which are closely related and which, furthermore, merge more or less in the metaphor used. To what reality it refers must remain largely hidden. But we can say a few things about it, even though a number of questions will remain.

The beginning and end are the establishment of a hallmark. The repetition indicates the importance which the author gives to the statement: 'from their fruits it will become clear, that one deals with pseudo-prophets'. The fruits must, therefore, be unacceptable. What could be the meaning? The first meaning offered is the possibility that these prophets demonstrate a discrepancy between what they say and what they do. Fruits are then the deeds which are evil, because they are not in accordance with what they impress upon others: they talk about it, but they do not do it.

The interesting aspect of this interpretation is that it fits in with a typically Matthean theme(103): integrity between saying and doing; the connection with his anti-Pharisee criticism especially in the beginning of chapter 23; and the connection with the main theme of the immediate context(104). In any case such an interpretation would not go beyond Matthew's intention.

The parable of the weeds and its authorised explanation (105) fill this in and give a closer concretisation. Only when the fruits appear does it become clear that weeds are sowed together with the good seed. Notwithstanding the protest of the slaves the lord of the field allows the weed to grow with the good seed, but at the harvest the weeds shall be burned(106). From Matthew's interpretation it appears that with the weeds are meant 'the sons of the evil one' who are σκάνδαλα and who 'act lawlessly'. The fruits of the weed are the evil deeds of people, the expression of their lawlessness, the offence in person(107). Even if this authorised interpretation of the parable does not coincide, as stated already, with the reality of the pseudo-prophets, the reverse is probably true. The fruits of the pseudo-prophets are fruits which one can expect from thistles and thorns: an imagary which runs completely parallel with what the parable says about weeds, i.e. the pseudo-prophets are, according to this interpretation, people who act contrary to what they say, people who do not respect the Law in their actions and thereby become an offence for people.

It is not possible to make it more concrete. As topos in the criticism of prophets it has a good future. The wrong actions will be colourfully described as carousing, guzzling at festive diners(108), as deceit, whoremongery, pedophilia etc(109). These descriptions appear, according to some authors, only in the later literature(110). They are descriptions in which reality and fantasy are not always clearly separated. Every action, which does not correspond to a strict norm, will be overemphasised from the viewpoint of an ascetical moralism.

The beginning of this way of thinking can, however, already be found in Philo. A prophecy can only be accepted if the prophet is prepared to impose strict norms on himself. He must be pure in soul and body, i.e. free of passion and cleansed from all that belongs to his mortal nature: eating and drinking and sexual contact. Philo can thus say about Moses: 'The intercourse with women he had disdained for many a day, almost from the time when, possessed by the spirit, he entered on his work as prophet, since he held it fitting to hold himself always in readiness to receive the oracular messages. As for eating and drinking, he had no thought of them for forty successive days, doubtless because he had the better food of contemplation'(111). In a similar vein he speaks about Tamar (112), and Samuel(113) and about Noah, Isaac and Moses (again): they could be prophets only, because they kept the Law faithfully(114). The human spirit must be freed in order to be capable to receive God's spirit(115).

Matthew is still at the beginning of this development, still fairly close to what the Mishnah says about the false prophet: the prophet who transgresses his words, his death is in the hands of heaven(116), cf. the story about the prophet from Judah who predicts the ruin of Jeroboam's altar, but who, by eating anyway in Jeroboam's city, transgresses the express command of God(117). The Lord is not to be ridiculed. The punishment for this transgression will come unfailingly.

no grapes from thorns, no figs from thistles

The interpretation, that the pronouncement about recognising by the fruits should be seen as an indictment of the discrepancy between acting and speaking, is, as we have said, only a possibility. For equally good reasons one could suppose that Matthew has taken these 'fruits' as 'what the prophets said': from the 'words' of the prophet one will know whether he is a good or a false prophet. That is an explanation of the metaphor 'tree and fruit' which Matthew himself gives. In a discussion about the question whether Jesus drives out demons with the help of satan or that he acts in the force of God's spirit - when the warning is given not to speak against the Holy Spirit -, the metaphor about the tree and its fruits is used and explained: 'from the fruit one can know the tree. Viperous brood, how can you say good things when you are evil? The mouth speaks from the fullness of the heart'(118). From the fact that the Pharisees say evil things about Jesus - that he drives out devils through Beelzebub - it is clear that they are evil. The fruits of this tree make clear what they are worth themselves.

J. Reiling(119) showed that this meaning connects with the LXX ideas on the pseudo-prophet. One must distinguish between two basic meanings. The verbal meaning deals with 'a prophet who tells things that are not true'; the nominal meaning is 'a person who falsely alleges to be a prophet'. The Septuagint translator(s) know only the verbal meaning, because they could not (yet) understand that within the same religion one can call upon the spirit of the Lord in two different ways. The pseudo-prophet speaks untruth and is associated with pagan fortune-telling and magic. In Matthew this is out of question. But it cannot be without reasons that his explanation is taken up in the context of the discussion about demonic powers and forces.

The only time Matthew gives the content of what the pseudo-prophets say, is found in his eschatological discourse, 'many will say in my name: 'I am the Christ', and they will lead many astray; many pseudo-christs and pseudo-prophets will rise who will do great signs and miracles'(120). Are we allowed to understand this as a total description of what Matthew understands by pseudo-prophets: this is what they say? And are these real persons whom Matthew, so to say, encountered in the flesh or is it only a literary topos in eschatology which Matthew borrowed from the text of Mark?(121).

It is difficult to decide whether, according to Matthew, the claim on being messiah is the only real false prophecy. It seems a form of reduction, but one should remember that in Jewish contemporary literature - in connection with Scripture - a similar reduction takes place: the pseudo-prophet is someone who leads to idolatry. The Mishnah states: even if such a one declares pure what is pure and impure what is impure - i.e. if he speaks according to the Halachah - he deserves death, because he speaks in the name of idolatry(122). The preeminent anti-model is again Balaam who, in many contemporary texts(123) in addition to Scripture, takes the initiative to lead Israel into idolatry by advising Balak to use the Moabitic women as a lure. Such a presentation connects with what the Torah has to say about the prophet who wants to bring the people to serve other gods. Although he performs signs and miracles and although what he says happens, he is not to be followed(124). The danger of idolatry is just around the corner. One should, therefore, always be aware of what a prophet has to say.

The second question - whether Matthew and his group have had concrete experiences with these pseudo-prophets - is also difficult to decide. This does not mean that the question remains without any answer. Matthew's pronouncements about pseudo-christs function in an era which has known such figures in abundance. Even if the hearers of the Matthew gospel have had no personal contact with these people, a connection is made via these texts.

Josephus is practically our only informant(125), but he is very informative in this respect. One can make a whole list of names and events which all belong in this context one way or another(126). There is mention of all kinds of people who, from prophetic consciousness, call the people to trust in God's help and to follow them. The time of the desert, the time of the signs of Moses, Joshua and Jeremiah has returned. They will prove it by their signs and miracles. But the Romans prevent time and again the decisive action from becoming reality: the crumbling of the walls of Jerusalem, the dividing of the Jordan, the finding of the holy vessels of Moses. The times are evil and liberation is still to be awaited.

The joy of discovery - to have found in Josephus an author who demonstrates that prophecy has not died out in Israel(127) - may not make us forget that all these people are cheats and swindlers for Josephus. Notwithstanding their prophetic consciousness and everything they achieve, their mission is a grand failure: the proof that they are not good prophets. They did not realise that the time for the liberation of Israel has not yet come. In the true prophecies - of Jeremiah and Daniel - we read that Jerusalem and the Temple will fall and that the Romans will be the victors in the battle. Whoever opposes that proves by his own words that he is a pseudo-prophet(128). In this way too we find a deep relationship between Matthew and Josephus.

a good tree has good fruits, a bad tree bad fruits

The metaphor of the tree and its fruits is brought one step further. Bad fruits point to a bad tree. One cannot expect good fruits from such a tree. The emphasis, which comes from the repetition, is on the negative aspect of the pronouncement. The pseudo-prophets are evil in themselves and one can only expect evil things from them. This is not anthropology(129). As ever, Matthew is pragmatic. He wants to warn his hearers of a danger which threatens them. Pseudo-prophets always cause disaster.

Three expressions show the direction of Matthew's thinking in this regard. First of all, the qualification of the fruits as σαπρός: a concept which points not only to the usefulness and worthlessness but also to the harmfulness(130). It is with the fruits as it is with the fish from the parable of the net: they are separated as good and bad fish: as useful, valuable and healty or as useless, worthless or harmful. Applied to the pseudo-prophets this means that it is wise and intelligent to leave them alone. They cannot bring one further. Secondly, already in the opening sentence it has been said that the pseudo-prophets are rapacious wolves. They are after their own interests which means disadvantage for the victims. They try to hide this, but one should not be deceived by outward appearances. Thirdly, the pseudo-prophets lead people astray. 'Error' is the only effect of their actions. This is an important theme for Matthew. In his eschatological discourse, it is a kind of leitmotiv; its final result is the 'cooling of love in many'. Time and again Matthew returns to this(131), foreseeing the error of many as a future event which puts pressure on the present. His telling of the parable of the lost sheep shows how much the author wants this theme to be understood in the context of divine concern and presence. God and his angels rejoice each time one of the lost is found(132).

The emphasis on the personal damage is again a topos in the critique on the prophets. The pseudo-prophets are not innocent people. Through guile, deceit and seduction they manage to get people to believe in them. A whole range of concepts is used to express this negative side: deceive (133), snare(134), seduce(135), lure(136);and on the other side we have words like: lead astray(137), be overpowered (138), be ruined and lose one's freedom(139). What kind of reality is involved cannot easily be guessed. The atmosphere is determined by polemics. One wants to warn the hearers because one foresees calamity or because one has seen, after the fact, where one made the wrong choice.

Josephus is a marvelous example of this. From the point of view of his general conviction that Jerusalem must fall according to the prophecies, he judges all other predictions. He sees a parallel with the history of former times, when the pseudo-prophets kept on predicting victory and the true prophets, who talked about the downfall, were maltreated and ridiculed(140). That is the way it has gone in his own time. All the signs pointed to the fact that ruin was imminent, but they were not seen. 'Numerous prophets, indeed, were at this period suborned by the tyrants to delude the people ... Thus it was that the wretched people were deluded at that time by charlatans and pretended messengers of the deity; while they neither heeded nor believed in the manifest portens that foretold the coming desolation but, as if thunderstruck and bereft of eyes and mind, disregarded the plain warnings of God'(141). The pseudo-prophets managed only because of their seduction to find a large following. The deluded people were the victims.

the tree with the bad fruit is cut down and thrown into the fire

The threat of punishment is the last topic. The image is taken from rural practices where a tree is used as firewood if the grafting is not successful or if it is not a fruit-tree. It is typical of Matthew that this threat must be taken eschatologically. There are two arguments for this.
1) The sentence is an exact repetition of what John the Baptist told his hearers according to Matthew(142). That is remarkable because, in order to achieve this effect, a transition from fruits (in the plural) to fruit (in the singular) is necessary. The metaphorical use of words is transparent in meaning also in the address of John the Baptist. The fruit, which is expected on the tree, is the fruit which should bring about μετάνοια. If this is absent there will be condemnation. All kinds of images are closely put together with the final meaning that the time is short and the threat of punishment serious. The axe at the root, baptism in water and in spirit and fire, the winnow in the hand with the double effect of the wheat in the granary and the chaff in the inextinguishable fire which stands for threat, punishment, judgment and condemnation. The fire which threatens the tree with the bad fruit is the punishment-side of the eschatological judgment.
2) There is a reference to the explanation of the parable of the weeds and the one of the net(143). The presentation is parallel to what has just been said. The eschatological judgment will come and there will then be a division between the good seed and the weeds, between the good and bad fish, between the just and those who act lawlessly, the evil ones. On the negative side there is the fire: an oven which is all ready where there is only weeping and grinding of teeth. The fact that the punishment has been developed more broadly - in the parable of the net it is developed as the only possibility - indicates how much emphasis this has for Matthew.

The threat of fire is thus a threat of condemnation, when the world comes to an end. There is no time indicated, but the initiative will be taken by the Son of Man, i.e. it will happen at the moment that the 'parousia' of the Son of Man comes.

The element of punishment is a general given as topos in the critique on the prophets. The pseudo-prophets will not be able to exercise their activities till the end without punishment. The moment will come when they will be exposed (144), when their deceit will be shown up because truth is stronger than lies(145), when the counter-forces, which they have called forth, will take the upperhand(146). Within the religious orientation of the literature of this era, this means that one sees that 'punishment at the end' is not separate from God's intervention. It is for God to execute the just punishment(147); or, as in the case of Revelation, where the Son of Man is speaking himself, a promise of heavenly intervention is announced(148). God himself is involved because prophecy is at stake.

One must read Peter's second letter to find a text which, in the same eschatological vein as Matthew, deals with the threat of fire for the pseudo-prophets. The treatise is one strong plea not to lose faith in the prophets and in the doctrine of the church on the parousia by listening to pseudo-prophets with their myths, their greed and licentiousness. Sentence has been pronounced, their downfall will not be long awaited. The downfall of the angels, of Noah's generation and that of Sodom and Gomorrah are brought in to prove how God knows to distuinghuish between good and evil. The pious will be saved, but He will keep the deepest darkness for the law breakers (149). The first world disappeared in water, this one will perish in fire(150), but a new heaven and a new earth will rise where justice will live. No false prophet will then be able to lead the pious astray and make them lose their stability. The punishment of the pseudo-prophet is a model for the punishment which threatens the whole cosmos.

the Christian prophets

Mt 7,21 -23

The picture of the Christian prophets is slowly being filled in with concrete images as in a jigsaw puzzle. The insight that they, according to Matthew, do not do anything else than what Jesus did before them, is important. He is the first and great prophet in whom the followers participate. It is a life in which the miraculous has its place, because it is filled with the force of Jesus' name: in the name of Jesus, the Lord, they prophesy, cast out demons and perform many miracles.

To begin with, I must refer to what has been said in the

beginning of the previous pericope about Jesus'prophetical activity: that his whole life was embedded in prophecy and, especially, that this power has been handed over to the apostles, according to Matthew. Similar sentences are used to describe the 'works of the Messiah'(151) as are used to describe the mission Jesus gives to the twelve, when he sends them to the lost sheep of Israel. They must heal the sick, resurrect the dead, and cast out the demons(152). To them is given to know the secrets of the dominion of heaven for which many prophets and just people have looked(153). They accept the word and understand it. Semantically, this is all mixed up in Matthew. And even if one may possibly not conclude that every follower of Jesus is given the same charism, the similarity in content between all these sentences, especially when one remembers here the 'fate of the prophets', forms an identity between Jesus, the twelve apostles and the Christian prophets. Not without reason Matthew speaks again of 'many' prophets. The Christian prophets are for him an important reality.

What kind of people must we think of? It is tempting to see an immediate connection with what is said about the pseudo-christs in the eschatological discourse. They make their predictions about who and where the Messiah is in order to lure the people to certain places. They perform their signs and miracles which will lead many astray. What the promises are, is not mentioned but, if we may look at Josephus' way of presenting matters, they are not unimportant(154): the crumbling of the walls of Jerusalem, the finding of the vessels of Moses, the division of the Jordan. In view of the cosmic character of Matthew's text we should in any case not think of anything less. They will be the last prophets and the threat is enormous. If it were possible even the elect would be led astray.

That Matthew, in this text of the Sermon of the Mount, is not thinking of these people follows, in my opinion, from his evaluation. While in the eschatological discourse only negative things are said, he does not distance himself at all from the prophetical activities mentioned in this saying of the Sermon on the Mount. There is criticism in the warnings given - I will come back to that - but there is no criticism of whát they do. These are people who want to be of service to their neigbours on a much smaller scale and with less pretences. One should think of something what is described in the secondary conclusion of Mark: 'and these signs will accompany the believers: in my name they will cast out devils, they will have the gifts of tongues, they will pick up serpents; even if they drink deadly poison, it will not harm them; and when they lay their hands on the sick, they will be cured'(155); or something like what is used as a refrain in Acts: 'and in Jesus' name miracles and healings occurred'(156), referring to the healing of the paralytic in the Temple, the revelation of the sin of Ananias and Saphira, the miraculous power of Stephen, and of Paul and Barnabas on their mission. It is a kind of small magic with which people can perform sensational actions related to persons and places: the viper at Paul's hand which does not cause him harm(157); the announcement of a famine while no one took precautionary measures(158); a spectacular casting out of a demon by a slave-woman and her masters cannot use her any longer(159). It refers to people like the Magi in Matthew who know the course of the stars; people like Joseph and Pilate's wife who have predicting and prophesying dreams; people like Simon Peter, the children in the Temple and the centurion under the cross who profess the Messiah through a force from without. The 'prophets' in this saying in the Sermon on the Mount are people who, sometimes incidentically and sometimes permanently, sometimes consciously and sometimes unconsciously, are in contact with supernatural and preternatural forces which enable them with the help of Jesus' name to make predictions, to overpower demons, to heal the sick.

I did not use the word 'magic' without reason. It has a negative connotation in exegesis because, in much of the primary literature of this era, a sharp distinction is made between the μάγος (the magician) and the γόης (the charlatan) who are under the influence of demonic and/or idolatrous forces, and the prophet, the miracle worker and the exorcist from the Jewish-Christian religion who operate under the inspiration of the Holy Spirit(160). In reality it is very difficult, if not impossible, to make a distinction in what is being done or said by these different people(161). They are much the same kind of people, each in his own way. Only when they demonstrate that they follow the rules of the foregoing saying without anxiety, it becomes clear whether they are upright in the context of their own religious values(162).

Researching the background against which Matthew's text has functioned, trying to clarify its ideological function, means an enormous expansion of the material. Also the texts, which speak negatively about magicians and swindlers of the people, must be taken into consideration, perhaps especially these texts, because they openly go into all that is evil. But the real question is what can be found out about our 'prophets' in the first century, with an emphasis on Palestine?

It should not surprise anyone that important information comes from Egypt. It is the melting pot of ancient magical lore(163). In various Jewish writings(164) these practices are discussed colourfully. We find it even in Philo who in several places goes after the μάγοι, because of their 'crimes', which are forbidden by Moses' Law. It gives as in a mirror an image of the totality of the varied Hellenistic world regarding mantic techniques. This is true for the methods used as well as for the content.

Our point of departure can be again the story of Balaam as told by Philo(165). Balaam is the 'pagan' fortune-teller par excellence. Highly proficient in augury he can predict whether rain-storms will come in summer, or dry spells in winter, and hot weather; whether after a good season there will be infertility or after abundance infertility; he foresees whether rivers will be full or dry and he knows about pests and all kinds of sickness. If he consults God, he goes away to find out with God 'what is better'(166). And while he makes use of the good omens through birds and voices while he stays with Balak, he understands at the end that he must reject that(167). This last is a theme which is dear to Philo. Moses forbids the appearance of anything which smells of pagan mantics. In his state no haruspices, purificators, augurs, interpreters of prodigies, incantators and those who put their faith in sound and voices will be allowed(168). All ventriloquists, soothsayers, charmers and witches are directed more to lies than to truth(169). They are people who promise purifications and disenchantments, who prepare love-charms and incantations to change friends into enemies and vice versa; but their art is very dangerous. They are scorpions and vipers. One must kill them before they can attack(170).

A whole world of prophetic practices is brought out here in a few short words, known also from other sources(171). It is difficult to determine what the reality is - we should remember that Philo lived in Alexandria where the whole Roman Empire met, and even more difficult to determine in how far these phenomena were also practised in Jewish circles. For that we have to refer to other literature. Three (or four) books especially are worthy of mention.

1) The Testament of Job deals with the use of some kind of magic amulets. Magic-mystical practices are described. The seven sons of Job get the whole inheritance to the sorrow of his three daughters. They are afraid that nothing will be left for them. But Job has kept something of far greater value for them. He asks the eldest daughter to fetch three gold chests in each of which a cord is hidden: a phylactery with great powers. It heals, it will make sure that they have an income, it keeps evil away, it enables them to speak and understand the language of the angels, it helps them to know invisible secrets, it preserves them for

eternal life(172). The way these miracle amulets are described makes clear how positive people thought about things like that in the circles in which the book originated.
2) The treatise of Shem shows a totally different reality. It is an astrological calendar which, for each year, precisely foretells what is going to happen on the basis of the course of the stars(173). One can imagine that it was used much like astrology is today: with all certainty speaking about future events in ambiguous language. Depending on the readiness of the questioner will the answer be positive or negative. The importance of this text lies in the fact that it is a téxt: a book of predictions which are still unfulfilled(174) and which are read and explained on request.
3) The novel Joseph and Aseneth(175) connects 'prophetism' to 'the reading in secret books'. It says of Levi: 'he was a prophet of the Most High and sharp-sighted with his eyes, and he used to see letters written in heaven by the finger of God and he knew the unspeakable (mysteries) of the Most High'(176). The theme of the existence of secret/heavenly books is rather general(177), but the combination of these books with prophetism is typical(178).
4) If the Testament of Solomon may be placed in the first century(179), we must conclude that thinking about controlling demons has really taken off. Again and again Solomon is presented as someone who, with a magic ring, manages to get in his power all sorts of demons, great ones and small, males and females, dangerous and not so dangerous. If the ring is placed on the breast of the demon he or she must obey Solomon, must reveal his or her name, and say what his or her function is. It opens an unimaginable world of contact with demonic powers.

Obviously, these are only small flickers of light in a large dark forest which one cannot just put together. But each one shows something about the manner in which also Jews in Egypt worked with this: amulets, books of predictions, knowledge of hidden secrets and fear of demons are the historical realities, or at least supposed realities, which give some indication of a possible background for the understanding of the saying from the Sermon on the Mount.

Even if the indications for Palestine are less colourful it is striking that in essence the same realities are in question. I put the data together.

In the first place we must mention the treatise 'The Lives of the Prophets'. Presupposing that it is written in the first century AD in Palestine(180), it is a first hand document on the contemporary understanding of 'prophetic activity'. A strange literary effect develops because 23 prophets are 'taken care of' in a short time. The text limits itself to a small number of phenomena. For our context this means: the prophets manifest themselves as miracle workers, the miracles are proposed as an answer to prayer(181), as a prediction(182), as a vision(183), or as a prophetic sign(184). Because only those events are narrated which have come true, the prophecies, which are still to come true, obtain a high value of veracity(185): they will undoubtedly come true. The fact that a number of burial places have a healing power is also relevant: their prophetic forces endure till the present time(186). The prophets of the past are still relevant today: their expectations of the future, about the end of the city and the world, are still awaited and because of them real miracles still occur. They are an example for the people who believe they have to function as actual prophets.

Following the narrative of the story we find a treasure of strange customs in the Book of Biblical Antiquities. The story about Cenez, the successor of Joshua, is the most elaborate. He lets all twelve tribal heads make a confession of guilt in order to cleanse the people of sin. The tribes of Issachar and Aser confess that they had contact with demons. The sin and punishment of Aser gets the most elaborate description of all. They possess seven gold statues of female deities of the Amorites set with seven precious stones. One can consult these to know what one should do every hour of every day. The stones give off light and heal blindness. Everything which is sinful is burned, but the seven stones and a book (!) receive special treatment. They must be put on a hill next to the altar. The dew of the hill will wipe out the letters of the book and the stones will be thrown in the deepest part of the sea by angels after which God will replace them for the twelve stones of the ephod(187).

This is not the only story in which magic plays the lead role. There are several kinds of magic stories. In a short episode the story of Aod is told, the magician who can let the sun shine in the night with the help of angels. The angels have lost their power because of their transgressions, but there are magicians who are capable of abusing this lost potential(188). The author elaborates much on the statue of the deity, when the story of Micah is re-told. They have become six with each their own function: an image of a dove when men come to ask something about their wives; an image of three children for questions about children; an eagle for questions about riches; a lion for strength; tree cows for slaves; a serpent if one wants to know how long one still has to live. The technique of the oracle is clearly stated(189). When Samuel is called during the night and still does not know who it is, the author let Eli say: 'From now it will be forever true; when someone is called during the night or at midnight and the voice speaks only twice, one will know that it is an unclean spirit. But if the voice calls three times, it will be an angel'. An a little later: 'The right ear hears the Lord at night, the left ear his angel'(190). We hear an exorcism-psalm in the story of David which he sings for Saul to cast out the unclean spirits(191). The book ends with the description of Saul and the witch from Endor with lots of horrors about death-exorcism: it causes Saul's death(192).

All these stories are negatively evaluated. The book's tendency is in line with the Mishnah about magic, as far as I could trace it. 'May the Zealots touch him who damns another by enchantment'(193). But these stories do make clear how much people are concerned with demons, casting them out, death-exorcism, oracles, future predictions and magic stones.

We find some more concrete indications in Josephus. We find there that especially the Essenes are involved in these things. Because of their knowledge of the ancient books, which they select on the basis of their value for the good of soul and body, because of their long training, their practices of cleanliness and their ascetic life they are able to make predictions. They seldom make mistakes (194). They do research in medicinal herbs and stones and they are able to cast out demons.

He tells an interesting story about this in his Book of Antiquities: in a hymn for Solomon: 'And God granted him knowledge of the art used against demons for the benefit and healing of men. He also composed incantations by which illnesses are relieved, and left behind forms of exorcism with which those possessed by demons drive them out, never to return. And this kind of cure is of very great power among us to this day, for I have seen a certain Eleazer, a countryman of mine, in the presence of Vespasian, his sons, tribunes and a number of other soldiers, free men possessed by demons, and this was the manner of the cure: he put to the nose of the possessed man a ring which had under its seal one of the roots prescribed by Solomon, and then, as the man smelled it, drew out the demon through his nostrils, and, when the man at once fell down, adjured the demon never to come back into him, speaking Solomon's name and reciting the incantations which he had composed. Then, wishing to convince the bystanders and prove to them that he had this power, Eleazar placed a cup or footbasin full of water a little away off and commanded the demon, as it went out of the man, to overturn it and make known to the spectators that he had left the man'(195). The root about which Josephus speaks is probably the Baaras-root which is found in the vicinity of Machaerus and is suitable for drawing demons out of men. To get the root out of the ground one must use urine from women or menstrual blood (196). It is clear that this is a very primitive culture.

It is surprising that precisely in Qumran all sorts of texts have been found which, however fragmentary, fit in with this very well. Partly, the ancient forefathers have been given these magical gifts. When Abraham goes to the land of Egypt he has a predicting dream. People will try to kill him and spare his wife. Therefore, Sarai must say that Abraham is her brother. When the emissaries from Pharaoh come to Abraham, he reads to them from the book (Enoch) that there will be a famine. The Pharaoh sends for Abraham's wife. In that same night Abraham asks God to send Pharaoh an evil spirit. God hears his prayer and for two years the Pharaoh cannot have contact with Sarai. None of the Egyptian doctors or magicians can heal him, until Pharaoh finds out that Sarai is Abraham's wife and sends her back to him. Abraham comes to Pharaoh, lays hands on him and heals him. Pharaoh sends Abraham home with many gifts(197).

In the same way we can suppose that Daniel is also presented as an exorcist. In 4 Q sNab we have a fragment of a thanksgiving prayer in which Nabonides, the king of Babylon, thanks God for being healed from an evil sickness which lasted seven years. 'And an exorcist remitted my sins for Him'; and in 4Q Mess Ar a blessing is said over a newborn baby in sentences which are filled with allusions to Daniel and Solomon: 'and he shall become skilled in the three books ... he will know the secrets of mankind ... his calculations will exist forever'(198). We should remember also that in the Book of Jubilees(199) an exorcist story is told about Noah. On his deathbed he asks God to jail the devils for him, because his grandchildren are beginning to listen to them. God does not hear his prayer completely. He leaves one tenth of the devils free to make sure that men will know their powers. In compensation God teaches Noah about all sicknesses which the demons bring and about their art of seduction. He also teaches him about the herbs which can bring healing. Noah writes all this down in a book which he gives to his eldest son Sem.

In the same way it is said of Isaac, when Jacob visits him with his sons Levi and Judah: 'And a spirit of prophecy came down upon his mouth'(200); and of Jacob himself that an angel is seen by him in a vision of the night. This angel makes him read seven tablets in which is written 'which would happen to him and to his sons during all the ages'(201).

Noah, Abraham, Isaac, Jacob and Daniel are miracle-workers, exorcists, dream-interpreters, future-predictors. It is not all that surprising that an astrological text has been found in Qumran(202). Its meaning is not so easily to trace, but it shows a special interest in the answer to the question how many parts of light and darkness go into a person(203).

Finally a last remark. In the book of Enoch, all sorts of demons teach people how they should handle stones, exorcism, liberation from them, how to cut roots, how to handle astrology, and the signs of the earth, the sun and the moon(204). These people may have died, but the mention of the learning process has had far more meaning for the readers in Qumran than a simple information about an historical fact, as moreover may be clear from the description in the Temple Scroll(205) of pagan practices. This description is linked up with Dt 18,9 - 13, but at the same time it wants to refer to real practices: it is forbidden to practice witchcraft, to predict, to enchant, to curse and to question ghosts of dead people and of oracles.

What is the value of this very special subject of this research into Jewish thought and practices? All in all it has become quite extended and needs some systematisation. Most striking is the fact that negative and positive evaluations are juxtaposed without much intermediation. 'Prophecy' is apparently a reality which evokes ambiguous feelings in people and which, therefore, brings out very explicit pro's and con's. In the negative evaluation, two motives play a role. Magic transgresses the Law of Moses (206) ánd magic is only possible with the help of the devil(207). These two motives are not independent of each other, but they are sufficiently different to distinguish them. At the same time, - even though not really at the sáme time in the same literature! -, there is a strong positive evaluation of magical practices: the forefathers themselves have done it: Noah(208), Abraham(209), Isaac (210), Jacob(211), Moses(212), David(213), Solomon(214), Job(215), Daniel(216) and all known prophets(217). The actual practitioners will not have lived with a lack of self-awareness.

It is surprising that Matthew's gospel connects very well with this whole cluster. It will be sufficient to point to a few facts: how Jesus is accused of blasphemy when he cures a paralytic; why he refuses to give a sign to Pharisees and Sadducees; how he is accused of working through Beelzebub when he casts out demons; how Matthew sees a connection between Jesus' practices of healing and casting out demons and the prophecies in Scripture. The same is true for the disciples: they also will be accused of being under the influence of the devil, the prophets whom Jesus sends will be persecuted and be killed but, precisely therefore, it is clear that they are like the prophets of old. The accusations comes from without, the support comes from within the group. For outsiders the Christian prophets are the devil's servants and trangsgressors of the Law(218). For insiders they are the prophets who bring to life the olden times: the predictions of the prophets are fulfilled in them.

We should read the warning in the Sermon of the Mount against this background: 'not everyone who calls 'Lord, Lord', will enter into the kingdom of heaven, but he who does the will of the Father in heaven'. 'Doing the will of the Father' is in Matthew the set phrase for 'being a disciple of Jesus in the correct way'(219).

Performing miracles, even if done in Jesus' name, is fruitful only when it is part of the whole context of his teaching. If one feels oneself above that, if the ego-consciousness is more important than the Christian community, one will be disillusioned at the final judgment. In other words, the elements of the Jewish criticism of magic - that it is in opposition to the Law of Moses - is taken up in an indirect way (there is no criticism of the practise itself) and it is modified (there is a connection with the will of the Father as taught by Jesus). Clearly not without good reasons, the saying ends with the curse 'away from me you who practise lawlessness'. The Law of Moses, as the will of the Father revealed by Jesus, is the last criterion by which every Christian will be judged (220).

the house on the rock and the house on sand

Mt 7,24 - 27

The opposition between words and deeds is the topic of the last saying of the Sermon on the Mount. The connection with what immediately precedes is clear: not words alone, but words which are given reality in practice, are the guarantee for the chances of survival at the last judgment. The saying has a greater emanation than the preceding sentences, because it does not mention concrete practices. 'Whoever hears my word and does it', is addressed to all hearers. The limitation to the pseudo-prophets of the last passage of the Sermon on the Mount is lifted in this concluding sentence. For that reason the mashal is a perfect closure, referring to all that has been said before.

After all that has been said already, there is no need

to prove anymore that the content of the saying expresses an idea which essentially connects with contemporary Jewish thought. In exegetical research we find an unanimous reference to the mashal of Rabbi Eleazar ben Azarja about the tree with its branches and roots(221), and the mashal of Rabbi Elisha ben Abuja about the house built with stones and bricks(222), comparisons which connect, in the same way as Matthew does, the Torah and the work, wisdom and action: without the deed the teaching remains an empty shell. The teaching has not reached its aim unless it brings men to follow the road. Teaching and road belong together.

This train of thought returns as a continuing refrain especially in the treatise 'The Saying of the Fathers'. Three realities provide the figurative material for the metaphors. 1) In the oldest sayings stands the distinction between learning and doing as a wisdom-sentence: do not talk too much but do something so that your words remain true: 'the man who talks more than he does, will not stay in the wisdom'. If Torah is not together with deeds, it leads to sin. Silence is sometimes more valuable than speaking(223). 2) Use is also made of a metaphor which is borrowed from labour relations: the work to be done is presented as commissioned by a foreman, a man who divides the work, who keeps an eye on it and who determines the wages: 'know for whom you are slaving because trustworthy is the person who is lord of the work and who pays the wages'(224). Rabbi Tarfon used to say: 'the day is short and the work is long and the labourers are lazy and the wage is large and the lord of the house is insisting'(225). The work must be done, but there is no reason to be afraid because the employer is trustworthy. 3) Thirdly, a metaphor is used taken from the reality of the beth-midrash: learning is necessary, but it must be directed to action: 'when someone learns to act, to him it will be given to learn, to teach, to maintain and to act'. The halachah belongs to the learning of the Torah, the road which must be followed in order to fulfill the Torah. Just is he who goes and does(226).

They are three aspects of the same reality, taken from the wisdom-tradition, the eschatology, and the rabbinical Torah-doctrine, which colour also the meaning of Matthew's saying. I will take them one by one.

The wisdom-aspect plays but a modest role in Matthew's mashal. One thinks of the opposition between wise and foolish. There is an allusion in the Sermon on the Mount in the saying about the salt which becomes 'foolish': Jesus' hearers are the salt of the earth, when they act according to his words; if they do not do that, they will be thrown out like worthless salt. Against the background of the whole gospel one should think, in the opposition between wise and foolish, of the parable of the wise and foolish virgins(227): a story which also deals with admitting and rejecting. As condition for admittance the story gives the readiness, always and immediate, to depart. The wise man knows what he does. The foolish man thinks he knows it, but he will be deceived.

The eschatological background is more immediately important. There are two reasons for understanding the mashal in an eschatological sense. Formally there is a comparison with a future event(228): whoever hears the words of Jesus and acts accordingly, will be like a house that stands firm or vice versa like a house that falls down. In this era there is a distinction between the two houses, i.e. the two persons, but they are both standing till the final judgment: a thought which is dear to Matthew and which he elaborates in various parables(229).

Not only formally, but also regarding the content, the eschatological elements play a role: the description of the judgment - storm, water, winds announcing the year's end- and the description of the result - the house stands or falls - must be seen as metaphors of the end of the world at the end of time. People invest their whole being to build a house. In the same way their whole being is at stake, when the forces of nature test it.

That the mashal connects with the rabbinical teaching about 'how to deal with the Torah', is in content determined by the opening sentence. Several exegetes are struck by the fact that Matthew does not make Jesus speak about 'these words', but that he emphasizes 'these words of mine'. Jesus is presented as the Messiah and the Son of God who takes over the authority from the Torah according to Christian exegetes(230); conversely, D. Flusser thinks that the saying originally referred to the words of the Torah and that, therefore, the ascription of these words to Jesus cannot be original(231).

But it is typical of Matthew that he is totally unaware of any opposition between Jesus and the Torah. Jesus' words are not a replacement of the Torah. They are the Torah. They are the expression of the will of the Father in heaven. How one can see that, also in an interpretation with a Jewish orientation, has become clear to me from a midrash explanation on Exodus 34,27 by M. Buber(232). It says in the midrash: 'Another explanation of 'write for yourself': the ministering angels began to say before God: 'you give Moses permission to write what he likes. He could say to Israel: I give you the Torah; I have written it and given it to you'. Then God said: 'I hope not, but even if he does this, he would still be faithful to me, as is written (in Numbers 12,7): 'not my servant Moses. He is faithful in my whole house'(233). This text is the point of departure in the chassidic story: 'Rabbi Jizchak of Worki was asked by his disciples how one should interpret this text. He answered with a parable: 'A merchant wanted to go on a journey. He hired a helper for his store; he himself was usually in the room next to the store. From there he heard his helper in the first year occasionally say to a buyer: 'My master cannot sell this so cheaply'. The merchant did not go on his journey. In the second year, he heard his helper say from time to time: 'We cannot sell this so cheaply'. He postponed his trip still longer. But in the third year he heard: 'I cannot sell this so cheaply'. Then he went on his journey'. The Jewish-Christians from Matthew's community probably understood how Jesus was the interpreter of the Torah in this way: not in contradiction to what Moses taught, but in line with what God wanted to express in his Torah.

For the last time, through this opening sentence of the closing mashal, a relation is expressed with everything which in the Sermon on the Mount has been said of Torah about Torah: the prolegomenon which introduced the legal texts; the legal texts themselves with their opposition between 'you have heard that it has been said to the people of old' and 'but I say to you'; the halachot about giving alms, praying and fasting; the joy of the Law for those who are capable of renouncing their riches for it; the relecture of the Law which leads to the torah about mutual love. Jesus announces the will of his Father in heaven. One should not just listen but one should also act.

Notes: INTRODUCTION

1. I base myself on L. Althusser, Pour Marx, Paris 1966, and Positions, Paris, 1976. Althusser has always been hidden in a cloud of commentaries which I cannot completely unravel. My own reception is influenced by E. Balibar, On the Dictatorship of the Proletariat, Manchester, 1977 (1976); N. Poulantzas, L'Etat, le pouvoir, le socialism, Paris, 1978; S. Stuurman, Kapitalisme en burgerlijke staat, Amsterdam, 1978; G. Therborn, The Ideology and the Power of Ideology, London, 1980; and escpecially H. Manschot, Althusser over het marxisme, Nijmegen, 1980 from whom I took some fundamental insights.
2. Position, Paris, 1976, 104
3. cf Letter of Engels to J. Bloch, Marx-Engels-Werke, 37, 462
4. Pour Marx, Paris, 1966, 241
5. cf e.g. H.D. Betz, Studien zur Bergpredigt, Tübingen, 1985. He emphasizes the Hellenistic side, but it can possibly be even more precisely localised. The fact that a Hellenistic culture exists, does not mean that everything is the same in Alexandria, Antioch and Athens. It is probably not without reason that very specific and very divergent models of interpretation arise in for example Alexandria and Antioch.
6. R.E. Brown - J.P. Meier, Antioch and Rome. New Testament Cradles of Catholic Christianity, London, 1983

Notes: chapter 1 SUFFERING OF THE PEOPLE AND ITS RESTORATION

1. Die Klassenkämpfe in Frankreich 1848-1850, Marx-Engels Werke VII. 79
2. Der Ursprung des Christentums, Berlin, 1908, 279
3. J. Dupont, Les Béatitudes, Louvain, 1954, II, 268
4. S.G.F. Brandon, Jesus and the Zealots, Manchester, 1967, 308
5. G. Strecker, Les macarismes du discours sur la montagne, in L' Évangile selon Matthieu. Rédaction et théologie, Louvain, 1972, 194 (in the following quoted as Macarismes) cf Strecker, Die Bergpredigt, Göttingen, 1984, 33
6. How the rich Philo solves this problem, can be deduced from a text like De Virt. 6: 'For under the grip of poverty multitudes have been laid low, and like exhausted athletes have fallen to the ground enfeebled by lack of manliness. Yet in the judgment of truth not a single one is in want, for his needs are supplied by the wealth of nature, which cannot be taken from him; the air, the first, the most vital, the perpetual source of sustenance, which we can inhale continually night and day; then the fountains in their profusion and the rivers spring-fed as well as winter brooks ever flowing to provide us with drink; then again for our meat (sic;it should be 'meal'), the harvest of crops of every sort, and the different kinds of trees, which never fail to bear their annual autumn fruitage. These no one lacks, but everybody everywhere has an ample and more than ample sufficiency' (Transl. as always in the following F.H. Colson of the Loeb-edition). Cf the same thought in De Praemiis et Poenis 98ff and De Somniis I, 92ff where it is used as proof that Ex 22,26ff (about pawning the undergarment) should not be taken in its literal sense. Moses definitely meant it allegorically!
7. Mt 5,8 and 5,28
8. & 197, see also L. Schottroff, Das geschundene Volk, in L. Schottroff - W. Schottroff, Mitarbeiter der Schöpfung, München, 1983, 164; Schweizer, TWNT s.v. πνεῦμα, 398, note 438
9. 2 Macc 5,11
10. Acts 18,25, see also Rom 12,11
11. Phil 2,30
12. Mt 11,29, see also 1 Cor 14,20: adult unto your very mind

13. 1 Thess 2,17
14. 1 Cor 5,3; see also Col 2,5
15. 1 Pt 3,18
16. It follows from the construction in 1 Cor 7,34 that an opposition is not necessarily implied, when a double dative is used: 'that she may be holy in body and in spirit'
17. The word πένης is used in Greek for this group of people
18. These people are called πτωχοί, see especially H. Bolkestein, Wohltätigkeit und Armenpflege im vorchristlichen Altertum, Groningen, 1967/2 (1939), 181-185; A.R. Hands, Charities and Social Aid in Greece and Rome, New York, 1968, 62-76 and M.I. Finley, The Ancient Economy, London, 1975, 41
19. see especially Schweizer, TWNT s.v. πνεῦμα, 398ff; also in Schweizer, Bergpredigt, Göttingen, 1982, 11ff
20. cf R. Zuurmond, Wie oren heeft om te horen ..., Zeist, 1979, 13
21. The list of the seven names for the poor in the Abot de Rabbi Nathan, B-version is very illustrative: 'The poor (man) is called (in the Scripture) by SEVEN names: poor (cny), needy ('bywn), poor man (mskn), lowly (mk), sparse (dl), crushed (dk), dispossessed (rš). Poor, literally. Needy because he desires everything; he sees one thing, but cannot eat (it); another thing, but cannot drink (it). Poor man because his life is in danger (!cf parallel in Mt, in ARN it is a word play on 'skn'). Lowly because he is as lowly as the threshold. Crushed because they are crushed. Sparse because his possessions are sparse. Dispossessed because he is trampled upon (cf Mt 5,5!). Another interpretation. Dispossessed because it (poverty) comes to him by inheritance' (Transl. A.J. Salderini, A Translation and Commentary of the Fathers According to Rabbi Nathan, Leiden, 1975, 270. See also his references to parallel texts).
22. In TWNT s.v. πνεῦμα; Jewish anthropology is, in fact, translated back to an aristotelian-thomistic way of thinking. It seems that we in the West cannot think any other way.
23. Mt 22,43
24. Mt 26,41
25. Mt 19, 16-30
26. see also the parables in Mt 13, 44.45 and 22,5: in this commentary discussed in Chapter IV
27. J. Dupont, Les Béatitudes, II, Paris, 1969/2, 19ff; Bammel, TWNT s.v. πτωχός; Botterweck, TWAT s.v. 'ebjôn'; R.A. Guelich, The Sermon on the Mount, Waco,

Texas, 1983/2 (1982), 67f

28. 1 QM 14,7
29. 1 QM 11,13
30. 1 QM 12,14
31. 1 QM 13,13
32. It is a pity that precisely 1 QM 14,7 is corrupted, because we do not know what these poor people do precisely with that 'obdurate heart' which later on can again be decyphered. From the parallel formulation immediately afterwards about 'the perfect on the road who demolish all the criminal nations', one could think that they will make the 'obdurate heart' disappear. An ethical religious connotation of the concept 'poor in spirit' is not improbable then, cf D. Flusser, Blessed are the Poor in Spirit ..., Isr Expl Journal 10 (1960) 1-13; J. Dupont, Les πτωχοί τῷ πνεύματι de Matthieu 5,3 et les 'anawey ruach' de Qumran, in, Neutestamentliche Aufsätze, Fs. J. Schmid, 1963, 53-64; S. Légasse, Les pauvres en esprit et les 'volontaires' de Qumran, NTS 8 (1961/62) 336-345.

    But if one connects the concept with what goes before, where there is talk of stumblers, a despondent heart, a mouth without sound, weak hands, knocking knees and a broken neck, it would seem better to understand 'poor in spirit' in a physical sense: those who lack breath, in the way that in 1 QM 6,12 the opposite is said about horses who are 'longwinded', see for this interpretation (and for yet other ones) E. Best, Matthew V.3, NTS 7 (1960/61) 255-258; J. Smit Sibinga, 'Zalig zijn de armen van geest', Vox Theol 30 (1959/60) 5-15
33. cf H. Giesen, Christliches Handeln, Frankfurt, 1982, 112 for a survey on modern exegetical ideas about the Matthean concept of basileia
34. On this problematic more extensive in D. Boer, Een fantastisch verhaal. De politieke betekenis van de lezing van de bijbel, and, J. Bonsen, Verworpenen der aarde en Gods materialiteit, in, Eltheto 65 (1981) 14-52. 53-71
35. Ketubot 4,4,; see also Vita Adae et Evae 13,2 (parallel Vita Adae et Evae 40): Seth says in anticipation of the death of Adam: 'I will put dust on my head and throw myself to the ground before the gates of Paradise and mourn with great lamentation'; in Joseph and Aseneth 10,8ff is mentioned a somber tunic, loosening of the hair, sprinkling of ashes on her head; strecking the breast with two hands; weeping bitterly; for a charged but not an unrealistic description of mourning practices, see also Lucianus, On Funerals, 12: '.. Next come cries of distress, wailing of women, tears on all

sides, beaten breasts, torn hair, and bloody cheeks. Perhaps, too, clothing is rent and dust sprinkled on the head, and the living are in a plight more pitiable than the dead; for they roll on the ground repeatedly and dash their heads against the floor ..' (Transl. A.M. Harmon, Loeb-edition).

36. Jos Bell Jud II.1.1.1, Transl. H. Tackeray
37. cf Jos. Ant XVII. 8.4.200: immediately after the πένθος Archelaos begins to feast; Jos Ant XVII. 9.5.234: the discourse of Antipater in which he accuses Archelaos not have kept the πένθος, but that he held a feast as one does in the case of a conquered enemy, with dancing and singing.
38. cf Sir 22,12; Ap Mosis 29,7; Vita Adae et Evae 1,1ff; 46; 51,1ff (parallel Ap Mosis 43); in 11 Q Temple 49,6.19; 50,15 differences between the first, third and seventh day; in Bell Jud III. 11.5.437 Josephus writes that on the rumour of his dead in Jerusalem: 'all alike wept for Josephus. Thus for thirty days the lamentations never ceased in the city, and many of the mourners hired flute-players to accompany their funeral dirge'. It changes quickly when it is known that he is still alive. In Jos. C. Ap II. 205 he states, however: 'The pious rites which it provides for the dead do not consist of costly obsequies or the erection of conspicuous monuments'
39. cf Sanhedrin 2,1: the correspondence with Philo, De Spec Leg I. 113-115 and Jos C Ap II. 205 dates this mishnah
40. Moed Qatan 3,9, cf also Jub 34,13-17 and Mt 11,17
41. LAB 24,6 on the death of Joshuah; 33,6 on the death of Deborah; 40,5ff on the dead of the daughter of Jephtah; for this last one: M. Philonenko, Iphigénie et Sheila, in, Les syncretisme dans les religions grecques et romaines, Paris, 1973, 165-177
42. Jos Ant III. 5. 1. 98: the opposition is between πενθεῖν with λυπεῖν and κατηφεῖν
43. Sanhedrin 6,6 where a distinction is made between 'abal' (to mourn for a dead person) and 'anan' (to be sad); cf also b Sabhedrin 11a: 'They wanted to sound the praises of Juda ben Baba, but it was a bad time, and it was not allowed to mourn for people who were killed by the government' (For the rabbinic time table, cf C. Albeck, Einführung in die Mishna, Berlin, 1971, 22ff. 47f
44. On the prohibition to mourn for somebody who has been sentenced to death, cf Tacitus, Annales, 6,19; Suetonius, Tiberius, 61: Tiberius gives his special orders when Seianus and his companions have been slaughtered;

for these texts and their relevancy for the NT, L. Schottroff, Maria Magdalena und die Frauen am Grabe, Evang Th 42 (1982) 3-25; cf also Jos Bell Jud IV. 5.3.331: 'To such consternation were the people reduced that none dared openly weep for or bury a deceased relative; but in secret and behind closed doors were their tears shed and their groans uttered with circonspection, for fear of being overheard by any of their foes. For the mourner (πενθεῖν) instantly suffered the same fate as the mourned. Only by night would they take a little dust in both hands and strew it on the bodies, though some venturous persons did this by day'

45. Is 61,1ff
46. Strecker, Macarismes, 194 note 20
47. S. Schulz, Q. Die Spruchquelle der Evangelisten, Zürich, 1972, 78
48. G. Eichholz, Auslegung der Bergpredigt, Neukirchen, 1965, 38
49. Mt 2,18
50. cf also A. Schlatter, Der Evangelist Matthäus, Stuttgart, 1929, 134ff
51. especially K. Stendahl, The School of St. Matthew and its Use of the Old Testament, Uppsala, 1954; Quis et Unde? An Analysis of Mt 1-2, in, Judentum, Urchristentum, Kirche, Fs J. Jeremias, Berlin, 1960, 94-105
52. On this 'high' concept of the magi, cf especially Philo, De Spec Leg III. 100: 'Now the true magic, the scientific vision by which the facts of nature are presented in a clearer light, is felt to be a fit object for reverence and ambition and is carefully studied not only by ordinary persons but by kings and the greatest kings, and particularly those of the Persians, so much so that it is said that no one in that country is promoted to the throne unless he has first been admitted into the cast of the Magi' (for his 'low' concept of the magi, cf De Spec Leg III. 93);
    The connotations in Matthew's story are clearly oriented more on the fact that the magi are 'important, powerful and rich people' than that they stand for 'the pagans' as is always stated in exegesis: see the reception at the court, the respect with which people listen to them, the royal gifts they bring. The fact that they are pagans (= not Jews?) remains implicit in the story
53. Mt 2,15
54. Mt 2,18
55. Mt 2,23; for this interpretation which refers to Js 11,1 cf R. H. Gundry, The Use of the Old Testament in St. Matthew's Gospel, Leiden, 1967, 94ff

56. cf among others R.H. Gundry, The Use of the Old Testament, Leiden, 1967; G.M. Soares Prabhu, The Formula Quotations in the Infancy Narrative of Matthew, Rome, 1976; R.E. Brown, The Birth of the Messiah, New York, 1979; B.M. Nolan, The Royal Son of God, Tübingen, 1979
57. Mt 21,35 and 23,34
58. Mt 10,28; 21,35; 22,6; 23,34; 24,9
59. Mt 10,21
60. Mt 10,22 and 24,13
61. strictly speaking only in Mt 2,19; cf also 9,18 and 22,25
62. Mt 24,31; 13,43
63. especially H.G. Kippenberg, Religion und Klassenbildung im antiken Judäa, Göttingen, 1978, 144-155
64. Transl. J. Fitzmyer-D. Harrington, A Manual of Palestinian Aramaic Texts, Rome, 1978, 159; cf also J.T. Milik, Deux documents inédits du désert de Juda, Bibl 38 (1957) 245ff. The date of the contract has not been preserved, but it can be set on the first decades of the second century.
65. In Murabba^{c}at 22 we find a text which explicitly refuses ownership to the buyer. It is probably an attempt to revive the old law, cf H. Kippenberg, Religion und Klassenbildung, 146. For the text, see J.T. Milik, Judaean Desert Studies, 118-121: '(et moi, Bar-Hizqa), le les ai reçus ... sans aucun droit de propriété pour toujours': 'belô rashût she^{c}ôlam'
66. Lev 25,8-34
67. De Spec Leg II. 110f
68. De Spec Leg II. 113
69. De Spec Leg II. 112
70. De Virt 122; De Spec Leg II. 85
71. Jos. Ant. III. 12.3.282
72. Jos. Ant. IV. 8.28.273: After seven years the bought slave may be released, 'but, if having had children by a slave woman at the house of the master who bought him, he, out of love and affection for his own, desires to continue to serve him, then on the coming of the year of the jubilee - let him be liberated'
73. Jos. Ant. III. 12.3.283f
74. Jos. Bell Jud VII. 6.6.216; for commentary E.M. Smallwood, The Jews under Roman Rule, Leiden, 1981, 340; S. Applebaum, Economic Life in Palestine, in, Jewish People in the First Century, Assen, 1976, 693ff
75. Gittin 5,6: one fourth of the price must be given to the original owner; Demai 6,2: the lease price of a parcel of land which belongs to a foreigner is lowered; the sales price is higher; Aboda Zara 1,8: one does not

lease parcels of land to foreigners in the land of Israel. It is not too clear whether these mishnayot refer to the situation after 70 AD or after 130 AD; besides the literature mentioned in note 74 see also M. Avi-Yonah, Geschichte der Juden im Zeitalter des Talmud, Berlin, 1962, 30ff
76. cf Ps 36,21.26 (LXX) and Mt 5,42
77. cf Strecker, Macarismes, 197; Bergpredigt, 37; J. Dupont, Béatitudes, Louvain, I, 1954, 251ff; Lohmeyer-Schmauch, Das Evangelium des Matthäus, Göttingen, 1967/4, 86; C. Michaelis, Die Pi-Alliteration der ersten 4 Seligpreisungen in Mt V. 3-6 und ihre Bedeutung für den Aufbau der Seligpreisungen bei Mt., Lk und in Q, NT 10 (1968) 148-161
78. For these reflections, cf the excellent article by Hauck-Schulz, TWNT s.v. πραΰς cf also H. Bolkestein, Wohltätigkeit und Armenpflege, Groningen, 1976/2, 108ff. 140.300ff which, however, is to be read together with the discussion on the other 'virtues' like justice, liberality, helpfullness. With those Bolkestein points out more clearly that one thinks from a position of wellbeing, see for example 114. 130ff. 147f
79. Sir 10,14; 3,17
80. cf for example Philo, Vita Mos II. 279: 'Moses, greatly hurt and grieved at this (= rebellion of the levites) though the meekest of men, was so spurred to righteous anger by his passionate hatred of evil, that he besought God to turn his face from their sacrifice'; Jos. Ant XIX. 7.3.330.333.334: the king does not take action against Simon, who in an assembly accused Agrippa I to be impure, other than to ask him what unlawfulness he committed: 'for he considered mildness a more royal trait than passion'; Bell Jud VII. 11.4.451: 'Catullus (= the governor of the Libyan Pentapolis who falsely accused Josephus himself) owing to the lenity of the emperors suffered nothing worse than a reprimand; but not long after ... he came to a miserable end'
81. L. Schottroff, Gewaltverzicht und Feindesliebe in der urchristlichen Jesus-tradition, in, Jesus Christus in Historie und Theologie, Fs H. Conzelmann, Tübingen, 1975, 197-221
82. cf Liddell-Scott, s.v. πραΰς
83. cf for example Jos. Bell Jud IV. 6.1.365; Philo, De Virt 88: 'The manual worker or load carrier who toils painfully with his whole body like a beast of burden, 'lives from day to day' as the phrase goes, and his hope rests upon payment'; or, De Spec Leg II. 83: 'Do not harnass him (= your slave) like an unreasoning

animal nor oppress him with weights too heavy and too numerous for his capacity, nor heap insults upon him, nor drag him down by threats and menaces into cruel despondency'. The attribution of πραύτης to these people is not to be expected in Philo; cf also Did 3,7ff which understands the beatitude as an imperative: 'be submitted', in connection with the ethical implication of fear and submission; but see also 5,2 which emphasizes more the reciprocal solidarity

84. Mt 21,5
85. Mt 11,27f
86. cf Hauck-Schulz, TWNT s.v. πραύς; Str-B., I, 499 on the expression μάθετε ἀπ' ἐμοῦ; Schweizer, Bergpredigt, 15
87. S. Schulz, Q. Die Spruchquelle der Evangelisten, Zürich, 1972, 77
88. Lc 6,21
89. Mt 3,15; 5,20; 6,1.33; 21,32. In this list 'the search for justice' approaches at most the supposed meaning of 'hunger and thirst for justice', but it will be difficult to maintain that Mt 6,33 is a typical Matthean sentence
90. Strecker, Macarismes, 198 + note 36 pretends to give a number of examples, but he fools the reader a little. In Zosimus, Hermetica IV, 111.3 we find an accusative, but that deals with τὰ δαιμόνια who are not only hungry for sacrifice, but also for the soul (of the woman who is addressed); in Philo, De fuga et inventione 139 it says: 'those who hunger and thirst for καλοκἀγαθίας (genitive!); the other references in Philo are irrelevant; Jos. Bell Jud I. 628 deals with 'drinking the blood' (!) cf Anthologia Palatina 16,137: 'you thirst for the murder of children'; in Plut., Moralia 460B it says: 'in case one hungers for food (dative), one acts according to nature (i.e. one must eat when one is hungry), yet punishment (dative) is indulged in by one who is not hungry or thirsty for it (genitive αὐτῆς as a repetition of the implied object, see contrary to this Mt 5,6b); in Strecker, Bergpredigt, 39 note 44 this list has become: 'Für diese Auslegung finden sich in der griechischen Literatur zahlreiche Belege', and then follows Philo, De fuga 139 and Athenaeus 10,43
91. Jos. Ant. XX. 2.5. 51ff; 5.2.101; Ant. III. 15.3.320 (probably on a famine under Nero); for more concretisations J. Jeremias, Jerusalem in the Time of Jesus, London, 1969; S. Applebaum, The Economic Life in Palestine, in, Jewish People in the First Century, Assen, 1976, II, 631-700; A.Schalit, König Herodes. Der Mann und sein Werk, Berlin, 1969; E.M. Smallwood, The Jews under Roman Rule, Leiden, 1981/2, 44-119

92. Mt 6,25
93. Mt 10,42
94. Mt 15,33
95. Mt 25,31ff; in Bolkestein, Wohltätigkeit und Armenpflege, Groningen, 1967/2, 6ff one can read how long the history of these sentences is: from ancient Egypt till our text. That obviously poses the problem whether and how these texts refer to reality. However, an indication in favour of such reference to actual reality lies in the fact that it is retained as a prescription - cf various pseudepigrapha as for example 4 Esr 2,20ff; 1 Enoch passim etc.
96. Mt 6,1
97. Mt 3,15
98. Mt 10,1-14
99. cf P. Hoffmann, Studien zur Theologie der Logienquelle, Münster, 1972/2,312ff; L. Schottroff - W. Stegemann, Jesus von Nazareth, Stuttgart, 1978, 62ff; G. Theissen, Studien zur Soziologie des Urchristentums, Tübingen, 1979, 79-141 next to very different opinions
100. for the connexion between justice and kingly power of God cf Mt 6,33
101. cf Bultmann, TWNT s.v. ἔλεος; Zimmermann, TWNT s.v. χάρις; N. Tromp, Harmonie van contrasten, beschouwingen over Exodus 34,6-7, Utrecht, 1980; Freedman/Lundbom, TWAT, s.v. 'chanan'; Zobel, TWAT s.v. 'chesed'; Weinfeld, TWAT s.v. 'berit'; H. Frankemölle, Jahwehbund und Kirche, Aschendorff, 1973 has brought the implications of the covenant-concept for the totality of Matthew to the attention
102. 1 Sam 20,15; in for example LAB 62 we find a contemporary comment on this text: see the relation between justice, persecution and the shedding of innocent blood (cf also LAB 65,5)
103. Ex 34,6-7 (LXX); for literature, see note 101
104. For the opposition with the Greek way of thinking, see H. Bolkestein, Wohltätigkeit und Armenpflege, Groningen, 1967/2, 141ff on the rejection of ἔλεος by Aristotle and the Stoa. Only in Epicurism there is an appraisal of the compassion; for criticism on Bolkestein, A.R. Hands, Charities and Social Aid in Greece and Rome, New York, 1968
105. For the totality of contemporary ideas on the covenant-concept I. Abrahams, Studies in Pharisaism and the Gospels, New York, 1967/2, I. 139-167; G.F. Moore, Judaism in the First Centuries, Cambridge, 1927, I. 386-400; in the collection Moïse, L'Homme de L'Alliance, the articles by B. Botte, La vie de Moïse par Philon; G. Vermès, La figure de Moïse au tournant des

des deux testaments; R. Bloch, Quelques aspects de la figure de Moïse dans la tradition rabbinique, Paris, 1955, 55-167; see the important article by D. Daube, Redemption, in, The New Testament and Rabbinic Judaism, London, 1956; R. le Déaut, La nuit pascale, Rome, 1963, 76ff; 122ff; on the relation with the Law, W.D. Davies, The Setting of the Sermon on the Mount, Cambridge, 1964, 109-190; E.P. Sanders, Paul and Palestinian Judaism, Philadephia, 1977, 147-182

106. Tos Sota 4,1ff which is an expanded halachah on Ex 20,5f

107. cf Jub. which returns time and again to the covenant-concept; concerning the compassion: 5,18: for everybody who does penance; 10,3: God to Noah; 45,3: God to Jacob; in Philo this way of thinking is found most concentrated in his doctrine on the δυνάμεις of God, cr De fuga et inventione 94f; 'first the divine power, then the creative power, the royal power, the gracious power (ἵλεως), in the exercise of which the Great Artificer takes pity and compassion on his own work (οἰκτείρει καὶ ἐλεεῖ), the legislative power, the prohibitive power'; cf also in Leg ad Gaium I. 6f; also LAB develops extensively a theology of the covenant: see 19,8-13; 23,4-6; 28,2-5; 32,7-8; on the compassion see 19,8.9.11; 12,10; 13,10; see further 4 Esr 7,132-139: notwithstanding the deep pessimism of this book, nevertheless this liberating comment; in Joseph and Aseneth 11,7-10 we find mention of the opposition between 'the jealous and terrible God' with 'the living and merciful God'; see also 11,18; 12,8; in the Mekilta on Ex most extensively in Massekta Beshallah I. vs 13,21

108. LAB 19,8 and 19,9

109. LAB 19,11

110. Prov 17,5 (LXX) is the most complete parallel, but see also Ps 18,15-27 and Os 2,25. It is the basis for thinking in oppositions: 'reward for the just' and 'punishment for the evil', which is so central in the Wisdom literature.

111. In certain manuscripts it has the title: 'on pity and mercy', cf M. de Jonge, Testamenta XII Patriarcharum, Leiden, 1970

112. I am not sufficiently conversant with the literature in this respect. However, see the limited number of the texts in Str.-B. I. 203: Tos Baba Qamma 9,30: Sifre on Dt 13,18 & 96; p Baba Qamma 8.6^{c}.19; b Shabbat 151b

113. Test Zeb 5,1

114. Test Zeb 5,3

115. Test Zeb 8,1, see also 8,2.3; 9,7
116. Mt 9,9-13; 12,1-8
117. Mt 23,23
118. That this cannot be taken as a Christian-Jewish controversy is clear from the traditions about Rabbi Jochanan in the Abot de Rabbi Nathan c. 4, which brings Os 6,6 in connection with the creation of the world (Ps 89,3), the destruction of the Temple and the possibility for reconciliation by 'acts of mercy' as Daniel did, see J. Neusner, Development of a Legend. Studies on the Traditions Concerning Yohanan ben Zakkai, Leiden, 1970, 113ff; for the exegesis of Mt 23, see D.E. Garland, The Intention of Matthew 23, Leiden, 1979, 136ff
119. Mt 9,9ff.27ff.36; 12,1ff; 14,15; 15,21ff.32; 18,23ff; 20,29ff
120. The parallel text of the saying in James 2,13 functions in the same way in the context of the opposition between rich and poor and the obligations of the Law; This is changed in Ep Pol 2,3 and 1 Clem 13,2
121. Ps 18,26
122. cf Baumgärtel, TWNT s.v. καρδία; H. Conzelmann, Grundriss der Theologie des Neuen Testaments, München, 1968, 195ff; R. Jewett, Paul's Anthropological Terms, Leiden, 1971, 305ff; K.-A. Bauer, Leiblichkeit - Das Ende aller Werke Gottes, Gütersloh, 1971, 142ff; R.H. Gundry, Sôma in Biblical Theology, Cambridge, 1976, 110ff
123. Mt 5,27f
124. Mt 23,25f: D.E. Garland, The Intention of Matthew 23, Leiden, 1979, 141ff gives an interpretation which respects the Jewish context of these sayings
125. For example A. Schlatter, Das Evangelium nach Matthäus, Stuttgart, 1969 (1961), 52: 'Jesus streitet damit scharf gegen das jüdische Verhalten: Da legte man sich allerlei auswendige Schmuck als Ehre um und erlaubte sich dabei, das Herz mit jeder Lust zu füllen'; see also Lohmeyer-Schmauch, Matthäusevangelium, 90; Strecker, Macarismes, 199; Bergpredigt, 42; without reference that the saying refers to a Christian-Jewish controversy, but in the supposition that the saying rejects ritual cleanliness, Beare, Matthew, 132; Schweizer, Bergpredigt, 17
126. Mt 15,1ff; in 23,23 one can see how Matthew sees this combination: one should do the one thing and not neglect the other thing
127. see for example also Philo, De Spec Leg IV. 84ff: the desire as the source of every evil: 'if the desire is directed to <u>money</u> it makes men thieves and cut-purses,

footpads, burglars, guilty of defaulting to their creditors, repudiating deposits, receiving bribes, robbing temples and of all similar actions; if its aim is reputation, they become arrogant, haughty, inconstant and unstable in temperament, their ears blockaded by the voices they hear etc.. they form friendships and enmities recklessly so that they easily change each for the other, and show every quality of the same family and kinship as these; if the desire is directed to office, they are factious, inequitable, tyrannical in nature, cruel-hearted, foes of their country, merciless masters to those who are weaker, irreconcilable enemies of their equals in strenght, and flatterers of their superiors in power etc; if the object is bodily beauty they are seducers, adulterers, pederasts, cultivators of incontinence and lewdness etc; of the tongue they cause an infinity of troubles etc; of the belly, it produces gourmands, insatiable, debauched etc'; see also Decal 142ff where Philo gives a description of the social evils caused by evil desire: war, murdering of nations etc; see also Apoc Mosis 19,3 and 4 Macc 2,1-16

128. The connection between the Law and Desire may be known from a text in Paul's Letter to the Romans: 'Through the Law I came to know Sin. I would not know about Desire, if the Law did not say: do not desire. Sin has used the Command in order to call forth Desire' (7,7ff). For the whole cluster, see J. Bowker, The Targum and Rabbinic Literature, Cambridge, 1969 which I complemented with elements from Targum Neophyti, see Neophyti, Barcelona-Madrid, 1968ff: for the connexion of Law and Covenant, see R. Mach, Der Zaddik im Talmud und Midrash, Leiden, 1957, 26-31 and E.P. Sanders, Paul and Palestinian Judaism, London, 1977 who, admittedly, did not take up texts from the targums; for the doctrine on the 'desires' in the midrashim, see G.F. Moore, Judaism in the First Centuries, Cambridge, I. 1927, 479-493

129. Apoc Mosis c. 13 (Transl. M.D. Johnson, OTPsepigrapha II); see also Test Levi: 18,9.10: 'In his priesthood sin shall cease and lawless men shall rest from their evil deeds, and righteous men shall find rest in him. And he shall open the gates of paradise, he shall remove the sword that has threatened since Adam' (Transl. H.C. Kee, OTPsepigrapha I); 1 En 5,8: 'And then wisdom shall be given to the elect. And they shall all live and not return again to sin' (Transl. E. Isaac, OTPsepigraphaI); PsSal 14,2-4: 'To those who live in the righteousness of his commandments, in the

Law, which he has commanded for our life. The Lord's devout shall live by it forever: the Lord's paradise, the trees of life, are his devout ones' (Transl. R.B. Wright, OTPsepigraphaII); 4 Esra 7,8.9: 'The seventh order, which is greater than all that have been mentioned, because they shall rejoice with boldness, and shall be confident without confusion, and shall be glad without fear, for they hasten to behold the face of him whom they served in life and from whom they are to receive their reward when glorified' (Transl. B. Metzger, OTPsepigrapha I)

130. see also G. Dalman, Die Worte Jesu, Darmstadt, 1965 (1930), 145; Str.-B., IV. 799-977; R. le Déaut, La nuit pascale, Rome, 1963, 237ff
131. This interpretation is a summary of a complete discussion which can be checked in resp. vRad, TWNT s.v. εἰρήνη; Theologie des Alten Testaments, München, 1962/3, I. 136; H.H. Schmid, Šalôm, 'Frieden' im Alten Orient und im Alten Testament, Stuttgart, 1971; E. Brandenburger, Frieden im Neuen Testament, Gütersloh, 1973
132. A description of the time between 70-125 AD in A. Büchler, The Economic Condition of Judea after the Destruction of the Second Temple, in, A. Corré, Understanding the Talmud, New York, 1975 (a reproduction of an article of 1912); S. Zeitlin, The Struggle between Secular and Religious Forces in Leadership, in the same reader, 107-118 on the leadership of the Beth-Din in Jamnia (of 1941); see also E. Smallwood, The Jews under Roman Rule, 1981, 331-387; M. Avi-Yonah, Geschichte der Juden im Zeitalter des Talmud, Berlin, 1962, 62ff
133. Mt 5,21ff; 5,43ff
134. Mt 5,44 with the concluding sentence: that you may become children of God
135. Mt 10,11ff
136. for literature, see note 99
137. 2 Kings 5,6-8 (LXX); in 11 QTemple 45,7-18 - a contemporary text of Matthew - one can see how these regulations - at least ideologically - influence some way of thinking: prohibited to enter the Temple are people who are ritually unclean owing to pollution or sexual contact (3 days); blindness (always); menstruation (7 days); unclean owing to contact with a dead person or to skin diseases (after purification); 1 QM 7,4ff and 1 QSa 2,3-11 where we find a similar list (they mention also the crippled and the lame) deal resp. with the participants of the holy war or with the members of the community.

138. E. Brandenburger, Frieden im Neuen Testament, Gütersloh, 1973, 33ff who sees the peace Messiah in Mt rightly in the image of the Shepherd of Israel who will bring back Israel to the pasture (2,6f). Jesus gives this form through his preaching and his healing (9,35ff); see also S. Légasse, Jésus et l'enfant, Paris, 1969, 257; M. Trautmann, Zeichenhafte Handlungen Jesu, Würzburg, 1980, 347ff
139. Jos. Ant. XII. 237-265; 1 Macc 1,16ff
140. Jos. Ant. XIV 54-74
141. Jos. Ant. XIV. 468ff
142. Jos. Bell Jud VI. 1ff
143. Mt 24,27.37.39
144. In Qumran a text is found which makes this connection - at least according to the reconstruction of J.A. Fitzmyer, A Wandering Aramean, Missoula, 1979, 92. In his translation the text says: 'O King. All men shall make peace, and all shall serve him. He shall be called the son of the Great God, and they shall call him Son of the Most High'. The official publication of this fragment in the Qumran edition which in Fitzmyer is indicated as 4Q psDan A^a (= 4Q 246), is still awaited for some time and is surrounded by mystery. Fitzmyer did not re-accept it in his Manual of Palestinian Aramaic Texts, Rome, 1978; see also M. Hengel, Der Sohn Gottes, Tübingen, 1975, 71ff
145. I placed the 'Messiah' in brackets, because, on the one hand, a close connection exists between the words 'son of David' and 'Messiah' while, on the other hand, it is not said explicitly anywhere in the Wisdom literature that the Messiah is the son of God
146. Ex 34,25; 37,26; Is 54,10
147. see especially R. Hummel, Die Auseinandersetzung zwischen Kirche und Judentum im Matthäusevangelium, München, 1966, 30, which study should be re-evaluated. It cannot be excluded that certain formulations could be understood also in another context; see Strecker's exposition in his explanation of Mt 5,11 later on in this commentary
148. In the Sermon on the Mount 5,10.11.44; in the discourse to the twelve disciples 10,16-24; as indication in the explanation of the parable of the weeds 13,21; in the parable of the criminal wine growers which serves as a mirror story for the whole of the gospel 21,33-45; in the tirade against the Pharisees and scribes 23,29-39; in the prophetic address about the end of Jerusalem and the end of the world 24,9-11
149. With the exception of 10,16ff but see 10,41; the other texts are to be found in resp. 5,44; 13,17; 21,32;

23,35 and 24,12

150. This understanding of justice is more or less common; generally one is not looking for a reference for the necessity of persecution, see G. Strecker, Der Weg der Gerechtigkeit, Göttingen, 1965/2, 151; Bergpredigt, 39; D.R. Hare, The Theme of Jewish Persecutions of Christians, Cambridge, 1967, 114ff. 130; A. Sand, Das Gesetz und die Propheten, Regensburg, 1974, 201; B. Przybylski, Righteousness in Matthew, Cambridge, 1980,98

151. see Jos. Ant XVII. 146ff; XVIII. 55ff; 257ff; XIX. 292ff; Bell Jud I. 648ff; II. 169ff; 184ff; Philo, C. Flaccum 36ff; 53-96; Leg ad Gaium 181ff; 349ff (especially this text deals with slander and ridicule); see also Hypothetica, in, Eusebius, Praeparatio Evangelica 6,9: 'they would even endure to die a thousand deaths sooner than accept anything contrary to the laws and customs which he (= Moses) had ordained'

152. Mt 24,15. For the connection with the whole history of persecution from the Seleucides via Daniel, see M. Hengel, Judentum und Hellenismus, Tübingen, 1969, 542; for the connection with the imperial cult, see L. Cerfaux - J. Tondriau, Un concurrent du christianisme. Le culte des souverains, Tournai, 1957, 189ff (on the Ptolemees); 229ff (on the Seleucides); 342ff (the time of Caligula)

153. Jos. Ant XX. 105ff; Bell Jud II. 223; see also the parallel in Taanit 4,6 where, connected with the 5 disasters of the 17th Tammuz, is mentioned: 'Apostomos burnt the Torah'.

154. Jos. Bell Jud II. 301

155. Mt 14,1-12; Jos. Ant XVIII. 116ff

156. Mt 23,35; Jos. Bell Jud. IV. 334ff, see O.H. Steck, Israel und das gewaltsame Geschick der Propheten, Neukirchen, 1967, 33ff who probably collected the whole literature on the identification of this Zechariah

157. especially Mt 27,4.19.24, and possibly Jos. Ant XVIII. 64, for literature on this question, J. Blinzler, Der Prozess Jesu, Regensburg, 1969/4,47ff and Schürer, History, I. 428ff

158. Strecker, Macarismes 204 with reference to codex D and Itala which write also in 5,11 'for the sake of justice'

159. Also in the other texts about persecution, the relation with the 'prophets' is always thematised: 13,17; 21,46; 23,29.30.31.34.37; 24,11 with the exception again of ch 10, but see 10,41

160. Strecker, Macarismes, 203 and Bergpredigt, 46
161. In opposition with R. Walker, Die Heilsgeschichte im ersten Evangelium, Göttingen, 1967, 98; for the complexity of the Israel-connection, see H. Frankemölle, Biblische Handlungsanweisungen, Mainz, 1983, 191ff
162. Str.-B. I. 236
163. Sir 39,26
164. Ez 16,4
165. J. Jeremias, Gleichnisse Jesu, Göttingen, 1965/7, 169
166. so for example Nedarim 6,3.4.6
167. so A. Jülicher, Gleichnisreden Jesu, Darmstadt, 1969/3 (1910), II. 17
168. The pun is made with the Hebrew-Greek words'tafal' and μωραίνω, M. Black, An Aramaic Approach to the Gospels and Acts, Oxford, 1967/3 (1946), 166
169. Mt 7,24.26 via the parallel μωραίνω and μωρός
170. b Bekorot 8b, Str.-B. I. 236 with the comments of T.W. Manson, The Sayings of Jesus, London, 1964/6 (1949), 132 and R. Schnackenburg, 'Ihr seid das Salz der Erde, das Licht der Welt', in, Evangelienforschung, Fs. J.B. Bauer, Graz, 1968, 138; see also Lev 2,13 about the salt of the covenant which should never be missing in a sacrifice.

     Whether b Berokot 8b can be seen as anti-Christian, is a question as is whether the saying about the salt could be an Israel metaphor. Joshuah's saying is found in the context of a demonstration to prove that Rabbi Joshuah possesses more wisdom than 60 (pagan) wise men from Athens (?; from the Atheneum in Alexandria?). When he has come in very cleverly, they ask him to tell them 'stories'; 'And he said: It happened that a mule bore a foal, which carried a placard on which was written, that he could demand from his father 100.000 zuz. They answered: Is it possible for a mule to bear a foal? And he said: It is only a story. (They said): How can one make salt salty, when its tang is gone. (-the verb 'serej' is used, not 'tafal'-) And he answered: With the placenta of the mule. (They said): Does a mule have a placenta? (He said): Can salt become evil smelling?'. And so it goes on: all kinds of fantastic stories and events. Rabbi Joshuah is the clever, intelligent, capable wise man who always wins from all wise men outside of Israel
171. neither Mc 9,50 nor Lc 14,34f are to be understood as metaphors of Israel
172. Is 42,6; 49,6; 60,3 and Lc 4,18f
173. Mt 3,15f; Is 9,1-2
174. It is defended as a thesis by W. Trilling, Das wahre Israel, München, 1958; among others it is taken up by

R. Schnackenburg, 'Ihr seid das Salz der Erde', in, Evangelienforschung, 1968, 134ff; implicit by J. Radermakers, Au fil de l'évangile selon saint Matthieu, Heverlee-Louvain, 1972, 87; G. Künzel, Studien zum Gemeindeverständnis des Matthäus-Evangelius, Stuttgart, 1978, 134ff

175. see the difference between Mt 5,1f and 7,28f

176. especially C.W.F. Smith, The Jesus of the Parables, Philadelphia, 1975, 156; see the difference with Lc 11,33 which deals with a cellar and with people who enter a house

Notes: chapter 2 THE LAWS FOR THE PEOPLE

1. This is a global interpretation to which I will return further on. The way one inserts Mt 28,16-20 in the whole of Matthew's gospel is determinant, cf the exegesis of Mt 7,3-5 with reference to the concept of ἀδελφός in Mt
2. Mt 26,64
3. This antithesis corresponds with the Hebrew juridical pair 'bṭl' - 'qum' as it appears time and again in the Mishnah, cf Abot 4,9; Gittin 4,1.2; Aboda Zara 4,4; for more texts, see D. Daube, The New Testament and Rabbinic Judaism, London, 1956, 60; the fact that the LXX does not translate these Hebrew words as καταλύω and πληρόω weakens the argument as is said by e.g. H.Th. Wrege, Überlieferungsgeschichte der Bergpredigt, Tübingen, 1968, 37, and R. Banks, Jesus and the Law, Cambridge, 1975, 207. But it is always difficult to evaluate argumenta ex silentio.
4. Because Guelich, Sermon on the Mount, 134ff gives a very good survey on all theories of this prolegomenon, I think that it is not necessary to repeat this. It is clear that in my interpretation I am making the choices which link up with a 'Jewish' reading of the text cf my starting-points; see also H.D. Betz, Studien zur Bergpredigt, Tübingen, 1985 and K. Berger, Zur Geschichte der Einleitungsformel 'Amen, ich sage euch', ZNW 63 (1972) 45-52
5. N.J. McEleney, The Principles of the Sermon on the Mount, CBQ 41 (1979) 552-570; E. Schweizer, Matthäus und seine Gemeinde, Stuttgart, 78ff; in Schweizer, Bergpredigt, 29 we find a rather strong emphasis on the 'fulfillment' in the second command of love of neighbour. Bot I do not want to underestimate the difficulty of the meaning of ἕως ἂν πάντα γένηται.
6. This is not completely correct. In its totality it is true only for 5,21 and 5,33; further parallels are 5,27. 38 and 43; the most typical formulation is 5,31; for an explanation of these matters, see ad hoc; see also G. Theissen, Studien zur Soziologie des Urchristentums, Tübingen, 1979, 176
7. D. Daube, The New Testament and Rabbinic Judaism, 55-66; E. Lohse, Die Einheit des Neuen Testaments, Göttingen, 1973, 73-87; see also W. Davies, The Setting of the Sermon on the Mount, Cambridge, 1964, 99ff; I. Abrahams, Studies in Pharisaism, I, 16; for the rabbinic termino-

logy, cf W. Bacher, Die exegetische Terminologie der jüdischen Traditionsliteratur, Hildesheim, 1965/3 (1899), I, 190

8. C. Albeck, Die Einführung in die Mischna, Berlin, 1971 in the first place of course; but see also the enormous project of J. Neusner, on the history of the mishnah law in the series Studies in Judaism in Late Antiquity, Leiden, 1974ff, and the German series, now published by Töpelmann, Berlin; for the literature of the time before the war, cf the introduction by M.S. Enslin, in I. Abrahams, Studies in Pharisaism
9. For this tradition and its exceptions, see the beautiful article by L. Finkelstein, The Ethics of Anonymity Among the Pharisees, in, Pharisaism in the Making, Selected Essays, New York, 1972, 187-198; see more general B. Gerhardsson, Memory and Manuscript, Lund, 1961
10. Especially De Decalogo, De Specialibus Legibus I/IV, De Praemiis et Poenis, De Virtutibus and the fragment Hypothetica in Eusebius, Praeparatio Evangelica 6,1-7, 18 and 11,1-11,18. For this last one, see the apodictic and anti-Jewish book by H. Conzelmann, Heiden-Juden-Christen, Tübingen, 1981, 171ff. 176ff
11. Antiquitates III. 90-286; IV. 176-302; Contra Apionem II. 145-219; for this see G. Vermès, A Summary of the Law by Flavius Josephus, NT 24 (1982) 289-303. The targums, TJ I, TJ II (cf M.L. Klein, The Fragment-Targums of the Pentateuch, Rome, 1980, I-II), T Neoph and the early midrashim I use because of the problems in dating, connected with the Mishnah parallels, more as support, when they clarify the relation to a text from scripture.

    For the halachah of the book Jubilees, cf L. Finkelstein, The Book of Jubilees and the Rabbinic Halacha, and, Some Examples of the Maccabean Halaka, in, Pharisaism in the Making, 199-204. There are no connections with Mt
12. especially Mt 23,3
13. Sifre on Num & 112, vs 15,31 shows how much of an inner-Jewish tradition this is. It gives a sevenfold explanation of the verse: 'the word of the Lord he despised'. Relevant for our context are the following interpretations: 'this indicates the Sadducees' (! for the Pharisees it are the Sadducees; for Mt it are the Pharisees); 'this indicates the person who says he will accept the whole of the Torah, except for one or another verse' (cf Mt 5,19); 'this indicates the one who learns the Torah but does not teach it' (cf Mt 5,19); a little further on in the text we find as

'kelal': 'because that is why the Torah is given: to learn and teach it, to keep and do it'. Only the emphasis on learning of the Torah study is typically rabbinical.
See also Sifra on Lev., Parasha Bechukkotaj II.3 vs 26,14: on Israel's breaking of God's Law: 'whoever does not learn the Torah and does not act according to it, whoever despises some commandments and hates the scribes, whoever does not induce others to fulfill the Torah, he will finally repudiate the commandments of the Sinai and their root (= God)'; or see Sifre on Dt & 48 vs 11,22: 'if one learns the Torah, he has fulfilled one commandment; if one learns the Torah and preserves it, he keeps two commandments; if one learns and preserves and keeps the Torah, there is no one greater'.

14. In M.McNamara, The New Testament and the Palestinian Targum to the Pentateuch, Rome, 1966, 126ff we can see how this halachah-expansion is present also in the targums: not in the texts where one would expect it (Ex 21,12; Lev 24,17. 21; Num 35,16ff), but in Gen 9,6 (to make clear that the commandment is binding also on the pagans, because it comes from Noah?)
15. For the biblical foundation, cf Sifre on Num & 160, vs 35,24
16. Ketubot 1,1; see also Sifra on Lev., Parasha IV.6 vs 4,15
17. Sanhedrin 1,1-3
18. Ant. IV. 8.14.214, but see also Sanhedrin 1,2 which mentions resp. 3.5 and 7 judges, and, Mekilta, Massekta Nezikin vs 22,8 which mentions a court of 3 and 5
19. Bell Jud II. 20.5.571; the use of the word εὐτελέστερος is interesting: it indicates an economic as well as a physical component, see Liddell-Scott; see also Ant IV. 8.38.287: if there is a loss of a deposit without fault, one must submit the case to the court of seven
20. CD 10,4-6: 6 Israelites plus 4 sons of Levi and Aaron; Sanhedrin 1,3 and Megilla 4,3 mention the δεκαπρωτοί of a city in which administration and jurisdiction come together
21. 4 Q 159. 2-4; for this references cf Schürer, History, II, 186ff
22. In certain situations the number of the judges can be raised till 71
23. It is a difficult question whether capital punishment is still historical reality in all these matters in the first and second century (and several others which I have left out, because they are clearly related to a more developed rabbinism). The historical question is

whether the Jews have been allowed to use their own judiciary system for such a long time within the context of the Roman law. In contemporary literature we find a great deal of agreement with the presentation from the Sanhedrin treatise:
see the parallels in Philo: De Spec Leg II. 242-256 (cursing one's parents, desecration of the sabbath, bearing false and rash witness, denial of God), III. 11 (adultery); III. 42 (emasculating sexuality); III. 51 (fornication); III. 83ff (murder); III. 94ff (witchcraft); IV. 19 (kidnapping); in Hypothetica 7,1: sexual intercourse with children; adultery; the rape of a girl or boy; prostitution; violence with regard to a slave or a free person; incarcerate him or sell him; theft of holy and profane things; godlessness, but also lack of respects for parents and benefactors;
and the parallels in Josephus: C Ap II. 145-217 which also follows the Decalogue more or less: sexual intercourse between males; dishonouring the wife of another; raping of a girl who is engaged; seducing a married woman; abortion; disrespect for parents; accepting gifts by a judge; godlessness; Jos. Ant IV. 171ff based on Dt 11-26 links capital punishment to blasphemy, falsely testifying in a capital case, adultery, disobedient son, kidnapping, poison, death premeditated; Ant III. 224ff which mostly treats ritual law, links adultery and incest again with capital punishment and gives as reason the (il)legality of the children;
In the Book of Jubilees capital punishment is prescribed for desecration of the sabbath (2,25; 50,8); manslaugther (4,32; 7,29); the eating of blood (6,12; 7,30; 21,19.20ff); whoremongery (20,4); to give one's daughter in marriage to a pagan (30,7); adultery (30,8); incest with the wife of one's father (33,10ff); with the wife of one's son (41,25); with the mother or daughter-in-law (41,26); for not observing the pesach (49,9) (cf J.C. VanderKam, Textual and Historical Studies in the Book of the Jubilees, Missoula, 1977: he uses a number of these data to date the book between 160 and 140 BC).
A similar list with capital punishments can be found in in LAB 25,8-13.
In opposition to T Neoph and T Onq we find in T J I continuous references to (actual?) juridical practices: see e.g. Ex 21,12: murder of an Israelite is to be punished by the sword; 21,15: abuse of father or mother should be strangled with a piece of cloth; 20,17: who curses father or mother, must be stoned; 20,19: if one

wounds someone, one must pay for the loss of labour, for pain damage and cost of sickness; 20,20: if one kills a slave, capital punishment by the sword is prescribed; 22,17: witchcraft demands stoning; 22,19: idolatry demands the sword; T J Lev 24,7: in case of blasphemy death by the sword; T J Num 35,19: if in a blood feud one kills the murders outside the city, one acts 'bdynj': in accordance with the Law; T J Dt 22,22: in case of adultery, death by suffocation; Dt 24,7: selling an Israelite as slave, death by suffocation. Are all these texts imaginary? In any case it corresponds to the demands of justice as people experience it, that for these matters the punishment is death. How long can this go on if there is no actual execution?
G. Vermès, A Summary of the Law by Josephus, NT 24 (1982) 296 connects this question only to the expositions of Josephus on the Temple and on sacrifices, but as demonstrated, there are a lot more factors which play a role.

24. see also T Neoph Lev 24,12; T Neoph Num 27,5: 'Moses was fast in civil cases but slow in capital cases to prevent that innocent blood was shed', parallel to T J I and T J II

25. Sanhedrin 1,1: a city should count at least 230 inhabitants to be permitted to have a sanhedrin, i.e. 1 judge on each ten inhabitants

26. the βουλή. For changes in the functions of the βουλή in the transition from the Seleucides/Herodians to the Roman city system, see A.H.M. Jones, The Greek City, Oxford, 1966/2 (1939), 112ff. There is more emphasis on the privileges of the rich. The possibility to judge remains for the time being, at least in the case of situations which touch their own citizens; on the function of the γερουσία in the Jewish πολίτευμα of Alexandria, cf V. Tcherikover, Hellenistic Civilization and the Jews, Philadelphia, 1959, 300ff; E.M. Smallwood, The Jews under Roman Rule, Leiden, 1981/2 (1976), 220ff

27. cf Z.W. Falk, Introduction to Jewish Law, Leiden, I, 79-92; S. Safrai, Jewish Self-Government, in, Jewish People in the First Century, Assen, I, 1974, 377ff; Schürer, History, II, 200ff; P. Vidal-Naquet, Du bon usage de la trahison, the introduction in the translation by P. Savinel, La guerre des Juifs, Flavius Josèphe, Paris, 1977, 69ff. Connected to texts of Qumran and patristic M. Weise, Mt 5,21f - Ein Zeugnis sakraler Rechtsprechung in der Urgemeinde, ZNW 49 (1958) 119; see also Jos Bell Jud II. 20.5.569f where he relates, how he calls together a sanhedrin of 70 as

leader in Galilee; see A.H.M. Jones, The Greek City, Oxford, 1966, 157ff for the broader context within Hellenism, especially with regard to the question of popular representation in the ecclesia

28. so e.g. Str.-B I.275ff; for a recent defense R.A. Guelich, Mt 5,22; Its Meaning and Integrity, ZNW 64 (1973) 39-52 in which other authors and an all-embracing exegesis of the discussed words ῥακά, κρίσις, συνέδριον, μωρός; cf also The Sermon on the Mount, 179ff. 239ff; Strecker, Bergpredigt, 70
29. Except Judea where Jerusalem functions as μητρόπολις, cf Schürer, History, II, 197ff, but see also 205f. 218ff. Different in S. Safrai, Jewish Self-Government, in, Jewish People in the First Century, Assen, I, 1974, 397, but see also 416. The Sanhedrin could impose legal interpretations, which lower courts had to follow, but that does not mean that there was a court of appeal. If other courts did not consider themselves competent, or if they could not agree, the case had to be referred to Jerusalem which then acted 'in first instance'; see Dt 1,17; 17,8 and Jos. Ant IV. 8.15,218; Bell Jud II. 20.5.570: 'with instructions to refer more important matters and capital cases to himself and the seventy'
30. See the difference in Greek between the dative with κρίσις and συνέδριον and the construction of εἰς plus accusative with γέεννα; a close parallel is found in 2 En 44,3 (J-text): 'He who expresses anger to any person without provocation will reap anger in the great judgment. He who spits on any person's face, will reap the same at the Lord's great judgment' (Transl F.I. Andersen, OTPsepigrapha I).
31. cf H.-Th. Wrege, Überlieferungsgeschichte der Bergpredigt, Tübingen, 1968, 57ff
32. This interpretation is possible only on the basis of equalization of court (5,22) = sanhedrin (5,22) = (representation of the) ekklesia (18,17); the arguments are: Mt 18,16 refers to Dt 19,15: the torah on the talio; the supposition is that it treats social inequalities, see also the sequel in Mt 18,21-35: pagan and publican are often understood only in their religious meaning; that they are also social realities of great importance, can be seen only, if one understands ekklesia in its social meaning; see also the explanation on 5,46; 6,9 and 6,19ff
33. so e.g. G. Strecker, Die Antithesen der Bergpredigt (Mt 5,21-48 par), ZNW 69 (1978) 49f; Bergpredigt, 70; H. Merklein, Die Gottesherrschaft als Handlungsprinzip, Echt, 1978, 260; Bertram, TWNT s.v. μωρός; Schweizer, Bergpredigt, 34. J.S. Vos, Antijudaismus/Antisemitismus

im Theologischen Wörterbuch zum NT, Ned Theol Tijdschr 38 (1984) 89-110, especially 98 shows impressively that this kind of reflection displays often a Christian anti-Jewish mentality

34. See Sifra on Lev., Parasha Achere Mot V. 8 vs 16,30 for this train of thought: 'Sins between man and God are forgiven through the Day of Atonement, but not the sins between man and his brother until man has been given reconciliation by his brother; ... until you have brought peace to your brother'. cf Joma 8.9 This is different from T Neoph Dt 22,4: 'you must forgive your brother what you have in your heart against him'. What is asked here, is far more difficult: to quieten the anger of the other
35. Sanhedrin 3,5; Test Isaac 5,10ff is even more strict about someone who has been angry with his brother for one hour or for five hours
36. We should not only think of the Mishnah; a man like Josephus acts this way too, cf the way he speaks easily about all kinds of Temple practices in C Ap II. 193ff. For an interpretation of the phenomenon, cf J. Neusner, A History of the Mishnaic Law, passim
37. Mt 18,23-35
38. H. Kippenberg, Religion und Klassenbildung im antiken Judäa, Göttingen, 1978, 142; J.D.M. Derrett, Law in the New Testament, London, 1970, 32ff, especially 40 note 2
39. Sanhedrin 3,1
40. e.g. Jos Bell Jud II. 569
41. Tos Sanhedrin 7,1
42. Abot 4,8: 'Rabbi Ismael ben Jose always said: Take care that you do not act as single judge because no one may judge except the One'
43. A.H. Sherwin-White, Roman Society and Roman Law in the NT, Ann Arbor 1981/2 (1963)133 has shown that the saying should not be understood against the background of Roman law.
44. Ketubot 4,4; Kiddushin 1,1; for the dating, see the exact parallel in Philo, De Spec Leg I. 107; III. 72
45. Ketubot 7,8
46. Ketubot 7,7
47. Ketubot 1,1
48. Kiddushin 2,8.9: there is here more respect for women's equality
49. Ketubot 1,1
50. Ketubot 1,1. The assertion about 'bying in error' is obviously essential. The precise rules will not have been the same all through the period. For possible dating, see J. Neusner, A History of the Mishnaic Law of Women, V, Leiden, 1980, 87.98.169. It is a real

deficiency in Neusner's study that he does not use contemporary literature at all: from Philo, De Spec Leg III. 80f and Jos. Ant. IV. 246 it appears that the virginity process is still active in the first century. Philo speaks of a γερουσία as court (the small sanhedrin of the politeuma of the Jews in Alexandria); Josephus uses the attic expression δίκην λαχὼν: obtain permission to start a court case: see especially the similarities and differences with Dt 22,13 ff

51. On the institution of the marriage of levirate, which probably stops in the first century, see Z.E. Falk, Introduction to Jewish Law, II, 317ff; via 11 Q Temple 57,17-19 and CD 4,12-5, 14, J.A. Fitzmyer, The Matthean Divorce Texts and Some Palestinian Evidence, Theol St 37 (1976) 197-226, shows that also within Judaism there is a criticism of polygamy (but see also D. Daube, The New Testament and Rabbinic Judaism, London, 1956, 85f. 298f). These texts do not prove much about actual practice, because they are mostly exhortative. It is certainly not correct to apply here 'quod licet Iovi non licet bovi', because according to Qumran the kings are usurpers pure and simple. For the influence of this thought on polygamy of kings and 'zenut', see Sanhedrin 2,4
52. Ketubot 4,4
53. Ketubot 5,8: for a calculation of the minimum of existence on the basis of these and some other parallel texts, see A. Ben-David, Talmudische Okonomie, Hildesheim, 1974, 306ff
54. Ketubot 5,9
55. Ketubot 10,1ff
56. Ketubot 13,2
57. Baba Batra 8,2; Ketubot 13,3: at least, this is the traditional opinion, cf P. Blackman, Mishna, London, 1953,III. 190, note 8; for the totality I. Abrahams, Studies in Pharisaism, I, 66-78
58. According to J. Neusner, A History of the Mishnaic Law of Women, Leiden, 1980, V. 100f this cluster belongs to the pre-Jabne or Jabne period, i.e. before 70 AD or between 70-140 AD
59. see also W. Schrage, Ethik des Neuen Testaments, Göttingen, 1982, 92ff
60. This interpretation seems obvious: see e.g. also Philo, De Decal 125 which says about adultery: it destroys three houses: the man's in whose house it happens, the man's and woman's who commit adultery; and Josephus C. Ap. II. 201: he who violates the honour of the wife of another man, must die; also he who rapes a girl who is betrothed to another man; and who seduces the wife of

another man; T J I Dt 22,22: 'when a man has sexual intercourse with a woman who is the wife of another man'; it seems important that this interpretation is 're-discovered' every time to prevent reading the halachah as an absolute prohibition against all desire: see e.g.! R. Guelich, The Antitheses of Matthew 5,21-48: Traditional and/or Redactional, NTS 22 (1975) 456; J.P. Meier, Law and History in Matthew's Gospel, Rome, 1976, 137; J.A. Fitzmyer, The Matthean Divorce Texts, Theol St 37 (1976) 203

61. Sanhedrin 7,4
62. Sanhedrin 11,1
63. For this discussion, cf Schürer, History, II, 218ff especially note 80 and 82; see also (already) I. Abrahams, Studies in Pharisaism, II, 129-137; A.H.M. Jones, The Greek City, 121ff although he supposes that capital cases belong to the procurator; recently also J.-P. Lémonon, Pilate et le gouvernement de la Judée, Paris, 1981, 74-97 who deals extensively with the juridical aspects and who concludes that the Sanhedrin has lost its competence in capital case. For the rest, one should not translate 'yšbh lh ḥnwt' with 'il (le Sanhédrin) tint ses séances à Ḥanut', nor 'glth' with 'exile'
64. see also note 23
65. in Mt 5,22 as well as in 5,29f
66. in Mt 18,17
67. Keritot from 'karet': excommunication, banishment, cut out
68. Keritot 1,1; for the dating J. Neusner, A History of the Mishnaic Law of Holy Things, Leiden, 1980, VI. 174f: this whole mishnah is a construction from the time after 140 AD; the actual text comes from scripture; the prescription of the atonement sacrifice is from the time of Jabne (70 AD); see also Sifre on Num & 125 vs 19,13 where Num 19,13 is compared with Lev 15,31 and where it becomes clear that the same infringement carries death as well as exile: 'to teach you that capital punishment is the same as the punishment of exile and that the punishment of exile is the same as capital punishment', i.e. the Torah has foreseen this interchange; see the difference in T J I Ex 21 between the different capital punishments: at the death of a goring animal whose owner has been warned thrice, the punishment is 'capital punishment sent from heaven' (because such punishment ran counter to Roman understanding of Justice?) (T J I Ex 21,29)
69. Cutting of the hand: see Dt 25,11 which speaks, however, about a woman who grabs the sexual organ of a

man; see also Philo's explanation of this text in De Spec Leg III. 175-177 who excuses the eye, but not the hand because it is freeer.

70. For C. Dietzelfelbringer, Die Antithesen der Bergpredigt, ZNW 70 (1979) are hand and eye expansion of lust rather than instruments. The saying can then be inserted in the context of Matthew's moralising tendency of the Law
71. Kiddushin 1,1
72. Gittin 5,2; Nedarim 9,5
73. On the historical aspects of the ketuba, cf Z.W. Falk, Introduction to Jewish Law, II, 295ff; J. Neusner, A History of the Mishnaic Law of Women, V, 119.166 gives as date for this mishnah a time before 70 AD
74. Ketubot 1,6; see also the comparison of the growth of the vagina with the growth of unripe dates to ripe ones in Nidda 5,7; Nida 2,5 uses the comparison of a house with rooms; see also Philo, De Spec Leg III. 33: 'Now nature also each month purges the womb as if it were a cornfield - a field with mysterious properties, over which, like a good husbandman, he must watch for the right time to arrive. So while the field is still inundated he will keep back the seed, which otherwise will be silently swept away by the stream etc'; Literary works from another setting like Ovidius' Ars Amatoria I. 360.755-58; II. 322.513. 667-68 show that the comparison of a woman with rural reality is wide spread and much used
75. Ketubot 8,3.4.5
76. Gittin 1,4.5.6; Kiddushin 1,2: for the position of the woman in this respect, see also H. Kreissig, Die sozialen Zusammenhänge des jüdischen Krieges, Berlin, 1970, 64ff
77. Gittin, 4,1-9
78. The latter, as further elaboration of the mishnah, must, obviously, be dated later (according to Neusner after 140 AD), but not the surprising point of departure that a woman and a slave are seen as the same (see Neusner, A History of the Mishnaic Law of Women, V. resp, 97.151ff and 168). G. Agrell, Work, Toil and Sustenance, Lund, 1976, 48.64.66 stresses more that the mishnah is connected with the name of Rabbi Eliezer (around 90 AD). He also mentions the rich economic background and situation of this rabbi, which one has to presuppose from such a mishnah
79. e.g. Gittin 2,7; Mt 10,35
80. Gittin 7,5
81. Gittin, 5,9, to mention is also Lc 15,8ff (the parable of the lost drachme)

82. Mt 27,55
83. As for the political implications of the presence of women at a crucifixion, see L. Schottroff, Maria Magdalena und die Frauen am Grabe, Evang Th 42 (1982) 3-25. Even though the patriarchal structure is not broken, the behaviour of the women in the NT is a break through in the women's image compared with for example the Mishnah and a man like Philo: there the opposition man-woman is determined by the opposition outside the house- inside the house (not even considering the mysogenous remarks in Hypothetica, Eusebius, Praeparatio Evangelica 7,3 and 11,14-18). The self-reliance, mobility and responsibility of the woman in the NT shows a very different picture.
84. Gittin 9,10
85. Mt 19,3-10
86. Mt 1,17ff
87. A. Fridrichsen, Excepta fornicationis causa, Svensk Exeg. Årsbok 9 (1944) 54-58; A. Isaksson, Marriage and Ministry in the New Temple, Lund, 1965, 135-142
88. J. Bonsirven, Le divorce dans le Nouveau Testament, Paris, 1948; H. Baltensweiler, Die Ehe im Neuen Testament, Zürich, 1967, 87ff; see also J.A. Fitzmyer, The Matthean Divorce Texts, Theol St 37 (1976) 197-226
89. Kiddushin 4,1; Makkot 3,1; Neusner dates the mishnah after 140 AD, but the point of departure - the care to keep pure the blood of the priestly class - in the time before 70 AD, see A History of the Mishnaic Law of Women, V, 173, but see also 37 and 264!; see also L. Finkelstein, The Pharisees, I, 16ff
90. We find in the Mishnah at least five different terms for children without parents: 'jatôm' (orphan), the child whose father has died; 'mamzer' (bastard), the child from an invalid marriage, while it is uncertain who the father is; 'shetuqi' (the silent one), the child whose father is unknown; 'asufi' (foundling), the child whose father and mother are unknown; 'natin' (wanderer), the child whose father is a 'gebeonite', see Jos 9,27, i.e. probably a slave in the Temple; see Kiddushin 4,1.2; for this text cf D.W. Amram, The Jewish Law of Divorce according to Bible and Talmud, New York, 1968/2, 93ff; S. Krauss, Die Mishna, IV. 4 und 5, Sanhedrin, Makkot, Giessen, 1933, 357
91. A.M. Dubarle, Mariage et divorce dans l'Évangile, L'Orient Syrien 9 (1964) 61-73; for the data with regard to the existence of the 'pagan' cult, see Mt 6,7ff
92. For a recent survey on these and other theories, see A.L. Descamps, Les textes évangéliques sur le mariage,

Revue de Théologie Louvaine 11 (1980) 5-50; for other proposals, cf J.B. Bauer, Bemerkungen zu den matthäischen Unzuchtsklauseln (Mt 5,32; 19,9), in, J. Zmijewski - E. Nellesen, Begegnung mit dem Wort, Fs H. Zimmermann, Bonn, 1980, 23-33: he connects the text with Prov 18,22 (LXX), Jer 3,1-10 and 1 Cor 6,15ff

93. J.J. Kilgallen, To what are the Matthean Exception-Texts (5,32 and 19,9) an Exception, Bibl 61 (1980) 102-105

94. Ketubot 3,4-7; for the dating, see the exact parallel in 11 Q Temple 66,4-11; see also Philo, De Spec Leg III. 65-71 and Jos Ant IV. 251-252 and C. Ap. II. 201 which states more clearly the possibility of choice-to accept or to refuse the marriage - in case of rape (cf Ex 22,16 in opposition with Dt 22,28f); Philo, De Spec Leg III. 82 gives this same choice to a woman who is wrongly accused of the premature loss of virginity

95. Ex 20, especially 20,20 and 20,25

96. K. Berger Hartherzigkeit und Gottes Gesetz. Die Vorgeschichte des anti-jüdischen Vorwürfs in Mk 10,5, ZNW 61 (1970) 1-47; J. Piper, 'Love your enemies', Cambridge, 1974, 1-14

97. D. Novak, Law and Theology in Judaism, New York, 1974, 1-14 shows how the discussion between Hillel and Shammai influences the present Jewish marriage practices and by the way we see how great the similarity is with the just mentioned Matthean theology.

98. see also Mt 5,38f

99. For this distinction, see Neusner, A History of the Mishnaic Law of Women, III. 3-8. It is a distinction which is far more clarifying than the division in oaths which assert something and oaths which promise something, and yet, notwithstanding the criticism, this division keeps turning up, see J. Schneider, TWNT s.v. ὀμνύω and ὅρκος who does not even mention the 'neder'; G. Strecker, Die Antithesen der Bergpredigt, ZNW 69 (1978) 58ff; J.P. Meier, Law and History in Matthew's Gospel, Rome, 1976, 151 note 65; Guelich, Sermon on the Mount, 213

100. Shebuot 4,1-13

101. Shebuot 5,1-5. For the dating, see Philo's exposition on the pawn De Spec Leg IV. 30ff, and Jos Ant, IV. 286; see also T Neoph Ex 22,8; T J I Ex 22,10

102. This is not to be found in Philo and Josephus. Therefore, this oath should probably be dated later, see Shebuot 6,1-7; but see also Ex 22,8.10

103. See the treatise Nedarim, but also Philo De Spec Leg II. 9-25; De Decal 92-95; in Hypothetica, Eusebius, Praeparatio Evangelica 7,5 one finds the custom that

priests can dissolve vows

104. For this interpretation of the vows, cf J. Neusner, A History of the Mishnaic Law of Women, III, Introduction

105. Ex 20,7: the Hebrew word 'lashaw' is translated in the LXX with οὐ ἐπὶ ματαίῳ: not on something idle; in Jos Ant III. 91 with ἐπὶ μηδενὶ φαύλῳ: not for a slight matter; Philo, De Spec Leg II. 2 idem as LXX; II. 224: μὴ συνόλως μάτην: not whatsoever without reason; De Decal 51.85: μὴ ἐπὶ ματαίῳ: not on something idle; LAB 11,7 gives a typical parallel: 'non accipies nomen Domini Dei tui, ne vie mee vane efficiantur'; see also 44,6 where it is connected with idolatry; in 40,3 it has become: 'in oratione preoccupatus est pater meus', a text which is more positive for Jephta than the Hebrew text cf D.J. Harrington, The Hebrew Fragments of Pseudo Philo's Liber Antiquarum Biblicarum preserved in the Chronicles of Jeraḥmeel, Missoula, 1974; for yet other quotes cf G. Dautzenberg, Ist das Schwurverbot Mt 5,33-37; Jak 5,12 ein Beispiel für die Torakritik Jesu?, BZ 25 (1981) 53

106. The use of words is somewhat confused, cf the opposition between Shebuot 3,7 and 3,9

107. Jastrow s.v. 'biṭuj' and 'bṭh' and 'shaw'; see also Sifre Num & 153 vs 30,3 (end): 'He should not desecrate his word in this way': Rabbi Eliezer says: This is said in order to put the rash saying ('hbṭ'h') on a level with an oath. Rabbi Aqiba says: He must act precisely as he expresses himself. It is said in order to put the rash saying ('hbṭh') on a level with an oath'; and Sifre on Num & 153 vs 30,7 (end): 'A rash word ('byṭwy') is the same as an oath, as has been said: 'when someone swears with a rash expression' (= Lev 5,4), cf also Mekilta, Massekta Baḥodesh VII. vs 20,7 which also sees a connection with Lev 5,4. Sifre on Lev does not give a comment in a significant way in vs 5,4, but see T Onq Ex 20,7; Dt 5,11 which translates the hebrew expression 'lashaw' by two different words: by 'lemagana' (for nothing) and by 'lešiqra' (false); see also the difference between T Neoph Lev 19,12; 'you should not swear falsely (lšqr)', with in the margin 'for nothing (ᶜl mgn)', and T J II (mss 110 Paris) Ex 20,7 which gives the double interpretation: 'to use the name of God for nothing (lmgn')' and 'to swear falsely' (tštbᶜ ... wtqšr)

108. Shebuot 3,1-11

109. See the derivations in G. Strecker, Die Antithesen der Bergpredigt, ZNW 69 (1978) 58f and G. Dautzenberg, Ist das Schwurverbot ein Beispiel für die Torakritik Jesu,

BZ 25 (1981) 50ff. If it is true what I am saying, their complete Formgeschichte must be revised

110. cf the introduction-formulas and the use of the article δε (only in 5,21 and 5,33), the connection between the court and the oath, the digression of the antithesis

111. ἀληθορκέω

112. εὐορκέω, Liddell-Scott s.v. ἀληθορκέω, ἐπιορκέω, εὐορκέω, ψευδορκέω. A good example can be found in Jos Ant XVIII. 9.1.335. The story is about Anilaios and Asinaios, two Jewish robbers who become officers in the Parthian army. When they appear at the court of Artabanus, one of the generals wants the king to give him permission to kill Asinaios. The king cannot do that, because he gave Asinaios his oath that he would be safe. But he says: 'my ἐπιορκία (= breaking my oath) is not necessary. You can save the honour of the Parths, if you kill him with your own army without my knowledge, when he leaves'

113. cf without any account the translation in W.F. Albright - C.S. Mann, Matthew, 66 but you cannot say that 'the translators misunderstood the Aramaic'; the opposite in Guelich, Sermon on the Mount, 212 who translates with 'you shall not swear a false oath' but then continues with the statement: 'The conjunction δε generally connotes the adversative meaning 'but'. Translated in this way, the second part of the premise stands in contrast to the first. Yet such an understanding would not make any sense'; see also his worrying on page 249;.
I am wondering whether this meaning of ἐπιορκέω should not be supposed in texts as Wisd 14,28: (see addition ταχέως and opposition with κακῶς ὀμόσαντες 14,29); Didache 2,3 (as different from the false witness; see also 2,5: 'your word shall not be mendacious, nor idle but filled with deed(s)'!; Phocylides 16 (vs 17 deals with the false oath); Test Aser 2,6: see parallel with ἀθετῇ

114. P.S. Minear, Yes or No: The Demand for Honesty in the Early Church, NT 13 (1971) 8 but he should not refer to Mt 15,18-20. This deals with ψευδομαρτυρία i.e. with the ninth/resp. the eighth command of the Decalogue

115. see also Mt 7,16-20. 24-27; for a close parallel, see 11 Q Temple 53,11-15

116. See especially the addition in T Neoph and T J I Ex 20,7. I quote the latter: 'That no one of you swears idly in the name of the word of JHWH, your God, because JHWH will not leave unpunished <u>on the day of</u>

the great judgment whoever has sworn idly in his name'; parallel to Dt 5,11; see also Jub 31,29

117. This is against the opinion of G. Dautzenberg, Ist das Schwurverbot ein Beispiel für die Torakritik Jesu?, BZ 25 (1981) 47ff; see e.g. Philo, De Spec Leg II,4f who knows of criticism of oaths but who nevertheless writes: 'Those persons too deserve praise whose unwillingness, tardiness and shrinking, if they are ever forced to swear, raise qualms not only in the spectators but even in those who are administring the oath: such people are in the habit of saying 'Yes, by ...', or No, by ...' and add nothing more, and by thus breaking off suggest the clear sense of an oath without actually making it. But also a person may add to his 'Yes' or 'No' if he wish, not indeed the highest and most venerable and primal cause, but earth, sun, stars, heaven, the whole universe'. For the rabbinic opinions, cf W.D. Davies, The Setting of the Sermon on the Mount, Cambridge, 1964, 239ff
118. as in Philo, De Spec Leg II. 16ff: these oaths are an expression of hatred for people, of a wild character, of pride, of lack of education and frivolity: the last two especially in the case of oaths of women.
119. Mt 23,16-21; for commentary D.E. Garland, The Intention of Matthew 23, 132ff
120. Mt 14,6-12
121. Mt 26,63
122. Mt 26,69-75
123. especially Jos Bell Jud II. 135 and 139: 'swearing they avoid, regarding it as worse than ἐπιορκία (a rash oath!)', a remark which admittedly is not supported by Qumran texts but which is completely parallel to Mt 5,33.34; cf also 11 Q Temple 53,11-15
124. Ex 21,12-22,26
125. Jos Ant IV. 196
126. Philo, De Spec Leg III. 181; for the actual existence of this πολιτεία cf V. Tcherikover, Hellenistic Civilization and the Jews, Philadelphia, 1959, 300ff; cf Hypothetica, Eusebius, Praeparatio Evangelica 6,1-6,10; and especially the explanation of the seventh commandment against stealing, De Spec Leg III. 144ff and IV. 1-40
127. Note how this train of thought returns in the midrashim in places where one would not expect it, e.g. Sifre on Num & 2.3.4. vs 5,5-8 which uses a possible infringement of the Law, by a woman who has slept with another man, to speak about goods which have been lost and are found, about theft and arson, a deposit and a debt in money; or Sifra on Lev, Parasha Wajikra,

XII.22 vs 5,21 where the torah on safekeeping, loans, theft and found goods is supplemented with the other parts of this law: arson, injury, rape, killing bull etc; T J I Ex 21,1 introduces the series with the expression: 'see, these are the 'sidre dinayya' (the juridical prescriptions) which you shall teach'; cf also Sifre on Dt & 16 vs 1,16

128. Baba Qamma 1,3; Sanhedrin 3,1, cf also Lc 12,14
129. e.g. Sanhedrin 1,4 on the killing of an animal which has killed a person: the bull, wolf, lion, bear, leopard, and snake; and the killing of the animal's owner and the correspondence with Baba Qamma 1,4
130. see also Mt 5,21
131. J.P. Meier, Law and History in Matthew's Gospel, Rome, 1976, 158
132. Jos Ant IV. 280; Philo, De Spec Leg III. 181 is yet pleading for a literary correspondence between crime and punishment
133. Also Baba Qamma 1,1; 1,3; 8,1; one estimates what a person would bring in as a slave before and after the accident; or how much someone would demand for the pain suffered, or how much a security man would get for guarding a gherkin field; see also T J I Ex 21,19 and especially 21,24 where the expression 'an eye for an eye' is changed into 'the price of an eye for an eye, the price of a tooth for a tooth etc'; parallel in T J I Lev 24,19f; T J I Dt 19,21 cf the commentary in Mekilta on Ex., Massekta Nezikin VIII. vs 21,23ff; for the datings, see Z.W. Falk, Introduction to Jewish Law, II. 165ff
134. Mekilta on Ex, Massekta Nezikin XIV. vs 22,4: 'Even if Scripture had not said so, I would have known it to be a logical conclusion (that the damage one's animals do in someone else's field, must be compensated), because the 'pit' is is one's money, and the 'grazing' is his money'; clearer yet is b Baba Qamma 5a: 'How does one arrive at such uniformity? By the uniform interpretation of the following terms: 'instead of', 'compensation', 'payment' and 'money'.'
135. b Baba Qamma 4b: 'There are 13 causes of damage: an unpaid surety, a lender, a paid surety, a renter, loss of value (- to which the loss of goods belongs -), pain, healing, loss of time, humiliation, and the four matters mentioned in the Mishnah (i.e. goring ox, open well, grazing and arson)'.
136. On the discussion with regard to this problem, cf R. Banks, Jesus and the Law, Cambridge, 1975, 196
137. How this is connected with a Jewish way of thinking, appears from Sifra on Lev., Parasha Qodashim II. 4 vs

19,17 where the prohibition of revenge is explained by the example of lending out a saw to his neighbour, notwithstanding the fact that he had not been willing to give you his axe the day before

138. Baba Metzia 8,4
139. G. Theissen, Studien zur Soziologie des Urchristentums, 1979, 177
140. Mt 23,35
141. Jos Bell Jud II. 350f
142. For a much better historical analysis, see P. Hoffmann, Tradition und Situation, in, Ethik im Neuen Testament, Freiburg, 1984, 50-118
143. For the immediate post-Jabne time, cf W.D. Davies, The Setting of the Sermon on the Mount, Cambridge, 1964, 256-315; for the revolution under Hadrian, as for the whole period, cf M. Avi-Yonah, Geschichte der Juden im Zeitalter des Talmud, Berlin, 1962, 62ff and E.M. Smallwood, The Jews under Roman Rule, Leiden, 1981. For the stories on Aqiba, cf L. Finkelstein, Aqiba, 1962. The discussions in the two wars run parallel. This appears clearly in the story of the meeting of Rabbi Hanina and Rabbi Joseph. Rabbi Hanina reads the Torah publicly, against the express prohibition of the Romans. Rabbi Joseph attacks him over this 'because the Romans have been given their power from heaven; they have destroyed the Temple, they have killed the just, murdered the nobility and still they live'. He calls this common sense, but Rabbi Hanina answers: 'God will have mercy', see b Aboda Zara 18a, and the similarity with the speech of King Agrippa II to the people in the war of 70 AD, cf note 141
144. L. Schottroff - W. Stegemann, Jesus, Hoffnung der Armen, Stuttgart, 1978, 80 who give a reference to Jos Bell Jud II. 338 and 417ff, but there are much more texts; see, for the rest, Theissen, Studien zur Soziologie, 191 where he speaks with more shades
145. Baba Qamma 8,6; see for this summary also Sifra on Lev., Parasha Emor IV. 20 vs 24,19; D. Daube, The New Testament and Rabbinic Judaism, London, 1956, 254-265 sees hitting the cheek as a case of 'injuria' (an offense) which the rabbis bring under the law of talio later. If we interpret it as a brawl, we do not have to look for such a complicated historical reconstruction, because it connects directly with Ex 21,18ff and the examples in Baba Qamma 8,6
146. Lc 6,29
147. Mekilta on Ex., Massekta Kaspa I vs 22,25; see also H.-Th. Wrege, Die Überlieferungsgeschichte der Bergpredigt, Tübingen, 1967, 76

148. Baba Metzia 1,1: for commentary and an historical reconstruction of the care for clothes cf A. Ben-David, Talmudische Okonomie, Hildesheim, 1974, 310; J. Broer, Friede durch Gewaltverzicht, Stuttgart, 1984, 26 supposes that it does not come to a lawsuit. The nudity scene takes place then in the street
149. Jos Ant XIII. 52: in the edict of Demetrius to Jonathan in which he gives exemption from the duty to provide post's horses
150. According to M. Rostovtzeff, The Social and Economic History of the Roman Empire, Oxford, 1957/2 (1936), I, 381 it is a word from the Persian or Aramaic language and the use comes originally from the East. It was, however, fully accepted by the Romans already in the first century, as we see in the edict of Germanicus on Egypt. For the further history, see p. 381-387; see also F.M. Heichelheim, Roman Syria, in, Economic Survey of Ancient Rome, IV. 242ff; M. Avi-Yona, Geschichte der Juden im Zeitalter des Talmud, Berlin, 1962, 93
151. Baba Metzia 7,8
152. see also Abot 2,9 where Ps 37,21 is quoted, and the interest of this mishnah for Mt 6,22ff
153. It is not without reason that one can see reminiscences with Paul in my commentary. There is an historical line from this halachah in Matthew and the series of statements of Paul in Rom 12,9- 21. For a more complete treatment of this text, see J. Piper, 'Love your enemies', Cambridge, 1979, 100ff; see also G. Strecker, Compliance, Love of Enemy - The Golden Rule, Australian Bibl Rev 29 (1981) 40ff. However, there is a real ideological difference between his interpretation and mine
154. recently J. Piper, 'Love your enemies', 19-63. Correctly, texts as 1 QS 1,9 and 1 Q 9,2ff are not considered as parallels, see R. Banks, Jesus and the Law, Cambridge, 1975, 200; for an extensive discussion of the texts from Qumran in relation with Mt 5,43 cf W.D. Davies, The Setting of the Sermon on the Mount, Cambridge, 1964, 245ff. He considers the Qumran people as the anti-type of Mt
155. cf I. Broer, Freiheit vom Gesetz, Stuttgart, 1980, 86
156. T J I Dt 20,19 gives as reason 'for these trees cannot hide themselves as humans can; T Neoph Dt 20,19 'for they cannot fly'; in Jos Ant IV. 299 'for they cannot speak or lament or move'
157. Jos Ant IV 257. 265. 292. 299; C Ap 212; Philo, De Virt 109-115. Philo is clearly more theoretical; and besides he mentions only the duty to negotiate and the

rule on the captured woman

158. Dt 20; 21,10-14. 22-23

159. Sota 8; in Sifre on Dt & 221 vs 21,10 it is expressly stated that these war laws treat a 'war of authority' i.e. a national war which is politically demanded; but in Sifre on Num & 42 vs 6,26 where peace is glorified in 20 sayings, the talk is only about peace in Israel: from the text of Dt only 20,10 is used; in T J I Dt 20,1 the exceptions for taking part in the war are interpreted according to levitical laws of cleansing: whoever has a house which does not yet have a 'mezuza' (a case with the text from Dt 6,4-9 and 11,13-21 and sometimes the Decalogue); a vineyard which has not yet been bought back from the priest; whoever is unclean because of sin; the same in Dt 20,19 which sees a connection between cutting fruit trees and the sabbath; 20,20 which calls a besieged city a 'rebellious' city (cf Sanhedrin 1,1; 10,5); 21,13: a captured woman must become a proselyte.

160. Ex 23,5 and Dt 22,4; see the difference between Philo, De Virt 96; 116 and Baba Metzia 2,10; see also T J I Ex 23,5 where the whole concept of enmity is depoliticized: 'your enemy i.e. the man which you despise on behalf of a fault in him which is known only to you'; also in T Neoph Ex 23,5 the enemy is an inhabitant of the country. It prescribes that one should do away with everything evil against him, cf T J II (ms 440 Vatican) Dt 32,4; in Sifre on Dt & 222 vs 22,4 there is a reference to Ex 23,5

161. This theory which is linked up with M. Rostovtzeff's thesis, has been disputed recently by H. Grassl, Sozialökonomische Vorstellungen in der kaiserzeitlichen griechischen Literatur, Wiesbaden, 1982. It all depends what one understands as 'questions of state'. Even as regards the economy and the insights in that which form in a certain sense the centre of his argument, Grassl must admit that his authors '(klare, wenngleich) vielfach hausbackene und auch von einer moralischen Grundhaltung getragene Positionen entwickelt (haben)' (p. 203). One could ask whether this is all that far removed from M.I. Finley's argument on the common sense insight of the ancient authors. (see The Ancient Economy, London, 1975). Notwithstanding the correct and impressive parallelism of the socio-economic way of thinking and the praxis of the state from the first to the third century, it remains that for the time being the real 'question of state' - i.e. the question about the political power structures- has been lost from sight

162. Sanhedrin 6,5; see also b Hagiga 15b owing to this word Rabbi Meir is given forgiveness for his error to have taught Ben Acher, the renegade
163. Sanhedrin 4,5; see also Mekilta on Ex., Massekta Baḥodesh VIII vs 20,17 where it is said that the first 5 commandments are put on the first stone and the last 5 on the second. Therefore, the first and the sixth commandment must be interpreted in relation to each other: 'This tells that if one sheds blood, it is accounted to him as though he diminished the divine image'
164. Lev 19,17.18; see for these texts of the Torah and their influence in the legal interpretation of Jesus, parallel to my own text but with much more ruach hachaja, P. Lapide, Die Bergpredigt. Utopie oder Programm, Mainz, 1982, 88vv
165. see Nedarim 9,4 which speaks about the possibility to 'undo' vows, if they are made in ignorance that they are against prescriptions or at least could be against prescriptions; and T Neoph Lev 19,16f (par T J I Lev 19,16) which interpret the texts with examples from the court: no triple tongue, no false or absent witnesses against one's neigbour. The parallel with the antitheses in Mt is then almost complete
166. Quoting some of them without any pretension of completeness: see Prov 24,29: Do not say 'I will do to him as he has done to me, I will pay the man back for what he has done; Prov 25,21: if your enemy is hungry, give him to eat bread; if he is thirsty, give him to drink water; Sir 28,2: forgive your brother his injustice; Jos As 23,9; 28,5; 28,14; 29,3: do not repay evil for evil to any man; Test Gad 6,3: expel the venom of hatred and do not harbor deceit in your heart; T J I Lev 19,18 and 19,34: you shall love your brother as yourself and what you consider to be unpleasant for yourself, you shall not do to him; Seneca, De Beneficiis IV. 26: if you are imitating the gods, you say, 'then bestow upon the ungrateful; for the sun rises also upon the wicked, and the sea lies open to pirates'; Epictetus, Diss. III. 22.54: the cynic needs to be flogged like an ass, and while he is being flogged he must love the men who flog him, as though he were the father or brother of them all.
For these and other references, see J. Piper, 'Love your Enemies', 19ff
167. L. Schottroff, Gewaltverzicht und Feindesliebe, in, Fs Conzelmann, Tübingen, 1975, 197-221 has made an impressive plea for this reality
168. L. Schottroff - W. Stegemann, Jesus. Hoffnung der

Armen, 21ff

169. A. Dihle, Die goldene Regel, Göttingen, 1962, 32 who gives a treasure of references
170. see Respublica 332 E; 334 C; 335 E; Meno 71 E; Gorgias 507 B; these references come from A. Dihle, Die goldene Regel, 33f and especially 61ff
171. see also the discussion in Mt 7,12
172. It is a pity that L. Schottroff, Gewaltverzicht und Feindesliebe, Fs H. Conzelmann, 197ff does not deal with this problem. If it is difficult even for a writer of a gospel to do without 'thoughts of enmity' ...!
173. cf I. Abrahams, Studies in Pharisaism, II, 138-182; Delling, TWNT s.v. τέλειος; J. Zumstein, La condition du croyant dans Matthieu, Göttingen, 1977, 323; R. Mach, Der Zaddik in Talmud und Midrash, Leiden, 1957, 19ff; for a survey, cf Guelich, Sermon on the Mount, 234ff: taking into account his view on the whole of the Sermon, he naturally makes a plea for an interpretation which is Wisdom-oriented.

Notes: chapter 3 THE PRACTICES OF JUSTICE

1. In Sifra on Lev., Introd. has been recorded how in the 15 middoth of Ismael the fifth middah of Hillel 'kelal uperaṭ uperaṭ ukelal' (the general and the specific, and the specific and the general) has been developed hermeneutically into 6 separate rules; for a discussion of these texts, W. Bacher, Die exegetische Terminologie der jüdischen Traditionsliteratur, Hildesheim, 1965/ 3 (1899-1905), I, 79f; II, 83f
2. H. Bolkestein, Wohltätigkeit und Armenpflege im vorchristlichen Altertum, Groningen, 1967/2 (1939)
3. For the critical remarks, A.R. Hands, Charities and Social Aid in Greece and Rome, New York, 1968; H. Grassl, Sozialökonomische Vorstellungen in der kaiserzeitlichen Griechischen Literatur, Wiesbaden, 1982, 4
4. Lev 19,9f; 23,22; Dt 24,19-21
5. For a clear description of the Pea treatise, A. van Iterson, Armenzorg bij de Joden in Palestina, Leiden, 1911, 8-100
6. L. Finkelstein, The Pharisees, Philadelphia, 1945/3 (1938), I, 69
7. On this complicated legislation and the differences in the contemporary literature, esp. on the question whether priests are meant or levites, W. Bunte, Maaserot - Maaser Sheni, Die Mischna, I, 7/8, Berlin, 1962, 1-50; cf also J. Jeremias, Jerusalem in the Time of Jesus, London, 1969, 126ff
8. Maaser Sheni 5,14 and its criticism on this practice
9. On the maintenance of the priests and the levites, Schürer, History, II, 257-274
10. Jos., Ant XX. 181ff
11. For instance Pea 1,6; Shekalim 5,2
12. TJ I Dt 26,12 says that the second tenth is for the poor and the third tenth for the sacrificial meal; in Tob 1,7.8 we find the reverse; the representation is more or less that it happens every year
13. cf Dt 14,24ff; Jos. Ant IV 240 states that a third tenth is added every third year
14. Pea 8,5; as a cubic measure a qab is about 2 litres, a log about $^{1}/2$ litre according to P. Blackman, Mishnayot, London, 1951, I, 18; the precise measures in A. Ben-David, Talmudische Okonomie, New York, 344: qab = 2,197 litre; log = 0,549 litre
15. Dt 26,13-15. This prayer has played an important role

in the history of the controversy between Pharisees and Sadducees. Johannes Hyrkanus (135-104 BC) abolished the prayer when he switched from the Pharisees to the Sadducees (Maaser Sheni 5,15; Sota 9,10; Jos., Ant XIII. 270ff; for commentary, Schürer, History, I, 211ff; W. Bunte, Maaserot, 243f). Therefore, the rabbis gave it a very special attention (see the midrash-like commentary in Maaser Sheni 5,10-13, but also TJ I and T Neoph Dt 26,13ff, which can obviously be used as an argument for the reality of the second (or/and third) tenth

16. Mekilta on Ex., Massekta Kaspa III., v. 23,10; Varro, De rerum rusticarum I.44.3
17. For the reality at the time of the kings, see D. Correns, Schebiit, Die Mishna, I, 5, Berlin, 1960,2ff, but see especially the beatitude of the meek
18. For this list, D. Correns, 17ff; more obsolete also in A. van Iterson, Armenzorg bij de Joden in Palestina, Leiden, 1911, 71f; cf. also R. North, Maccabean Shabbath Years, Bibl 34 (1953) 501-515 who has a wide ranging discussion about the problems of dates and who arrives at a more negative conclusion; as to the celebration of the sabbath year cf. also Tacitus, Historiae, V, 4: 'dein blandiente inertia septimum quoque annum ignaviae datum': 'with the progress of time they spent the sabbath year doing nothing, seduced into this because of their laziness'; cf. also Sota 7,8 which probably gives the description of the closing ceremonies of the sabbath year of 41 AD by Herodes Agrippa, S. Zeitlin, Some Stages of the Jewish Calendar, in, Studies in the Early History of Judaism, New York, 1973, I, 183-193 proposes a completely different theory which presupposes that the sabbath year and the jubilee year coincided: after a cycle of 49 years a period of 49 days was inserted - necessary because one day a year was lacking; this period was the jubilee year and the sabbath year.

    The supposition that people could buy food from the 'pagan' inhabitants of the country, is juridically excluded, because the halachah forbade this, cf Shebiit 6,1-2.5-6. But there was import of grain and flax from Egypt and Syria, cf S. Applebaum, Economic Life in Palestine, in, The Jewish People in the First Century, Assen, 1976, 669
19. Shebiit 10,3.4
20. On this interpretation, Z.W. Falk, Introduction to Jewish Law, Leiden, 1978, I, 25; II, 208
21. I am following here A.R. Hands, Charities and Social Aid in Greece and Rome, New York, 1968 and H. Grassl,

Sozialökonomische Vorstellungen, Wiesbaden, 1982, 11-34

22. See for instance the letters of the younger Pliny X. 39.40.70 in the beginning of the second century; or Dio Chrysostomos, Discourses 40,5ff; 41,6ff; 44; 45,6ff. For a general survey, A. Jones, The Greek City, Oxford, 1966/2 (1939), 121ff; 139ff.; M. Finley, The Ancient Economy, London, 1975, 150ff
23. Nedarim 5,5
24. Lc 7,4f; for the discussion on the text, I. Howard Marshall, Commentary on Luke, Grand Rapids, 1978, 280
25. S. Krauss, Synagogale Altertümer, Hildesheim, 1966/2 (1922); Schrage, TWNT s.v. συναγωγή; in The Synagogue: Studies in Origins, Archaeology and Architecture, Selected by J. Gutmann, especially the studies of M. Hengel, Proseuche und Synagoge: Jüdische Gemeinde, Gotteshaus und Gottesdienst in der Diaspora und in Palästina, 27-54; Die Synagogeninschrift von Stobi, 110-148; for the texts, Corpus Inscriptionum Iudaicarum (CIJ I-II), ed. by J.B. Frey, and, J. Fitzmyer - D. Harrington, A Manual of Palestinian Aramaic Texts, Rome, 1978, Appendix.

    There is a wealth of inscriptions beginning from the 3rd century BC, especially from Egypt, going till the 5th-6th century AD in the Byzantine empire. These examples from different centuries show a certain uniformity. This can prevent an undervaluation of the building activities in the first century. Even though we have fewer archeological data than we have from the 2nd century, it must have been considerable as attested by the literary data (Jos., Philo, NT). I believe that it is not correct historically to consider all first century synagogues as private synagogues or private buildings.

    Most important for our era is the inscription from Jerusalem which is definitely from before 70 AD (cf. Supplementum Epigraphicum Graecum, VIII (ed. Hondius), Leiden, 1938, nr 170 (= CIJ II, 1404): 'Theodotos, son of Vettenos, priest and archisynagogos, son of an archisynagogos, grandson of an archisynagogos, built the (this) synagogue for the reading of the law and the teaching of the commandments. He also built the guestquarters and the houses and the bathhouse for the foreigners who might be in need. The cornerstone has been laid by his fathers and the elders and Simonides'. A. Vincent, Découverte de la 'Synagogue des Affranchis' à Jérusalem, RB 30 (1921) 247-277 gives an interpretation of this text. He considers the time after Herod as the most probable time for its construction and dates the destruction in 69 AD. H. Lietzmann, Notizen, ZNW 20

(1921) 171-173 states that one does not have to consider this indication of a synagogue as an historical proof of the existence of the synagogue of the freed slaves; he places the inscription in the early empire; also A. Deissmann, Licht vom Osten, Tübingen, 1923, 378ff; H. Bolkestein, Wohltätigkeit und Armenpflege, Groningen, 1967/2 (1939), 416f; 481

26. Jewish slaves had to be set free in the sabbath year or, at least, they should be given the chance to become free men; a husband was obliged to buy freedom for his wife and children (Ketubot 4,4); something which often could be done only with borrowed money or with the help of the whole family. To prevent abuses - it was obligatory to buy freedom for Jewish slaves in the diaspora - it was agreed that in the case of 'voluntary slavery' the children's freedom may be bought only after the death of the father (Gittin 4,9); Horajot 4,7 gives the rules of precedence.
For the documents of release, CIJ I, 683 (80 AD); 684 (the release of all slaves with the permission of the community of the Jews); 690 (41 AD); 709-711 (the sale of Jewish slaves (men and women) to Delphi; in 709, a mother with two daughters); for the system, A. Deissmann, Licht vom Osten, 270-280; for criticism, R. Gayer, Die Stellung des Sklaven in den paulinischen Gemeinden, Frankfurt, 1976, 182ff
27. For instance Tos Megilla 1,5 on the collection for the feast of purim: one buys calves which are to be eaten during the feast; see also Corpus Papyrorum Judaicarum (ed. by V. Tcherikover - A. Fuks), I. 139: an Egyptian papyrus from the first century AD which makes the record of a feast meal of two days
28. 1 Cor 16,1-4; 2 Cor 8-9; Rom 15,25-28; Gal 2,10; Acts 20,1ff
29. Acts 6,1-6
30. Especially in 1 Cor 11,17-34, but there are also indications in Lc and Acts; see also Jas 2,1-9
31. See the introduction of Mt 14,13-15 and 15,29-32; also 9,35ff and the relation of the 'compassion' with the people which is as a herd without a shepherd, and 'the labourers of the harvest'.
32. See for instance the inscription in Aigiale, Amorgos in Aegea, about 50 AD, Inscriptiones Graecae, XII, 389 Transl. Hands, Charities, 186): 'Since Kritolaos and Parmenion, the sons of Alkimedon, on becoming 'choregoi', provided all that was needed for the staging of the plays ... and in addition supplied a ration of corn for the people and for all those dwelling in Aigiale and for the foreigners lodging in the city, and,

sacrificing oxen to Apollo and Hera, they provided meat and a feast for the people on two days, with no thought for expense and in a spirit of ambitious service; so that our city may be seen to honour men of ambitious spirit and honest worth ...'. For other texts, See Hands, Charities, 187ff

33. W. Stegemann, Lasset die Kinder zu mir kommen, in, W. Schottroff - W. Stegemann, Traditionen der Befreiung, München, 1980, 114-144; for the Jewish background, see Ketubot 5,6 and the commentary of the this text in the Talmud, b Ketubot (50a). 67b

34. Pea 8,7.8.9 and the commentary of the Talmud of Jerusalem; see also b Baba Batra 7b-11a and Schürer, History, II, 437 who believes that the distinction between the purse and the plate for the time of the Mishnah cannot be proved. H. Kreissig, Die sozialen Zusammenhänge des judäischen Krieges, Berlin, 1970, 53ff doubts the existence of the institute, but this is connected with the fact that he cannot see it as a local institute

35. W. Davies, Setting of the Sermon on the Mount, Cambridge, 1964, 306ff is of opinion that this institute is very complicated; W. Bauer, Pea, Mischna, I. 2, Berlin, 1914, Einleitung writes: they are anonymous sayings which are difficult to date; G.F. Moore, Judaism in the First Centuries, Cambridge, 1927, II, 174: 'For the preceding period our sources give but scanty intimations. For the second century they are ample'; if the inscription on the synagogue in Jerusalem, built by Theodotos, is from before 70 AD (cf note 25 for the text) we have proof that in Jerusalem people thought before 70 AD about a place, bath and food for people 'who might need it'. Probably these are pilgrims, but see also H. Bolkestein, Wohltätigkeit und Armenpflege, 416ff on the meaning of ξενών; see also the name used for the leaders from Beth-Mashiko who write a letter to Galgula, chief of the army of Bar Kochba, about the sale of a cow. They are called 'parnasin', derived from 'pirnes', meaning 'support of the poor' (Jastrow, s.v. 'pirnes'), P. Benoit - J.T. Milik, - R. de Vaux, Les grottes de Murabba'at, Oxford, 1961, 155ff

36. cf Shekalim 5,6: 'There were two boxes for offerings in the Temple. One was the box of the secrets, the other the box of the implements. The box of the secrets: people who feared to have committed offences, made their offerings in secret and the money was used to provide ('pirnes') secretly for the poor who came from good families. The box of the implements: who wanted to donate an implement deposited it there. Once every 30

days the treasurers of the Temple opened the box leaving in the box all implements which could be useful for the maintenance of the Temple; the others were melted down and its monetary value was given to the box for offerings, used to restore the Temple'; synagogues had the same system, cf Tos Shekalim 2,16

37. Experts will miss in my description of the care of the poor precisely the practice which in exegesis often functions as the only example of the saying: the fact that on certain days of fasting alms are publicly promised; this is an older interpretation as is shown by A. van Iterson, Armenzorg bij de Joden, Leiden, 1911, 109. Str.-B., IV. 1.549 gave it authority cf J.C. Fenton, Saint Matthew, 1963, 91; W. Grundmann, Matthäus, 193; F.W. Beare, Matthew, 165. But there is probably no proof that it existed in the first century. Anyway, it is only found in texts of the Talmud and, furthermore, the rabbis, who are linked to this tradition, belong to the third century at the earliest
38. cf. the relation of ἐλεημοσύνη (alms) with 'sedeka' (righteousness) and vs 6,1 προσέχετε τὴν δικαιοσύνην ὑμῶν (take heed for the quality of your righteousness); the mention of the honour from the people in 6,2; the financial words and expressions: they have received their reward in 6,2 (ἀπέχω as well as μισθός); the repaying in 6,4 (ἀποδίδωμι).
39. With exception possibly of the institute of the collection for the poor, at least in as far as we reconstruct it in its origins round the care for the poor in the Temple in Jerusalem. This (possible) exception indicates that Jesus - not necessarily the historical Jesus, but the Jesus in Matthew - does not intervene 'ab ovo'. That would anyway be difficult, because in his own practice he is dependent on this way of care for the poor
40. Wilckens, TWNT, s.v. ὑποκριτής; W.F. Albright - C.S. Mann, Matthew, Garden City, 1971, CXV-CXXII; S. van Tilborg, The Jewish Leaders in Matthew, Leiden, 1972, 8-26; D.A. Garland, The Intention of Matthew 23, Leiden, 1979, 91ff brings in the expression 'dwrśy ḥlqwt' from Qumran: the 'hypokritai' as 'spoilers of the law', as people who give false interpretations of Scripture.
41. The word has as basis the Hebrew word 'chanef'
42. Obviously this is as Jewish as it is Christian. In the Jewish tradition we can think of Abot 5,13, which describes the type of donors; cf also the way this admonition has been worked out in Abot de Rabbi Natan, in both the A- and B-recension; Mekilta shows how

giving itself is promoted (Mekilta on Ex., Massekta Amalek IV vs 18,27). It is a commentary on Proverbs 22,2 'rich and poor meet': 'Rich and poor meet. The Lord has made them all. This verse speaks about the alms giver. How? The poor man opens his hand to the landlord to beg for alms but the landlord refuses to give him. The eternal one has made them all. He who made one man poor, will make him rich in the end, and he who made the other one rich, will make him poor in the end'; cf also Sifra on Lev., Parasha XII, 20, vs 5,17, which states that the alms collector, those who give food to the poor and those who perform works of charity, will receive life: a reward far greater than the punishment for breaking the Law, in the same way as happened to Adam: the reward has no relation to the punishment

43. Mt 23,23, cf D. Garland, The Intention of Matthew 23, 104f one should think of people who give false interpretations of the Law
44. This is not typically Christian either. It already exists in the practice in Jerusalem for the double box for offerings and it continues in the institute for the collection for the poor, which demands a difference between the collectors and the dispensers; cf also the stories in b Ketubot 67b on Mar-Uqaba who would rather let his feet be burned than publicly insult his neighbour (by divulging who the donor is); also b Baba Batra 9b: 'Rabbi Eleazar said: 'Whoever gives alms in secret, is greater than Moses, our teacher', cf Prov 21,11
45. I think specifically of groups of people, who in Paul's as well as in Luke's writings, are responsible for the management of the capital, 2 Cor 8,16ff; Acts 6,1ff and 20,1f
46. cf Philo, Leg ad Gaium 132-137; in Flaccum 45f and the legendary descriptions of this synagogue by the rabbis in Tos Sukka 4,6; b Sukka 51b: the double colonnade, the 71 seats of gold, the wooden platform on which the 'chazan' gave his instructions for the service with a piece of cloth, the rows for the artisans: the goldsmiths, the silversmiths, the weavers of cloths and carpets; cf S. Krauss, Synagogale Altertümer, 261f; M. Hengel, Proseuche und Synagoge, in, The Synagogue, New York, 1975, 166ff
47. cf the inscription from Side, CIJ II, 781: 'Isakis, the administrator of the holy and first synagogue ...'
48. A.M. Jones, The Greek City, Oxford, 1966/2 (1940), 79ff, 120ff, 272, but it should be remarked that this book is mainly written from the 'Greek' point of view

49. cf. Megilla 1,3: 'What is a big city? Every city where there are ten 'baṭlanim'' These 'jobless people' are gradually devalued in the history of the synagogue. The δεκαπρῶτοι of the city about which Megilla 1,3 speaks, become jobless, who are being paid to make sure that there will be 'minjan' in the synagogue also during weekdays so that the services may go on, see Krauss, Altertümer, 103-106; L. Tetzner, Megilla, Berlin, 1968, 25-27; on the difference between a private synagogue ('shel-jachid') and a public synagogue ('shel-rabbim'), Krauss, Altertümer, 306; M. Hengel, Die Synagogeninschrift von Stobi, in, The Synagogue, New York, 1975, 162

50. cf the inscription from Aigina (CIJ, I, 723): 'During the time when Theodoros, the younger, was manager, this building was beautified with a mosaic, paid for with money from the synagogue ... 250 denars of gold were collected as income and 275 as gifts to God'; especially in Egyptian inscriptions we find 'the Jews' mentioned as a collective: cf the inscriptions from Schedia, Arthibis and Xenephyris (CIJ II, 1440. 1443/44. 1441); see also the correspondence between the inscription from Kasjum (CIJ II, 972) and the one from Schedia. This does not mean that the Jews financed the building. These texts are rather political: regal or imperial protection is connected with such a dedication.
In the later Palestinian inscriptions (6th - 8th century) 'all the people' are mentioned several times: Fitzmyer-Harrington, ᶜAin Duk Synagogue (A5): 'everyone who gathers his resources and contributes ..'; Beth Alpha (A 11): 'all the people of the town volunteered'; Beth Shean (A 13): 'all the members of the holy community'; Jericho (A 34): 'all the holy assembly, the elders and the youth'; Maᶜon (A 40): 'the whole assembly' cf also M. Avi-Yonah, Geschichte der Juden, 239f

51. cf the Greek inscriptions from Beth Shean (Krauss, Altertümer, 210): 'Maleichathos built the above sanctuary'; Ṭafas (Hauran) (CIJ, II, 861): 'Jacob, Samuel and their father Klematis built this synagogue'; especially the inscription from Jerusalem (CIJ, II, 1404): 'Theodotos built this synagogue for the reading of the law etc'

52. For a survey on the question, Krauss, Altertümer, 302ff, and Schrage, TWNT, s.v. συναγωγή, 812ff

53. The Aramaic texts say for this 'mtḥzqin'

54. cf previous paragraph on the giving of alms: most striking in Berenike (Schürer, Geschichte, III, 79f, note 20): Marcus Tittius receives on the occasion of

each new moon an olive wreath and a knot of honour (!), for commentary M. Hengel, Proseuche und Synagoge, 182; the text from the Tosephtah, Tos Baba Metzia 11,23, which speaks about 'mutual force exerted to get the synagogue built', reflects probably the time of the later empire where 'leitourgia' has become less attractive because of high taxes, cf M. Rostovtzeff, The Social and Economic History of the Roman Empire, Oxford, 1957, I, 380-392.
Megilla 3,1.2.3 describes how one should act in case a synagogue needs to be sold or in case a synagogue cannot be maintained. The sellers are called 'beney ha^{c}ir': people who have full citizen's rights, while the real sellers are considered to be 'ṭobey ha^{c}ir', the 'optimates' (j Pea 21a); for the whole history, A.M. Jones, The Greek City, 177ff; for the distinction between private and public, see Megilla 3,1, cf L. Tetzner, Megilla, Berlin, 1968, 89

55. Jos., Ant., XIX, 6.3.300: in this text even a non-Jewish city council is supposed to be responsible for the synagogue, cf Schürer, History, II, 118f
56. Jos., Bell Jud II, 14.2.289; the word used here is οἵ δυνατοί; the money-lender is the publican Johannes so that the commision in & 292 is even called οἱ περὶ τὸν 'Ιωάννην δυνατοὶ δώδεκα; see also Schürer, History, II, 115ff; other texts can be found in Philo, In Flaccum 47ff where the height of Flacus' criminal behaviour is the imprisonment of the 38 elders of his own Jewish γερουσία; and Jos., Ant XX. 8.11.194 which speaks about a conflict between the Sanhedrin of Jerusalem and Festus with regard to changes in Temple buildings. The Sanhedrin sends an envoy to Rome with a party composed of the δεκαπρῶτοι, Ismael, the highpriest and Helkias, the manager of the Temple treasury.
57. cf for instance Horatius, Odes, III, 4; III, 30; Ovidius, Amores, II, 16; Plinius, Epistulae, IV, 13; Martialis XII, 31; Anthologia Palatina, VII, 417: they are all texts which glorify, compare, recommend etc the own native town
58. Megilla 4,3 forbids reciting the Shema, if there are less than 10 persons present, or to pray the Tefilla, to give the priestly blessing, to read the Torah concluding with the Prophets, to fulfill the mourning rite of sitting and standing, to bless the mourners or the newly weds and to use the name of God in saying grace at table
59. Tos Megilla 3,7. For a completely different interpretation, see S. Zeitlin, The Tefillah, the Shemoneh Esreh, in, Studies in Early History of Judaism, 1973, I,

237ff. According to him this text should be seen as part of the discussion between rabbis who consider the synagogue as a place of prayer, and the people who maintain the old custom, which sees the synagogue as the 'house of the people', used mostly for ordinary things.

60. The Hebrew word is 'sarban': let yourself be invited and you do not know whether the invitation is sincere so that you are in doubt and you make the other insist, Berakot 5,3; cf also the sequence which b Taanit 16a presupposes for the public address on days of fasting: first the 'zaqan' (the elder), then, in his absence, the 'ḥakam' (the scribe) or if he is also absent an 'adam shel ṣurah (a man of standing)
61. I am using his description from Quod omnis probus 81ff; Vita Contempl 30ff; 65ff; Vita Mosis I, 180; II, 256; De Somniis II, 127f; De Spec Leg II, 60ff; Hypothetica 7,12.13. His description is not complete fiction as is clear from the inscription from Jerusalem which shows the same emphasis on passing on the Law: 'Theodotos built this synagogue for the reading of the law and the teaching of the commandments'; and from the description of the service in the main synagogue of Alexandria where the chazan gave liturgical directions to the people from a wooden dais, b Sukka 51b
62. The therapeutists use a double choir of men and women as there was after the passing of the Red Sea where Moses and Mirjam led the people in a song of praise, cf Vita Contempl 83ff; Vita Mosis I, 180; II, 256
63. cf especially the treatises Berakot, Megilla, Taanit and Rosh Hashana
64. Whether Num 15,37-41 has to be added or left out in the evening Shema, see Berakot 1,5; for commentary O. Holtzmann, Berakot, Berlin, 1912, 44
65. cf Rosh Hashana 4,5 on the sounding of the shofar with the prayers; Taanit on the fast days; Pesachim on the slaughter of the lamb and on other practices of pesach; Bikkurim on the feast and the procession of the first fruits; Joma on the Day of Atonement etc
66. Contra Elbogen, Der jüdische Gottesdienst in seiner geschichtlichen Entwicklung, Hildesheim, 1962/4 (1913), 247 who defends the theory: 'Die Belehrung tritt zurück, der Hauptzweck wird jetzt Gebet und Andacht'. The absence of texts to regulate the didachè does not indicate that this aspect was neglected; the best proof are the targumim and the midrashim
67. Megilla 4,1-2; 3,4-6; 4,4.10; 4,6-8
68. Mt 4,23; 9,35; 12,9; 13,54; also 10,17 and 23,34
69. G. Strecker, Der Weg der Gerechtigkeit, Göttingen,

1965/2 (1962), 20 thinks that the use of this expression is an indication of the fact that 'die Kirche über den Schranken des Judentums hinausgewachsen ist'. How can it be written?!

70. Acts 19,9f
71. Jo 20,19.26
72. Mt 10,17 and 23,34
73. Mt 24,26; see also J. Heinemann, Prayer in the Talmud, Berlin - New York, 1977, 191f who describes 'the force of Jesus' instructions to his disciples and of his exemplary prayer' in terms of intimacy, briefness, simple popular style, the choice for the vernacular and the independency from a Prayer Leader
74. Berakot 1,1-15; for commentary and other texts, Str.-B., IV.1. 189ff; Schürer, History, II, 454; Elbogen, Jüdische Gottesdienst, 14ff
75. Berakot 2,1.5; remember also the famous story about the martyrdom of Rabbi Aqiba: 'When they led Rabbi Aqiba away to kill him, it was the time of the Hear Israel prayer. They tore the flesh from his body, but he accepted the yoke of the kingdom of God. His disciples said: it is enough, rabbi. But he answered: My whole life long I have spent on the verse: 'with all your soul', i.e. also when He takes my soul unto Him. I thought: when will I have the chance to fulfill this verse? And now that the chance is there I would not do it? He said the word 'only' at such length that his soul departed from his body on this word 'only' ... A voice was then heard saying: Happy are you, Rabbi Aqiba, because you are destined for the life of the world to come,' cf b Berakot 61b
76. Berakot 4,1ff; 5,1ff; commentary in O. Holtzmann, Berakot, Berlin, 1912, introd.; Str.-B., IV. 1,208; Schürer, History, II, 455; Elbogen, Jüdische Gottesdienst, 27ff
77. The text of Berakot 4,4 is not without importance to understand ἐν ταῖς γωνιαίς τῶν πλατειῶν: 'Rabbi Joshua says: If you go to a dangerous place, you should say a short Tefilla: 'Save, Lord, your people, the rest of Israel, on every crossroad. Their needs may be in front of you. Blessed be you, Lord, who hears a prayer'. Crossroads are dangerous places, where decisions have to be taken. Often there was a dais (a mass of stones or an altar) where one could bring God an offering; cf Aboda Zara 3,7; 4,1; also b Sota 21a; in Hellenistic religion it is an altar for Hekate or Hermes and the offering is food which could be eaten by hungry passers-by; cf Pauly-Wissowa, s.v. Hekate and Quadruviae which also mentions some inscriptions, especially

from the region of Dalmatia, Pannonia and Germany; cf also Hastings, s.v. Cross-Roads with a lot of information on concrete practices; D. Flusser, Paganism in Palestine, in, The Jewish People in the First Century, II, Assen, 1976, 1087f; M. Hadas-Lebel, Le paganisme à travers les sources rabbiniques, in, Aufstieg und Niedergang der römischen Welt, 19,2, 450ff

78. As to the real intention of the saying one finds also in Judaism many statements which admonish the hearer to make sure that the prayers are a real prayer. Basic for the rabbis is the saying: 'Whoever makes his prayer into a 'qèba', i.e. whoever makes it an obligation, does not say a prayer of mercy', cf Berakot 4,4 also Abot 4,4. For the relation between 'public' and 'hidden', cf Sifre on Num & 115 v. 15,41: 'Know what I did to the Egyptians whose deeds were done in secret- I made them known. One should use a 'qal wachomer'-reasoning here. If God makes known what happens in secret in case of punishment - which is the lesser, how much more will he do that in case of a good deed- which is the more important'; see also the texts which treat the difference between short and long prayers with as point of departure: everything has its own time. Do not make your prayers longer than Moses did- who threw himself down before the Lord for 40 days and 40 nights. But do not make it shorter either than Moses who for his sister Mirjam only said: Lord, heal her, cf. Sifre on Num §105 v. 12,13, also Mekilta on Ex., Massekta Beshallah III, v. 14,15
There is a lot of literature on Jewish prayer, especially on its spirituality, see for instance, I. Abrahams, Some Rabbinic Ideas on Prayer, in A. Corré, Understanding the Talmud, New York, 1975, 360-372 (orig. 1908); G.F. Moore, Judaism in the First Centuries, Cambridge, II, 1927, 212-237; L. Finkelstein, The Pharisees, Philadephia, I, 1946/3 (1938), 60ff; W.D. Davies, The Setting of the Sermon on the Mount, Cambridge, 1964, 309ff; B. Martin, Prayer in Judaism, New York, 1968; J. Heinemann - J. Petuchowski, Literature of the Synagogue, New York, 1975

79. It is strange that B. Gerhardsson, Geistiger Opferdienst nach Matthäus 6, 1-6. 16-21, in, Neues Testament und Geschichte, Fs O. Cullmann, Tübingen, 1972, 69ff elaborates the meaning of the Shema in the whole of this passage, but does not mention the more striking relation with Mt 6,5

80. see L. Finkelstein, The Pharisees, Philadelphia, I, 1946/3 (1938), 60ff who lets it be introduced under Simeon the Just (230 BC) and who supposes that the

addition 'blessed be his name in blessing for ever and ever' after the first sentence, is a reaction on the triumphal entrance of Pompeius the Great in the Temple. For the addition itself, see T JI Dt 6,4 who ascribes it to Jacob. Proof, anyway, that it is seen as a very old tradition.

81. cf Jos., Ant IV. 212: 'twice each day, at the dawn thereof and when the hour comes for turning to repose, let all acknowledge before God the bounties which He has bestowed on them through their deliverance from the land of Egypt'; Philo, De Spec Leg IV. 141: 'Indeed he (the timid man) must be forward to teach the principles of justice to kinsfolk and friends and all the youth at home and in the street, both when they go to their beds and when they arise, so that in every posture and every motion, in every place both private and public ...'; Aristeas' Letter 160: 'He (Moses) recommends that we take to heart the prescriptions of the Lord when we go to sleep, when we get up and when we walk ...'.
82. Mt 23,5f
83. cf J.T. Milik, Discoveries in the Judaean Desert, IV, 2: Tefillin, Mezuzot et Targums, (4 Q 128 - 4 Q 157), 47ff
84. It is to be remembered that women, slaves and children were not allowed to wear it, cf Berakot 3,3. The relation between the Shema and the tefillin is here also presupposed, because the same group is relieved of the obligation to recite the Shema
85. Dt 6,4-9; 11,13-21; the absence of the Num-text is striking, also in the edition which has become the definitive version, cf the hesitation whether the Num part may be added in the evening. The argument is based on the interpretation of Dt 16,3: 'only during the day one should remember the exodus from Egypt', cf O. Holtzman, Berakot, 44
86. Is it not better to speak of an earlier and a later type, supposing that the evolution is from greater freedom to more strict observance. Calling the 'later' type 'Pharisee', a connection is made with Mt 23,5, which connection is strictly speaking not proved
87. cf also Megilla 4,8 where the same kind of criticism is found: there is resistance to show and to the setting-oneself-apart: 'One should not make round tefillin; not put them in other places: high on the forehead or on the hand; they should not be made of gold or placed on the arm'.
88. from the verb '^{c}amad': to stand up
89. Berakot 4,1ff; 5,1f
90. cf the relation of Eccl 51,12 with Blessings 1.8.10.

14.15; I. Elbogen, Jüdische Gottesdienst, 29ff

91. The well known story of the addition by Samuel, the minor, of the prayer against the 'minim' (b Berakot 28b-29a) in the Eighteen-prayer makes clear that the text of the Tefilla has changed considerably over a longer period of time. Textually there are several versions which make it difficult to determine the original form. See next to the mentioned literature, J. Pedro, A First Century Jewish Sage, in, A. Corré, Understanding the Talmud, New York, 1975, 198-215 (orig. 1958); K.G. Kuhn, Achtzehngebet und Vater Unser und der Reim, Tübingen, 1950; the latter believes he can prove that the Eighteen-prayer as a whole has its origin in the first half of the first century. With Elbogen he believes that the blessings on the restoration of the Temple and on the return from exile do not necessarily date to the period after 70 AD, p. 10.15. 18; S. Zeitlin, The Tefillah, The Shemoneh Esreh, in, Studies in the Early History of Judaism, New York, I, 1973, 92-133, cf especially p. 122ff dates the origin after 70 AD: his argument is clouded in extravagant theories (medieval origin of the Hebrew Sirach text; b Berakot 28b presupposes an original Seventeen-prayer etc.); S. Safrai, The Synagogue, in, Jewish People in the First Century, Assen, II, 916f presupposes that a nucleus of the prayer existed before 70 AD. See also J. Heinemann, Prayer in the Talmud. Forms and Patterns, Berlin - New York, 1977, 224 who writes: 'The custom of reciting precisely eighteen Benedictions must have crystallized sometime during the century before the destruction of the Temple (at the very latest)'. He argues from the routine usage of the term 'Eighteen Benedictions' by the Sages who lived during the generation following the destruction, which would seem to indicate that the custom was not a relatively recent one

92. cf D. Garland, The Intention of Matthew 23, Leiden, 1979, 104ff who does not give this interpretation for Mt 6,4ff

93. This in opposition with D. Flusser, Paganism in Palestine, in, The Jewish People in the First Century, Assen, II, 1976, 1095: 'By speaking so (= Mt 6,7), it was not necessary that the speaker knew much of actual paganism. It would have almost been enough for him to have read his Bible where the priests of Baal are said to have prayed in vain to Baal from early morning to midday'

94. 4,15

95. 8,18.28; 14,22; 16,5; 19,1

96. 16,5 with the continuation in 16,13
97. 19,1
98. 8,28 and 15,39
99. 15,21ff
100. 4,24.25
101. 2,13ff
102. For this area, O. Eissfelt, Tempel und Kulte syrischer Städte in hellenistisch-römischer Zeit, Leipzig, 1941; L. Vidman, Isis und Sarapis bei den Griechen und Römern, Berlin, 1970; D. Flusser, Paganism in Palestine; J. Teixidor, The Pagan God, Pagan Religion in the Greco-Roman Near East, Princeton, 1977; Schürer, History, II, 29ff; just a few weeks before presenting my text to the publisher, I have become acquainted with the studies of R. MacMullen, especially Roman Social Realities 50 B.C. to A.D. 284, New Haven, 1974, and Paganism in the Roman Empire, New Haven, 1981. In comparison with his erudition, my text is not much more than an extended footnote but, at least, I hope to have given a correct and defensible description of this special era and location
103. See e.g. the criticism of Flusser on the use of a late source as Stephanus Byzantinus, p. 1987 and his description, anyway, more reserved, of the actual situation in opposition to what Schürer writes. Obviously there is a great deal of difference between an inscription on a pillar on the spot or on one located on the island of Delos or in the Piraeus, between an existing ruin and one single coin, between a text as that of Josephus and the Expositio Totius Mundi
104. But remember that these ruins are mostly from the second century and even later
105. For a short history A. Jones, The Greek City, Oxford, 1966, 227; M. Nilsson, Greek Folk Religion, New York, 1961/2 (1940), 98ff
106. L. Friedländer, Sittengeschichte Roms, Wien, 1934, 461-548 gives a very vivid description
107. Schürer, History, II, 55 based on texts of Josephus. Probably JHWH played the most important role here; think e.g. of the attempts of Ezechiel the Tragedian, to dramatise the Jewish history, making God speak in words; see M. Hengel, Judentum und Hellenismus, Tübingen, 1969, 137 on the question of the gymnasium of Jerusalem
108. Jos., Bell Jud VII. 2.1.24ff; see also Y. Meshorer, Jewish Coins, Tel Aviv, 1967: the temple of Caesarea Philippi; Agrippa I as chariot-driver; Agrippa II with Nike, Tyche and Pan

109. Bell Jud VII. 3.1.37-40
110. Bell Jud VII. 5.1.96
111. Bell Jud VII. 5.5.132ff
112. The treatise Aboda Zara; for commentary, see the most instructive study of M. Hadas-Lebel, Le paganisme à travers les sources rabbiniques des IIe et IIIe siècles, in, Aufstieg und Niedergang der römischen Welt, 19/2, 397-485
113. M. Nilsson, Geschichte der griechischen Religion, München, 1967/3 (1940), II, 381ff; precisely in the beginning of the time of the empire the practice of the daily sacrifices and hymns develops in the temples of the Hellenistic deities under the influence of Egyptian religions. There is no documentary evidence that this penetrated into Palestine. One was probably dependent on available personell i.e. dependent on the richness of the temple
114. One would like to know how this figured in the Syrian and Nabataean cults. Apart from Palmyra I have not found anything on this, cf J. Teixidor, The Pagan God, 133 where the author describes communal meals with invitations, membership etc. At the very least this presupposes a cult community which meets several times a year, but how much Hellenistic influence is there in this?
115. Aboda Zara 1,1
116. cf especially Nilsson, Geschichte der griechischen Religion, II, 24f. 61ff, 70ff.82ff; E. des Places, La religion grecque, Paris, 1969, 87-110. From the many texts it may be interesting to point out the inscription from Andania (92 BC). For the text, see W. Dittenberger, Sylloge Inscriptionum Graecarum, Leipzig, 1907, II, 736 l. 28-35. This is about a 'mystery' feast but, because it is such a typical description, it can be taken as an example. I will translate part of the text: 'On the procession': Mnasistratos will lead the procession, followed by the priest of the gods whose mysteries are celebrated together with the priestess; then follow the leader of the games, the priests for the offering and the fluteplayers. Behind them come the holy maidens according to the place determined by lot and the wagon carrying the boxes with the secret holy implements. Then follow the leader (fem.) of the feast meal of Demeter's temple and her helpers who are actually in service and the priestesses of Demeter at the hippodrome and Demeter in Aigila. Then come, separately, the holy women in the order determined by lot and the holy men as determined by the commission of ten. The

women's supervisor must determine the order of the holy women and maidens by lot and he will see to it that they take their place according to lot. Sacrificial animals will come along in the procession to wit: a pregnant sow for Demeter, a young sow for the great gods, a wild boar for Apollo Karneios, an ewe for Hagna ...'; see also Pausanias, IV 1-2; 3,10; 14,1; 15,7; 16,2; 26,6-27,6; 33,4ff; for commentary E. des Places, Religion grecque, 98ff; Nilsson, Geschichte der griechischen Religion, II, 96ff

117. Aboda Zara 1,4 presupposes that not every shopkeeper places these ornaments. It says, there was such a case in Beth Shean

118. The prohibition not to co-operate with the building of a basilica (Aboda Zara 1,7) has to do with this practice.

119. L. Vidman, Isis und Sarapis bei den Griechen und Römern, Berlin, 1970, 48ff, 106ff gives the typical development, applied to the cult of Isis and Sarapis.

120. Aboda Zara 1,3: Kalendas, in the beginning of the year: one own's housegods are venerated and small gifts are exchanged such as figs, dates and honey cakes (see the prohibition to sell these in Aboda Zara 1,5), with the public cult at the Capitol of the city; the Saturnalia (17-23 December) with a festive meal, sacrifices, congratulations and a special market; the κράτησις: probably the commemoration of the 'transfer of power' by Augustus at Actium which was seen as the beginning of a new era, or otherwise the day of the enthronement of the emperor of the moment; the γενεσία: the birthday of the emperor with circusses and a popular meal, cf M. Hadas-Lebel, Le paganisme, 427-433; Nilsson, Geschichte der griechischen Religion, II, 388f. 489f

121. On the κράτησις, Jos. Bell Jud I. 21.8.415; Ant XVIII. 2.1.26; on the γενεσία, see the texts of Josephus on the feasts of Titus but also Mt 14,6; Mc 6,21; further Schürer, History, I, 346, note 26

122. Aboda Zara 1,6 prohibits the sale of bears and lions to pagans, because these animals can hurt people: this proves that the memory of the terrible history of the Jews after the war, is not yet forgotten

123. cf Schürer, History, II, 32 + note 13; 38 who locates this cult in Ashkelon, Dora, Caesarea, Raphia, Gaza. The famous statue of the nursing mother - Isis with Harpokrates - (see Tos Aboda Zara 5,1) has been found in Ashkelon, see M. Hadas-Lebel, Le Paganisme, 401 and D. Flusser, Paganism in Palestine, 1085; L. Vidman, Isis und Sarapis, 45.60 mentions also an inscription

from Samaria (3rd century BC) and from Tyre

124. See e.g. the description by Apuleius, Metamorphoses XI of the famous feast of the navigium Isidis where a ship, dedicated to Isis, is brought to the sea in a great procession. There are several testimonies of this feast, cf L. Vidman, Isis and Sarapis, 76ff; F. Cumont, Les religions orientales dans le paganisme romain, Paris, 1929/3 (1911), 152; Nilsson, Geschichte der griechischen Religion, II, 622f

125. Sanhedrin 7,6; I give a slighlty different interpretation than M. Hadas-Lebel, 452 who thinks that the sweeping (from 'kbd' = to sweep, Jastrow s.v.), cleaning, washing and anointing refers to the temple floor

126. Nilsson, Geschichte der griechischen Religion, II, 622ff; L. Vidman, Isis und Sarapis, 55ff; 60ff; 271f; F. Cumont, Les religions orientales, 148ff; see especially Apuleius, Metamorphoses XI, 20; Plutarchus, De Iside et Osiride 372 D (52) and 383 A (78)

127. Aboda Zara 3,5.7-10; see also F. Cumont, Les religions orientales, 181ff

128. Aboda Zara 4,1ff; M. Hadas-Legel, Le paganisme, 450ff; Nilsson, Geschichte der griechischen Religion, I, 501ff

129. Aboda Zara 1,3.5.8; 3,1.2.3

130. cf discussion in Bauer, Wb; Liddell-Scott, s.v.; Delling, TWNT s.v.: there are doubts on spellings, manuscripts and meaning

131. Well known examples are the hymn to Demeter, the hymn of Kleanthes to Zeus, the aretologies to Isis, the Carmen Saeculare of Horatius. E. des Places, La religion grecque, 153-170 gives as examples which most probably functioned in liturgies: the dithyrambe of Elis of Dionysos; a prayer of the Atheneans to Zeus to ask for rain and fertility; the hymn of Telesilla on the Mother of the gods; several peans to Asklepios; the hymn to Zeus Diktaios; several hymns to Isis; the hymn of praise of Mesomedes on the Nature and the Sun; the morning hymn to Asklepios; the pean on Hygia. In his references he then develops the innumerable private prayers and ways of praying which can be found in Greek literature. For the hymn to Demeter, p. 207ff; for the hymn to Zeus, p. 262ff.

132. cf L. Friedländer, Sittengeschichte Roms, Wien, 1934, 462 who claims that the processions are seen as too long prefaces. He probably refers to a text as Ovidius, Amores 3,2

133. I do not know any texts. P. Lagrange, Matthieu, Paris, 1927, 123 refers to the stoic criticism on prayer as 'tiring the gods': Seneca, Epistulae 31,5; Martialis,

Epigrammata VII, 60,3. This, however, deals with something different: one should not ask the gods for the wrong things such as riches, honour, and an easy life which tires the gods; one should ask for moral maturity wich will bring harmony in every eventuality. Maybe one should think of Isis' attribute that she is πολυώνυμος (E. des Places, La religion grecque, 165), which at the very least led to the extraordinary Isis-litany, see B.P. Grenfell - A.S. Hunt, Oxyrhynchus Papyri, London, 1915, XI, nr 1380. A long list of places is mentioned where Isis is venerated with a special name for each place. There are also mentioned Palestinian cities from which on I quote: 'In Dora (you, Isis, are called) friendship; in Hellas Straton's Tower, the good one; in Ashkelon, the mightiest; in Sinope (this is sligthly outside the series), you-with-the-many-names (! the same in Delos); in Raphia, the mistress; in Tripolis, the helper; in Gaza, the superabundant one; in Berytus, Maia; in Sidon, Astarte; in Ptolemais, the understanding ... etc'. (see also Schürer, History, II, 32, note 13). Cf Apuleius, Metamorphoses XI, 2: 'quoque nomine, quoquo ritu, quaqua facie te fas est invocare; XI. 5: 'cuius numen unicum multiformi specie, ritu vario, nomine multiiugo totus veneratur orbis'; and Plutarchus, De Iside et Osiride, 372 E (53): 'she is called μυριώνυμος by many because, changed by the logos, she takes on all forms and figures'

134. Grammatik & 40
135. TWNT s.v. βατταλογέω
136. In j Aboda Zara 43a on Aboda Zara 3,6: I am following the translation of G.A. Wewers, Tübingen, 1980; see D. Flusser, Paganism in Palestine, 1075 and note 1 + 2 for a commentary on the text of the Talmud babli
137. Suggested by Liddell-Scott through a connection with βατταρίζω (to stammer); βάταλος (stammerer); ἀκαιρολογία (nonsense); ἀργολογία (?), see also Delling, TWNT s.v.
138. cf Nilsson, Geschichte der griechischen Religion, II, 345-372; F. Cumont, Les religions orientales, 148ff; 181ff; 339ff; A.J. Festugière, Les mystères de Dionysos, RB 44 (1935), esp. p. 192-211 where we find a report of an epigraphic research. Celebrations of Demeter's mysteries and certainly of Dionysos are documented for the whole area of Greece and Asia Minor. The closest places are Tarsus and Alexandria where Antony and Cleopatra have held their Dionysia (if these can be called mysteria), see L. Cerfaux - J. Tondriau, Le culte des souverains, Tournai, 1956,

295ff. It is not ruled out that the bad memories of the forced Dionysos-mysteries under Antiochus Epiphanes (175-164 BC) have played a negative role, see especially 2 Macc 6,7; for the whole history, Schürer, History, I, 155ff

139. cf L. Vidman, Isis und Sarapis, 125ff: Isis' mysteries are epigraphically known for the first century in Italy. From there they spread over the mediterranean area. Also Nilsson, Geschichte der griechischen Religion, II, 622ff; even R. Reitzenstein, Die hellenistischen Mysterienreligionen, Stuttgart, 1966, (1927/3), 38ff - the latter had enough reasons to date the texts as early as possible, as is well known. They do not know any earlier mysteria of Isis. They only develop the texts of Plutarch and Apuleius (i.e. first decades of second century AD)

140. cf the reconstruction of the sarcophagus from Ravenna by L. Vidman and A.J. Festugière, Isis and Sarapis, 132ff; see also the discussion in Nilsson, Geschichte der griechischen Religion, II, 626ff; that one thought of stuttering in connection with the mysteries is probably connected with the presentation of things as e.g. Euripides does it in his Bacchantes, and Titus Livius (39, 8-19) in relation to the first appearance of Dionysia in Southern Italy. It is now generally accepted that this definitely did not apply anymore in the time of Christ and later times; cf the description of Nilsson, II, 350ff A.J. Festugière, Les mystères de Dionysos, RB 44 (1935) 192-211; 366-396; even in W.F. Otto, Dionysos, Myth and Cult, London, 1965 (orig. 1933); recently in H.J. Klauck, Herrenmahl und hellenistischer Kult, Münster, 1982, 91ff. 106ff. It would indeed be difficult because the development of the mysteria brought a progressively greater emphasis on 'gnosis' in the broad sense of that term

141. As for instance is made clear by the story of Apuleius, Metamorphoses, XI. 22 and 28; and Juvenalis, VI, 511ff; see also R. Reitzenstein, Die hellenistischen Mysterienreligionen, 142ff; H.J. Klauck, Herrenmahl und hellenistischer Kult, Münster, 1982, 124ff

142. This even applies when the list of magical practices of Tos Shabbat 6-7 is taken into consideration, cf M. Hadas-Lebel, Le paganisme, 456-474

143. cf Nilsson, Geschichte der griechischen Religion, II, 698; E. des Places, La religion grecque, 288; A.J. Festugière, L'idéal religieux des Grecs et l'Évangile, Paris, 1932, 281ff. Most outspoken is M. Nilsson, Opuscula Selecta, Lund, 1960, III, 129-166: 'Alle grossen und wichtigen Stücke stammen aus dem 4. oder

sogar dem 5. Jahrhundert, die älteren sind so kurz, dass es kaum möglich ist zu konstatieren, ob Unterschiede vorhanden sind'(p. 132)

144. cf E. Lohmeyer, Das Vaterunser, Göttingen, 1962; J. Jeremias, The Lord's Prayer in Modern Research, Ev. Theol 71 (1959/60) 141-146; R.E. Brown, The 'Pater Noster' as an Eschatological Prayer, in, New Testament Studies, Milwaukee, 1965, 217-253
145. S. van Tilborg, A Form-Criticism of the Lord's Prayer, Nov Test 14 (1972) 94-105; it is recently criticised by Strecker, Bergpredigt, 111ff
146. cf 'exhaustively' by J. Carmignac, Recherches sur le 'Notre Père', Paris, 1969, 118ff. 214ff
147. But see for example also chapter II on the juridical structures; chapter IV on the sociological composition of the group: that Matthew's community has progressed economically; chapter V on the system of the brotherly correction; chapter VI on the activities of the 'prophets' in the Matthean community
148. 6,5-6
149. 10,17
150. 4,23; 9,35; 12,9; 13,54
151. 6,5
152. cf ch. II, note 32: ch. V, note 36
153. cf Mekilta on Ex., Massekta Bahodesh vs 20,24 (resp. 20,21 in the traditional, Jewish counting) and b Berachot 6a
154. cf Abot 3,6
155. In the texts of the Mekilta and of Berachot the number 5 is missing; the probable reason is the fact that the scriptural text (Amos 9,6) is not very clear in itself
156. in, Die Frau im Urchristentum, Hrsg von G. Dautzenberg, u.a., Freiburg, 1983, 29ff
157. 5,22ff; 7,3ff; 18,15.35
158. this at all events in 23,8 because there the subject of 'being called rabbi' is raised which excludes women; and in 28,10 where 'the brothers' appear to be 'the eleven disciples' in 28,16
159. in 5,47, connected with the becoming υἱοὶ τοῦ πατρὸς in 5,45 and 5,48; cf also 13,38 on 'the sons of the evil one' and 'the sons of the kingdom'; and in 25,40 where no sexual differences are supposed or even wanted
160. 12,46-50
161. 26,6-13
162. 23,8-12
163. see for example G. Dalman, Die Worte Jesu, Darmstadt, 1965 (1930) 276; S. Sandmel, The First Christian Century in Judaism and Christianity, Oxford, 1969,

9.70, and above all C. Spicq, Une allusion au Docteur de Justice dans Matthieu XXIII, 10?, RB 66 (1959) 387ff: not because of his concrete suggestion on the καθηγητής, not because of his study of this concept in Hellenistic literature

164. 7,22; 10,40; 13,17.52; 23,34
165. cf Schweizer, Bergpredigt, 92f: are also the 'wise men', the 'disciples' and the 'little ones' functions? I think that it is a little less probable. One could give arguments for the 'wise men' because there is a possible connection with the rabbinic 'chakamim' (which, nevertheless, are always historical figures), but according to Matthew every follower of Jesus has to be a disciple and 'small'
166. cf ch. VI which treats the phenomenon of the prophets more extensively
167. 10,1; 11,1; 26,60; in 28,16 they are 'the eleven disciples'
168. 14,28; 15,15; 16,16; 18,21; 19,27; 26,33
169. 4,18; 10,2
170. 17,24
171. see for example 14,31ff; 16,6ff; 16,23ff; 20,25ff; 26,75ff. For the totality G. Strecker, Der Weg der Gerechtigkeit, 198
172. 28,19
173. cf above all the commentary in ch V on Mt 7,2-3
174. 1,18.20; 3,11.16; 4,1; 10,20; 12,18.31.32; 22,43
175. cf commentary ch V on Mt 7,2-3
176. 3,11.12
177. 13,30 and 13,42
178. For the context of these questions, J. Jeremias, Die Abendsmahlsworte Jesu, Göttingen, 1960/3 and recent H.-J. Klauck, Herrenmahl und hellenistischer Kult, Aschendorff, 1982
179. For this concept see, 20,28 in the same sense
180. H. Frankemölle, Jahwehbund und Kirche Christi, Aschendorff, 1973, 37ff
181. in 14,19 as well as in 15,36
182. 19,12
183. Reich Gottes und Eheverzicht im Evangelium nach Matthäus, Stuttgart, 1983. From the title itself it is already clear that he argues in favour of the meaning 'unmarried because of the kingdom of heavens'
184. so the comparisons in Sir 20,4 and 30,20; and in the denial of the 'kashrut' in Jebamot 8,4 with the possibility of recovery
185. see especially b Jebamot 80b and the physical characteristic of a 'saris' and b Jebamot 81a (on Jebamot 8,6: a priest who is 'a saris from his birth' and who

is married) on the differences between a 'môlid' and a 'non-môlid': i.e. to be capable to beget children or not.

186. 1,19: the opposition of 'in secret' is 'to deliver someone to contempt'

187. cf 9,15; 22,1ff; 25,1ff

188. 1,21

189. 9,6

190. 26,28

191. as is stated expressively in Mc 2,7 and Lc 5,21

192. cf 6,14.15 and 18,35

193. One could think on for example 28,18-20 and 18,19-20; so far as 1,21 is concerned, see the continuation in 1,22: Jesus = Emmanuel = God with us; in 9,1ff the Pharisaic argumentation on God's sole power to forgive sins has been left out; in 26,28 it is expressed by the concept of the covenant and its reconciliation which has become valid through the Kyrios

194. Der Weg der Gerechtigkeit, Göttingen, 1966/2,220

195. 18,15ff

196. in ch. V, the commentary on Mt 7,2ff

197. 12,31.32

198. 6,14.15

199. 18,21-35

200. Didachè 8,5ff

201. The text of the Lord's Prayer in the Didachè is different from the text in Matthew in a few places, but these are rather typical: the sg. 'heaven' in the title; the sg. 'the trespass' in stead of the pl. 'the trespasses'; the present-form of the verb in 'we forgive' in the prayer on the forgiveness so that an immediate dependency is almost excluded

202. Bl.-D. & 387; μή εἰσενέγκῃς is parallel

203. see above all J. Carmignac, Recherches, 110ff who has discovered that this is already a suggestion from Origen

204. TWNT, Foerster, s.v. ἐπιουτιος; R.E. Brown, The 'Pater Noster' as an Eschatological Prayer, in, New Testament Studies, Milwaukee, 1965, 217ff; Carmignac, Recherches, 118ff; H. Bourgoin, ἐπιούσιος expliqué par la notion de préfixe vide, Bibl 60 (1979) 91-96

205. your father who is in heaven; your heavenly father: 5,16.45; 6,1. 4.6.8.18. 26.32; 7,11; 18,14 (l.v.); 23,9; your father: 10,29; their father: 13,34; my heavenly father; my father who is in heaven: 7,21; 10,32.33; 12,50; 15,13; 16,17; 18,10; 18,14 (l.v.); 18,19. 35; my father: 11,17; 20,23; 25,34; 26,29.39. 42.53; father (said by Jesus): 11,25.26; his father (said of Jesus): 16,27

206. cf in this commentary Mt 7,9-11
207. see 5,5 and 5,42 and the relation with Ps 36,21.26 (LXX)
208. b Berakot 32b
209. Apart from concrete information Behm's article (TWNT s.v. νῆστις) is, under this aspect, really bad. One can taste the author's aversion in every sentence. This even brings him to the faulty historical reconstruction that in the early church there would have been a period when fasting was not practised
210. cf 11 Q Temple 27,8; Philo, De Spec Leg I, 186; II, 193 - he defends this opinion against his Greek audience -; Vita Mosis II, 23; see also LAB 13,6, notwithstanding the fact that it is not too clear how the day of fasting is connected with the 'feast of the trumpets' (= Rosh ha-Shana); Joma does not describe Jom Kippur as a 'feast day'. It is considered as 'mo^{c}ed', connected with the joy because of the liberation from sin which it brings about (Joma 8,9), but see also Taanit 4,8: 'There were no better days (jom ṭob) for Israel than 15th Ab and the Day of Atonement'.
211. Joma 1-7, see also the short commentary of J. Meinhold, Joma, Giessen, 1913; for the last mentioned ceremony - the dance of the daughters of Jerusalem -, Taanit 8,9 cf L. Finkelstein, The Pharisees, Philadelphia, 1946/3 (1938) I, 54-58
212. cf Joma 2 where precisely in connection with the Day of Atonement rules are described on the cleaning of the altar, the offering of sacrifice etc because of the disorder and the pulling and pushing which occurred every time; cf also Philo, De Spec Leg I, 186: 'even the evil ones compete with the good ones to prove their self control and their virtue'; the exaggeration does not prevent us from seeing the popularity of the feast, also in the diaspora.
213. L. Tetzner, Megilla 32. I did not found the proper rules; Joma 1,4 even seems to contradict it
214. For the whole question, Joma 8; concerning the sexual taboos one should consider how much trouble is taken to prevent that the officiating highpriest falls asleep and gets a pollution, cf Joma 1,5.6.7.; cf also Jos. Ant. XVII. 165: it relates that Matthias could not officiate as highpriest on the Day of Atonement, because he dreamed in the preceding night that he had intercourse with his wife
215. Taanit 1,1.2; cf also LAB 13,7 where the feast of Tabernacles is connected with the promise of rain: 'et memor ero in pluvia totius terre': the dew of the

night is considered as an eternal sign; the seasons will come in their own order; stars, clouds, winds, lightnings and thunders will come and go according to their appointed time; in Tract Shem 8,3; 10,17 one can see how the fast for rain is presupposed to be connected with praying and alms!

216. P. Blackman, Mishnayot-Moed, London, 1952, II, 515 on the three periods of the 'rebiyah': 1-17 Marcheshwan; 18-23 Marcheshwan; 24 Marcheshwan - 1 Kislew: for the history of the meaning of 'rebiyah', cf S. Krauss, Talmudische Archäologie, II, 149f

217. cf Taanit 1-2; for commentary, L. Tetzner, Megilla, Berlin, 1968, 27f. in the notes; Str.-B. IV, 1, 83ff

218. M.D. Herr, The Calendar, in, Jewish People in the First Century, Assen, 1976, II, 844 gives this exact date. He probably has come to this opinion because rather many events of the Jewish war have been mentioned which are outdated by later events so that they cannot be considered any more as 'feast days': see 3 Kislew (if the images of the emperor are meant); 22 Shebat (the cessation of the (pagan?) service); 25 Siwan (the removal of the tax-collectors from Juda and Jerusalem); 17 Elul (the departure of the Romans from Jerusalem); he does not say what he thinks of 'yom ṭwrynws' - if this is to be translated with 'Trajan's Day', but see J. Fitzmyer - D.J. Harrington, A Manual of Palestinian Aramaic Texts, Rome, 1978, 187. See also N.N. Glatzer, Megillat Taanit, in, Encyclopaedia Judaica; A. Pelletier, Le nomenclature du Calendrier juif à l'époque hellénistique, RB 82 (1975) 229; G.F. Moore, Judaism in the First Centuries, I, 160; II, 54; III, 127; S. Zeitlin, The Judaean Calendar, in, Studies in the Early History of Judaism, New York, 1973,I, 194-211; Schürer, History, I, 587, but above all H. Lichtenstein, Die Fastenrolle. Eine Untersuchung zur jüdisch-hellenistischen Geschichte, HUCA 8/9 (1931/32) 257-351. For the historical importance of the Trajan's Day, see E. Smallwood, The Jews under Roman Rule, Leiden, 1981, 425f

219. cf H. Lichtenstein, HUCA 8/9 (1931/32) 272

220. Jos. Ant. XIV. 22. Josephus dates the story in the time of Aristobolus and Hyrkanus II (= 67-40 BC); according to the scholion on Megillat Taanit: 'until Choni stood before the arc and said a prayer, and the rain came down; they declared the day that the rains came down, a 'yom ṭob' - the scholiast apparently knows Taanit 3,8 -, the story belongs to the time of Simon ben Shetach (103-76 BC), cf H. Lichtenstein, HUCA 8/9 (1931/32) 299

221. Taanit 3,8
222. Taanit 3,4; see for example Behm, s.v. νῆστις; Str.-B. IV, 1. 82: how is the relation between the sounding of the shofar and the fasting? See the discussion in Taanit 3,3.5.6.7 and the different practices when wolves were only seen, or when it is known that children were actually killed by wolves
223. Taanit 3,5.7: as is also the menace of wild beasts
224. Judith 4,9ff
225. 2 Macc 13.9ff
226. Jos. Ant XX. 89: for commentary, E. Smallwood, The Jews under Roman Rule, Leiden, 1981, 416ff; for the connection of war and fasting in the rabbinic tradition, see J T I Ex 17,9; Mekilta on Ex. Massekta Amalek I vs 17,9 and 17,12
227. Jos. Bell Jud III. 8.1. 340ff; also Test Mos 9,5f where the same story is found: Taxo, the man from the tribe of Levi, prefers to hide himself with his seven sons in stead of transgressing the commandments of the Lord
228. Pesachim 4,5; Taanit 2,10; 4,7; Rosh Hashana 1,3; Megilla 1,3
229. Taanit 4,6: the prohibition to enter the land refers to Num 14,29ff owing to the disobedience of the Israelites; the first destruction of the Temple, 2 Kings 25,1ff; Jer 39, 1ff; 52,4ff; the capture of Bethar belongs to the war of Bar Kochba, cf E. Smallwood, The Jews under Roman Rule, Leiden, 1981, 424f; 541f; 455f, as does the ploughing up of the City as the start of the foundation of Aelia Capitolina, cf Smallwood, 432ff esp. 459
230. cf Sifre on Dt & 31 v. 6,4 where Zach 8,19 is commented: the fast in the 5th month is explained as the fast of the 9th Ab 'when the Temple was destructed for the first and the second time'; Jer 52,4ff speaks of the 10th day; Jos. Ant. X. 131 follows 2 Kings 25,1ff; Jer 39,1f but harmonizes with Jer 52,4ff by saying that the events took place at midnight; according to him the second capture took place at the same day but it is called the 10th Lois (= Ab) (Bell. Jud VI. 249). The rabbinical tradition solves this problem by saying that on the 9th day the fire started and on the 10th day spread around, see b Taanit 29a
231. b Erubin 41a; b Taanit 12a, cf L. Tetzner, Megilla, Berlin, 1968, 28 who mentions also the later literature on this topic.
232. L. Finkelstein, The Pharisees, Philadelphia, 1946/3 (1938) 731-734; Schürer, History, I, 371
233. Jos. Ant. XIV. 66; Bell Jud I. 149; Ant XIV. 487f

234. E. Smallwood, The Jews under Roman Rule, 564; Schürer, History, I, 239, note 23; 284, note 11 who mention all problems on these texts with all possible solutions. In my suggestion the difficulty remains that it should be the third month. Besides, it would have been a too nice coincidence to 'forget' these captures in the list of disasters

235. A. Schalit, Herodes, Berlin, 1969, 764-768 proposes to understand these texts as 'special fast days' in view of the 'sword': a real possibility as we have seen. In that case they would be real indications of such popular fasts which are only 'legendary' ornaments in other texts

236. 11 Q Temple 25,11.12 and 27,6.7': 'everybody who does not fast on this day, will be eradicated from your people'; Joma 8,3: 'if one both ate and drank, one is liable to one 'chattah'; if one both ate and worked, one is liable to two 'chattoth'

237. This should not lead to the misconception that the rabbis had no idea of the limited value of fasting. They are especially explicit with regard to the Day of Atonement: cf Joma 8,8 where the necessity of 'teshuba' is pointed out; Joma 8,9: if one says: 'I will sin and the Day of Atonement will effect atonement', then the Day of Atonement does not effect atonement; for transgressions between a man and his fellow man the Day of Atonement does not effect atonement until he shall have first appeased his fellow man'; cf Sifra on Lev., Parasha Achere Mot V.8, vs 16,30 for the same way of thinking. How is it possible that Behm, TWNT does not know these texts? For a survey I. Abrahams, Studies in Pharisaism, New York, 1967/2, I. 121-128; G.F. Moore, Judaism in the First Centuries, Cambridge, 1927, II, 62-69; 257-265

238. Lc 18,12

239. Didache 8,1; Didaskalia V. 14,18.21.22 point out the passion of Jesus as the reason for this change: they arrested Jesus on Wednesday; they crucified him on Friday. In spite of W. Rordorf - A. Tuilier, La doctrine des douze apôtres, Paris, 1978, 173 who agree with this motivation, it seems more probably that the reason of the change was identical to the reason why the Jews fasted on Monday and Thursday: one should not fast before and after the sabbath, resp. immediately before and after Sunday. It remains to be explained why the Christians left out Thirsday

240. 2 days: Test Zab 4,2;
3 days: Test Mos 9,6;
7 days: Apoc Baruch 5,7; 12,5; 20,5 (21,1); 43,3

(47,2); 4 Ezra 5, 13.20; 6.35; 9,24;
12 days: Test Benj 1,4;
40 days: Vita Adae et Evae 6;4 Ezra 14,42; 3 Baruch 4,14 (slav); History of the Rechabites 1,1ff; also in Mt 4,1ff;
2 years: Test Simon 3,4;
70 weeks and twice 60 weeks: Apoc Ezra 1,3.4;
7 years: Test Jos 3,4; Test Ruben 1,9.10;
always: Judith 8,6; Lc 2,37; Test Isaac 4,1 (and trice 40 days a year! 4,4);
remember also Philo, Vita Contempl. 34f which describes people who only use food after every 3 days and some of them even after six days; besides, one does not eat before sunset

241. This mourning refers to the official procedure: the standing and sitting for the condolence and the blessing of the mourners. cf Megilla 4,3 and commentary in L. Tetzner, Megilla, Berlin, 1968, 119ff
242. Mt 9,14ff
243. Test Benj 1,4: Rachel fasts 12 days and then conceives Benjamin
244. Joseph and Aseneth 10 where Aseneth expresses her grief over the absence of Joseph by a fast which is described with abundant romantic details; and Test Zab 4,7: because Joseph has been sold
245. Test Ruben 1,10; Test Juda 15,4; History of the Rechabites 8,3
246. Apoc Baruch 5,7; 4 Ezra 10,4ff where one finds a combination of fasting on account of a private grief and of the destruction of Jerusalem, with a discussion; Test Mos 9,5 with its concrete descriptions of the destruction of Israel in c. 8 (dependent on the dating of this tractate this refers to the time after Herod or after 70 AD); Taanit 4,7 presents Rabbi Juda as someone who wants to promulgate the 9th Ab as a national day of grief
247. cf Apoc Abr 9; Apoc Baruch 5,9; 12,5; 20,5; 43,3; Apoc Ezra 1,3.4; 4 Ezra 5,13; 5,20; 6,35; 9,24-26: it is connected with Dan 9,3; 10,2.12
248. 4 Ezra 9,24-26
249. Apoc Baruch 21,3; 4 Ezra 9,27: for the totality, G. Dautzenberg, Urchristliche Prophetie, Stuttgart, 1975, 90ff
250. Apoc Elia 1,20-22 (Transl. O.S. Winter, OTPsepigrapha I). Parallels which are influenced by their own context, are LAB 30,4; Test Jos 9,2; 10,1; Test Simeon 3,4; Ps Sal 3,9; Test Jacob 7,17
251. Mt 10,1ff
252. Mc 9,29 = Mt 17,21, if these texts are original, see

textcritical apparatus

253. Plutarchus, De Iside et Osiride, 361 B (26): μέγαλας μὲν ἰσχυράς, δυστρόπους δε καὶ σκυθρωπάς; cf also the combination of evil spirits, mourning and fast with the concept σκυθρωπός in Test Simeon 4,1

254. b Hullin 107b and b Joma 77b: one is not allowed to put a piece of bread in someone's mouth - be it one's own child - without washing his hands because of Shibbeta, the demon which dwells on unwashed hands: she should not get the chance to enter; see also b Joma 76b-77a where the prohibition of the anointing is connected with Dan 10,3; Ez 8 and 10. Test Sol where one could expect to find something, does not make a connection between demons and eating. But the washing of hands (13,2), the sprinkling with water (18,18), the anointing (18,34) are used as apotropeics

255. see for example A. Sand, Das Gebet und die Propheten, Regensburg, 1974, 91ff; S. van Tilborg, The Jewish Leaders of Matthew, Leiden, 1972, 8ff; H. Giesen, Christliches Handeln, Frankfurt, 1982, 150ff

256. cf D. Garland, The Intention of Matthew 23, Leiden, 1979, 104ff; cf also the interesting parallel in Test Aser 2,8ff: it refers to someone who, although fasting, commits several crimes. This is διπρόσωπος. He is as a hare: although halfway clean, it is unclean. The-having-two-faces is connected with an example from the Law, just as the fasting itself has to be imbedded in the fulfilling of the commandments.

Notes: chapter 4 THE PROBLEMS OF THE RICH AND THEIR SOLUTION

1. For Beth-Sachur (47-45 BC) and En-Gedi (before 60 AD because the latest coin is a coin of Felix; there are 139 coins, particularly of Agrippa I and Felix), see Y. Meshorer, Jewish Coins of the Second Temple Period, Tel Aviv, 1967, 50 and 106; for Isfija, see A. Ben-David, Talmudische Okonomie, Hildesheim, 1974, 192; the youngest coin is 52/53 AD. For other hoards, see A. Kindler, The Jaffa Hoard of Alexander Jannaeus (851 coins; 90-85 BC) and H. Hamburger, A Hoard of Syrian Tetradrachms and Tyrian Bronze Coins from Gush Halav (= Gischala) (237 coins, 201-226 AD), in, Recent Studies and Discoveries of Ancient Jewish and Syrian Coins, 1954, resp. 107-185 and 201-226
2. H. Grassl, Sozialökonomische Vorstellungen in der kaiserzeitlichen griechischen Literatur (1.-3. Jh n.Chr), Wiesbaden, 1982, 142ff gives a number of texts which should prove that this 'idea of treasure' is not generally accepted. Most notable is the text of Philostratos, Vitae Sophistarum, 547 in which the author makes Herod Atticus say that money in a treasury is 'the prison of wealth'. One should be aware, however, that this advice does not point in the direction of 'making money fertile' in trade etc, but that money should be given to friends, cities, nations: this 'giving' should be seen as 'helping' (ἐπαρκέω): something which is not completely outside the ambit of self interest. Furthermore, Grassl has probably gathered all the texts and even so, there are only a few; and, finally, they have hardly influenced the economic thinking of the time, however 'intelligent' they were, if seen from the point of view of our capitalistic ideas
3. Representants of the classic point of view are A. Ben-David, Talmudische Okonomie; H. Grassl, Sozialökonomische Vorstellungen; F.M. Heichelheim, Roman Syria, in, An Economic Survey of Ancient Rome, ed. by T. Frank, Vol IV, 121-257; also, An Ancient Economic History, Leiden, 1970. Vol III; M. Rostovtzeff, The Social and Economic History of the Roman Empire, Oxford, 1957 (1926), I-II; representants of the more critical point of view are M. Weber, The Agrarian Sociology of Ancient Civilizations, London, 1976 (orig. 1924/1896-1909) and M.I. Finley, The Ancient Economy, London, 1975
4. as for example H.G. Kippenberg, Religion und Klassenbil-

dung im antiken Judäa, Göttingen, 1978 and H. Kreissig, Die sozialen Zusammenhänge des jüdischen Krieges, Berlin, 1970

5. see for instance F.W. Beare, Matthew, 180. It is interesting to see where this opinion leads to: 'Are we to take these words of Jesus as flatly forbidding his followers to put by any kind of savings at all? If so, we should have to regard them as utterly impractical and even unwise (! sic). Without some accumulation of capital, no new venture could ever be undertaken, from the opening of a shop to the building of a factory. The words assume that the treasures are hoarded; they are prized for their own sake, not put to work to create jobs and produce goods'. In this interpretation the whole capitalistic way of thinking is taken up in a unreflected and care-free way. In this exegetical tradition we find also H. Riesenfeld, Von Schätzesammeln und Sorgen, in, Neotestamentica et patristica, Fs O. Cullmann, Leiden, 1962, 47ff; J. Radermakers, Au fil de l'évangile selon s. Matthieu, Heverlee, 1972, 101 ('il s'agit de se détacher des trésors illusoires (!?); Guelich, Sermon on the Mount, 365 and passim; the basic text remains Bultmann's formulation: 'Diese Absage an die Welt ... ist aber nicht etwa Askese, sondern die slichte Bereitschaft für Gottes Forderung. Denn was dieser Absage positiv entspricht und worin also die Bereitschaft für die Gottesherrschaft besteht, ist die Erfüllung des Willens Gottes' (Theologie des NT, 10). Fortunately there are more exegetes who take up the economic components of this text
6. Mt 23,16.17 and 27,6, see Jos. Bell Jud II, 175: ἱερὸς θησαυρός, καλεῖται δὲ κορβωνᾶς, Bauer Wb. s.v. κορβανᾶς
7. Shekalim 1,3; Jos. Ant III, 195: he speaks of four attic drachms; in fact it had to be paid in Tyrian silver money; see also S. Applebaum, Economic Life in Palestine, in, The Jewish People in the First Century, Assen, 1976, 678; H. Kreissig, Die sozialen Zusammenhänge, 48
8. Shekalim 1,3
9. Mt 17,24ff; see the system of the payment by way of a pledge as an indication of the exerted compulsion, Shekalim 1,3; 2,1
10. Jos. Ant XVIII. 19.1.310: Nehardea and Nisibis as the rallying-place for the didrachma; Philo, De Spec Leg I, 78: in every town a pay-desk; an election of the escort-people; Leg ad Gaium 216: on the contribution from Babylon; see also F.M. Heichelheim, Roman Syria, 247f; A. Ben-David, Talmudische Okonomie, 254ff
11. Jos. Ant XVI. 6.2.163ff; Philo, Leg ad Gaium 311

12. Applebaum, Economic Life, 678
13. Jos. Ant XIV. 16.4.488
14. Jos. Bell Jud V.13.6.562; Philo, Leg ad Gaium 319
15. Jos. Bell Jud V.5.3.205
16. Joma 3,10
17. Joma 3,10
18. Jos. Ant XIX. 6.1.294
19. Joma 3,10; 3,9
20. Middot 3,8: we need to mention the six offering boxes in the form of horns where visitors could deposit their money offering
21. cf 2 Macc 3 on the whole cluster: the wrong notion on the richness of the Temple treasure by the Temple servant Simon; the deposit of Hyrkanus; the money of the widows and the orphans; the seizure by Heliodorus; cf. also 4 Macc 4,3: 'many millions in private capital are deposited there'; Jos. Bell Jud VI. 5.2.281; see J. Jeremias, Jerusalem in the Time of Jesus, 1969, 56; Applebaum, Economic Life, 683
22. For the system of the temple as a banking institute in aniquity, see R. Bogaert, Banques et banquiers dans les cités grecques, Leyde, 1968, 279-304
23. cf Lev 27,14ff; in Sifra op Lev., Parasha Bechoqoti 10,5 v. 27,14ff we find yet a discussion on the rules; E. Lambert, Les changeurs de la monnaie en Palestine, REJ 52 (1907) 27
24. Shekalim 4,1.2
25. On this difference between main-capital and rest-capital in the Greek temples, see R. Bogaert, Banques et banquiers, 289; in Hebrew it is called 'terumat ha-lishkah' and 'shejarej ha-lishkah'
26. Shekalim 4,3.4; Jos. Bell Jud V. 5.1ff; see also H. Kreissig, Die sozialen Zusammenhänge, 58ff
27. Shekalim 4,2
28. cf Bell Jud V. 5.1ff (one can suppose that Herod is the subject here, but this is not completely certain. It is possible that Herod paid this from his own resources, see Applebaum, Economic Life, 666); Bell Jud II. 9.4.175 = Ant XVIII. 3.2.60 (on Pilate and his aqua-duct); Ant XX. 9.7: on Agrippa II: the inhabitants of Jerusalem had proposed to rebuild the east gallery, but Agrippa does not believe that they have sufficient funds for that
29. Some amounts are mentioned in Joma 3,7. This text does not speak about the most expensive garment of the high priest, adorned with jewels and gold and silver clasps. The garment is even given a political significance, because there is an argument over the place where it should be kept: in the fortress of Antonia or in the

Temple. The disagreement becomes so strong that the Jews send an emissary to Rome, with the help of an personal intervention of Agrippa II, Jos Ant XX. 1.3.5ff

30. 2 Macc 3,11
31. Ant XIV. 4.4.72; Bell Jud I. 7.6.152
32. Ant XIV. 7.1; also Bell Jud II. 3.3.49 (= Ant XVII. 10.2.264) which mention a plundering by Roman soldiers after Herod's death: 400 talents are been taken away
33. Bell Jud V. 13.6.565
34. Bell Jud VI. 5.2.282
35. Bell Jud VII. 5.5.132ff
36. cf Jos. Ant XV. 9.1.299; Herod's income is reduced to nothing because of an ongoing drought. To overcome this problems he smelts 'his own' gold and silver and buys grain in Egypt to distribute, but also to be sold as seed, using the coming harvest as collateral; see A. Ben-David, Talmudische Okonomie, I, 223. For a description of the court and the court personnel of Herod, see Jeremias, Jerusalem in the Time of Jesus, 87ff
37. M.I. Finley, The Ancient Economy, 113ff
38. Jos. Ant XIV. 3.1.34; see also A. Ben-David, Talmudische Okonomie, 167
39. Jos. Ant XV. 4.2.96 = Bell Jud I. 18.5.361; Strabo, Geographia XVI. 2.41 (the balsam serves to fight headaches, catharacts and other eye sicknesses and is, therefore, very expensive); XVII. 1.15 (it is prohibited to plant it somewhere else which limits the production); Plinius, Naturalis Historia XII. 54.111-125 (before the war the ownership was with the kings, now it belongs to the imperial fiscal authority; in the five years since the war it produced 800.000 sesterces); see also F. Heichelheim, Roman Syria, 145; Applebaum, Economic Life, 665
40. Jos. Ant XV. 6.7.200ff: all other 'services' are mentioned here given by Herod to Augustus, especially the provisions for his army on its sortie to Egypt; see also Ant XVI. 2.2.16f: the journey of Herod to Ionia in occasion of the visit of Agrippa, the co-regent of Augustus: no amounts are mentioned but it will have cost 'something'
41. Jos. Ant XVI. 4.5.128: on this occasion Augustus gives Herod half of his income from the coppermines in Cyprus as a return donation: it should thus be valued at the same amount, if not more
42. Jos. Ant XVIII. 2.3.31 = Bell Jud II. 9.1.167: for the history, see Ant XVII. 11.1.301; Ant XVII. 11.5.321. One should mention here what the procurators take or allow to be given them, such as the seizure of Arche-

laos' money by Quirinius (Ant XVIII. 1.1); the bribe of Cumanus (Ant XX. 6.1.118); the daily gifts of Ananias to Albinus (Ant XX. 9.2.206ff); the freeing of the captives for money by Albinus (Ant XX. 9.5.215; see also Bell Jud II. 14.1.271) and the abuses in management by Florus (Ant XX. 11.1.252 = Bell Jud II. 14.2.277ff, see especially 293 which tells the story that Florus steals 17 talents from the Temple in favour of the imperial fiscal authority)

43. Bell Jud II. 6.3.93; one finds the higher figures in Ant XVII. 11.5.321; see also Ant XVII. 6.1.146 and 8.1.190ff where other figures are mentioned; see also the legacy of Salome to Julia in Ant XVIII. 2.3. 31; the events about the legacy of Archeloas in Ant XVIII. 1.1; the mentioning of the high income of Agrippa I, Ant XIX. 8.2.352 which consists of 12.000.000 drachmas according to a textual conjecture of L.H. Feldman (Loeb ed.); see also Kreissig, Die sozialen Zusammenhänge, 82; Jeremias, Jerusalem in the Time of Jesus, 91
44. Ant XVIII. 6.3.158
45. see resp. Mt 18,23ff; 25,14ff and 14,1ff; see also 11,8 on the μαλακά which are worn in the palaces of the kings
46. On the discussion of the relation between the office of the highpriest with the class of the highpriests, Schürer, History, II, 227ff who takes on the proposal of Jeremias, Jerusalem in the Time of Jesus, 175ff
47. Jos. Ant XX. 8.8.179ff; also Tos Sota 14,6: it gives an interpretation of 1 Sam 8,3 but at the same time it is apparently not without historical reminiscencies: 'Rabbi Meir says: 'They openly demanded their portions.' Rabbi Judah says: 'They forced goods on private people'. Rabbi Aquiba says: 'They seized the gifts'. Rabbi Jose says: 'They took a basket of tithes by force'.' (Transl. J. Neusner)
48. Jerusalem in the Time of Jesus, 181ff
49. Ant XX. 9.2.206ff
50. Ant XX. 8.8.179f. For reasons which are not very clear H. Kreissig, Die sozialen Zusammenhänge, 41ff believes that whatever is spoken in the Mishnah literature, has no reality. These texts could teach him better
51. Joma 3,9; cf also b Pesachim 57a which by way of a lamentation enumerates the abuses practiced by rich (and) high-priestly families: the use of clubs, fists, viper's venom, (backbiting?), abuse of writing materials, nepotism and violence by slaves, cg Jeremias, Jerusalem in the Time of Jesus, 195ff; Kreissig, Die sozialen Zusammenhänge, 96
52. Jos Bell Jud V. 5.7.230: every sabbath, every new moon,

on New Year and on the Day of Atonement

53. On the income of the Temple for the priests, see Schürer, History, II, 238ff: the main source of income is the yearly tithe on the harvest. This is made clear once again from the abuses mentioned
54. resp. Mt 26,14-16 and 27,3-10; 28,11-15; 23, 16-22
55. end second century AD: Daneko, Issur and Rabbi Chija ha-Gadol, cf b Baba Qamma 99b
56. I am following here the not yet improved study of E. Lambert, Les changeurs et la monnaie en Palestine, REJ 51 (1906) 217-244; 52 (1907) 24-42
57. Shekalim 1,7; R. Bogaert, Banques et banquiers, 325ff shows that the average in Greece was about 5%. As reason for this big difference in agio he mentions that there was little cash available: an argument which certainly must have been true for Jerusalem; see also S. Egjes, Das Geld im Talmud, Giessen, 1930, 87
58. Sifra on Lev., Parasha Bechoqoti 10,5. v. 27,14ff
59. j Shekalim IV. 1.48a and Tos Shekalim 2,13
60. cf Tos Shekalim 2,13: 'all kinds of coins were to be found in Jerusalem'; for the practice itself and the profit from this exchange, see R. Bogaert, Banques et banquiers, 317f
61. Meila 6,5; Tos Meila 2,11; Baba Metzia 3,11: the Hebrew words for 'closed' and 'open' are resp. 'tserur' and 'mutar'; for the whole system, R. Bogaert, Banques et banquiers, 332ff
62. Mt 25,27ff
63. Mt 21,12-17
64. On this history, E. Badian, Publicans and Sinners, Oxford, 1972
65. see also Mt 17,25 where a difference between κῆνσος and τέλος is supposed
66. 1% on sale; 25% on trade of freed men; 20% on inheritances; 20% on emancipation of slaves, see O. Hirschfeld, Die kaiserlichen Verwaltungsbeamten, Berlin, 1963/3 (1876) 93.95.106
67. Maybe with the exception of Gaza where the quarta mercatura = 25% has to be paid, cf S.J. de Laet, Portorium, Brugge, 1949, 366; see also the report of the discussion between Schürer and Rostovtzeff on p. 342, and Schürer, History, I, 372ff
68. Archelaos abolishes it in the beginning of his government, Jos. Ant XVII. 205; Vitellius (35-39 AD) does the same for the sale of fruits in Jerusalem, Ant XVIII. 4.1.90
69. S.J. de Laet, Portorium, 334ff; Michel, TWNT s.v. τελώνης, 98; for Capharnaum, see F.M. Heichelheim, Roman Syria, 230

70. However, this is not as certain as is sometimes thought. The arguments are often taken from one author to another without argument, see for instance the difference of formulation in Michel, TWNT s.v. τελώνης, 97 line 20 and 98 line 18/19. The real argument is the Palmyra inscription, but it is a question whether the situation of this city state can be transferred to Palestine, see Schürer, History, I, 375f
71. Tacitus, Annales, 13,50f and the inscription from Palmyra, cf S. de Laet, Portorium, 371ff
72. S. de Laet, Portorium, 420ff; E. Badian, Publicans and Sinners, 75; see also L. Schottroff - W. Stegemann, Jesus von Nazareth. Hoffnung der Armen, Stuttgart, 1978, 16ff and J.-P. Lémonon, Pilate et le gouvernement de la Judée, Paris, 1981, 105ff. This is all the more cogent when one considers that the plain of Jericho fell directly under the imperial fiscal authority
73. Jos. Bell Jud II. 14.4.284
74. Mt 5,46; 9,9-13; 10,3; 11,19; 18,17; 21,31-32
75. cf b Baba Metzia 42a; for the merchants is used the Greek/Hebrew word 'praqmataja' = πραγματευταί
76. Notwithstanding the fact that Rabbi Isaac comes from a later time, about 300 AD; cf M.I. Finley, Ancient Economy, 118 on Plinius, Epistulae X.54: 'The first (thing to be noted) is the familiar trinity, cash on hand, land, money on loan'
77. cf Applebaum, Economic Life, 658 who refers to the landed estates of Eleazar ben Harsum (b Joma 35b); Flavius Josephus (Vita 422-429); Ptolemeus, the servant of Herod (Ant XVIIIsic!, has to be XVII. 289; Bell Jud II. 69); Compsos (Jos. Vita 33: there are mentioned several people who are εὐσχήμων - which presupposes landed property -; Krispos is mentioned as actual owner of κτήματα); Philippos (Vita 47); see also A. Ben-David, Talmudische Okonomie, 314 who refers to Rabbi Tarfon (b Nedarim 49b. 62a) and Rabbi Gamaliel II (Berakot 2,7; Demai 3,1; Baba Metzia 5,8); the most rich large landowner was Herod of course (Bell Jud I. 20.4.398); H. Kreissig, Die sozialen Zusammenhänge, 29ff refers to texts of the NT where (large) landowners are mentioned: Acts 4,34.36ff; 5,1ff; 12,12ff; Mc 10,22; 15,21
78. Baba Batra 4,7: is 'shed for hides' not a better translation for 'beit shelachin' than Applebaum's 'irrigated fields'. Jastrow says it means 'a field which needs irrigation'; apart from this philological argument we must point to the linguistic argument, that the surrounding area is mentioned only at the end of the mishnah, at least, if 'sanṭer' means 'guarded land

outside of a township' and not 'vilicus', see also W. Windfuhr, Baba Batra, Giessen, 1925, 43. In Baba Batra 3,1 we find the same distinction: the utensils of the villa which compromises also the 'beit ha-shelachim', are juridically part of the property, if they have been undisputed for three years without interruption; a different arrangement is made for the 'beit ha-ba^{c}al'; but, Baba Metzia 7,2 is clearly about a field in which a well brings water for irrigation. For the system of the Roman villa, see Varro, De rerum rusticarum, and Columella, De re rustica. For the extensitivity of the cattle-breeding in Palestine, see Philo, De Spec Leg I. 136

79. cf Erubim 5,6; Applebaum, Economic Life, 641; Ben-David, Talmudische Okonomie, 50
80. Bell Jud II. 21.2.591/2; in Vita 74f different ciphers are mentioned: there the profit is 10:1; Ben-David, Talmudische Okonomie, 111.231; Heichelheim, Roman Syria, 229; Kreissig, Die sozialen Zusammenhänge, 68ff
81. Y. Meshorer, Jewish Coins of the Second Temple, Tel-Aviv, 1967, nr 5.7.8.9.10.11 (Alexander Jannaeus); nr 50.51.52.53.55 (Herod); nr 56.57.58.59.60 (Archelaos); nr 90.92 (Agrippa I); nr 98.118.124 (Agrippa II); see also Ben-David, Talmudische Okonomie, 277ff
82. For the risks of the shipping, cf Arachin 4,3; Gittin 3,4; Aboda Zara 1,3
83. cf Mt 22,5; 13,31-33 and 19,6ff: the classic place for the synoptic evaluation of ownership
84. cf A. Jülicher, Gleichnisreden Jesu II, 98 who rejects the idea that there would be a second spiritual organ of light (F.W. Beare, Matthew, 183 seems to presuppose something like that); 'light in you' has no other meaning than 'the eye is the lamp of the body'. For this anthropology, see E. Sjöberg, 'Das Licht in dir', in, Studia Theol 5 (1951) 98ff
85. That is the general opinion as far as I know; for the older literature, see C. Edlund, Das Auge der Einfalt, Uppsala, 1952, 11ff; more recent in J. Amstutz, ΑΠΛΟΤΗΣ, Eine begriffsgeschichtliche Studie zum jüdisch-christlichen Griechisch, Bonn, 1968, 96ff; S. Schulz, Q. Die Spruchquelle, Zürich, 1972, 468; E. Schweizer, Die Bergpredigt, Göttingen, 1982, 75. Formgeschichte has had a great influence on this opinion, pointing out the difference between Mt 6,22ff and Lc 11,34ff Therefore, it was less inclined to see the saying in Matthew as a separate unit with its proper logic. However, in Luke something like in Matthew happens, but his point of view is more positive: a light without any shade of darkness. Luke also

presupposes that there are two kinds of eyes

86. E. Sjöberg, Das Licht in dir, Studie Theol 5 (1951) 98ff discusses all posibilities which go from 'tam', 'shalem', 'tob' with digressions on 'jashar', 'sèdèq', 'hèèmin' etc., see also J. Amstutz, ΑΠΛΟΤΗΣ, 39
87. J. Amstutz, ΑΠΛΟΤΗΣ is the most fundamental study of this concept, see also C. Edlund, Das Auge der Einfalt, Uppsala, 1952 and M. de Jonge, Testament Issachar als 'typisches' Testament, in, M. de Jonge, Studies on the Testament of the Twelve Patriarchs, Leiden, 1975, 291-316. I base myself for my own research mainly on those texts where the concept is used with a certain coherence and consistency: 1) in Test XII Patr it is a central concept: Test Ruben 4,1; Test Levi 13,1; Test Simeon 4,5; Test Benj 6; Test Issachar uses the concept as title because several chapters deal with it; 2) in the New Testament it is used, besides Acts 2,46; Jas 1,15, in conspicuous places of the pauline literature: 2 Cor 8,2; 9,11.13; 11,3; (Eph 6,5 = Col 3,22); 3) as a third unit we find the texts in the Shepherd of Hermas: Visio I. 2.4; II. 7.2; III 9.9; 16,5; 17,1; Mandatum I. 1.2; II; Similitudo IX. 24.1-4; 4) the specific use of the word in Philo's theology and in the gnostic (and gnosticising) literature is not all that interesting for an understanding of the Matthew text. I used the Septuagint more as added material
88. Job 1,1.8; 2,3.9 (LXX A) (God); Test Levi 13,1 (the Lord); Test Iss 4,3 (the will of God); 5,1 (Law); 5,2 (the Lord); 6,1 (the commandments); Test Aser 1,6; 3,1 (the Good); 4,5 (commandments); 6,3 (Law); 2 Cor 11,3 (Christ); Pastor, Visio II. 7.2 (God)
89. Test Ruben 4,1; Test Benj 6,3; Test Iss 3,6; 4,4; 7,2; Pastor, Mandatum II. 2.4
90. Test Ruben 4,1; Test Iss 3,1; 5,3
91. Eph 6,5; Col 3,22
92. 2 Cor 8,2; 9,11.13, see also Rom 12,8
93. Test Iss 7,5; parallel with this boasting of oneself is the use of the word in Ps 7,9; 25,1; 40,13; 63,5 (LXX A); 1 Macc 2,37, cf Amstutz, 28ff
94. Pastor, Mandatum II; Prov 28,6 (LXX A); see also the use of ἁπλοῦς as an attribute of the king in 1 Chron 29,17 (LXX O); Jos. Ant VII. 332; 3 Macc 3,21
95. Test Iss 4,2: Test Benj 6,3; Jos. Bell Jud II. 151; Philo, De Somniis, II. 156; Leg All III. 140
96. Acts 2,46 in relation with 2,45; Pastor, Similitudo IX. 24.2
97. Test Iss 4,2; against the πλεονεξία; 4,5: against the ἀπληστία (also 6,1)
98. Test Benj 6,2

99. Test Benj 6,5.6.7. and Jas 1,8 in relation with 1,5. For the representation of the διπρόσωπος, διπλοῦς and δίψυχος against the μονοπρόσωπος, cf Test Aser 1,3.4.5; 2,1.3.5.7.8; 3,1.2; 4,1.3.4; 5,4; 6,1.2; the anthropological-theological argument is found in Test Zab 9,3: 'all that the Lord has made, has only one head'
100. Test Benj 6,4; Test Iss 4,5; 7,4
101. Test Simeon 4,5; cf Amstutz, ΑΠΛΟΤΗΣ, 67ff as archetype of Cain
102. Test Iss 3,3; Pastor,Mandatum II. 27.2ff
103. cf G. Baumbach, Das Verständnis des Bösen, Berlin, 1963; Harder, TWNT s.v. πονηρός; S. van Tilborg, The Jewish Leaders in Matthew, Leiden, 1972, 27ff
104. especially the texts in Matthew on the ἀνομία: 7,23; 13,41 in relation with v. 38 (sons of the evil one), v. 39 (the devil), v. 43 (the righteous ones); 23,28 (opposition with righteous ones, relation with ὑποκρίσις); 24,12 (v. 11 the relation with πλάνη)
105. C. Edlund, Das Auge der Einfalt, 105ff where one finds a survey of the older authors who have pronounced themselves on this question
106. see also J. Amstutz, ΑΠΛΟΤΗΣ, 99f; this connonation appears also in the LXX, although there are only few texts: Dt 15,9; Hab 1,13; Sir 14,8.9.10
107. Mt 20,1-15.16 for this interpretation, see especially J. Jeremias, Die Gleichnisse Jesu, Göttingen, 1965/7 (1947) 29ff; L. Schottroff, Der Gott der kleinen Leute, München, 1979, 71ff; V. Fusco, Oltre la Parabola, Roma, 1983, 115ff. In my interpretation the social-economic components are taken seriously up to the narrational interpretation of Matthew himself
108. Abot 5,13; see also 2,9.11 and 5,10, as also the commentary on these sayings in Abot de Rabbi Natan
109. Mt 8,12; 22,13; 25,30
110. Mt 13,42.50: if these texts are to be accepted textcritically
111. Mt 8,11; 22,1ff; 25,21.23
112. Mt 15,14; 23,16.17.19; 23,26
113. Mt 23,16ff
114. Mt 23,26
115. In Test XII Patr it is a constant topic, but it gets the broadest treatment in Test Juda which carries the title ΠΕΡΙ ΑΝΔΡΕΙΑΣ ΚΑΙ ΦΙΛΑΡΓΥΡΙΑΣ ΚΑΙ ΠΟΡΝΕΙΑΣ: see esp. 13,4-8 (the gold, the bazzling by the wine, the temptation of pleasure which brings about the absence of ἀκράτεια); 17,1 (silver and an alluring form bring a person to error); 18,2 (with the long list of evil consequences: 18,3-19,4); in 1 Qp Hab 8,10-12 (to

leave God for the sake of possessions, robbery and gathering possessions); 9,5 (the last priests in Jerusalem gather riches for themselves and possessions from the spoils of the peoples); 12,10 (the possessions of the poor have been robbed from the cities of Juda) -- in these Qumran-texts these practices are not directly connected to blindness but, considering the correlation between '[c]awel', 'shaw', 'sheqer' etc with 'chôshek', this is only relatively true (see 1 QS 1,9ff; 4,9ff.13; 3,19 esp. in relation with, for example, 1 Q pHab 10,9f; 11,1); surprising is Philo in his exposition on rentals; he calls the δανείζων blind, because he demands interest on his money out of greed, presents himself as a philanthropic person but represents in reality ἀπανθρωπία. cf De Spec Leg II. 75ff; see also II. 23 (on seeing and blind wealth as εἰκών of the virtuous and evil person) cf De Virt 82ff and De Abr 25; see De Fuga et Inv., 28ff on how this position is used ideologically to maintain one's own wealthy position, but see also De Spec Leg IV. 74: 'so then let not the rich man collect great store of gold and silver and hoard it at his house, but bring it out for general use that he may soften the hard lot of the needy with the unction of his cheerfully given liberality' (Transl F.H. Colson); for Philo, see J. Korver, De terminologie van het credietwezen in het grieksch, Amsterdam, 1934, 82.92.105.118

116. Gittin, 4,5 and Eduyot 1,13; see also Sanhedrin 11,1 on the theft of a half-slave, half-free man; Pesachim 8,1 on the eating of the pesach-lamb

117. In the Mishnah one finds this only in Pesachim 8,1, but see also Acts 16,16.19 which proves that the institute existed in the first century. See Kelim 18,9; Erubim 6,7; Shekalim 1,7; Chullin 1,7; Bekorot 8,3; Baba Batra 9,4 for the use of brothers acting as 'shutafin' (partners). H. Kreissig, Die sozialen Zusammenhänge, 35 maximalises textual occurence but minimalises the meaning. According to him the texts are simply exercises in logical juridical thinking. This, however, cannot be proved from Acts 16,16.19

118. On the whole system of slavery in Palestine, S. Krauss, Talmudische Archäologie, II, 83ff; Ben-David, Talmudische Okonomie, 58ff: on slavery at Herod's court esp., Jeremias, Jerusalem in the Time of Jesus, 87ff; also 110f; 312ff; 334ff

119. At any rate from Str.-B., I. 433f on. I did not find it in the older literature

120. But it is less than one could expect, see, however, Jeremias, Gleichnisse Jesu, 192; S. Schulz, Q. Die

Spruchquelle, 460; Grundmann, Matthäus, 213 who - to say the least - has read Strack-Billerbeck (cf note 18); Beare, Matthew, 183

121. Read Baba Batra 1 to know about the laborious settlements

122. For the whole literary Roman tradition on agriculture, W.E. Heitland, Agricola, A Study of Agriculture and Rustic Life in the Greco-Roman World, from the Point of View of Labour, Cambridge, 1921: on Cato, 164ff; Varro, 178ff; Columella, 250ff. He particularly takes on the social context of these texts in the agricultural history of Italy

123. Varro, De rerum rusticarum, I. 17.3-7 (Transl Lloyd Storr-Best, London, 1912, 50ff). The decisive latin words are: 'despicere' from the point of view of the dominum; 'restituere voluntatem ac benevolentiam in dominum' from the point of view of the slave. For other texts of Varro on slaves, see I. 13.4 (the place where the slaves' privies are to be located); I. 16.4-6; 18.1-8 on slaves as utensils and the number of slaves required; I. 54.3 on 'lora' (a much diluted wine) as drink for slaves; II.10 on shepherds as slaves; III. 9.7 on a keeper of chicken and the place for living in the chickencoop

124. Columella, De re rustica, I. 7.1; 8.1-10; 8,15-20 (Transl. Harrison Boyd Ash, Loeb. ed.). Typical for Columella is the attention he gives to specialisations among slaves, see esp. I.9; the division in small units to maintain supervision; the extensive attention for the wife of the vilicus who is primarily responsible for everything what happens in the home and for the preparations for the wine harvest, for the preserving of fruits, for the slaughtering of cattle, see esp. book XII.
He uses as typical words to describe the relation dominus-servus: 'comiter agere' and 'comitas' against 'offensio'; and 'severitas'/'crudelitas' against 'detestare' and 'spernere', see I. 7.1; 8.10; 8.15; 8.18; 8.20

125. cf Mt 21,33-46 in comparison with Mc 12,1-12 but also with Lc 20,9-19 who does not use the plural at all

126. Mt 22,1-14 in comparison with Lc 14,15-24

127. Mt 25,14-30; Lc 19,11-27 and Mt 18,21-35

128. Mt 13,24-30 and 36-43

129. Could this possibly be an explanation for the phenomenon that Matthew begins his saying with οὐδείς instead of οὐδεὶς οἰκέτης as in Lc 16,13? Matthew does not speak from the point of view of the slave

130. Str.-B. I. 434; Schlatter, Matthäus, 102; Hauck, TWNT,

s.v. μαμωνᾶς; H.P. Rüger, μαμωνᾶς, ZNW 64 (1973) 127-131

131. cf L. Schottroff, Die Güte Gottes, in W. Schottroff, Der Gott der kleinen Leute, München, 1979, 84ff who thinks that in Matthew the problem has been shifted to Christian ethical principles about pride and charity. The emphasis she places om Mt 19,30 is, in view of Mc 10,31, maybe less typical than she seems to think. Anyway, I believe that I can point out that the 'problem of the rich' is still an actual problem in the Matthew community
132. Mt 19,16-30; see also the difference with Mc 10,30 and Lc 18,30 with regard to the reward. Matthew does not speak any more of a reward ἐν τῷ καιρῷ τούτῳ
133. Mt 13,22-23; notice the clear distinction in four groups in Matthew; the disapppearance/respectively addition of 'the other desires' (Mc 4,19); the clearer opposition in Matthew with regard to the fruits: see καὶ ἄκαρπος γίνεται in Mt 13,22
134. Mt 13,44.45
135. Mt 6,19-21; 22,5
136. so Bultmann, TWNT s.v. μεριμνάω
137. S. Schulz, Q. Die Spruchquelle, 152
138. Jeremias, Gleichnisse Jesu, 212; M.F. Olsthoorn, The Jewish Background and the Synoptic Setting of Mt 6,25-33 and Lk 12,22-31, Jerusalem, 1975, 24 ff.
139. L. Schottroff - W. Stegemann, Jesus von Nazareth. Hoffnung der Armen, 59 which deals with Q, however; it does not express its opinion on the text as incorporated in Mt (resp. Lc)
140. S. van Tilborg, Geloven tussen utopie en werkelijkheid, Hilversum, 1980, 26
141. M.F. Olsthoorn, The Jewish Background of Mt 6,25-33,47 who refers to Shabbat 7,2, a text which sums up the activities forbidden on the Sabbath. One of these is the manufacture of clothes: see also b Berakot 58a which sums up the laborious activities of Adam. Firstly, the works to get the food: he had to plough, to sow, to reap, to bind and pile sheaves, to thresh, to winnow, to sift, to mill, to knead, to bake. And secondly the works to get clothing: he had to shear, to cleanse, to beat, to spin, to weave'.
142. I have used M. Weber, The Agrarian Sociology, London 1976 (1924/1896) 237ff; W.E. Heitland, Agricola, Cambridge, 1921; F.M. Heichelheim, Roman Syria, 147ff; H. Kreissig, Die sozialen Zusammenhänge, 26ff; Ben-David, Talmudische Okonomie, 58ff; M.I. Finley, The Ancient Economy, 95ff; Applebaum, Economic Life, 631ff
143. Applebaum, Economic Life, 657.665: a whole series of

areas can be pinpointed through Josephus; as for the organisation we can think of what happened under Nero in North Africa, cf Heitland, Agricola, 203ff; 325ff; especially we know the income of the date palms and balsam plantations around Jericho, probably because they were exceptional, cf note 39 for further data

144. On the private large landowners in Palestine, Applebaum, Economic Life, 641ff.658; Heichelheim, Roman Syria, 146ff; Kreissig, Die sozialen Zusammenhänge, 29ff who tries to establish a figure; see also notes 77-79 supra where I collected the historical data

145. When this transition from the vilicus system to the colonus system happened, cannot be dated very precisely as is obvious. Heitland, Agricola determines that at the time of Columella definitive forms are established in Italy. These are the first traces of a transition to the feudal system which is impeded in Palestine because of the extensiveness of small land holders, cf. Kreissig, Die sozialen Zusammenhänge, 26ff who tries to limit himself as much as possible to data from the first century; see also the discussion with him by Applebaum, Economic Life, 662; Ben-David, Talmudische Okonomie, 58ff can explain the whole system of lease and rent with more freedom, because he treats a much longer period in history

146. The Mishnah does not yet know the other lease systems like the 'shoker' who must pay in cash, and the 'shatla' who makes fallow ground fertile; see esp. Applebaum, Economic Life, 659 who refers to Pea 5,5: the 'aris' is described in this text as '^{c}ani': a poor man who takes on the 'arisut' contract: promising to pay half, a third or a fourth part of the harvest; see also Heichelheim, Roman Syria, 147ff and Ben-David, Talmudische Okonomie, 61ff

147. For literature, see note 146. The basic mishnah is Baba Metzia 9,2 which states that the contract depends on the explicitly mentioned conditions; and Baba Metzia 9,4: the lessor may add his own conditions; cf also Baba Batra 10,4 describing the 'chakirut' contract in terms of 'qabal' = receive. From Muraba^{c}at it appears that this lease system is from a fairly early date, cf P. Benoit - J. Milik, Les grottes de Muraba^{c}at, Oxford, 1961, nr 24 where a lease contract reads: 'I, Chalipha, will pay you, Hillel, yearly in wheat of good quality (...) Kor, a lease subject to tithe (...) after having deducted the tithe'

148. Kreissig, Die sozialen Zusammenhänge, 26ff leans clearly in this direction. Even if the data are insufficient to prove the extension which Kreissig

defends, it is clear that the small holding system was present in Palestine for a longer time and in a more extensive way than in other places

149. Talmudische Okonomie, 297ff
150. Mt 24,45-51; see also 24,42: 'you do not know on which hour the kyrios will come'
151. Mt 21,33-44, see also the difference with Mc 12,2 and Lc 20,10, resp. ἵνα .. λάβῃ ἀπὸ τῶν καρπῶν τοῦ ἀμπελῶνος and ἵνα ἀπὸ τοῦ καρποῦ τοῦ ἀμπελῶνος δώσουσιν αὐτῷ.
152. Mt 13,24-30; the workers are not called δοῦλοι but ἄνθρωποι and later on θερισταῖ: 13,24.30
153. Mt 20,1-16
154. Mt 13,44; 22,5
155. Mt 13,31.32
156. Mt 3,11.12
157. Mt 13,3-8
158. Mt 13,31-33
159. Mt 21,28-32
160. Mt 18,12-14
161. Mt 24,18.40.41
162. Mt 13,31: ἐν τῷ ἀγρῷ αὐτοῦ; Mc 4,31: ἐπὶ τῆς γῆς; Lc 13,19: εἰς κῆπον ἑαυτοῦ
163. Mt 21,34: ὁ καιρὸς τῶν καρπῶν ... λαβεῖν τοὺς καρποὺς αὐτοῦ
Mt 21,41: οἵτινες ἀποδώσουσιν αὐτῷ τοὺς καρποὺς ἐν τοῖς καιροῖς αὐτῶν
Mc 12,2: ἵνα ... λάβῃ ἀπὸ τῶν καρπῶν τοῦ ἀμπελῶνος
Lc 20,10: ἵνα ἀπὸ τοῦ καρποῦ τοῦ ἀμπελῶνος δώσουσιν αὐτω
164. Mt 22,5: ὃς μὲν εἰς τὸς ἴδιόν ἀγρόν, ὃς δὲ ἐπὶ τὴν ἐμπορίαν αὐτοῦ
Lc 14,18: ἀγρὸν ἠγόρασα, ζεύγη βοων ἠγόρασα πέντε
165. Mt 24,45: δοῦναι τὴν τροφὴν ἐν καιρῷ; Lc 12,42: διδόναι ἐν καιρῷ σιτομέτριον Although L. Schottroff, Das geschundene Volk, in L. Schottroff - W. Schottroff (Hg), Mitarbeiter der Schöpfung, München, 1983, 184 comes to the same conclusion with relation to the option of the parables, she gives a different interpretation of the facts. According to her the historical readers of Matthew remain hidden behind this language of another class. The argumentation I have given may be sufficient to make one own's judgment. Remember also the proposal (with argumentation) of G.D. Kilpatrick, The Origins of the Gospel according to St. Matthew, Oxford, 1946, 124ff: 'The reference to a wide range of money and the little concern about poverty would agree more with a rich community than with a country one with its limited economy'; see also J.D. Kingsbury, The verb ἀκολουθεῖν ('to follow') as

an index of Matthew's view of his community, Journ Bibl Lit 97 (1978) 76f

166. From 1 Cor 7 it is clear that this is true also for the NT. Therefore, there is no need to bring in other literature. Paul sees a connection between the 'cares' and the fact that one is married or not and the attention one must give to the partner as opposed to the undivided attention for τὰ τοῦ κυρίου; Lc 10,41 speaks about the concern which results from hospitality; Lc 12,11 speaks about the concern in relation to a process which deals with one's own life. In 1 Cor 12,25; 2 Cor 11,28; Phil 2,20; 1 Pt 5,7 it carries the positive meaning of caring for one another and the concern that everyone is doing well; see for a larger explanation of these texts - however with very different interpretations - Bultmann, TWNT s.v. μεριμνάω; Jeremias, Gleichnisse Jesu, 212; M.F. Olsthoorn, The Jewish Background of Mt 6,25-33; G. Agrell, Work, Toil and Sustenance, Lund, 1976, 68ff; the latter is very logical, starting from a too dogmatic question and little attention for the context and the semantics of the text

167. Abot 2,7: a saying which addresses also a lot of strange things: it can be understood only from the viewpoint of the milieu where it originated: the palace of Juda ha-Nashi. Gamaliel uses the Hebrew word 'da'aga', cf. also I. Abrahams, Studies in the Pharisaism and the Gospels, New York, 1967/2, II, 106: he pleads for the Hebrew word 'qapad'. The train of thought is obviously a very old Wisdom tradition, cf Sir 31,1ff

168. Lc 12,16ff

169. cf also Jas 4,13.14 where the plans for the future are compared with a person who is like a fog which is there one moment and gone the next. For Mt 6,34[c], I. Abrahams, Studies in Pharisaism and the Gospels, New York, 1967/2, II, 209 who points out the parallel in b Berakot 9b: 'every hour has enough on its own worries', see for the rest Str.-B. I. 441

170. Mt 13,22. There is apparently no good Hebrew background for the concept 'care for the world'. Most authors are silent. In Dalman, Die Worte Jesu, Darmstadt, 1965/3, 125 we find at least an attempt, even though he cannot find a good univocal translation either. He can only point to similar Hebrew-Aramaic expressions. He too believes that the opposition of 'aeon' is not the 'the coming aeon' but 'God'

171. The closest rabbinical parallel can be found in Kiddushin 4,14: 'Rabbi Eleazar said: Did you ever see

a wild beast or a bird with an occupation. And yet, they find food without having to worry about it. But are they not created to serve me? But I am created to serve my creator. How much more then will I find food without having to worry about it'

172. For a short but complete exposition of this verse, see G. Schwarz, προσθεῖναι ἐπὶ τὴν ἡλικίαν αὐτοῦ πῆχυν ἕνα, ZNW 71 (1980) 244-247. If one wants to understand the precise meaning, it is quite difficult. However, one need not worry about the intended meaning

173. cf Mekilta, on Ex., Massekta, Wajassa III v. 16,14; V v. 16,19; V v. 16,27; T J I Num 11,32. It could have been known for a longer time as is made clear by I. Abrahams, Studies in Pharisaism, New York, 1976/2, II, 91 and L. Finkelstein, The Pharisees, Philadephia, 1946/3, I, 258; see also M.F. Olsthoorn, The Jewish Background of Mt 6,25-33,52ff

174. Mt 16,8, see also Mt 8,26 and 14,31 where the word is used in the context of a pressing danger for life in case of drowning

175. G. Strecker, Der Weg der Gerechtigkeit, Göttingen, 1966/2, 152-154: 'Gottes Gerechtigkeit und menschliche Gerechtigkeit schliessen sich nicht aus, sondern sind identisch ... Sie sind nicht 'Gabe' sondern gegenwärtige, der ethischen Forderung entsprechende Tat des Menschen'; R. Walker, Die Heilsgeschichte im ersten Evangelium, Göttingen, 1967, 135ff.143; A. Sand, Das Gesetz und die Propheten, Regensburg, 1974, 204; B. Przybylski, Righteousness in Matthew, Cambridge, 1980, 89; somewhat more complicated, with more attention for the fact that the basileia is in the future, in H. Giesen, Christliches Handeln, Bern, 1982, 166; Schweizer, Bergpredigt, 78 takes it in a more Pauline sense. No author even speaks about the content of this 'will of God': that it is a message addressed to the rich from whom something is being asked and to whom something is being promised. That is symptomatic for the exegetical research

176. Contra J. Dupont, Les Béatitudes, Louvain, 1954, 250ff and many other authors who see this πρῶτον as a weakening. It is surprising that Dupont does not refer to Mt 18,21. But this text treats exactly the same reality. The 'perfection' which is lacking in the rich man, is fullfilled through his will to divest himself of his wealth and to follow Jesus, i.e. by entering into the Kingdom of God.

Notes: chapter 5 THE LAWS FOR THE PEOPLE: MUTUAL RELATIONS

1. G. Bornkamm, Der Aufbau der Bergpredigt, NTS 24 (1978) 419-432 for whom Mt 6,17-7,11 is a connected unit in the form of a commentary on the Lord's Prayer, has been followed by Guelich, Sermon on the Mount, 321ff. He has worked out this suggestion consequently with enormous consequences for the interpretation. E. Schweizer, Bergpredigt, 78,83 splits up the pericope in 7,1-6: von der Bruderlichkeit die nicht richtet, and 7,7-12: von der Freude des Betens; Beare, Matthew, 188 calls the pericope 'miscellaneous instructions'.
   From B.W. Bacon, Studies in Matthew, 1930, 277ff who gives 7,1-6 the title: 'self-judgment' and 7,7-12 'answer to prayer, colophon', it appears that we are dealing with an old discussion; T.H. Robinson, Gospel of Matthew, 1928, 59 calls the whole chapter 7 'miscellaneous instructions'; W.C. Allen, Matthew, 38 puts 6,19-34; 7,1-5 and 7,6 together as 'three prohibitions'; A. Schlatter, Der Evangelist Matthäus, 1948, 237 says: 'Der feste Zusammenhang der Rede scheint sich auf zu lösen'.
2. see e.g. Beare, Matthew, 189 implicitly in the statement 'our judgments must not be harsh'; Gundry, Matthew, 120ff referring to Mt 18,15-18, but see to the contrary Grundmann, Matthäus, 219; Schweizer, Bergpredigt, 80.113
3. Mt 5,21ff and 18,15ff
4. Lc 6,37
5. see especially the treatise Sanhedrin which teaches how in the 'dîn' (the court) the decisive questions are always directed to 'zekût' (acquittal) or to 'chôba' (conviction), notwithstanding the differences between the 'dînei mamonot' (the evil cases) and the 'dînei nefasot' (the capital cases): Sanhedrin 3,6.7; 4,1.5; 5,4.5
6. For a very individualistic interpretation, see Marshal, Luke, 266; it seems to come from fear that with a different interpretation all law and punishments will be abolished in society. We have to think of the sociological composition of the group in which such a saying has its origin: they may have had bad experiences with κριταί; maybe they react against all forms of subordination. One should compare this prohibition with the sayings against the rich. These sayings do not bring up the problem either, how society can go on, when everyone would renounce his possessions; see also Schürmann,

Lukas, 361; Schweizer, Lukas, 82; Schneider, Lukas, 158; and again Marshall, Luke, 266: none of them develop the relation with the Jewish juridical system

7. Mussner, Jakobusbrief, 187; see also James 3,1; Pastor, Mandatum II. 27.2ff and especially Test Iss 3,3: 'I was no meddler in my dealings, nor was I evil or slanderous to my neighbor. I spoke against no one, nor did I disparage the life of any human. I lived my life with singleness of vision' (Transl. H.C. Kee, OTPsepigrapha I), see also Test Iss 4,1; 5,2; 7,4ff
8. Rom 2,1ff and 14,3.4.10.11
9. Over these texts themselves not much discussion exists, see the commentaries Wilckens, Römer, 123 which for Rom 1,2 also points to the difference with Mt 7,1, in which τὰ αὐτὰ πράσσεις is not presupposed per se; Schlier, Römerbrief, 68.406. 410; Käsemann, Römer, 50.356.360 which fits in with Bultmann's suggestion to understand Rom 2,1 as a glossa. 'Αναπολόγητος is then, 'sad to say', no longer a word from Paul, and also, the reference to 1,20 disappears
10. See especially the difference in the LXX where 'sônei bètsa' (accepting gifts) has been changed in μισοῦντας ὑπερηφανίαν (hating recklessness): a form of spiritualization which speaks for itself!; see also Ex 23,6-8. In T J I Ex 18,21 and T Neoph Ex 18,21 'the gifts' are explained as 'falsely acquired riches'
11. It would be to wished that on these texts a similar study existed as W. Schottroff's study, Arbeit und sozialer Konflikt, in, Mitarbeiter der Schöpfung, München, 1983, 104-148, on Neh 5
12. In the Septuagint there is again a typical change. The striving for equality in which the position of the 'qatôn' is strenghened against the 'gadôl', has become: κατὰ τὸν μικρὸν καὶ κατὰ τὸν μέγαν κρινεῖς: because the comparison has disappeared, the legal status of the μικρός has become worse; see further Dt 16,19; Ex 23,3 (see here also the difference between TM and LXX; Philo will exploit this formulation of the LXX).

    In T J I Ex 23,3 and T Neoph 23,3 is expressly added that the poor must be guilty. Interesting is also Tos. Sota 14,4 (the long list of transgressions of the Torah surrounding the ruin of the Temple): 'When Dt 1,17 was abolished, the yoke from heaven was lifted from them and they accepted the yoke from people'. Once Dt 1,17 is no longer respected, one is delivered up to the hands of men.

    In T J I Dt 1,16.17 we find some typical additions also: in 1,16 the prescription that every accused person should have an equal chance to explain his case;

and in 1,17 that one should not be afraid of a rich and powerful man, because God sees all hidden things

13. Without any pretension of completeness, see Is 1,21-24; 56,9-12; 61,4-9; Jer 22,13-19; Ez 22,12-17; Amos 3,9-11; 6,3ff; Hab 2,6-11; Prov 1,19; 24,23; 28,16.21; Job 34,1ff. 17ff. For a summary D. Kellermann, TWAT s.v. 'bts[c]'
14. Sir 35,11-14 (LXX) where God is presented as a judge who is without respect of persons and, who, therefore, speaks justice also for the poor and the widow: opposite to what is threatening the lawabiding person in his impotence
15. The context of the saying leads to this interpretation: do not try to obtain power (ἡγεμόνεια); or a seat of honour; but on the other hand also: do not lower yourself before the masses (the ὄχλος), see Sir 7,4.5.7; fidelity to Law must shine by itself
16. De Spec Leg IV 57 where three of the four cardinal ἀρεταί are summed up: σύνεσις, δικαιοσύνη, ἀνδρεία
17. De Spec Leg IV 59ff where Philo takes Ex 23,1 LXX as starting point of his expositions
18. De Spec Leg IV 62ff where Philo explains 23,8 in combination with Dt 16,20
19. De Spec Leg IV 70 with references to Dt 1,17 and 16,19
20. De Spec Leg IV 72 as explanation of Ex 23,3; but see also De Spec Leg IV 172 where he describes the lawsuits against the commoners, poor and obscure as the μεγάλαι ὑποθέσεις. In this text he also tells the story of Moses and Jethro, and the connection with the theologoumenon that Israel is an orphan between the peoples (see IV 179)
21. Jos Bell Jud II 20.5.569: Josephus acts as if he is Moses. He institutes a general court of 70 people and appoints in each city a college of 7 judges to take care of minor matters. Major cases and all capital cases must be sent on to the court of 70 or to himself
22. Jos Ant IV 8.14.214-218, see also C Ap II, 207 on capital punishment in case of bribery for the judges
23. Abot 1,8; the meaning of '[c]orekei hadaiianim' is disputed, see K. Marti - G. Beer, Abot, Giessen, 1927 who want to translate it as 'judges of the inquiry'; but see also Jastrow s.v. '[c]rk' who translates: 'do not make thyself to be like legal advisers, i.e. be careful as judge not to suggest an advice to one of the litigants'
24. Abot 4,8; see also Pea 8,9: 'and any judge who takes bribes and perverts justice will not die of old age before his eyes have grown dim, as it is said, 'And a bribe shalt thou not take for the bribe blindeth the

seeing' (Ex 23,8)

25. In the Mt-commentaries these texts are often found; often with the negative qualification that the Mt-text has a much broader range, see for example Schweizer, Bergpredigt, 80: 'Er (=Mt) besagt dass wir verloren sind, solange wir noch in der Kategorie des Zumessens, Abwägens, Einstufens leben. Das geht freilich über jüdische Sätze hinaus, die formal ähnlich sind', and Abot 2,4 and b Shabb 127a! are quoted then; the same also in Schulz, Q. Die Spruchquelle, 148; Büchsel, TWNT s.v. κρίνω, 937; Deissner, TWNT s.v. μέτρον, 636ff and often in the German literature
26. Abot 1,6, see especially the commentary on this in Abot de R. Nathan ch 8, where, in a thrilling story about a rabbi who spends the night with a girl freed from slavery, the teaching is given how one can think good or bad about a person
27. Abot 2,4
28. Abot 4,7, see K. Marti - G. Beer, Abot, 192 for the textcritical variants with regard to the name. Ismael ben Jose belongs to the fourth generation of the tannaim, i.e. ±140-220 AD; around 180 AD according to Billerbeck
29. For the pseudepigrapha, see e.g. 2 En (J-text) 42,7: 'Happy is he who carries out righteous judgment, not for the sake of payment, but for justice, not expecting anything whatever as a result; and the result will be that judgment without favoritism will follow for him'; 42,9: 'Happy is he who judges righteous judgment for orphan and widow, and who helps anyone who has been treated unjustly'; yet closer to the text of Mt: 60,4: 'He who lies in wait for a person in judgment, his judgment will not be slackened in the great judgment for eternity' (Transl F.I. Andersen, in OTPsepigrapha I).

    See also Test Moses 5,6f: 'For those who are the leaders, their teachers, in those time will become admirers of avaricious persons, accepting (polluted) offerings, and they will sell justice by accepting bribes. Therefore their city and the full extent of their dwelling places will be filled with crimes and iniquities. For they will have in their midst judges who will act with impiety toward the Lord and will judge as they please' (Transl J. Priest, in OTPsepigrapha I);
30. Mt 10,17-22; 24,9-13
31. Mt 12,7
32. Mt 25,36.39.43.44
33. see also the difference in expression: Sir 7,6: μὴ

ζήτει γενέσθαι κριτής

34. It is not completely clear in which way the judges are nominated, see De Spec Leg IV 55; IV. 177ff; Jos Bell Jud II. 20.5.569
35. see Mt 23,32ff. R. Stuhlmann's commentary, Das eschatologische Mass im NT, Göttingen, 1983, 102ff is really unsatisfactory. Firstly, the comparison with 1 Thess 2,16 is too simple as if 'the Jews' from 1 Thess 2,16 are the same as the Pharisees and scribes; Secondly, Mt 23,32f is not the only place in Matthew where μέτρον is used. 'Measure for measure' is a strong eschatological expression
36. see the explanation in 5,21ff and 6,9ff
37. B. Couroyer, 'De la mesure dont vous mesurez, il vous sera mesuré, Rev Bibl 77 (1970) 366-370
38. How different this can be, appears probably from 2 En (A-text) 44: 'Happy is he whose measure will prove to be just and whose weight just and scales just! Because on the day of the great judgment every measure and every weight and every scale will be exposed as in the market; and each one will recognize his measure. And according to measure, each shall receive his reward' (Transl F.I. Andersen, OTPsepigrapha I); see also c 49; c. 53 'keep your hearts from every injustice in balance'
39. In H.P. Rüger, 'Mit welchem Mass ihr messt, wird euch gemessen werden', ZNW 60 (1969) 174-182 one can find a good introduction to this history, even if the author summarizes it all a little too much. The difference will become clear in my text. He cannot prove either his pretence of completeness. One should add: Tos Sota 3,2; Mekilta on Ex, Massekta Pisḥa, VII vs 12,12 and Massekta Beshallaḥ II vs 14,4. In conformity with my point of departure I limit myself to the oldest texts, Mishnah, Tosephtah and Midrashim on Ex., Lev and Deut
40. Sota 1,7-9
41. On this unpersonal plural as indication of the name of God, see Str.-B. I.443 and the commentary by M. McNamara, The New Testament and the Palestinian Targum, Rome, 1966, 140; see further H. Bietenhard, Sota, Berlin, 1956, 42
42. Sota 1,9: 'weken le^{c}injan ha-ṭôbah'
43. cf Bietenhard, Sota, 46 note 2
44. Is 58,8 is applied to the just
45. Tos Sota 3,1-19; 4,1-17
46. In Tos Sota 4,10-17 this list of punishment is again taken up with some repetition and with additions with new names: the generation of the Flood, the people from Sodom, the Pharaoh, the spies, the neighbours of

Israel, the prophets in Jerusalem, the serpent of Adam and Eve, and finally, a list of evil people from Cain to Hamam

47. It is, at the same time, an occasion to solve a number of problems which the Mishnah brings out, with a lot of haggadic material about the burial of Joseph and about the crossing.
48. As in Sifre on Num & 106, vs 12,15 which has taken up Sota 1,9; and in the Mekilta on Ex., Massekta Beshallaḥ I vs 13,19.21 where Tos Sota 4,7.8; Sota 1,9 and Tos Sota 4,2-6 are quoted
49. So in Sifra on Lev., Perek XX Parasha XII vs 5,17: 'which measure is greater: the reward or the punishment? Say, the measure of the reward', with an elaboration of the heavy punishment of Adam's sin and the hope this brings for anyone who converts and does penance; and in Sifre on Dt & 26 (end) (or beginning of & 27) vs 3,24 where the measure of the good is set against the measure of punishment on account of the divine name JHWH and Elohim: wherever it says JHWH, the measure of mercy is meant, wherever Elohim, the measure of punishment
50. Mekilta on Ex., Massekta Pisḥa VII vs 12,12; XIII vs 12,33; Massekta Beshallaḥ II, vs 14,4 (on the Pharaoh); VI vs 14,25 (on the chariots of the Egyptians); Massekta Shirata IV vs 15,4 (on the Pharoah); V vs 15,5 (a pun on 'eben': stone and delivery chair of Ex 1,16); VI vs 15,8 (the gathering of the water and the guile, via the pun with 'ᶜormah' (guile) and 'ᶜaram' (to gather)); Massekta Amaleq II vs 17,14 with the application on Amaleq, the Pharaoh and all people who want to harm Israel. Only in this last text we find the reference to Ex 18,11 (end) on which Rüger insists so much
51. In Massekta Beshallaḥ VII vs 14,26 are summed up Ex 18,11; Ps 7,16.17; Qoh 10,8.9; Prov 12,14; 26,27; Is 59,18; 65,7; Jer 32,19; 50,29; in Massekta Pisḥa VII. vs 12,12 are quoted: Gen 7,23; 19,11; Ex 14,4; Dt 13,16; Num 5,27. Therefore, there are many more than the modern commentaries show: they often refer only to Wisdom 11,16
52. T J I; T Neoph Gen 38,25.26; in P. Rüger, 'Mit welchem Mass ...', ZNW 60 (1969) 177ff and McNamara, The New Testament and the Palestinian Targum, 138f all textual traditions are summed up. In this case there are many
53. An interesting parallel is to be found in 2 En (J-text) 44,3ff: 'He who expresses anger to any person without provocation will reap anger in the great judgment. He who spits on any person's face, insultingly, will reap

the same at the LORD's great judgment ...' 43,5 '(and in accordance with that measurement) each shall receive his own reward' (Transl F.I. Andersen, OTPsepigrapha I)

54. I mention the text here because of the indicated comparison between action and punishment. E. Brandenburger, Das Recht des Weltenrichters, Stuttgart, 1980, 67ff enters more precisely into the nature of this comparison; see also P. Christian, Jesus und seine geringsten Brüder, Leipzig, 1975, 37ff

55. It is precisely this aspect which one finds quite often in the commentaries: see Grundmann, Matthäus, 219; Gundry, Matthew, 121; Wrege, Überlieferungsgeschichte, 124 who quotes similar lists from 1 Clemens and Polycarp (interesting that in these lists, which take as their point of departure ἔλεος, the μέτρον saying is taken up, see also James 2,13); Beare, Matthew, 189

56. The typical is obviously relative, see e.g. also Test Zab 8,3: 'To the extent that a man has compassion on his neighbor, to that extent the Lord has mercy on him'

57. The author of this saying is Jochanan, from the second generation of the amorites, the founder of the school in Tiberias, end of the 3th century AD, therefore, a late text which clearly should not be taken as a historical source for Matthew. But that does not alter the fact that these thought structures are still alive apparently around this time

58. Rabbi Samuel ben Nachmani is a Palestian about 260 AD cf Str.-B., VI. 230

59. It is an explanation of the text which is only understandable from the Hebrew: Ruth 1,1: 'wajehi bimei shefoṭ ha-shofeṭim' is explained as 'dôr she-shofeṭ et shofeṭaw'

60. Is 2,22 as will be said further on: a lament on Jerusalem which violates law and justice

61. Arakin 3,5; the literary translation says: 'The law of the one that 'hath brought up an evil name' has a light side and a severe side. How so? It is all the same whether one 'hath brought up an evil name' against the greatest (woman) of the priestly stock or against the least important (woman) of the (lay) Israelite community: he must pay a hundred selas. Thus we find that he who speaks with his mouth (pays) more than one that commits a (wrongful) act. Thus we find also that the judgment (not to enter the Promised Land) was sealed against our ancestors in the Wilderness because of (their) evil talk, as it is said, 'Yet they have tried My these ten times, and have not hearkened to My voice' (Transl Blackman)

62. Dt 22,14

63. Num 14,22
64. He is a Babylonian around 300 AD
65. b Arakin 15b, with reference to Job 20,22: 'when the abundance is complete, the distress will come upon him'
66. Lev 19,17
67. He is a tanna, about 110 AD. b Arakin 16b is, therefore, a text which is probably much earlier to date than b Baba Batra 15b
68. This deals with 'lets', a word which plays an important role in the Qumran literature; it is used there in the context of 'faulty interpreters'. For the connection with the Matthean concept ὑποκριτής see D.E. Garland, The Intention of Matthew 23, 103ff, especially 107
69. Prov 9,8
70. see note 68
71. In two others places, Sifre on Dt & 1 vs 1,1 and Sifra on Lev, Parasha Qedoshim II. 4 vs 19,17 (!) the Arakin-text (with some slight variations) is repeated literally but exclusive of the saying on the splinter and the plank. I do not know what could be the meaning of this
72. The Jesus-word is, according to Schweizer, Bergpredigt, 80, ridiculed by a Jewish rabbi; according to Grundmann, Matthäus, 220, it was taken in an ironic way in Jewish literature. One can only come to this conclusion, if one reads Str.-B. only and if one does not study the text in its own context. For Grundmann this is probably more a question of Christian anti-semitism than of a lack of knowledge of the basis-text, cf J.S. Vos, Antijudaismus/Antisemitismus im Theologischen Wörterbuch zum Neuen Testament, Ned Theol Tijdschr 38 (1983) 95ff
73. i.e. Lev 19,17, see also the foregoing text in Lev 19,15 where the abuse of law is discussed. This combination appears time and again
74. see D.E. Garland, The Intention of Matthew 23,103.121: especially his reflections on the interpretative context of ὑποκρισία
75. see also the commentary on Mt 6,1-18
76. Mt 23,23; 23,29ff
77. cf D.E. Garland, The Intention of Matthew 23, 121fff, although he starts from the supposition that the 'Christians' as such are addressed. From the following it becomes clear that the situation is somewhat more complicated
78. Mt 5,22.23.24.27; 7,3.4.5
79. Mt 28,10 in connection with 28,7; for the whole cluster of the 'brotherhood' in Matthew, cf J. Lange, Das Erscheinen des Auferstandenen, Echt, 1973, 375ff; H. Frankemölle, Jahwehbund und Kirche Christi, Aschen-

dorff, 1974, 177-189; J. Zumstein, La condition du croyant dans l'évangile selon Matthieu, Göttingen, 1977, 386; W. Weren, De broeders van de mensenzoon, Amsterdam, 1979, 102f

80. For this interpretation, see G. Strecker, Der Weg der Gerechtigkeit, Göttingen, 1966/2,212, although the totality of interpretation which I propose, goes in a completely different direction than Strecker. For him Israel's time is past. For the problem of the combination in Mt of different traditions which are contradictory, see H. Frankemölle, Biblische Handlungsanweisungen. Beispiele pragmatischer Exegese, Mainz, 1983

81. Mt 28,16-20 has, of course, an extensive amount of commenting literature. Referring only to the more recent titles: J.P. Meier, Two Disputed Questions in Matt 28:16-20, JBL 96 (1977) 407-424; B.M. Nolan, The Royal Son of God, Göttingen, 1979, 199f (very short); B. Przybylski, Righteousness in Matthew, Cambridge, 1980, 112ff

82. Mt 4,13ff

83. Mt 9,33

84. see the explanation of Mt 6,7f

85. In H. Frankemölle, Biblische Handlungsanweisungen, Mainz, 1983, 197ff one finds a lot of other texts: pagan-oriented would be: 1,1.3.5.6; 2,1-12; 4,15f; 5,13.14; 8,5-13; 10,18; 12,18-21; 13,38; 15,21-28; 24,14; 25,31ff; 28,16-20; Israel-oriented: 10,5f; 10,23; 15,24 (one should discuss about some texts and one could add others: one could ask e.g. whether the Sermon on the Mount and the mission discourse are not directed in their totality to Israel). He sees this double perspective as a denotative system: from the community in Matthew mission is practised to Israel as well as to pagans. It is possible. In any case, it is an ideological taking of position of Matthew. I am not sure whether one should go further than that

86. Mt 12,46-50: see especially the difference with Mc 3,31-35 and Lc 8,19-21; Mt deals with the τὸ θέλημα τοῦ πατρός μου. That for Matthew this 'will of the father of Jesus' coincides with the 'Torah as explained by Jesus', follows from texts as 5,45.48; 6,1-18; 7,21; 9,13; 11,25ff; 12,7; 12,50; 18,14; 18,35; 26,39. Because the Torah of God is involved, Israel is present

87. It is important to keep the perspective of this discourse in mind: Jesus is presented as speaking to the masses and to the disciples. Mt 23,8-10 is not a purely ecclesiological pronouncement no more than 12,46-50, although obviously 'church'-people are addressed. By placing it in the context of the liste-

ning crowds, it is first of all a critique on Israel as model for the own community which, by imitation, will make Israel's light shine

88. Not without good reason do I come back to this text time and again, while I am giving a commentary on the Sermon on the Mount. The description of the needs is, however conventional it is expressed, denotative for the suffering of the people and points to the whole of the beatitudes. In the proposed interpretation the Son of Man identifies with the suffering person, because he recognises Israel as suffering. The peoples will be judged on the basis of the way in which they have dealt with this Son of Man who identifies with suffering mankind: have they recognised Israel as suffering? The identification 'Son of Man' with 'suffering Israel' would simplify a number of 'traditionsgeschichtliche' problems of the text. Regarding the literature on the text, see J. Lange. Das Erscheinen des Auferstandenen, Echt, 1973, 295ff; P. Christian, Jesus und seine geringsten Brüder, Leipzig, 1975; J. Zumstein, La condition du croyant, Göttingen, 1977, 327ff; W. Weren, De broeders van de mensenzoon, Amsterdam, 1979; E. Brandenburger, Das Recht des Weltenrichters, Stuttgart, 1980
89. Mt 18,23-35; 18,15-22
90. Gen 4,24 (LXX). For this suggestion cf H. Frankemölle, Jahwehbund und Kirche, Aschendorff, 1972, 182
91. According to G. Schwarz the first trial has been made by J.A. Bolten, Der Bericht des Matthäus von Jesus dem Messias, in 1792
92. cf J.A. Fitzmyer, A Wandering Aramean, Missoula, 1979, 14 there is no more any necessity to suppose a Hebrew or Syrian background, for 'qds di dhb' in 11 Q tg Job 38,8 proves that is has existed as first century Aramaic expression
93. For the discussion see successively F. Perels, Zur Erklärung von Mt 7,6, ZNW 25 (1926) 163-164; M. Black, An Aramaic Approach to the Gospels and Acts, Oxford, 1967/3 (1946) 200f; J. Jeremias, Abba, Göttingen, 1966, 83-87 (originally 1936); G. Schwarz, Matthäus VII.6a, NT 14 (1972) 18-25. I am quoting here his translation
94. especially J. Jeremias, Abba, Göttingen, 1966, 87, but see also H. and R. Kahane, Pearls before Swine? A Reinterpretation of Matt 7,6, Traditio 13 (1957) 421-424; Michel, TWNT s.v. κύων
95. How far did the possibility of choice go with donkeys, what price had to be paid; for the halachah on this, see the treatise Bekorot, about the donkey esp. Bekorot 1,6.7; from the agreement between Philo, De Spec Leg I.

135ff who says that one pays a ransom for the first born of camels as well as for horses and donkeys, and Jos Ant IV. 4.4.70 who also states that for all unclean animals a ransom is to be paid, it is clear that one does not think all that unanimously about this

96. and for animals with defects, but that is not essentially different for the halachah, see Teruma 6,5 and Bekorot 4,4
97. Sifre on Num & 118 vs 18,15; see C. Albeck, Einführung in die Mischna, Berlin, 1971, 64
98. Teruma 6,5 (cf J. Jeremias, Abba, Göttingen, 1966, 87) ascribes this same halachah to Chanina ben Antigonos, a rabbi who lives a little later than Rabbi Tarfon, resp. 150 and 110 AD
99. Bekorot 2,2.3; Chullin 10,2; Zebachim 8
100. There is a discussion about this in the Mishnah, not 'money' can be meant ('kesafim' cannot be contaminated, cf Philo, De Spec Leg I 104), but rather 'naturalia' as a lamb, wine, oil and flour which are normally offered at the altar, cf Temura 6,2 and 6,4
101. Jos Ant IV. 8.9.206
102. cf Zebachim 8,1; 9,3; 14,2; Temura 6,1 and 6,3. The 'earnings of the dog' are parallel, therefore, to 'the earnings of the whore' cf Temura 6,2 and 6,4
103. Temura 6,3
104. Mt 15,21-28; see especially the difference with the text of Mark where the mission of Jesus to the 'lost sheep of the house of Israel' has not been used (could not be used?)
105. Consider Temura 6,3: 'What is understood by 'exchanged for a dog'? (Thus), if one said to his fellow, 'Here is for thee this lamb for this dog' (Transl Ph. Blackman). Sheep and dogs have a relation of exchange in which the sheep represent purity and the dogs impurity
106. I have to come back on the used equivalence 'the holy' = 'Israel'; 'the dogs' = 'the pagans'
107. 1 Baruch 6,3.7.10.23.38. 50.54.57.69.70
108. 1 Baruch 6,8 and 6,11.32.71
109. 1 Baruch 6,12.13
110. 1 Baruch 6,26 and 6,29
111. Aboda Zara 1,8
112. cf Pauly-Wissowa, Orth, s.v. Schwein
113. Mt 8,28-34 and parallels
114. Nedarim 2,1
115. Mt 5,47; 6,7.8; 6,32
116. a.o. Js 44,9-20; Wisd ch 13.14.15; 1 Baruch ch 6; Apoc Abraham 1-8

117. The Greek/Latin authors are filled with it; for our era think of authors as Menander, Plautus, Ovidius, Petronius, Lucianus
118. Prov ch 5
119. Prov 29,3
120. Sir 9,3-8; see also 19,2
121. see Is 57,3ff; Jer 5,7ff; Nah 3,4ff
122. cf K. Schneider, Pauly-Wissowa, s.v. Hetairai who, based on Athenaios, gives a list of nicknames of hetaerae among which also ὗς figures; cf also Hepding, s.v. Hieroduloi; in the (relatively) long text from Qumran on a whore (4 Q 184), only the seduction and the punishment in the pit of destruction are mentioned
123. S Brandon, Jesus and the Zealots, Manchester, 1967, 174
124. Brandon is silent on this question. He refers only to the meaning 'torah' referring to Black, see Brandon, 174, note 3
125. For the image of the swine in Jewish literature, see Str.-B. I, 499; cf the dogs, Str.-B. I, 722ff; I can add T J II Ex 22,30 (ms 110 Paris) and T J II Ex 22,30 (Vatican ms): 'You shall cast it to the dogs: you shall give it to the gentile who is likened unto the dog' (Transl M.L. Klein, The Fragment-Targums of the Pentateuch, Rome, 1980, II. 56.135); I. Abrahams, Studies in Pharisaism, II, 195 opposes against the equivalence dog = pagan and calls attention to the equivalence dog = persecutor cf Ps 22,16. But one equivalence does not exclude another one
126. Apoc 21,9-27
127. especially 2 and 3 Enoch
128. 4 Esra 10,25ff
129. Twice, in traditional material: in the description of Jesus' temptations (Mt 4,5), and in what happens after his death (Mt 27,53). It is an indirect indication of the importance which Matthew gives to Jerusalem in the context of its relation to Israel
130. Again typical of Matthew, in the eschatological discourse, Mt 24,15
131. cf D.R.A. Hare, The Theme of Jewish Persecutions of Christians, Cambridge, 1967, 123; Gundry, Matthew, 122 (about non-disciples, disciples who profess a false confession); Beare, Matthew, 191 (about missionaries of the gospel, but not in the context of the gospel); J. Schmid, Matthäus, 146, idem; W.D. Davies, Setting of the Sermon on the Mount, 326.392 as gemarah on the foregoing verses to keep livable the prohibition to judge; idem in Dupont, Les Béatitudes, I, 127-171
132. Besides the texts in Str.-B. I, 477, see also Sifre on

Num & 5 vs 5,15; it is evident that one discusses references to 'the holy'; as to trample and tear apart the reference is to the persecutions of the missionaries in a pagan environment

133. In connection with 2 Pt 2,22 where a saying about a dog and a swine is used in the context of apostasy
134. Didache 9,5, see also 10,6
135. see note 1 of this chapter where several authors are quoted about the division of this passage and the connection in the context
136. Lc 11,9-13 and 6,31
137. Mt uses this particle a lot of times. According to Moulton-Geden at least 54 times, always in a consecutive sense. For the texts in the Sermon on the Mount, see 5,19.23.48 (!); 6,2,8.9 (!). 22.23 (!). 31 (!). 34 (!); 7,11.12.24 (!)
138. K.-H. Rengstorf, 'Geben is seliger denn Nehmen', in, Fs für Köberle, Hamburg, 1958, 23-33; J. Jeremias, Neutestamentliche Theologie, Gütersloh, 1971, 186; N. Brox, Suchen und Finden. Zur Nachgeschichte von Mt 7,7/Lk 11,9b, in, Fs für J. Schmid, Freiburg, 1973, 17-36 (see p.18); G. Theissen, Wanderradikalismus, in, Studien zur Soziologie des Urchristentums, Tübingen, 1979, 94; but see also the criticism of L. Schottroff - W. Stegemann, Hoffnung der Armen, Stuttgart, 1978, 81, note 43 (why?: the context in Mt indicates to think of the 'have-nots')
139. Lc 11,8
140. See especially N. Brox, Suchen und Finden, 18 who points to this silence. He shows that 'asking' and 'searching' must have been regularly combined, because otherwise the triad ask-search-knock would not be plausible. I think I can give a good context
141. The treatise Pea indicates that an own terminology has been developed: 'lèqèt' for the corn; 'pèreṭ' and '[c]olelôt' for the vine, 'chabata' for the olive cf Lev 19,9.10; 23,22 and Dt 24,19-21; 'pea' for the corner of the field which has to be left cf Lev 19,9.22; 'shikcha' (cf Dt 24,19) for the forgotten sheaf, the forgotten grapes and olives. Remember also the adjudgments about the 'hèfqer': the declaration that certain fruits are public possession, cf Pea 6,1
142. see a.o. Albright-Mann, 83: 'if, then, you who are sinful' (!?); Guelich, Sermon on the Mount, 359: 'if you being evil'; J. Radermakers, Au fil de l'évangile selon saint Matthieu, I, 23: 'si donc vous qui êtes méchants'; cf Lagrange; Beare, Matthew, 'wicked'; Schulz, Spruchquelle, 163, 'böse'; idem Schottroff-Stegemann, Jesus. Hoffnung der Armen, 81; Schweizer,

Bergpredigt, 84; G. Baumbach, Das Verständnis des Bösen, Berlin, 1963, 80; Strecker, Bergpredigt, 153

143. cf Liddell-Scott, s.v. πονὴρος

144. W. Ott, Gebet und Heil. Die Bedeutung der Gebetsparanäse in der lukanischen Theologie, München, 1965, 102ff is undoubtedly the best commentary on these verses; see also p. 107 on the relation between 7,7-11 and 7,12

145. Mt 13,47ff

146. In N. Brox's article, Suchen und Finden, this is developed for the use of the meshalim in gnosticism, in which the saying about searching especially is used creatively as indication of the gnosticus on the way to gnosis; and in orthodox exegesis where searching becomes an alternative for believing

147. A shortened reflection of this exegetical question can be found in the discussion between exegetes whether Matthew can have meant material or spiritual goods with τὰ ἀγαθὰ, see especially W. Ott, Gebet und Heil, 109ff and G. Baumbach, Das Verständnis des Bösen, 80

148. K. Berger, Die Gesetzesauslegung Jesu, Neukirchen, 1972, 243

149. Mt 19,21

150. Mt 5,42

151. Mt 10,8

152. Mt 14,19 and 15,36: in this last text the distribution of the fishes is mentioned

153. N. Brox, Suchen und Finden, 18 is against it; Baumbach, Verständnis des Bösen, 80 is in favour. Brox's interpretation is more correct in my opinion

154. A. Dihle, Die goldene Regel, Göttingen, 1962: a rare all-encompassing study which describes the history of this ethical rule with an enormous knowledge

155. see p. 80ff. In Dihle's opinion one should not see this 'consequence' as an historical process, in which vengeance is so much rationalised that nothing is left of the first phase. The three phases are typologies of ethics which go together. Even today elementary feelings of vengeance play a role in the administration of justice: some form of equality with the damage suffered is necessary to satisfy the damaged sense of justice

156. For this formulation, see K. Berger, Die Gesetzesauslegung Jesu, Neukirchen, 1972, 209ff: 'Es ist der Versuch, die Stellung der beiden Hauptgebote zum Gesamt des Gesetzes zu definieren' (p. 230). It deals with 'die Gesamtheit des verpflichtenden Willens Gottes' (p. 224)

157. Most extensively in Dihle: for antiquity, p. 103; for

the Christian literature, p. 107; for Jewish literature, see Str.-B. I. 460. An older list in A. Resch, Das Aposteldekret nach seiner ausserkanonischen Textgestalt, Leipzig, 1905, 132ff. From my own research I can add: Jos Ant XVI 2.4.37ff.47: the speech of Nicolas before Agrippa which presupposes (negatively) the golden rule in its argumentation, parallel to Dio Cassius, Roman History, LII. 34.1 in the speech of Maecenas to August

158. Mt 22,34-40
159. Rom 13,8-10
160. Gal 5,14
161. James 2,8
162. For commentary, see I. Abrahams, Studies in Pharisaism, I. 18ff and G.F. Moore, Judaism, II. 85ff; Didache 1,2 gives a same connection of Lev 18,19 and the golden rule
163. Mt 5,17
164. For the references I depend on A. Resch and A. Dihle, supplemented by Str.-B., cf note 157
165. Herodotus, 3,142 and 7,136
166. Isocrates, Ad Nikokles 24
167. Isocrates, Nikokles 49; the treatise Demonikos (for the saying, see 21) is wrongly ascribed to Isocrates. It deals with the education in which the son is urged to become equal with his father; he should be for his parents what he would want his children to be for him etc. It is a similar context as Tob 4,5 where Tobit gives his son all kinds of admonitions in his farewell discourse. The Torah background remains obviously strong as a Jewish text
168. Isocrates, Panegyricus 81.

Notes: chapter 6 NOT WORDS BUT DEEDS

1. V. Fusco, Il 'vissuto' della Chiesa in Matteo -appunti metodologici con esemplificazione da Mt 7,15-23, Asprinas 27 (1980) 21
2. Test Abr 11; see E.P. Sanders, Introduction to the Test Abr in OTPsepigrapha, I, 869; G.W.E. Nickelsburg, Jewish Writings of the Second Temple Period; Assen, 1984, 60-64; M. Stone, idem 420; and especially 'Studies on the Testament of Abraham', ed. by G.W.E. Nickelsburg, Missoula, 1976, 27ff which supposes a double influence (from Plato and from Jewish Psepigrapha)
3. The formulation of Test Abr 11,2.10.11 of the longer version is so typically parallel with Matthew's text, that it seems best to think of a reworking and rewriting of this Mt-text (cf commentary Sanders). It may be clear that this is not necessary a dependence in writing. The shorter version (Abr 8) is also here quite different from the longer version. The influence of Matthew's text is either less or possibly completely absent: the roads are not mentioned; the gates are not explicitly accompanied by exegesis in this chapter; in ch 9 it it understood that it deals with sinners, resp. just people
4. Test Abr 11,7.10 in opposition with 11,12
5. Test Abr 11,10.11, transl Sanders. This interpretation finds its supporters till in recent time, cf Grundmann, Matthäus, 231; Jeremias, TWNT s.v. πύλη
6. Most instructive is the article by Michaelis, TWNT s.v. ὁδός, but it is good to realise that, already in Lucianus, obviously in a funny way, the real essential steps are distinguished cf The Teachers of Rhetors 3 (two roads), 6 (Pinax of Cebes), 7 (Hesiodos and Xenophon), 7ff: an extensive description of the roads in the 'wrong' manner
7. Quoting in a more or less arbitrary order: cf Xenephon, Memorabilia B.I. 21-34 (ἀρετή or κακία); Ps 1,16 (justice or wickedness); Ps 118,29 (LXX) (untruth or truth); Prov 2,10; 4,18 (light or darkness); Prov 12,28 (life or death; justice or injustice); Jer 21,8 (life or death); Test Aser 1,3-5 (good or evil; justice or sin); En 91,18f (justice or unjustice; rightness or badness); sl En 30,15 (light or darkness, good or bad); sl En 42,10 J-text (the secular path of this vain world against the right paths); A-text (path of change against right paths); Philo, De Spec Leg IV. 108f (ἀρετή or

κακία); Plantatione 37 (life or death); De Abr 204 (distress and fear or εὐπάθεια); De Virt 51 (holiness or uncleanness); 1 Q S 3,3f (light or darkness); Did 1,1.2; 5,1 (life or death); Barn 18,1; 19,1; 20,1 (light or darkness, eternal death and punishment); Abot 2,9 (good or bad)

8. so for example in Did 1-6; Barn 18-20
9. Test Aser 1,3ff, transl. Kee, OTPsepigrapha I, cf also 1 QS 3,3f; see also the discussion of the Xenophon text, Memorabilia B. I.21-34 by Michaelis in TWNT s.v. ὁδός
10. Jer 21,8
11. Prov 2,10f; cf also 4,27 LXX
12. Prov 4,18
13. Prov 15,19
14. λεωφόρος, cf e.g. Vita Mosis II. 138; De Opif Mundi 144; De Virt 51; cf also De Gigantibus 64; Quod Deus 159 on the kingly highway which does not branche off but which goes straight on
15. De Abr 269
16. ἀνοδία, see e.g. De Spec Leg IV. 109
17. De Abr 269
18. Dio Chrysostomos, Discourse, I. 66ff; for the reference, see G. Mussies, Dio Chrysostom and the New Testament, Leiden, 1972, 51
19. Transl J.W. Cohoon (Loeb-edition); the opposition is between an ἔφοδος πλατεῖα and στένη
20. Hesiodos, Works and Days, 85ff, transl D. Wender, Harmondsworth, 1979, 67, except the last phrase. The Greek text does not read 'she is not hard to find', but 'then the road is easy for the difficulties are done away'
21. 4 Esr 7,3-13 is not a complete parallel because there is no double road, cf Michaelis, TWNT s.v. ὁδός, 57
22. I have used a text edition of J. van Wageningen, Groningen, 1903 with a beautiful 17th century drawing of the περίβολοι
23. Cebes 15,2-16,5
24. In De Agricultura 102ff and Leg All II. 98. In De Agricultura 101 one sees that Philo really thinks that the only road leading to good is the broad and easy road: 'For lack of self-control ... and all pleasures ... never allow the soul to go along the straight course by the highway, but compel it to fall into pits and clefts'. It is this waried train of thought which is responsible for the differences between the two texts
25. De Agricultura 102f
26. Leg All II. 98

27. Cebes 6,2
28. Cebes 9,1-10,4
29. Cebes 11,2, cf also 12,3; 14,4; 24,3
30. Cebes 12,3
31. Cebes 15,2; mostly it is the only text which is quoted, cf J.D.M. Derrett, The Merits of the Narrow Gate, Journ for the Study of the NT 15 (1982) 21; Michaelis, TWNT s.v.ὁδός 73, note 103; but see also Jeremias, TWNT, s.v. πύλη, 922 note 15 who gives references to 17,2; 18,1; 20,2 but not to 15,2
32. Cebes 15,1-16,5
33. Cebes 24,3
34. J.D.M. Derrett, The Merits of the Narrow Gate, Journ Study NT 15 (1982) 20-29 who is mainly based on G. Schwarz, Matthäus vii 13a, NT 12 (1970) 229-232. He seems to have missed the article by A.J. Mattill, 'The Way of Tribulation', JBL 98 (1979) 531-546. This author develops with other matters the fact that there is a small gate within the large one. Derrett mentions correctly that this is not necessary to understand the mashal. Anyway, how could it then be said that it is difficult to find?
35. One could also point to the fact that πύλη has the double meaning of 'gate' and 'custom-house', cf Liddell-Scott s.v.; and to Jos. Bell Jud V. 6.5.284: 'suddenly all (Jews) dashed out together through a concealed gate near the Hippicus tower'
36. see A.J. Mattill, 'The Way of Tribulation', JBL 98 (1979) 531ff who rather strongly emphasizes the connection with θλῖψις as eschatological danger; in any case it means 'to be oppressed'; also according to Gundry, Matthew, 127f the figurative organisation of the mashal is restricted to a mountain-city
37. Bell Jud III. 7.7.158ff λήγοντι τῷ ὄρει is possibly better to translate with 'where the mountain stops'
38. Bell Jud III. 7.14.190
39. Bell Jud IV. 1.1.5ff
40. Bell Jud IV. 1.7.52
41. Bell Jud IV. 1.9.62
42. Bell Jud VII. 8.3.281ff
43. Bell Jud VII. 8.4.293
44. see Jeremias, TWNT s.v. πύλη who proves that the gate is meant by the δι' αὐτής
45. Bl.-D. & 339 who gives references to two other Matthew texts: 23,13 and 27,40. In this supposition the Matthew text is very close to Lc 13,24
46. Mt 22,13 cf 8,12; 14,51; 25,30
47. Mt 25,12 cf 7,23
48. Mt 3,10-12: the wheat in the granary, the chaff in the

unextinguishable fire; 5,30: descend into the gehenna; 13,30.40.42: the wheat in the granary, the weeds in the fire, resp. shine in the dominion of the father against the oven of fire; 13,47-50: the good fish in baskets, the bad fish outside it, resp. in the oven of fire; 18,8.9: enter into the life paralytic, lame or with one eye against to be thrown into the gehenna of fire; 25,34.41.46: eternal fire prepared by the devil and his angels against the dominion prepared from the foundation of the world.
The metaphors concretise the oppositions inner-outer, above-below, life in light-life in fire; see also 8,12; 22,13; 24,51; 25,21.23.30 cf note 46 where the opposition joy-sorrow and light-darkness are mentioned
49. Mt 24,5.6.10.11.12.24.28
50. Mt 16,17ff, and the parallel in 18,18ff. I am wondering whether the couple δέω - λύω does not suppose in first instance the Hebrew/Aramaic couple na^{c}al-pataḥ: to close and open doors with keys. For the fact that doors are not only opened with keys but also closed with them, see S. Krauss, Talmudische Archäologie, I. 39ff who refers to Tos Erubim 10,1 and Kelim 14,8. The last text gives a description of the closing of the Temple gate from the inside. In this supposition the used metaphor is much more coherent than generally supposed
51. Mt 23,13
52. Mt 21,28-32; concerning John and the road he has gone, see also Mt 3,3 and 11,10; in 22,16 the whole didache of Jesus is subsumed under the theme of the road
53. Mt 19,16ff: it is the only text where the entrance into the eternal life resp. into the dominion of heavens is presented as 'difficult'. J. Mattill, 'The Way of Tribulation', JBL 98 (1979) 531ff even tries to reconstruct a connexion via the equivalence 'needle of the eye' = 'the small gate in the great gate', but the linguistic arguments are insufficient
54. cf V. Fusco, Il 'vissuto' della Chiesa in Matteo, Asprinas 27 (1980) 21
55. Mt 24,5.11, but see infra
56. When there is mention in the exegesis of prophecy in Matthew's gospel, people too often start from the concordance and limit themselves to texts which speak explicitly about 'prophets', as in Mt 5,12; 10,40; 13,17; 23,34, so in Cothénet, DBS s.v. Prophétisme; E. Schweizer, Gesetz und Enthusiasmus in Matthäus, in, Das Matthäusevangelium, Darmstadt, 1980, 350ff; E. Aune, Prophecy in Early Christianity, Grand Rapids, 1983, 213ff. They leave out, almost matter of factly, the corpus of Matthew's vocabulary - the mention of the

prophets from the Old Testament -; the idea is that these people are, for Matthew, historical figures who have nothing to say about his ideas on prophecy.

57. Mt 16,14; 21,11.46; 13,57 is the only text where Jesus uses it as an self-identification, but also there in a very indirect way; see also 27,68
58. Mt 1,22; 2,15.17.23; 4,14; 8,17; 12,17; 13,35; 21,4; 26,54.56; 27,9
59. Jos Ant IV. 6.5. 125, see also Ant X. 10.4.210 about the prophecies of Daniel about the hard stone (which indicates the fall of Rome and which, therefore, is not explained by Josephus?) and e.g. Ant X. 4.4.66ff where is determined that the prophecy of Jeroboam after 361 years is fulfilled; for the Greek side of the question one could think of the system of the chresmologues and their collection of prophets, see R. Flacelière, Devins et oracles grecs, Paris, 1961, 87ff
60. Mt 1,20; 2,12.13.19.22
61. For this description, see E.R. Dodds, The Greeks and the Irrational, Berkeley, 1959, 107 who distinguishes three types of dreams: the symbolic dream which uses metaphors as a kind of puzzle where the meaning cannot be understood without explanation; the dream as a vision: a straightforward pre-enactment of a future event; and the dream as an oracle: an important figure for the dreamer reveals to him, without symbolism what will happen or not happen, or, what should happen or not happen. The dreams in Matthew belong to this last category
62. Mt 27,19
63. Mt 27,51f; 28,2f; 17,9; for the Greek context of this phenomenon, see R. Bloch, Les prodiges dans l'antiquité, Paris, 1963, 19f
64. For parallel-lists, see Mt 10,8 and 15,30f
65. Mt 9,35ff; 12,15ff; 15,29ff: J.M. Hull, Hellenistic Magic and the Synoptic Tradition, London, 1974, 116ff thinks that in Mt, as far as the miracle stories are concerned, a 'cleansing' has taken place from what we find in Luke and Mark about magical customs and practices. This thesis is connected with his specific vision on magic which is demonstrable especially in the exorcist stories of the gospels. But, if we read Matthew in the larger contemporary context of 'prophecy', this reservation is no longer valid
66. Mt 12,38ff; 16,1ff, for commentary, see J. Hull, Hellenistic Magic, 118ff
67. Mt 8,28ff; 12,22; 17,16ff
68. cf the explanation of the parable of the seed (13,18ff) and of the weeds (13,36ff) and the parable of the

wedding (22,1ff) and the final judgment (25,31ff)

69. Mt 16,21ff; 17,22; 20,17ff
70. They do not foresee the evil which will come over them, see classical Lucianus, Alexander, 59: 'In spite of his prediction in an oracle that he was fated to live a hundred and fifty years and then die by a stroke of lightning, he met a most wretched end before reaching the age of seventy, in a manner that befitted a son of Podaleirius; for his leg became mortified quite to the groin and was infested with maggots. It was then that his baldness was detected ...' (Transl. A.M. Harmon, Loeb-edition); and Apuleius, Metamorphoses, II, 12,3-14,6 (see note 144 of this chapter)
71. Mt 5,11ff; 10,17ff; 23,34ff; 24,9ff also 16,17ff
72. Mt 10,15f; 11,20ff
73. Mt 24
74. Mt 4,1ff parallel to Lc 4,1ff
75. Mt 17,1ff and 11,15ff parallel to Lc 9,28.36 and Lc 10,21ff
76. Mt 21,15
77. cf the correspondence between 11,25 and 21,16
78. For this unit see also E. Cothénet, DBS s.v. Prophétisme
79. Mt 13,13.16 and 13,23
80. Mt 5,11f; 23,34ff.37ff
81. see especially the discussion in D.E. Aune, Prophecy in Early Christianity, 409/410, note 165 between Aune, Kingsbury and Schweizer. Obviously one cannot give an estimate of factual figures. Matthew himself cannot be cleared from some ambiguity: on the one hand the disciples are usually addressed as prophets (5,11ff; 13,16; 23,34) which seems to presuppose that every follower of Jesus has prophetic qualities, but on the other hand hospitality is asked for the prophet (10,41) which suggests a distinction between giver and receiver, between host and prophet
82. D.E. Aune, Prophecy in Early Christianity, 224; see also E. Schweizer, Gesetz und Enthousiasmus bei Matthäus, 362; idem Bergpredigt, 93; V. Fusco, Il 'vissuto' della Chiesa in Matteo, Asprinas 27 (1980) 23 who supposes the unity of the pericope 7,15-23, distinguishes between 'errors in the teaching' (7,15ff) and 'wrong ethical behaviour' (7,21ff)
83. Otherwise the pseudo-prophets would be meant in Mt 13,41 and 23,28. I presume that D. Hill, False Prophets and Charismatics, Bibl 57 (1976) 327ff would not disagree for 23,28, but his plea for two different groups in 7,15f. 21f would then fall to pieces
84. O. Böcher, Wölfe in Schafspelzen, TZ 24 (1968) 405f

85. There is also a clear connection with the classical criticism on the wandering cynics: a group which probably is not completely separate from the system of prophets as Matthew knows them, see G. Theissen, Studien zur Soziologie, Tübingen, 1979, 90ff.106ff; especially in Lucianus, Peregrinus (nr 3,17.36.40) we find a number of negative remarks about their clothing (the wallet, the cloak, the Heracles-club), their hair and their behaviour
86. Is it not normal that clothing is made from sheep's wool? Then we have linen and silk which is used only for festive, rich garment and which not everyone can afford to use every day. Linguistically his story would be correct if Mt had used μηλωτή as the LXX calls the cloak of Eliah, or if the sheep's clothes were somewhat nearer the description of John the Baptist: clothing made from camel's hear with a leather belt around his middle (Mt 3,4). Now the author has to write 'dem Schafspelz ist das Kamelhaargewebe gleichwertig ... und die Vokabel μελωτή wird verdeutlichend durch ἔνδυμα προβάτων ersetzt' (p. 412)(?!)
87. Mt 23,25. Obviously I do not want to say that for Matthew the Pharisees are pseudoprophets, as D. Hill, False Prophets and Charismatics, Bibl 57 (1976) 327f tries to prove. The opening sentence should have said then something different from the cleansing of the cup and the plate!
88. The thesis of Böcher, Wölfe in Schafspelzen, TZ 24 (1968) 405ff that the wolves are meant to indicate that these pseudoprophets are under magic-demonic influence is based on an argument which is as weak as his suggestion about the clothing of the prophets. There is an associative connection of texts, from very old mythological texts to Grimm's fairy tales, in a mishmash of all kinds of animals where surprisingly few wolves appear. It seems better to forget this suggestion. I find it unbelievable that so many people have accepted his proposal
89. see also Sef 3,3
90. Striking because precisely this text is lacking in the parallel editions of Mark and Luke, see Mt 10,8 and parallel in Mc 6,7ff and Lc 9,1ff. Typical of Matthew are the additions: for nothing you have received, for nothing you should give; the labourer is worthy of his keep (see Lc 10,7 who speaks of 'salary'); and in the list of forbidden gifts apart from copper (so Mc) and silver (so Lc), also the gold
91. J. Reiling, Hermas and Christian Prophecy, Leiden, 1973, 53 has made the most extensive list of referen-

ces, as far as I know; Hellenistic authors - except Lucianus - are not represented

92. Acts 8,20
93. Acts 16,16ff
94. Acts 19,24ff
95. Did 11,12
96. Acts 11,27ff
97. 1 Tim 6,5; 2 Pt 2,3; Did 11,6.9.12; 12,3.4.5.; Pastor Hermas, Mandatum XI.12; The Lives of the Prophets 22,12ff about Gehazi, the slave of Elishah; Martyrdom of Isaiah 3,28ff; LAB 18,11
98. There is not so much attention for this in Josephus, but that he knows about it is clear from the fact that it appears in significant places in opposition to the text of Scripture, see especially Ant VI. 4.1.48 and Ant X. 11.3.241; for commentary, W.C. van Unnik, Flavius Josephus als Schriftsteller, Heidelberg, 1978, 23f
99. Vita Mos I. 266
100. Vita Mos I. 268, see also 275
101. Vita Mos I. 293
102. I am quoting these texts explicitly because they tend to be forgotten in research; in D.E. Aune, Prophecy in Early Christianity, they are only mentioned in the notes
103. cf the observations on Mt 5,19
104. see the introduction of this chapter
105. Mt 13,24-30.36-43
106. parallel to Mt 5,19
107. For this 'person-oriented' interpretation of σκανδάλον, see Stählin, TWNT, s.v. σκανδάλον
108. 2 Pt 2,13; Jud 12
109. Asc Js 3,28; Lucianus, Alex 19.41
110. cf G. Strecker, Bergpredigt, 170; J. Reiling, Hermas and Christian Prophecy, 52; H.D. Betz, Lukian von Samosate und das Neue Testament, Berlin, 1961, 114; M. Caster, Études sur Alexandre ou le faux prophète de Lucien, Paris, 1938, 65. Remember also 2 Pt and Jude-if, at least, these texts are not to be dated much later than Matthew
111. Vita Mos II. 69
112. Quod Deus sit imm 136ff
113. De ebrietate 143ff
114. Quis rerum div. heres 258ff
115. This is the most essential philonic conception about prophecy, cf. Vita Mos I. 57. 157.201; II. 250-252. 272. 280f, see especially E. Fascher, ΠΡΟΦΗΤΗΣ. Eine sprach- und religionsgeschichtliche Untersuchung, Giessen, 1927, 159ff

116. Sanhedrin 11,5; see also Did 11,10: 'every prophet who does not do what he learns, is a pseudo-prophet'
117. 1 Kings 13
118. Mt 12,33f
119. J. Reiling, The Use of φευδοπροφήτης in the Septuagint, Philo and Josephus, NT 13 (1971) 147-156
120. Mt 24, 4.24
121. so e.g. Strecker, Bergpredigt, 168; Beare, Matthew, 195 differentiates rather strongly between Mt 7,15ff and Mt 24,24; for Schweizer, Bergpredigt, 88 the appearance of factual pseudo-prophets is a 'vorzeichenhafte Erscheinung' of the eschatological pseudo-prophets
122. Sanhedrin 11,6; see also in 11 Q Temple 54,8-13 where the pseudo-prophet predicts signs which come true
123. Philo, Vita Mos I. 294; Jos. Ant. IV. 6.6.129f; T J I Num 24,14, but not in Neoph (here the advice is given to make the Israelites sin); LAB 18,13ff; see also the intensification of Balaam's own idolatry in different texts
124. cf Dt 13,1 and commentary in Philo, De Spec Leg I. 315 and IV. 51: 'in quite a short time such manoevres are exposed, for it is not nature's way to be concealed for ever but when the right time comes she uses her invincible powers to unveil the beauty which is hers alone'; see also Jos. Ant VIII. 13.1.318; IX. 6.6.133, although in Josephus this is not the dominating implication; see also Apoc 2,20-24 where the idolatry is connected with adultery
125. but see Acts 5,36.37 and 21,38
126. Samaritan prophet (Ant XVIII. 4.1.85); Theudas (Ant XX. 5.1.97); anonymous imposter(s) (Ant XX. 8.6.167; 8.10.188; Bell Jud II. 13.4.258); Egyptian (Ant XX. 8.6.169; Bell Jud II. 13.5.261); pseudo-prophet (Bell Jud VI. 5.2.285). See for this list P.W. Bernett, The Jewish Sign Prophets, NTS 27 (1980/81) 679ff who for the rest opposes the idea that these people would have a messianic consciousness; the Samaritan prophet is not to be found here for some reason or other
127. see the description of this development in D.E. Aune, Prophecy in Early Christianity, 1ff with as predecessors the studies by E. Fascher, ΠΡΟΦΗΤΗΣ Eine sprach- und religionsgeschichtliche Untersuchung, Giessen, 1927 and R. Meyer, Der Prophet aus Galiläa, Darmstadt, 1970/2 (1940)
128. For this conception of prophecy in Josephus, see- with the seemingly necessary differences - J. Blenkinsopp, Prophecy and Priesthood in Joseph, JJS 25 (1974) 239-262; G. Delling, Die biblische Prophetie

bei Jospehus, and M. de Jonge, Josephus und die Zukunftserwartungen seines Volkes, in Josephus-Studien, Göttingen, 1974, resp. 109-211 and 205-219; W.C. van Unnik, Flavius Josephus als historischer Schriftsteller, Heidelberg, 1978

129. Strecker, Bergpredigt, 169 seems to presuppose this: 'Der Vers enthält eine Erklärung über das Wesen der Verführer und über das Verhältnis ihres Seins zu ihren Taten'

130. Bauernfeind, TWNT s.v. σαπρός

131. Mt 24, 4.5.11.24, always in the context of the pseudo-prophets

132. Mt 18,10-14

133. Pastor, Mandatum XI. 13; Acts 13,10, but also Qumran, 1 QH 4,10.20 (lie and deceit); CD 6,1; 8,13; 20,15 (lie); 1 Q pHab 5,9; 10,9ff (lie, deceit, city of blood)

134. 2 Pt 2,20

135. 2 Pt 2,14.18

136. Josephus generally connects the word ἀπάτη to the 'imposters' during the great war: cf. Bell Jud II. 13.4.258; 13,5.261; VI. 5.2.288f; Ant XX. 5.1.97; 8.6.167. 169; 8.10.188

137. 1 Jo 4,6; 1 QH 4,20 (the seers of the error); 1 Q pHab 10,10; for Qumran and prophetism, cf T.M. Crone, Early Christian Prophecy, Baltimore, 1973, 115ff; D.E. Aune, Prophecy in Early Christianity, 132ff

138. 2 Pt 2,19.20

139. Jos. Ant XX. 8.10.188; Bell Jud VI. 5.2.285; see also 2 Pt 2,1.3.19.20

140. See the history of Jeremiah (Ant X. 6.2.88; 7.3.111) who predicts the downfall of Jerusalem, but is not believed and is even accused of magic against the king; and Ezechiel (Ant X. 7.2.104) who is brought in contact with Jeremiah and where Josephus shows how both their prophecies are fulfilled; the same in the history of Achab and Josaphat: it is a pseudo-prophet who urges Achab to start a war (Ant VIII. 15.4.401) pointing back to the history of Jeroboam and Jadon (Ant VIII. 9.0.236) where the old (pseudo-)prophet brings Jadon down by trickery

141. Bell Jud VI. 5.3.288ff after which we find a whole list of such portents: a star as a sword, a comet, light around the altar, a cow which gives birth to a calf in the Temple, the eastergate which opens by itself, chariots in the air with armies, a voice which says, 'let us get out of here', Jesus, son of Ananias with his prophecy, an oracle about a square temple and about a future lord over the whole world

142. Mt 3,10
143. Mt 13,36-43; 47-50
144. see e.g. the story in Apuleius, Metamorphoses II. 14.1 about Diophanes, the fortuneteller from Chaldea who makes a clean breast of it, when he tells his friend how terrible it was during the sea voyage
145. so Philo, De Spec Leg II. 52: 'truth will come back and shine again, illuminating the far distance with its radiance, and the lie which overshadowed it will vanish away'
146. see Josephus about his charlatans and imposters who accompany the war: the Romans persecute them to death
147. Sanhedrin 11,5 distinguishes between a punishment at the hands of men (in the case of a false prophet who speaks about what he has not heard and about what has not been told him) and a punishment at the hands of heaven (in the case of a false prophet who keeps back his own prophecy (cf Mt 12,32?); who is disobedient to a prophet who transgresses his own words); see also Did 11,11 (about a prophet who does not learn to do everything he does)
148. Apoc 2,22f
149. 2 Pt 2,9.17, see parallel in Jud 13. This last text quotes En 1,9 to prove the immensity of the punishment
150. 2 Pt 3,7.10.12; Jud 7.23; for the ruin in the fire, see also Sib Or 2,85ff. 196ff; 4,44.173. 815
151. Mt 11,5; 15,30ff
152. Mt 10,18: notice especially that only Matthew includes this assignment in his mission-address
153. Mt 13,11.16
154. Messianism and Exodus to the desert are parallel representations; for the references, see note 126
155. Mc 16,17ff
156. Acts 4,30; 5,11; 6,8; 14,3; 15,12
157. Acts 28,1ff
158. Acts 11,27
159. Acts 16,16ff
160. One does not find in the literature till now the clear distinction in time, place and customs. M. Smith, Jesus, the Magician, London 1978, wants to prove that Jesus was a magician. For contemporary literature he can point only to the Testament of Solomon (if that is contemporary!). For the rest, there exists an abundance of second and third century source material, but one should remember that precisely in the second century the golden era of the magical literature begins; in J.M. Hull, Hellenistic Magic and the Synoptic Tradition, London, 1974 the distinction in time and place is done with much more care. Quite

correctly this author limits himself to the redactional level. Regarding Mt, see note 65 and 66.
For literature about the θεῖος ἀνήρ, see L. Bieler, ΘΕΙΟΣ ΑΝΗΡ. Das Bild des 'göttlichen Menschen' in Spätantike und Frühchristentum, Wien, 1935; D. Tiede, The Charismatic Figure as Miracle Worker, Missoula, 1972 and C.H. Holladay, ΘΕΙΟΣ ΑΝΗΡ in Hellenistic Judaism, Missoula, 1977. Especially Holladay has shown that the 'theios anèr' does not exist as type in the relevant literature of our era (Josephus, Philo (and Artapanus))

161. The chapter about the Christian mantis in J. Reiling, Hermas and Christian Prophecy, Leiden, 1973, 79ff made this clear to me. What he showed for the second century I would like to try to make clear about the (Palestine) area in the first century AD
162. cf A.D. Nock, Paul and the Magus, in, Essays on Religion and the Ancient World, Oxford, 1972, I, 308-330: in Greek antiquity not everything what we call magic has been seen as such: rainmakers, love potions, (medicinal) herbs, incantations do not fall into this category according to the ancients. Greek speak about magic, when people claim to be able to give to another the means which can be used in their own interest and against the interest of their enemies; if such means are used against enemies; if foreign religions are in question (p. 314); see also M. Smith, Jesus, the Magician, 68-80
163. cf D.C. Duling, OTPsepigrapha I. 943
164. which are to be localised in Egypt with more or less probability: Test Job, Treatise of Shem, Joseph and Aseneth, Test of Solomon, see OTPsepigrapha and Jewish Writings of the Second Temple, ed. by M.E. Stone
165. Vita Mos I. 263ff
166. Vita Mos I. 277 cf the Hellenistic oracular question: 'Is it better and more beneficial that I (he/she) shall marry/travel/lend etc; for a positive evaluation, see Vita Mos II. 192ff where Moses is described as a prophet who arrives at divine pronouncements διὰ πεύσεως καὶ ἀποκρίσεως. cf D.E. Aune, Prophecy in Early Christianity, 52ff; H.W. Parke, The Oracles of Zeus, Dodona, Olympia, Ammon, Oxford, 1967
167. Vita Mos I. 282.284.287
168. De Spec Leg I. 59-65; IV. 48ff
169. De Somniis I. 220
170. De Spec Leg III. 93.95.100ff
171. For a complete description, see D.E. Aune, Prophecy in Early Christianity, 23ff
172. Test Job 46,1-50,3; a number of these themes come back

in an even more romanticised form in Joseph and Aseneth: see the story about the apparition of Michael and the miraculous meal with the honey comb 14,1-17,10 with the result access to eternal life, invulnerability in battle and access to the future 26,1ff

173. For the text, cf OTPsepigrapha I.473; in Artapanus Fr 1,6 and 3,50ff - an early Egyptian text - one can see how astrology and thaumatourgy have been annexed by Egyptian Jews; for commentary, see C.H. Holladay, ΘΕΙΟΣ ΑΝΗΡ in Hellenistic Judaism, Missoula, 1977, 200ff

174. F. Flacière, Devins et oracles Grecs, Paris, 1961, 87 about the collectors and vendors of oracles

175. JosAs 22,11-13; see also 23,8 and 28,16

176. Transl C. Burchard, OTPsepigrapha II

177. cf En 103,1; 106,19; Jub 32,21; Vita Adae et Evae 51,3ff; Prayer of Joseph Fragm B

178. see also Jub 32,21

179. Especially the very specific domination of the demons argues against a too early dating. I would like to know how the Testament has been influenced by/or resp. has influenced the magical papyri

180. D.R.A. Hare, in OTPsepigrapha II, 381 pleads for the first quarter of the first century AD, in Jerusalem. Is not the fact that a rather strong emphasis is on the destruction of the city and the Temple an indication of a somewhat later date?

181. Isaiah prays for water and God let the Siloam flow; Jeremiah prays that serpents and crocodiles may stay away; Ezekiel prays for fish; Daniel for Nebuchadnezzar; Elijah for rain to come and to stay away; the resurrection of the son of the widow; with the priests of Baal; for fire from heaven; Elisha for water in Jericho; birth and resurrection of the son of a woman from Shunem; blindness of enemies

182. Jeremiah on the tumbling down of the images of the idols; Ezekiel on the signs of the return; Obediah and Nahum on the destruction of Niniveh; Habbakuk on his journey to Babylon; Zephaniah on the city; Haggai on the restoration of the Temple; Zechariah on the birth of a son of a priest, the victory of Cyrus; Nathan on the sin of David; Ahijah on Solomon and Jeroboam

183. Ezekiel and Daniel the Temple; Daniel the situation of Nebuchadnezzar; Habbakuk on the conquest of Jerusalem; Zechariah on the end of the pagans; Ahijah: an ox who tramples the people and the priests

184. see especially Zechariah on the victory of Cyrus; Elijah and Elisha on the passage through the Jordan; and also the long lists of Elijah and Elishah

185. Jeremiah: the consummation of his mystery: the resurrection of the arc and of the saints; Ezekiel: the return from Media; Daniel: the downfall of Babylon and of the whole earth; Hosea on the coming of the Lord; Jonah on the downfall of the city; Habbakuk on the downfall of the Temple; Zechariah on the end (or is this a prophecy which has already come true?)
186. Isaiah's tomb gives water to the Siloam; Jeremiah's tomb cures people from snake bite; visible signs in the Temple from the death of Zechariah and Jehoiada
187. LAB 25,9-26,15
188. LAB 24,1-5, see also Martyrdom and Ascension of Isaiah 4,5ff
189. LAB 44,1ff
190. LAB 53,2ff
191. LAB 60,1ff
192. LAB 64,1ff
193. Sanhedrin 9,6; obviously the remark about the Zealots does not apply; witchcraft is connected to capital punishment, but see also 11 Q Temple 60,18.19
194. Bell Jud II.8.6.136; 8.12.159; Ant XV. 1.1.3. and Ant XVII. 2.4.41ff attributes the same power to the Pharisees; about this 'confusion', see R. Meyer, Der Prophet aus Galiläa, Darmstadt, 1970/2 (1940), 58
195. Ant VIII. 2.5.45ff
196. Bell Jud VII. 6.4.180ff; the Loeb-edition gives here a rather victorian translation: 'pouring upon it certain secretions of the human body'(!)
197. 1 Q apGen 19,4-20,34
198. Transl J. Fitzmyer - D.J. Harrington, A Manual of Palestinian Aramaic Texts; about the identification with Daniel, see G. Nickelsburg, in, Jewish Writings, Assen, 1984, 35; for Daniel as 'magos', see also Jos. Ant X. 10.3.195f and 10.6.216 where Daniel is put on the same line with the Chaldeans and magicians of the king, or better, as a 'magos' who is better and bigger; for 4 Q Mess Ar, see J. Carmignac, Les Horoscopes de Qumran, Rev de Qumran 5 (1964-66) 206ff
199. Jub 10,1ff. This fragment has not been preserved in Qumran, but the close relation between Qumran and Jubilees is known; see J.C. VanderKam, Textual and Historical Studies in the Book of Jubilees, Missoula, 1977, 18-95 on the Hebrew fragments
200. Jub 31,12
201. Jub 32,21; see also 44,3ff: these texts are not found in Qumran
202. 4 Q 186
203. For the text, J.J. Allegro, Discoveries in the Judaean Desert, Oxford, V. 88-91; for commentary J. Carmignac,

Les Horoscopes de Qumran, Rev de Qumran 5 (1964-66) 199-206 and M. Delcor, Recherches sur un horoscope en langue hébraique provenant de Qumran, Rev de Qumran 5 (1964-66) 521-542. The last one gives an overview of a number of astrological texts and theories from antiquity. Contemporarily - pace Delcor -, one cannot point to any text from Palestine

204. 1 En 8,3; neither this fragment has been found in Qumran but because of the many surviving fragments it is certain that the book is read in Qumran
205. 11 Q Temple 60,16ff
206. so Philo and LAB with a certain constancy. One could also think of the targums, especially when they mention Jannes and Jambres as the opponents of Moses, see T J I Ex 1,15 (par Jos. Ant II. 9.2.205); Ex 7,11; Num 22,22 cf 2 Tim 3,8; CD 5,17-19, see M. McNamara, The New Testament and the Palestinian Targum, Roma, 1966, 82ff; in T J I Num 22,22 Jannes and Jambres are the helpers of Balaam; in T J I Num 23,23 is stated against this that there are no augurs and witches in Israel; see also T J I Ex 7,15; 8,16 where Pharaoh himself is represented as a magician; see opposite T J I Ex 9,14; for the whole tradition on Jannes and Jambres, see recently A. Pietersma - R.T. Lutz, OTPsepigrapha II. 427ff
207. so in LAB 24,1-5; LAB 64,1ff; 1 En 8,3; Jub 48,9ff
208. Jub 10,10-15
209. 1 Q apGen 20,1ff
210. Jub 31,12
211. Jub 32,21
212. Jos Ant II. 13.3. 284ff
213. LAB 60,1ff
214. Test Sol; Ant VIII. 2.5.45ff
215. Test Job 46.3
216. 4 Q sNab; Jos Ant X. 10.3.195; 10.6.216
217. The Lives of the Prophets
218. In Acts 8,1ff; 13,4-12; 19,11ff one can see how this applies vice versa from one religion to the other: a Christian author rejects the Jewish magicians
219. especially Mt 12,50 and 21,31
220. A similar message is found in Hermas, Mandatum XI, see J. Reiling, Hermas and Christian Prophecy, Leiden, 1973, 96; for the eschatological background of the saying, cf H.D. Betz, Studien zur Bergpredigt, Tübingen, 1985, 111ff
221. Abot 3,17
222. Abot de Rabbi Natan 24; see a.o. F.H. Breukelman, Bijbelse theologie, Kampen, 1980; Strecker, Bergpredigt, 178; Schweizer, Bergpredigt, 98; D. Flusser, Die

rabbinischen Gleichnisse und der Gleichniserzähler Jesus, Bern, 1981, 98ff

223. Abot 1,17; 2,2; 3,9
224. Abot 2,14; 2,16; 6,5
225. Abot 2,15
226. Abot 1,17; 4,5; 5,14
227. Mt 25,1-13
228. Schweizer, Bergpredigt, 98; Breukelman, Bijbelse theologie, 72
229. Mt 13,24-30.36-42; 13,47-51; 18,35; 22,10-14
230. Guelich, Sermon on the Mount, 413: 'it underscores Jesus' person and ministry as the fulfillment of the Old Testament promises'; Strecker, Bergpredigt, 178: 'Die Autorität die das Judentum der Tora zugesteht, nimmt in der Bergpredigt der Gottessohn für sich in Anspruch'; see also Schweizer, Bergpredigt, 98
231. D. Flusser, Rabbinische Gleichnisse, 100
232. M. Buber, Die Chassidischen Bücher, Berlin, 1927, 566
233. Midrash Rabba on Ex 34,27.

INDEX

1. Scripture

9. Tosephtah

10. Talmud

11. Targums

12. Midrashim

13. Jewish and Christian Pseudepigrapha

THE SERMON ON THE MOUNT
AS AN IDEOLOGICAL INTERVENTION